North Africa, Operation Torch, 1942. A shell went through the bogie wheels, under the tank and out the other side like a rabbit, bouncing off across the desert. Then, with a sound like a giant bell, a shell hit our turret, but didn't penetrate. Another hit made our ears ring, but we kept working on that jammed breechblock. As soon as our gun was unjammed, we began firing again, but now a German 75mm shell smashed the bottom of our left rear gas tank and blazing gasoline spurted out over the back of the tank. Heavy black smoke began to roll up from our hull. I shouted to my boys, "Now is the time to git," and we boiled out like peas from a hot pod.

Bong Son, RVN, 1967. Fire had broken out everywhere in the hamlet, and there were hundreds of broken-off coconut stumps that acted just like WWII-style dragon's teeth and would peel a track off or belly-up a tank. The drivers lived in a lonely world of their own while the turret crews fought. Only men who have been in close-in ground fighting at hand-grenade range can understand what it is like to be in a life-and-death struggle for not just surviving but winning. The action was so close that I got blisters on two fingers of my left hand . . . from pulling hand-grenade rings and dropping the grenades around the tank.

The Iraqi desert, 1991. Suddenly the platoon sergeant, Dennis McMasters in HQ 21, reported that Stephens was taking incoming fire from an undisclosed location. All he could see were the ricochets bouncing off the hull. Then something got through the armor, and Stephens's ammo began to cook off and explode, with the crew still in the vehicle. . . .

TANK ACES

STORIES OF AMERICA'S COMBAT TANKERS

RALPH ZUMBRO

POCKET BOOKS

New York   London   Toronto   Sydney   Tokyo   Singapore

An *Original* Publication of POCKET BOOKS

 POCKET BOOKS, a division of Simon & Schuster Inc.
1230 Avenue of the Americas, New York, NY 10020

ISBN: 0-671-53612-5

First Pocket Books printing January 1997

10 9 8 7 6 5 4 3 2 1

POCKET and colophon are registered trademarks of
Simon & Schuster Inc.

Cover photo credits: front cover top, courtesy of Magnum Photos;
front cover middle left, courtesy of *Armor Magazine;* front cover
middle right, courtesy of the author; front cover bottom, courtesy
of the author; spine photo courtesy of *Armor Magazine;* back cover
photo courtesy of *Armor Magazine*

Printed in the U.S.A.

ACKNOWLEDGMENTS

This book began as a concept in the imaginative minds of Paul McCarthy and Doug Grad, of Pocket Books' military history department. When I was offered the job, I jumped enthusiastically, right into a research project of monumental proportions. Fortunately, I already had a few connections. One of the first was Major General R. J. Fairfield, Jr., who provided me with names and consented to write the story of just how the tanks came to Vietnam under his guidance. Then, Brigadier General Stan Sheridan came up with a list of people going back to WWII and before, and we were off and running.

Colonel Jimmy Leach, a prominent historian, also came up with some critical names and suggested that I contact the Patton Museum at Ft. Knox. Ms. Katie Talbot, the research librarian there, provided some critical information on WWI and the first primitive tankers.

Recognition is also due to Mr. Richard Hunnicutt, author of many technical tank books, for his help over the years since my first effort at writing tank history.

A letter to Mr. David Fletcher, Chief Librarian at the British Tank Museum in Bovington, England, supplied much information, including the story of the first American tanker, and material for a future book.

ACKNOWLEDGMENTS

The story of the 192nd and the Bataan tankers would not have been complete without the help of Mr. Ervin J. Sartell, Jr.

Ms. Diane Dempsey of the Eisenhower Center in the University of New Orleans was kind enough to find the reports of two D-Day soldiers, and she put me in touch with Mr. Rockwell and Mr. Ahearn, who graciously gave permission to use their stories in that part of the book.

Brigadier General Albin F. (Al) Irzyk, who was a battalion commander in France and Germany has allowed the use of two chapters from his own book to be adapted to this work. They are in the Europe chapter and are titled, "Near Martille France, November 13, 1944," and "East of Mainz, Germany, March 18, 1945," from the book, *He Rode up Front for Patton,* published by Pentland Press, Inc., 5124 Bur Oak Circle, Raleigh, NC 27612.

Mr. James Turner submitted his battle history especially for this book.

Next came the Marine tankers of WWII, and that seemed to be a closed door until I called Colonel Cesare Cardi of the Marine Detachment at Ft. Knox and suddenly a whole new world opened up. He provided me with the roster of the Marine Corps Tanker's Association and I began calling around, resulting in an interview with Mr. Robert Swackhamer and Mr. Wilson McClendon and the creation of the Iwo Jima chapter. In addition, I received encouragement and references from Mr. "Red" Saunders, Mr. Philip Morell, and Mr. Joseph O'Donnell, all retired USMC tankers.

The story of the Amtankers came from historical references in *Armor Magazine,* but also from the history, *One if by Land, Two if by Sea,* by Mr. Cordell Smith, a veteran of the Philippines campaign.

The staff of *Armor Magazine,* to which I contribute, gave me much help also. Colonel Terry Blakely, Jon Clemens, Vivian Oertle, Mary Hager, and Jody Harmon all helped with both the selection of stories and the provision of the photographs to illustrate the work.

For the Vietnam segment, I am indebted to Mike Stewart

ACKNOWLEDGMENTS

for his story of his return to Vietnam, to Frank Cole for background on the Ben Het Battle, to Charles Hazelip for his reminiscences, and to Major Spurgeon and Mr. Russell for the final battle of the 69th.

Mr. Patrick Sims furnished the vital connection with Ken Patch, whose diary forms the framework of the Desert Storm chapter.

Major Mike Campbell, USMC, generously provided me with a copy of his combat log of the experiences of the Marine Provisional Tank Detachment, Mogadishu, Somalia, which concludes the book.

Mr. Tristram Coburn, our working editor at Pocket Books, has gone the course with this project, even though he had another crash priority job dropped on him in the middle of our book.

My many and heartfelt thanks are due to all of the people who made this book possible. It stands as a tribute to America's armored warriors.

Last, but definitely not least, I must thank my lovely and enduring wife, Louise, whose moral support and tireless editing made this entire project possible from the beginning.

CONTENTS

CONTENTS

PROLOGUE

As far back as memory reaches, the commander's lever, the arm of decision on the battlefields where humanity writes its history, has been the mounted armored man, or group of men. Even at the end of the Bronze Age, where our formal records fade from the pages of Herodotus into the dust of archaeology and the mists of legend, we find royal lists of the "Chariotries" that protected the old city-states and projected their power faster and farther than marching spearmen. Before the birth of Israel, Thutmose III, Pharoah of Egypt, faced the Canaanites on that already bloodied ground. In a copper-armored, gold-trimmed chariot that carried archers, the priest-king led his "Arm of Decision" on the plains of Meggido . . . where Armageddon is prophesied to take place.

There is a constant evolution in the art of war, as available time, terrain, and hardware affect the intents of commanders; but one thing never changes. There has always been a need for a mobile protected source of firepower, be it the chariots of Ramses II or the armored knight who dominated the Dark Ages. In the year 1500, Leonardo da Vinci invented a man-powered "combat vehicle," and in 1519, Jan Ziska created his war wagons—horse-drawn mobile fortresses. Soldiers and technicians have long needed a machine to break stalemates, but the problem, until this century, has always been motive power.

In 1916 in France, men were dying by the hundreds of thousands, entire regiments slaughtered by barbed wire, poison gas, and machine guns. Something was desperately needed to stop the awful slaughter and end the war that had begun at Sarajevo . . . which is still a flashpoint of nations.

In Britain, men of vision with such names as Ernest Swinton and Winston Churchill saw possibilities in the American Holt artillery tractor and began to experiment. Their first creation was called "Little Willie," and never saw combat. The second machine, oddly enough, was called "Mother, Mark I," and saw combat in the Somme. In order to conceal their real purpose, the MkIs were covered with canvas and shipped as water tanks. TANKs are what they've been called ever since.

The story of the motorized fighting tank began in bloody battle on August 15, 1916, just west of the little French village of Flers, in the Somme. Badly used and sent in small groups and sometimes alone, they nonetheless proved their worth beyond doubt, and warfare was forever changed by these "rude mechanical types." On November 20, 1917, at Cambrai, they got it right. Nearly 400 British tanks hit the German fortifications with little or no warning, rolled up the wire, and spanned the trenches.

Suddenly there was a new contestant in the killing zone. That breakthrough, coupled with the new technique of observer-controlled artillery, six divisions of infantry, and scouting aircraft, was one of history's pivot points. It was no fault of the tankers that the advance was not exploited properly. They bestrode the trenches in their clanking, smelly, crawling, slab-sided monsters, spitting machine gun bullets and cannon shells, and the Germans coined a new phrase: "Tank terror."

It got worse, much worse. On September 12, 1917, in what was then known as the St.-Mihiel Salient, Americans, under an obscure colonel named George S. Patton, jumped in, and these men played *rough*. Patton's orders read in part as follows: "No tank is to be surrendered or abandoned to the enemy. If you are left alone in the midst of the enemy, keep shooting. If your gun is disabled, use your pistols and squash the enemy with your tracks. . . . In any case, remember you are the first American tanks. You must establish the fact that *AMERICAN TANKS DO NOT SURRENDER. . . .*" They also established Murphy's law, but that's another story.

The period after the unsatisfactory peace of 1918 was just a breathing spell in this century of war, during which all belligerents regrouped, rebuilt, and gathered forces for the next round, which we call World War II, the Russians call the Great Patriotic War, and the Japanese don't like to talk about. Innovations in the field of armored warfare came thick and fast and were tested in places such as Manchuria, where General Georgi Zhukov taught the Japanese a few lessons in tactics.

All through the 1930s, border wars, civil wars, and revolutions set the stage for WWII. In Spain, the Germans sided with Franco and sent tanks and dive-bombers. The Russians, for a change, sided with the Republicans and sent tanks and advisors. In Ethiopia, the Italians waged war on the Abyssinian natives with tanks and poison gas until the British ran them off. In Russia, with Stalin's approval, the Germans took the first steps toward the creation of their visualized Panzer Force . . . with Swedish technical help.

When war broke out for real, the Poles and the French felt the German armored fist, while the Japanese received their first setback, near the Manchurian town of Nomonhan. In late August 1939, General Zhukov destroyed three of their divisions and so traumatized them that the record has been expunged from their history. At this point, the history of armor splits. Formal historians and the news media concentrated on the great sweeping battles of history while down in the jungles of Southeast Asia and the Philippines, the first of the jungle tankers were learning their deadly trade the hard way, by on-the-job training!

Newly designed M-3 light tanks, the famed Stuarts, named for a slashing Confederate general, J.E.B. Stuart, fought against Japanese infantry and their crude tanks in the gloom of jungle, swamp, and rain forest. In Burma, the British fought a long guerrilla war, using American light and medium tanks. On the island of Luzon, the Stuarts fought side by side with the last of the old American horse cavalry.

Deep in a foreign jungle, the saber was passed, and the tradition still lives. On the Bataan peninsula, in 1942, the 26th Regiment of horse cavalry fought alongside the newly formed 192nd Light Tank Battalion. Light horse cavalry screening for tanks was a lethal innovation. Possibly, just possibly, their heroism saved Australia, for they upset the precision timetable of General Homma by almost four months.

All across the line of Pacific atolls and islands, at places with names like Guadalcanal, Tarawa, Tinian, Iwo Jima, and Okinawa, the Stuart, Grant, and Sherman tanks fought savagely, punching high-explosive (HE) shells into bunkers and canister rounds into bamboo thickets. Some, converted to flamethrowers, burned the Sons of Nippon out of heavy cover and roasted them in their foxholes and caves. Others, mounted in landing craft, became temporary gunboats. The drivers became masters at broken field running. The loaders could feed better than a dozen shells a minute through their cannons while looking out for snipers in the palm tops.

The tank commanders stood crouched in their turrets like gunfighters, firing from the hip, without needing the sights. A crew like that doesn't just operate a tank, they wear it like their clothes. It is their home and place of business—the business of death.

Half a world away, freshly trained American tankers were getting their first hard knocks from Erwin Rommel and the famed Afrika Korps. Nothing like being sent in, raw and inexperienced, against the best tank general the world had yet seen. They learned fast, though, under George Patton, Creighton Abrams, and others. Rommel himself said that "Americans knew less but learned faster than any other soldiers that I have fought." Turned loose in Sicily, they

4

defeated most of a German army. Then they slugged their way up the length of Italy, waded ashore in southern France, and punched their way ashore at the bloody Normandy beaches. Now up against the first team and superior German tanks like the MkIV, the Panther, and the dreaded Tiger, they were the armored fist that crushed forever the megalomaniac dreams of an Austrian corporal named Adolf Hitler.

When the war was over, those battle skills lived a precarious half-life in the memories of a few old tankers who soldiered on, through the Korean unpleasantness and the long, dreary cold war. When, in the 1960s, the contest became hot, in Vietnam, which used to be French Indochina, America got involved for convoluted political reasons and sent first advisors, then ground troops. The Pentagon had decided that it would have to be an infantryman's war, the jungle supposedly being no place for tanks. The lessons of the past had been buried in the planning for the great coming European war, and jungle tanking wasn't even taught at the Armor School.

The French had had a disaster on highway 19E just west of the town of An Khe, and the world armor community was traumatized. No one had noticed, however, that 13 Chaffee tanks almost saved the French foreign legion at Dien Ben Phu. So, when the Americans arrived, they were supposed to have left their heavy armor at home. The first troops in, though, were U.S. Marines who didn't get the word and took a few tanks along. Ambassador Maxwell Taylor was outraged to see those tanks on TV, as he considered that Vietnam wasn't "tank country." That was the prevailing expert opinion, although nobody had asked the tankers.

Slowly, the tanks proved their value. The M-113 armored personnel carrier became, in effect, a light tank because of its superior mobility. With an armored cupola and extra machine guns, it became an armored cavalry assault vehicle (ACAV). Then the heavy M-48s took the plunge into the paddies and jungles, and the jungle tankers were reborn. First the armored cavalry regiments, the famed 11th Cav, the 3/4 Cav, and the 1/4 Cav, were allowed in to test the waters with their mix of ACAVs and tanks.

General Westmoreland, the American commander, began to overcome his doubts, and when the 25th Division was sent in, in 1965, he allowed its integral heavy armor battalion, the 1st Battalion of the 69th Tank Regiment, commanded by Lieutenant Colonel Ronald Fairfield, to go with it, and the war was never the same. The 69th, you see, had a few old jungle tankers left over from the Pacific war who'd also slugged their way up the length of Korea. The colonel, whose personal military experience dated back to before WWII, had taken that background and hammered the battalion into a fighting machine unequaled in any army. When those old soldiers rolled their iron monsters out into the Vietnamese countryside, they weren't in strange country; they were home, and they remembered the first motto of the old tank corps: "Treat 'em rough."

Again, parceled out in penny-packet lots, the tankers rode their steel steeds into an infantry war. Like knights-errant of old, they prowled the jungles, mountains, and paddies, sometimes in platoons, sections, or even alone. We escorted convoys, smashed bunkers, climbed jungled mountains, rode in landing craft, poured out 90mm cannon shells by the thousands and machine-gun bullets by the millions of rounds. In the Tet assault of 1968, the Viet Cong died as a military force. In 1972, the North Vietnamese Army (NVA) came south and lost 100,000 men (their figures). That war was lost, as Leonid Brezhnev said it would be, not on the battlefields, but on American streets.

From the unnecessary death of Vietnam through the long flickering of the cold war, the tankers trained and watched the Fulda Gap through which we always expected the hordes of the Soviet Union. Then, with unexpected swiftness, Russia curled in on itself, for the time being, and the world again became dangerously unstable. Places like Grenada and Panama began to require American attention, and then came the big one. Saddam Hussein, who'd been seen as a counterbalance to Iranian ambitions, came howling into tiny Kuwait, and the armored divisions were on the loose again. Desert Storm proved that we'd been preparing correctly for mass warfare, but then came the little quagmires like Somalia and Rwanda, where soldiers are now learning a new/old trade. From St.-Mihiel to Somalia, this is our story, told by the men who fed the guns and the officers who commanded us.

1

THE FIRST WORLD WAR

Since the fall of Rome, the old men who rule Europe have been writing their history with the blood of their sons. For uncounted thousands of years, swords, spears, and now bayonets and machine guns, had been the pens that recorded the fate of kingdoms, republics, and empires. The assault of infantry, the sweep of cavalry, and the pounding of the guns have always sealed the fates of the nations of Europe . . . until June 28, 1914, a bright, sunny Sunday afternoon.

On that date, Archduke Ferdinand of Austria had been reviewing the troops of the Austro-Hungarian Empire, along with his wife, at the city of Sarajevo, capital of the province of Bosnia. One bomb had already been thrown into his open limousine, and several of his entourage were wounded in an earlier attempt that morning. Ferdinand, perhaps foolishly, ignored the threat and went on with the affairs of state. Suddenly a young Bosnian separatist named Princip stepped out from the crowd and opened up with a Belgian automatic pistol, critically wounding both the duke and his wife, who stepped between him and the assassin, trying to shield her husband with her body. They were taken to the nearest hospital for treatment . . . and the administering of the last rites. Before the day was done, they were dead, and shortly thereafter, Europe was again in flames. But the question is often asked, What did they want, those old men who sent their sons to war? What was the reason for the slaughter? Only world domination. Here are their words.

"God has called on us to civilize the world. We are the missionaries of human progress. We are the salt of the earth. . . . It is a tradition in our house [Hohenzolleren], that we regard ourselves as chosen by God to govern and guide the people. . . . We Germans fear God and nothing else in the world. . . . The German people will be the block of granite on which our Lord will be able to elevate and achieve the civilization of the world. . . ." Assorted comments by Kaiser Wilhelm in addresses to the German people prior to 1910. (It should be remembered that the word *Kaiser,* like the title *Czar,* is a corruption of *Caesar,* and the dream of empire is habit-forming.)

"Do not let us forget the civilizing task which the decrees of Providence have assigned to us. . . . In order that no one shall be left in doubt, we proclaim that henceforth our continental nation has a right to the sea, not only the North Sea but the Mediterranean and the Atlantic. Hence we intend to absorb, one after another, all the provinces which border on Prussia. We will annex successively Denmark, Holland, Belgium, Northern Switzerland, and then Trieste and Venice; finally northern France from the Sambre to the Loire. This program we fearlessly announce." This quote is from the writings of Field Marshal Bronssart von Shellendorf . . . and all this while Hitler was in rompers.

For yet more specious reasons, young men were again being led into "glorious" war. Unlike previous conflicts, though, this time the infantry and cavalry were pinned, like flies against a screen, against the barbed wire that had been invented to contain cattle in the American West. Worse, they were trapped by mines and then murdered in counted hundreds of thousands by the machine guns invented by Hiram Maxim and John Moses Browning, both Americans.

The conflict that created the need for the modern battle

tank may have been a European neighborhood feud, but the technology that made the armored fighting machine necessary was distinctly American. This nation, at that time, was mostly of European descent, and it was inevitable that, eventually, we'd be drawn into their battles. Even back then the "aeroplane" and the steam-driven warship were shrinking the planet, and nations were reaching out across the globe . . . and taking their quarrels with them. That war was about whether Germany or the English-speaking peoples would rule the planet.

The flower of European youth was being slaughtered in the trenches and barbed-wire entanglements like cattle, and even the aid we tried to send across oceans was being sunk by yet another American invention, the ocean-going submarine. The international patents of John Holland and Simon Lake had been perverted by German designers into the first of the commerce-destroying U-boats. History and technology were dragging us, kicking and screaming, into world conflict . . . and a century of war that isn't over yet.

One of the first attacks of Germany into France, after their sweep through Belgium, had been into a region south of Verdun, known as the St.-Mihiel Salient. The battle for Verdun was so bloody that it is a name, like Shiloh or Antietam, that is only whispered, not spoken aloud when soldiers gather to tell the tales. The Germans had spent 300,000 lives in an attempt to take that land, and the French had spent at least 200,000 more in defense of it, then, stalled by wire and the machine gun, both sides had dug in to wait out the war being fought out on other fronts. That was the longest, costliest battle of the conflict and just outside of that ancient city is a mass grave containing both German and French soldiers. The battle had broken the hearts of the soldiers, and the total list of the dead is estimated to exceed 800,000 men. After that point, they just quit fighting. The front had become, in effect, static, both Germans and French regarding it as almost a recuperation area, where exhausted troops from more recent battles could be sent to rest. . . . Until the Americans decided to strike their first blow as an organized military force, under

11

an obscure cavalryman named George S. Patton. But first there would have to be the invention of the tank and its test in combat.

Trench warfare had cost so many human lives for so little gain that something had to be done to break the deadlock. When almost a million young men die for no visible gain, a more efficient killing machine is actually a humanitarian service, if it will make the conflict stop. What had to be done was to so traumatize the German commanders that they would take their dreams of empire and go home. The tank, more than any other factor, was the cause of the end of that war—that and mass production. The British built almost a thousand heavy tanks, while the Germans managed to build only 20, and those too late.

When the first tanks, fresh out of the factories and shipped under cover as "mobile water tanks," went into action, it was too little, too soon. The battle of the Somme had begun in June 1916, and by September, the British commander, General Sir Douglas Haig, had little enough progress to report and was desperate to make some progress of any kind. In his desperation, he seized on the new, untried machine, the tracked tank. Over the protests of the tank's creators, who wanted to wait for greater numbers of their Mark I tank to become available, he sent what he had into battle on September 15.

Of 50 machines present, only 32 would run reliably enough to see combat, and they were spread out over a five-mile front, with infantry that not only had never seen such a sight, but didn't know how to work with them. Of all the ways to confound a battle, secrecy between allies and especially from one's own troops is one of the better ones. Then to compound the error, the tanks were sent in too spread out to do much good. Thirty-two tanks on a five-mile front figures out to one tank per 275 yards. A distance of almost three football fields separated each tank. Most soldiers can't even shoot a rifle accurately that far.

They crushed the defenses though and then got into serious trouble. Capable of only four miles per hour, they nonetheless ground down the barbed wire, spanned the trenches, machine-gunned the terrified Germans . . . and then outran their own infantry and, when they got in among the Germans, attracted the attention of every artillery piece within range. The MkI's armor was only 10mm, or less than half an inch thick, and the Germans had already developed a bullet that would pierce that much steel plate. Lone tanks without accompanying infantry died quickly.

Where terrain forced the tanks to clump up, though, they quickly smashed all resistance and took ground measured in miles rather than yards, with very light infantry casualties. Lessons were being learned, and the fertile mind of an English officer, John Fredric Charles Fuller, absorbed and analyzed all of them. J.F.C. Fuller was one of the keenest military minds of his generation, and his writings on the use of tanks would change history. Unfortunately, one of those who derived the most good from his theorizing was named Erwin Rommel, who at the time was a lieutenant of infantry . . . and in the Austrian army there was a private named Adolf Schicklgrüber, who, according to official reports, conducted himself quite valorously.

Blitzkrieg is usually thought to have been a German invention, but it was invented, quite by accident, by the British. A single strong point in the Somme network of trenches, known as the Gird Trench, was attacked by a lone MkI tank, and it was aided by a strafing Sopwith Camel fighter and locally controlled artillery. There were shockingly few British infantry casualties. Again, a few people took notes, one was Fuller, the others were Germans, who coined the phrase "tank terror." Although they used mostly captured tanks and their few cumbersome A7Vs, "The Boche" were learning. And the German mind has a long memory.

On April 9, 1917, there was a small tank action at Arras, where a few MkIV tanks were successful in reducing a fortress known locally as "The Harp." But Haig was learning, slowly, and was collecting more tanks for a massed assault. He still, however, couldn't quite make himself release them without warning. The long preparatory artil-

13

lery barrage was firmly ingrained in the military mind of the time. At Messenes and Passchendaele, he tried it again.

Dawn, June 7, 1917: With an eye-searing, earth-trembling blast like the eruption of a small volcano, the land in southern Belgium known as the Messenes Ridge lifted into the air and came down as dust, mud, and mangled human bodies mixed inextricably with the other debris. The third battle of Ypres was under way, and the corpse factory was at maximum output. The British had mined the ridge under the noses of the defending Germans and then set off a million pounds of explosives. The ridge, what was left of it, was captured with only moderate casualties, about 25,000. Then things got a bit more serious, for this was imagined by the British commander, General Sir Douglas Haig, as a two-stage operation, the objective being to secure the Passchendaele Ridge and from there menace the German rear. General Haig, it should be noted, was obsessed with gaining a significant military victory before the Americans arrived, and this probably clouded his judgment.

He should have known better. The general had been advised by his engineers that the land now in front of the British positions was reclaimed marshland and, if subjected to a lengthy bombardment, would turn back into a swamp. Better, he was advised and importuned, to try the new war machines—the tanks, of which he had some 200, and attack immediately. In his hurry for success by traditional means, he ignored all advice, massed 3,000 guns in front of Passchendaele Ridge and worked them for ten days.

One hundred and three thousand *tons* of artillery shells turned the already-wet ground into a sea of mud. The land became so treacherous that slime-filled craters large enough to swallow small houses and large vehicles became death traps for the unwary. Many soldiers simply slid helplessly down into the craters and died ignominiously in quagmires, weighted down with weapons and choking on trapped pools of mustard and chlorine gas. Into this, General Douglas Haig sent the first armored mass assault in history. Predictably, it failed. The tankers, still new at their trade, had to spend more time pulling each other out of craters than engaging the enemy.

That offensive had been predicted to last only three or four days. One hundred days, 4,300,000 artillery shells, and 400,000 British casualties later, they gave it up. Meanwhile, there had been some serious wrangling going on behind the lines as to just how to use the tanks most profitably, as the costs in material and human lives were mounting rapidly, to no observable military gain.

The commander of the British Tank Corps, General H. J. Ellis, had been arguing with the commander of the British 3rd Army, Sir Julian Byng, that his tanks, if used properly, could end the stalemate once and for all . . . and he had a target, the great railroad marshalling yards at Cambrai. The Germans had heavily fortified this segment of their ill-gotten gains as part of the defensive works that they called the Hindenburg Line. General Ellis wanted a free rein to set up his attack with no preliminary ten-day artillery barrage to muddy the field. Finally, he convinced Byng, and then the two of them went to work on Haig, who was looking at the collapse of the Eastern Front as the Russians went into the throes of revolution. That, he knew, would release several dozen German divisions for a renewed assault on his lines. Finally, on October 20, 1917, he gave Byng and Ellis the go-ahead . . . on their terms.

First, though, the two generals had to convince all concerned, including themselves, that those fearful fortifications could actually be breached by tanks. To that end, they put the Royal Engineers to work, building an exact duplicate of the Hindenburg Line in a hidden training area. Working from combat reports, aerial photographs, and maps, they built a section that was 40 feet deep and 140 feet long. Heretofore, the only way to breach such entanglements and trenches had been days of bombardment and thousands of human lives. The tanks tore through it in a space of time measured in minutes, and that point in time was the beginning of the end of trench war. Their hammering treads flattened the wire, and gigantic bundles of timber carried on their bows, called *fascines,* filled in the worst of the trenches. The rest were simply spanned by vehicles as long as 37 feet. After that demonstration, the tankers and their commanders were ready to try Cambrai.

For weeks, the supplies had been gathering and the shops had been going full bore, making fascines and fuel and ammunition carriers to be towed up front by the armored vehicles. Lacking the time to make wheels, or even roads on which to roll them, the carriers consisted of steel-runnered sledges with tow chains to connect them to the tanks. With no warning, in the dim dawn hours of November 20, 1917, the sky fell on the German army at Cambrai.

In the early light, with little artillery preparation to muddy the ground, just under 400 tanks churned through the wire, tumbled fascines into the trenches, and produced a gap big enough for an army to pour through. Unfortunately, that army was already almost exhausted and couldn't follow through on the opportunity that the tanks had created. Most especially, the British horse cavalry seemed almost traumatized by the few remaining German machine guns and simply couldn't perform their traditional role of pursuit and encirclement.

The totally predictable German regrouping and counter-attack did two things, neither of them good for the Allied cause. First, the Germans took back almost half of the ground that they'd lost. Second, they captured many British tanks that had broken down and been left for the repair crews to retrieve. They were retrieved, all right . . . by German mechanics, and *nobody* has ever faulted German mechanical expertise. Those MkI tanks were soon fighting again, this time wearing the Maltese Cross of Germany.

So it went, for many months of seesaw bloodletting, until March 21, 1918, when General von Ludendorff launched what would turn out to be his final great offensive, gaining dozens of miles of French territory: Here, the tanks were for the first time forced to fight on the defensive, operating from hidden dugouts and stabbing the onrushing horde in the sides and rear. Unfortunately, the German artillerymen were in that rear, and their antiaircraft gunners had discovered that their 77mm guns made fearsome antitank weapons as well. Gleefully they went to work, slaughtering the new MkIV tanks, one of which bore a hangman's gibbet painted on its bow, between the words *Judge Jefferys*.

That particular tank was commanded by an American officer, Captain James A. McGuire, who'd been on loan to the British army in order to gain battle experience that could be passed on to the now forming AEF (American Expeditionary Force). Captain McGuire had been born on Manhattan Island and had joined the army as an infantryman. In that role he had been sent to France as a liaison officer to the British. He'd fought through the fearful carnage of the Somme, and when he heard of the formation of the new Royal Tank Corps, he instantly volunteered his services. McGuire and his small group of "Yanks" would become the first American tankers to roll a track or fire a tank's gun in anger. His first tank, a MkIV, had been in combat in March 1918, a full eight months before the new American Tank Corps had its combat baptism in the St.-Mihiel Salient.

2

THE FIRST AMERICAN
TANKERS

James A. McGuire and his American group were accepted into "J" Company of the 10th Tank Battalion and given a tank and training. Since the tradition had been adopted that a tank's name should begin with the company letter, the name *Judge Jefferys* was painted on her bow. After the tank had taken her mortal hit, south of Achiet-le-Grand, McGuire and his Americans were given a new mount, the state-of-the-art Mark V.

The new tank, which they received just in time for the battle of Amiens in August 1918, needed a name, though, and with this thought, let's read the story of Captain McGuire in his own words.

Since the name had to start with a "J," I selected the sinister death sign of Africa: "Ju-Ju." What more fitting symbol for a war chariot, a fighting tank? I found a confederate in the letterer of the battalion, who, besides inscribing the name on the nose of my new tank, painted a large white grinning skull between the words. The Ju-Ju, a MkV male, was the latest of its kind. Powered by a Ricardo engine and equipped with a one-man driving control, it was miles ahead of the old MkIV, which required four men to handle its shifting and steering.

18

Our battlefront in this effort to relieve the threat on Amiens was 11 miles long. On the left (north), it started just south of the village of Morlancourt, which is north of the River Somme, and extended in a zigzag wave to the southward. Sandwiched in between contingents of Americans, Australians, Canadians, and various French units were more of the British line regiments. The 10th Tank Battalion, my own, was assigned the post of honor in the assault, the extreme left end of the attack. The flank of any storming army is a point of vital weakness because if it is turned by an enemy, the whole attack can be shattered, which is what the Germans had done at Cambrai.

On the evening of August 7, I listened with a fluttering heart to the doubtful distinction that was being conferred on me. Our major had designated the Ju-Ju to fight on the extreme left of the battalion; this meant that our tank was to be on the left of the entire attack—a place for glory and other possibilities well known to old soldiers. At mess, the commanding officer, excusing himself for talking "shop," asked if there were any questions on the morrow's show. Having answered the few we asked, he added, "Eat heartily, gentlemen, for we are leaving early in the morning and there is little likelihood of obtaining any breakfast." He might well have added that the meal would probably be the last for many of us.

The crews had already been warming the powerful Ricardo engines, and soon the tanks began lumbering from their shelters. Due to the overflowing of the Somme and the fact that artillery had destroyed the centuries-old agricultural drainage system, the tank park was a swamp, and we had to use unditching procedures just to get out of it. A check on solid ground showed that everyone had made it.

Following one another, avoiding roads which were taboo, we trekked eastward. Most of us elected to walk alongside the tanks, breathing in the cold, wet air before being cooped up inside for what might be our last jaunt. Suddenly a tank stopped, then another. Two drivers had fainted from the heat. If the heat was stifling enough to bowl us over in the cold, gray dawn, what would it be like when the sun got up and all the ports were closed tight? Two more drivers got in, and the column lumbered on.

Stragglers came drifting by like flotsam on a restless sea. Transport streamed to and from the forward area like ghostly wraiths in the early morning mist. A group of walking wounded stopped and watched the tanks crunching and groaning along. They made no comment. Soon the old familiar rumble of guns became clearer. From time to time, the lowering sky was split with crimson light as nearby batteries went into action. Despite the relative quiet, a sinister something brooded over us; we sensed the lull before the storm. A runner appeared, and we changed direction, moving through a labyrinth of shell holes.

Suddenly we were there, the jump-off point. White tape was laid on the ground to guide the following infantry. Each tank was assigned its position, and the major called a whispered conference in the lee of a tank. The time for the kickoff was set for 4:20. I glanced at my luminous dial: a matter of minutes remained. Tank commanders moved off to their stations with a typical British "Cheerio." I made a last check of the Ju-Ju, and my driver pointed to the compass. The nose of the bus was pointed north instead of eastward! Calling the crew to me, I sat on the ground with my back against the warm metal of the Ju-Ju. It felt good on that cold morning. Talking hardly above a whisper, I explained. The enemy had captured a piece of high terrain directly to our front. Our section would have to trek north for a short distance and then swing to the right.

"Ridout," I said to my driver, "be sure to watch the tank on your right; when it swings right, so do we. Remember that we are on the extreme left flank and if we fail to keep in touch with our right, we are in the blue."

Everything was ready, and planes hummed low over us like giant bats out of the night. They served to drown the clatter from our tanks and keep the enemy guessing. Suddenly the sky at the back of us turned red as if lit by huge torches. Our batteries had gone into action! What an inferno! The roar was deafening. The tortured air above us screamed and moaned as a rain of projectiles sought targets in enemy land. A shrill whistle pierced the din, and tank engines came to life with splitting crashes. We were off.

I dove through the sponson door, which clanged shut at my heels as I took my accustomed place, in the center of the tank with my eyes on a level with the vision slits. As I became accustomed to the murk, I looked down and saw my men, good lads and true, all of them. You need such in a game like that. I could visualize that long line of ours stretching away to the south, across the old Somme Canal—British, Americans, French—soldiers of many lands all tense as coiled springs . . . waiting. Then the signal came, and suddenly the Devil's Playground was peopled with scurrying figures. Some went over for king and country, some for democracy, some for la patrie, some for Allah; a few probably went over simply because they were essentially sons of Mars.

The white ghostly radiance of a Boche rocket brought out in cameo the barbed wire and the grisly reminders of war in no-man's-land. The light lasted only a minute or two, and then the darkness closed in, deeper than before, with the mist thickened by battle smoke. Seconds passed, and then another flare broke with a tiny *plop* overhead.

Now the German trenches literally spouted flares and colored lights, and his machine guns began their staccato beat along his entire front. On the left end following the 10th Tank Battalion came the 7th Queen's Imperials, and on the right, a regiment from the American 33rd Division. Proper playboys, these, for this staggering bash at the enemy. In the Ju-Ju, we could sense the battle by the dull thuds of exploding shells and the vicious spatter of machine-gun bullets on our sides as the gunners wasted their futile streams on our armor.

Sharing my small seat was a Corporal Bayley of the Queen's, who was my liaison with his outfit. I touched him on the elbow and shouted at him to warn my driver, Ridout, to keep close in order not to miss that turn. He was back in a jiffy. His face told me before his words did. We had lost contact and gone out into the blue. But Ridout was not too much to blame at that. The fog had thickened too quickly for calculation. It was simply one of those unfortunate and unforeseen developments that characterize every battle.

We bumped and lurched over German trenches, but saw no

sign of the enemy. After a bit of this, I decided to have a look around outside to get our bearings. The Ju-Ju had slowed down to a slow waddle, and I squeezed out with a map to try and get an orientation. Suddenly I stopped; I'd seen movement. A group of men were pushing their way toward me through a curtain of fog. Was it an enemy patrol? My hand stiffened on the Smith and Wesson I'd brought over from America, three long years ago. Then my breath went out in a glad exhalation. I had recognized British Tommies led by a lieutenant. We were both glad to see one another. The infantry and the tanks were both developing a brother-in-arms feeling. But we had another tie that binds. We were both lost.

The infantry officer and I sat on the edge of a shell hole and compared notes. Apparently we were in Fritz's second line of defenses, but well north of our original objectives. While we were talking, an infantryman approached and asked permission to put some of his gear on the tank, which was beginning to roll slowly forward. Apparently, he had missed nothing when the quarter-bloke passed out the tools of combat. Shovels, picks, even sandbags. With my approval he went over to the tank that was slowly waddling about, and began to unload. Suddenly there was a terrified yell.

The lad who'd had too much to carry was halfway up the back of the bus. He'd been picked up by the seat of his pants by a bit of barbed wire that was tangled in the tracks. While I ran to the front to signal Ridout to halt, there was an even louder peal than before. In order to stay his progress, our unhappy doughboy had grabbed the hot exhaust pipe.

Since haphazard wanderings in enemy lines would gain us nothing, the infantry officer and I decided to head northwest by west, hoping to find a headquarters for instructions. We encountered nothing much except some enemy artillery retaliation, which was fortunately, we thought, well scattered. Then I detected the sweet crushed-apple smell of phosgene gas, which explained those carefully spaced shells. Neither of us were using our gas masks, which I regretted later. After almost falling into a sunken road, we found a regimental HQ and parted company with our infantry patrol. We'd been sent to the headquarters of the 35th Infantry Brigade, which we eventually found, after some smart cross-country work with the Ju-Ju, which was now prowling alone.

There, I was questioned by a tall, lanky brigadier with a bandage over his eyes, due to some gas this morning, as to whether I would be pleased to function with him. I had clicked for more dirty work. I told him that I would be pleased to do so if he could service my tank with fuel and ammunition and notify my headquarters where I was, and supply rations for my crew. He agreed quickly, then asked, "What is your name, Tanks?"

"McGuire, sir."

At this he jumped up and, taking me by the arm, led me to a room cut into the side of the dugout. Apparently this was the officer's mess, as there were several officers there, assembled around an ornate table which had been salvaged from some nearby manor house. The general, it turned out, was an Irishman and introduced me around as such, without asking where I'd been born, which was on Manhattan Island. I later found out that he was a baronet to boot. I accepted a tot of whisky, which on an empty stomach would ordinarily have meant a sudden extinction of my higher faculties. However, the gas that I had inhaled must have served as a buffer. More drinks for various worthy causes were proposed and downed, but I still navigated under my own steam. I had no desire to eat. Perhaps some chemist can supply the answer.

Once I'd gotten the plan of the proposed operation, I went back to my tank, which had now been serviced, and my crew was supplied with rations. As I looked at my bewhiskered Ju-Ju fighters, I knew what the crew of Blackbeard the pirate must have looked like. Briefly, I explained what the good general wished us to do. He wanted us to "go over" with his Cambridgeshire Battalion. Since we were outside the normal area of operations, this attack was to be in the nature of a demonstration to conceal the real flank of our force. The general was fully aware that another Cambrai-style counterstroke might be tried on his front, which was actually the flank. To give support to this suspicion, it had been found out that we were facing the German 27th Division, who were normally used as shock troops; they were Würtemburgers and not used for simple line-holding. I'd met them before in the Salient and on the Somme in 1916.

I had of needs to do a commander's recon and decided on a stroll up to the front line to look over our jumping-off spot. Our own front line was just ahead of me as I found the high ground. Boche shells were landing in no-man's-land and shrapnel was breaking overhead as I found an infantry officer standing with his back to the parapet. Gory remains of what had once been cheerful, smiling Tommies were piled on one another in an indescribable shambles in muddy water.

"A bit of a mess," the infantryman said, with a gesture. "The Boche must have spotted us manning the trenches and—" Another wave of the hand that covered the bleeding, shattered horror.

"The brigadier instructed me to take my tank and go over with you chaps at 1:35," I said. "My bus is just over the ridge and is ready. Is that news?"

"No, a runner was just sent up."

I retraced my steps to the tank and gave Bayley and Ridout the final orders. I pointed out the best way down the slope and gave them the time. I wouldn't make the jump-off with them but would climb aboard as they went by the front line. The crew were drinking coffee and eating hardtack, and when I took some of the strong black coffee, my stomach turned. That gas. After a while I got up and went forward.

The Cambridgeshires were going over the top as I arrived, and I jumped up on a little knoll and gave the double-time signal to the oncoming Ju-Ju, and down the slope he came like a charging rhinoceros. As the tank ranged alongside, the sponson door flew open, and Corporal Bayley pulled me inside. I found my seat and gazed through the slits. Then my knee was nudged by Bayley, who was pointing through his gun-sight opening. A long gray column of mud-stained Boche were following a tiny Cambridgeshire infantryman. What a catch, a couple of hundred at least, but they were beginning to waver, and were about to head back toward their own lines.

Like the flip of a gnat's wing, I was out the sponson door,

telling the crew to keep me covered. Hitting the column in a subway rush, I shouldered my way to the leaders, who were all underofficers. "Over that way, Fritz," I barked, school German forgotten, jerking my thumb toward the lone infantryman. With the tank's guns and that grinning skull looming over them, they obediently turned and linked up with their solitary captor.

When we again linked up with the Cambridgeshires, they had the situation well in hand, but needed some machine-gun nests ironed out, which we did with gusto. We headed back to brigade headquarters and their brigadier was visibly pleased. He was also interrogating a Boche prisoner in fluent German. "Pay attention, Tanks," he said, then shot a stream of questions at a small disheveled German. The little Boche answered in some animation, and it turned out that he was much put out with his superiors.

They'd told him that he was going to be sent to a bomb-proof job in a peaceful spot directing traffic, not occupying a front-line trench. Accordingly, he wanted to do them as dirty as possible and gladly told about dugouts and emplacements and gave other military information.

"Tanks," the brigadier boomed. "Take your tank into Mor-lancourt tomorrow afternoon and do a reconnaissance to verify all this information. I do not think you will find many of the enemy, he appears to be retiring." There was an off chance that he might be right, but I had the feeling that that hamlet was as full of Boche as a soldier's shirt is full of itchy-coo.

Business was picking up. A runner from the line appeared. A Cambridgeshire officer had inquired if the tank would please bring up some hand grenades, Stokes mortar bombs, machine-gun ammunition, and a few other items. So it came to pass that, at dusk, the Ju-Ju sallied forth and delivered its load as per specification. The infantry officer asked us to try to take out a pesky machine gun, but the slope was just too great for the Ricardo engine from where we were. That particular Boche would just have to wait for morning. We settled down right in the front lines for a bit of sleep. The crew were inside, and I took a blanket and settled down underneath the nose of the bus. The grumbling of the guns was increasing as I scooped out a place for hip and shoulder on the floor of the sunken road. Would Morpheus take me in his arms? Not a chance. The artillery of the opposing sides had gotten into a counter-battery duel, which continued all night.

The next morning, after a bit of breakfast, we humped off. The day was already hot and dusty, and the ground was hot as the floor of a desert. We stopped under cover of a small rise of ground and were met by a squad of Tommies under a corporal. It still being the brigadier's idea that this place was deserted, these few men had been detailed to occupy it. Still obeying my orders, I also decided to play my hunch.

"The tank is to make a reconnaissance of the village," I told them. "My orders to you are that if we meet any resistance, you will return immediately to the trench. In any case it should not take long. We will be back for tea."

We rocked over the trench and set off. It was hard going. The Ju-Ju lurched like a drunken man. An empty ration tin careened crazily across the metal floor. I tried to make out objects through the turret openings, but the angles were too steep; I saw either a piece of blue sky or piled masonry. Suddenly there was a grating noise overhead, our unditching beam had worked loose and gone by the board. One of my gunners keeled over backward—heat prostration. Then another. I jumped down and pulled their collars loose and dumped water on them. I got back to my post as the going smoothed out and saw bits of colored glass, the village church, and we were moving through the village square. Everything seemed deserted, but I saw a dark oblong like the entrance to a dugout and fired a few shots into it from my Smith and Wesson. Out spewed a torrent of Boches, and not only from this dugout. They raced through the square, and suddenly all my guns were belching at once. The Germans were heading for the exit, a wide road leading out of town, but so was my driver, Ridout.

What a racket. My six-pounder cannons and Hotchkiss machine guns cut down those fleeing figures in batches. The firing ceased as suddenly as it had begun. The road was carpeted with gray figures. Some were crawling to the side. Three things had happened: The general was wrong, I was right, and a Boche prisoner had his revenge. The Ju-Ju resumed his progress out of town, and running into an open space, the guns resumed the Devil's Tattoo.

This time the target was the crew of a Boche field artillery battery. My gunners went after the gun crews, but failed to break the wheels off the guns themselves, and when I yelled at them to hit the guns, Bayley showed me the broken extractor of his six-pounder. It was out of action for a while. We were now in the outskirts of the town, and I decided to take a quick hop outside and locate our observation balloons and get some kind of orientation. There, on the road, about 35 yards away was a trench mortar on little wheels with two Boches getting ready to fire it at us. I reached for my revolver, wondering what my forward machine gunner was doing, when another Boche opened up with a hidden machine gun.

A long kellerman dive got me back into the bus as the door slammed at my heels with bullets drumming on it. A rifle muzzle was thrust in through the hatch normally used for dumping expended shells, and Bayley shot through the hole with his Webley revolver, ending that menace. Fritz by now must know that this was a serenade by a lone tank and was hitting us with everything he had.

Bullet splashes, illuminated the interior like fireflies in a tropical gloom. Bayley had burns on his arms from those bullet splashes, and I had some on my face. Then a bullet smacked the engine between my legs. An armor-piercing shell had got through the skin . . . but not damaged the Ricardo. We'd better get out of here. Back we came to where that light battery was, and the gunners were frantically swinging those tank-killing guns to bear on us. Ridout saw them, and to avoid giving them a target, he suddenly swung the tank around on its heel and drove straight through a house and then a barn. Luckily there were no cellars.

The corporal drew my attention by barking in my ear. "The six-pounders are out of action and no ammunition. One Hotchkiss has a bent barrel and the other has a jam and most of the machine-gun ammunition is gone too, sir." Now it was up to the driver. Fritz had us in range and under observation from his balloons, which could talk to their artillery batteries with telephones. Just about then the heat brought me to my knees. Ridout had to get us out of there or we were done for.

The tank seemed to hesitate, then lurched forward again with an earsplitting crash of dirt, masonry, and timbers as Ju-Ju plowed through yet another building. The dust finally settled, and through the slits I saw a glorious sight, the wash-basin helmet of a British Tommy. Unbelievingly, he stared at this lone unescorted monster coming out of enemy lines. We lumbered to a halt in the lee of the same hill we had started from several hours ago and tumbled out. We removed our unconscious comrades from the stifling interior. Ridout, gallant lad, was speechless, just laying on his back and gazing up at the sky.

An infantry subaltern of a Scottish regiment approached.

"Where did you chaps come from?"

"Just did a reconnaissance of that village for the brigade."

"We're going over at five, why not come along?" asked this gentleman from the north of the Tweed.

"Sorry, we must report back to the brigadier."

Then, I don't know why, we shook hands silently.

I got the crew back into the tank and we began to trek back. Passing through a cluster of houses, one of the boys jumped out and ran into a ruined dwelling. I thought perhaps the strain had affected him, but he soon returned with a small chair and a stovepipe hat. Signaling to Ridout to stop, he climbed on board. I did not interfere because I was feeling that way myself. Solemnly he climbed on top of the bus, plumped down the chair, and installed himself thereon. From this perch he proceeded to bandy words with the passing infantry.

When we came to the old sunken road, I reported in from that CP so that they could telephone in to our own outfit. While waiting, a group of walking wounded from the 10th came by. One, a corporal, came over to me. It was Reed, one of my old Judge Jefferys warriors.

"You did a fine show, sir," he said. "At first we thought you'd been taken prisoner."

He was bleeding from the jaw and I said, "Thanks, Corporal. Where did you get that wound?"

"Shrapnel, sir," he said diffidently, and I chased him off to the dressing station. Reed was a simon-pure fighting man from Ohio.

A runner dashed up. I was to report to brigade HQ. Great, a lone tank out in the open under the telescopes of balloon observers.

I directed Ridout to zigzag back to the 35th to make us a hard target, just in case. I was right. An artillery observer tried to bracket the Ju-Ju but must have had buck fever. At any rate, the zigging of the bus was too much for the Boche artillery. I tried to time the turns of the tank myself, but had no better luck than the enemy. Ridout outguessed everyone. When we finally vanished out of range, a heartfelt sigh bubbled up out of my diaphragm.

Outside brigade HQ, I saw my Irish brigadier talking to another general. I gathered he was waiting for me. "I say, Tanks, over here," he said. I came up to him and gave him my best salute. Returning it, he spoke to the other general, who was relieving him.

"Let's take a look at this great tank of his."

We circled the Ju-Ju. He certainly looked the part of a battle-scarred war wagon. Everything on the outside was gone by the board. The unditching beam and the Boche helmet that had hung from the jaws of the skull were both missing. In the back there remained but a few splinters where a wooden box of grenades had been. And then the relieving brigadier remarked, "By Jove, the thing is nickle-plated with bullet splashes."

I was told that I could report back to my battalion. Both generals shook my hand and praised me too much. After a strain, this is liable to make one unglued. I was preparing to swing aboard when a Tommy, who had been standing in a group nearby, approached and said, "You know, sir, you said you'd be back for tea." I nodded at the recollection. He was one of the squad who'd been given to us for an escort.

"Well, sir, you were," he added, and the admiration shining in his eyes beat what the generals had said. That symbol of the

African death sign brought luck, for we came through without a casualty. Without doubt, that grinning skull scared off the evil spirits.

So ends the tale of Ju-Ju, the first recorded American tank crew in action in any war. They started many of our traditions, and we carry them on proudly.

This story was first printed in a British military publication called The Legionary. *It is condensed here by the author from an article in the* British Tank Journal, *courtesy of the Tank Museum at Bovington, England, Mr. David Fletcher, Chief Librarian and author.*

3

TANK BATTALIONS AND HORSE CAVALRY

General Samuel Rockenbach, a career cavalry officer had been appointed by General Pershing to command the fledgling U.S. Tank Corps in late 1917. In this task he was ably assisted by two young captains: Dwight David Eisenhower and George S. Patton. While Eisenhower stayed behind in the States to oversee the training of prospective tankers, the fiery Patton, another transplanted cavalryman, was sent straight to France to get his hands on the tanks and to look over the ground. Literally. After he'd gotten his men and tanks together at the training ground at Langres, he, knowing that a battle at St.-Mihiel was imminent, set out to reconnoiter the ground personally, in true cavalry fashion.

There had long been a live-and-let-live attitude between the Germans and the French in the sector, which had been occupied and continuously fortified since 1916 . . . until the Americans became part of the Allied forces. On a night patrol in no-man's-land with the French infantry, Patton crawled quietly toward the German lines, probably thinking that this was no way for a cavalryman to approach the enemy. According to accounts, he was approaching the German wire and was surprised to hear the Germans whistle at them, quickly answered in kind by the French, who, satisfied with the status quo, turned and glided back to their trenches. That was the prevalent attitude in the whole salient, but Patton had at least gotten a good look at the ground. Tanks could work here, *if* the artillery didn't get carried away and pulverize the area into mush. Since the tactics developed for this operation were of the try-and-hope variety, now known as a "Hail Mary," the result was likely to be unpredictable and, in fact, a bit wilder than a novelist could have imagined.

Patton and Rockenbach had studied the British and French experiences and evolved their own version of how to run tanks in a combat zone. The planning stages were a nightmare compounded by the French railway system. They didn't get the last of their tanks off the flatcars until 0300 on September 12, 1918, two hours before the initial attack was to begin, which meant that the tankers were going into battle minus several nights' worth of sleep. Worse, the artillery commander who was to deliver the initial bombardment developed a terminal dose of impacted bureaucracy and refused to deliver the smoke shells needed to blind the Jerries. Patton complained directly to Rockenbach and got the smoke. . . . The name of the artillery commander who nearly queered the assault has survived time. It was Major Murphy.

Everything seemed to go wrong at once. The tanks began to run out of fuel, the infantry didn't know how to work with them, and then their commander vanished from the field HQ. Captain Patton, now brevetted to major, was limited in communications to runners . . . and pigeons. Frustrated by lack of communications with his tanks, he abandoned his HQ and went forward into the fight on foot, chasing down his tanks and directing them personally.

Seeing that his tankers were, for the most part, leading the infantry and doing their part, Patton stopped to pass some words with Brigadier General MacArthur (yes, that MacArthur) next to a railway cut where some French tankers were pinned down by light shell fire. Disdaining to take cover, the two officers stood in the open and discussed the battle while a creeping artillery barrage rolled over them. Then Patton, who'd gotten his tactical update from MacArthur, strode on to the town of Essey, where he rounded up five of his tanks and sent them over a stone bridge and into the town. For this action, Patton was roundly reamed out by General Rockenbach, for getting out of contact with higher headquarters.

The attack, however, kept on. Pannes, Beney, Nonsard— all fell to the rumbling, clanking, fire-spitting monsters. They arrived in Nonsard out of gas, and Patton, still out with his tankers, walked back seven miles to round up more gasoline. Forty tanks had been either stuck in trenches or had run out of fuel, but all were recovered and put back into action. The night of the 13th, some 50 tanks laagered up near the town of Vigneulles to await resupply. Around them, having come through the wire after the tanks smashed it, "B" Troop, 2nd U.S. Cavalry (horse mounted) scouted for any remaining Germans. Here, on the battle-fields of France, was where the last of the American cavalry troopers, some of whom had fought in the Old West, passed on their traditions to the new arm of decision, the tankers.

CAPTAIN ERNEST HARMON, 2nd Cavalry
September 12, 1918
West of Vigneulles, Eastern France

The night of September 11–12 was dark and rainy. Our squadron (provisional) started from its hiding place at 8 P.M. with only six miles to go. The march was very trying because the road was filled with troops and the ground to the sides was very swampy, which made it impossible to turn out of the column. The last platoon arrived at our position at 12:55 A.M. The squadron was formed in platoon mass with 100 yards between troops and 75 yards in depth between troops. The artillery preparation was to begin at 1:00 A.M., and the men stood by their horses' heads in order to control them in case of fright. While many of the animals were experienced cavalry mounts, many were not, nor were they used to the clanking and roaring of the new machines of war, the tanks.

We'd not had our own horses shipped from the States with us. Instead, the 2nd Cav had been mounted on a collection of animals from half the veterinary hospitals of France and England. We had everything from Spanish ponies to Belgian draft horses. We'd not had the chance to train them under fire, so their reaction to artillery fire was in some doubt, especially seeing how close we were to the gun batteries. Guns were all around us; we could hear the clang of the breechblocks as the guns were loaded at 12:55. The rain still fell gently as, at 12:58, two signal guns were fired. The night was so dark that one could not see the horses from one platoon to another. At exactly 1:00 A.M., all the guns fired at once.

It seemed as if all hell had broken loose. The sky became as light as day from the continuous artillery discharges. The horses did not seem to mind after the first few discharges, even though some of the guns were as near as 200 yards from our position. The bombardment was to continue until 5:00 A.M., when a rolling barrage was to be laid down and the infantry were to follow the tanks over the top. Once we'd ascertained that the horses wouldn't stampede, they were ordered unsaddled, and the equipment was placed in front of them. The men tied their reins to their mounts' legs, lay down, and in spite of the frightful din, nearly everyone fell asleep, so exhausted were they from the marching and confusion.

At 0500 hours, a drumfire barrage was thrown in front of our advancing troops. So many guns were in action that one could scarcely distinguish between reports. The large guns increased their range, firing from map coordinates and began firing on crossroads behind the German lines. As we heard the next day, they did great execution on the retreating Germans as our infantry, their path cleared by the tanks, closed on them.

We watered our horses in mud holes nearby, saddled up, and made ready for instant duty. About 1130 hours, we received orders to move up to Seicheprey. This was a town situated on the front-line trenches, which had long since been battered to ruins. We passed through batteries of 155mm guns and larger pieces. On our way, we passed long files of prisoners and lines of ambulances filled with wounded. We crossed the lines of the trenches with great difficulty, except at points where the tanks had already broken them down.

Throughout the latter months of WWI, there was much experimenting with the combined use of horse cavalry and the new mechanized cavalry. Some ideas worked, some did not. Oddly enough, it was the Russians, not the Germans, Americans, or British, who finally made the combination work, 20 years later. Captain Harmon's report continues:

At 0215, we received orders to proceed to Nonsard. This town was situated some nine kilometers behind the original front lines, and had been reached by our infantry and tanks early in the afternoon. The infantry had established outposts and rested at this point. The road was choked with artillery and ambulances, and we were forced to make our way between barbed-wire entanglements and trenches. Fortunately, our tanks had plowed their way through the barbed-wire entanglements, which greatly helped our advance. We reached Nonsard about 4:00 P.M. Our mission was to reconnoiter toward Vigneulles, a town seven kilometers north of Nonsard. A thick wood lay between Nonsard and Vigneulles with the main road running through it, crossed by several military roads and local woodcutter's roads.

"F" Troop formed the advance guard. Specific instructions were given by the squadron commander to march rapidly, to put out a strong left flank patrol but not to put out a right flank patrol as that was covered by the infantry. This was a great error. Immediately on entering the woods, the point patrol encountered a dismounted German who tried to run. One private tried to shoot him with a pistol, missed twice, and then dismounted and shot the Jerry between the shoulder blades with his rifle. A few minutes later, a mounted man was captured, and we discovered many horses running loose in the woods. In some of the huts, cooking fires were still burning.

"H" Troop, followed by part of "D" Troop, now suddenly appeared from the left flank and came onto the main road just ahead of the advance party of "F" Troop. This part of the force had been sent across the field through an opening in the woods 300 yards to the left of the main road, with directions to proceed toward Vigneulles paralleling the main road. The unit commander had not received instructions as to the duties or even the exact whereabouts of "F" Troop and, to avoid an impassable stretch of road, had swung into the main road. This situation was very confusing. At this moment, the two troop commanders rode forward to a slight ridge from where the point patrol had signaled enemy in sight. Down the slope they could see a continuous column of men, vehicles, and horses only 300 yards in front of them, crossing the main road from left to right. It was a column of retreating Germans, and the decision was made to take them under fire.

As an experiment, our troops had been equipped with Browning auto rifles at the ratio of one per troop with 2,500 rounds of ammunition. This was one instance where the heavy draft horses were invaluable. It was decided to cover the crossroads at once with fire from the auto rifles and to move through the woods by the right flank and cut the column off. However good this plan might have been, it was doomed by the fact that the auto rifles opened fire before the troops were ready, thus losing the element of surprise. As our leading elements moved off the road to form a line of foragers, the Germans set up a machine gun at the crossroads and opened up on us. We were in woods so heavy that the enemy could not be seen.

The American cavalrymen, unlike the British troopers who were armed with revolvers and sabers, carried Colt auto pistols, Springfield rifles, and their own integral automatic weapons, the famed BARs. Also, unlike the Brits, they were experienced in heavy cover and ambuscades, having soldiered in such places as the Philippines and the Panama

Canal Zone. Not traumatized by having had their commanders order charges against machine guns, they faced German Maxim guns with considerably more flexibility. Captain Harmon continues:

We quickly decided to move about 300 yards to the rear, dismount the troops, and move forward as skirmishers on foot, as the heavy woods made mounted action difficult. The command "fours left about, trot" was given. Our horses were green, and under the present excitement a command to gallop back would have stampeded them, as some horses had been hit.

The men were falling back to the next crossroads in good order when suddenly a machine gun opened up on the column from a small trail leading from the main road on the right. This was our unprotected flank. The Germans had allowed our patrols to go by and had brought their guns to the edge of the woods as the column started back. Fortunately, the Germans, trained to shoot at infantry, shot too low, only wounding a few horses in the legs. All our men opened fire with their pistols as they passed the machine gun, killing its crew. Of course, the untrained horses broke into a gallop. The head of the column, being without a leader, dashed past the crossroads before an officer could get in front.

Then a second machine gun opened fire from the left, and the cavalrymen seemed to automatically turn *into* the stream of fire and charged the gun, emptying their magazines down into the startled crew as their horses leaped the position. The Germans had hardly fired before they were all killed by the pistol fire of the cavalrymen as they passed at a gallop. No commands were given to our men, the firing was done from a sense of self-preservation and was effective. After this incident, the men had all the confidence in the world in their Colt auto pistols.

There were several more incidents of this type as the campaign wore on, and the cavalrymen performed good service, gradually replenishing their untrained horses with good German stock; meanwhile, the tanks, which had done yeoman service had pulled back to reorganize, repair, and restock. They would be back in action next month when the battle reopened.

Throughout the remaining months of the war and in the long dry period between the wars, there was always interaction between the older horsed cavalry, whose traditions went back past Rome and the chariots of the Bronze Age, and the modern "rude mechanical types" who were changing the face of battle all out of recognition. The saber was passed, however, and we hold their tradition dear, as will be seen in later chapters. Their traditions are ours, and our guidon flags are still trimmed with the gold of the cavalry.

4

THE MEUSE-ARGONNE OFFENSIVE

SGT. ARTHUR SNYDER
October 4, 1918, St.-Mihiel Salient,
South of Verdun, Eastern France

The little Renault FT series tank known as the "Five of Hearts," commanded by Arthur Snyder, was in trouble. Its mission was to support the American infantry who were trying to evict the Germans from a position they'd held for nearly two years. Snyder and his seven-ton combat machine were supposed to be part of a platoon of five tanks commanded by a Lieutenant Wood, but during the previous four days, the platoon had been whittled down to just two, one commanded by Lieutenant Wood, the other by Sergeant Snyder.

Major George Patton, who'd formed and trained these two American light tank battalions, the 344th and the 345th, had originally chosen playing card suits for easy combat identification of his tanks. As a result, each tank in a company got a heart, spade, diamond, or club, plus a number, in this case, number five. The platoon had originally gone into battle on September 12 in what was known as the Meuse-Argonne offensive, west of the Argonne Forest, in an assault on the Hindenburg Line. That battle had lasted until September 18, when the exhausted tankers and their battle-worn machines had been withdrawn. There had been a period of rest and refit, and then again the little French Renault tanks had been thrown into battle with American crews. Again they were going to assault the massive, almost impregnable Hindenburg Line, Germany's last defense against invasion. *"Break this line,"* they thought, *"and the war is over."*

The jump-off in the current assault was on September 26, 1918, but the 344th Battalion had quickly bogged down in the soft, shell-pulverized soil. Mechanical attrition had quickly set in, and the battalion, which had originally boasted almost 70 tanks, was quickly trimmed down to only 30 "runners," by October 4. The Hearts platoon of "C" Company, 344th Bn. was down to two tanks on that dismal morning, and its job was to support the whole 16th Infantry Regiment of the 1st Division. This is the way Sgt. Snyder tells the story:

We were out into the salient, and Lieutenant Wood was on my right, proceeding along a hedgerow from which the Germans were producing a severe volume of machine-gun flank fire. My orders were to keep strict formation on Lieutenant Wood's tank, and when I saw it change direction, I did likewise, turning away from the attack. If we had had radios, this wouldn't have happened, because Wood was wounded and his driver, Corporal Rogers, was taking him back behind the infantry assault line.

Then Rogers, who was only a kid in his teens, under great danger to himself, got out of his tank and crawled beyond the assault wave and signaled me to continue with the attack. As I was turning, a German shell exploded under the right track of my tank, severing it in two, like a piece of string. Of course the tank could then go only in circles. My driver, Kelly, got it swung around, facing our lines and we got out through the driver's door and had a crawling race to the rear of our assault line.

Here we found Wood and Rogers and their tank, the Five of Hearts.

I took command of it and using Rogers as my driver, returned to the attack. The enemy machine guns in the hedgerow had been practically silenced, but the infantry could make little progress because of heavy frontal machine-gun fire. As we proceeded, we suddenly encountered at close quarters, an extremely large machine-gun nest that was well concealed in a big shell crater. The position had undoubtedly been improved by field fortification methods, and it contained at least three machine guns . . . maybe more.

We were fortunate that the position was not supported by an accompanying light artillery piece, because in the fog and smoke, we were practically on it before observing it. I saw a German raise a potato-masher-shaped hand grenade to throw at us, but if he let it go, it did no harm, and we were causing confusion and damage in that nest with our 37mm cannon fire.

The armor plate on those old French Renault tanks was good, but when you came to close quarters, the splinters from bullets hitting around the vision slits did considerable damage to our personnel. Wood got wounded this way. As Rogers and I were trying to get around the right flank of that big machine-gun nest, he was hit about the eyes with splinters. He fell forward in his driver's seat but, fortunately, did not stall the motor, which was an easy thing to do with those old tanks.

I knelt behind Rogers, cautioning him as to the use of the foot throttle, and reaching forward to the steering levers, steered the tank back to our lines. The blood from Rogers's wounds was blinding him, and when I left him at the dressing station, it was obvious that he was no longer fit for duty. I took his .45 so the Five of Hearts would be sure to have a full complement of weapons, and then I looked for another tank mate. I was in the process of trying to get an infantryman when I saw a runner wearing the Tank Corps armband (a triangular patch divided into yellow, blue, and red segments, similar to today's armor patch). I found that he was of the 345th Battalion and had become lost from his organization. He told me that he had graduated from our driver's school at the

Tank Center at Langres, so I immediately pressed him into service as my third driver for the day.

We at once returned to the attack and found that the big machine-gun position had been taken. Some of its personnel were being taken to the rear as prisoners. We proceeded down the Exermont Ravine. At the bottom of this defile is a stream and to the west of Exermont was a stone bridge that spanned it. Orders had been issued not to use this bridge because of its being mined.

At this time a carrier pigeon arrived at battalion HQ bearing the following report in its message capsule:

No. 14 Oct 20   Pigeon Service

Arrived in EXERMONT RAVINE at 10:30 A.M. with tanks 500 yds west of EXERMONT. Much antitank gun fire vicinity (11). Two tanks disabled 200 yds south of ravine. Four tanks seen on right approaching EXERMONT. 18th Infantry entering ravine. Enemy active and in force about EXERMONT and hills north of this ravine. Our barrage about 600 yards beyond this ravine. Will proceed on gaining contact with infantry. Place (1.0-0.8) Time 10:30 A.M.

Signed Jones
2d Lieut T.C.

Sgt. Snyder's report now continues:

My driver and I were just getting ready to reconnoiter for a stream crossing when I was approached by a captain from the 16th Infantry. He informed me that his company was being held up by machine-gun fire from the other side of the ravine. I told him that I would support his company as soon as I could find a place to ford the stream. He asked my why I didn't use the bridge, and I explained the orders. He mentioned having received similar ones, but had discovered that if the bridge had ever been mined, it was no longer so.

He then asked me where my officers were, and I told him about my platoon leader having been wounded early in the morning. I did not know where any of the Tank Corps were, as the Five of Hearts was now covering a whole company front. I told the infantry officer that I would be glad to cross the bridge under existing circumstances if so ordered. This he did with a smile, and the Five of Hearts crossed the bridge safely.

Upon gaining the heights on the north side of the Exermont Ravine, we immediately made enemy contact, in the form of heavy rifle and machine-gun fire. Those outposts gave way rapidly, and several machine guns were abandoned. I have little doubt in my own mind that the enthusiasm to follow in pursuit made me go too far ahead of the infantry. The terrain flattened out, and there was little cover available, and though the going was rough, it afforded a rare opportunity to fire at moving targets. I fear that the backs of those Germans with their packs and heavy overcoats were impressing me more than keeping liaison with our infantry. However, the party was not to last long, for when the cover for which they had been running was reached, we met with enemy resistance. Upon being fired on at close range, my driver was shot through the throat, and at the same time, our engine stalled. I made many attempts to crank it from the gunner's compartment, but to no avail.

We were in much the same condition as a disabled man-of-war. Our mobility was gone, and with it all chance of maneuver and the ability to seek cover. Our firepower was not far from zero because the 37mm cannon was jammed in a depressed position from the bullets fired at it from close quarters. Several times I had put my full weight on the breech so as to elevate the piece, but now even this had become ineffective. Our projectiles would hit the ground only a few yards from the tank. The turret, also, could not be rotated because it too was jammed with embedded bullets. To our left was a German 77mm artillery piece, which could easily have killed the tank. There was plenty of ammunition beside its trail. The breech-block had been removed in the Germans' retreat when the gun was abandoned, but now the Germans began to reappear. It was a local counterattack. If one of them had that gun's breechblock, we were doomed.

My wounded driver kept filling pistol clips, and I produced as much fire as possible with our pistols and the crippled 37mm. I paid more attention to the volume of fire than to its accuracy, for I feared that the enemy could close in if the volume diminished. They set up three machine guns just out of range of our piece, with its limited elevation. I continued to fire, and the continued fragmentation of our shells did afford some protection, but I could not train direct fire on the German guns, which were trying to shoot us to pieces.

The constant hammering of these machine guns at close range was terrific. The hinges on the doors could not stand up for long, I knew, but it was the mushroom ventilator on top of the turret that gave way first. I was hit on the top of the head with fragments of it, accompanied with bullet splinters. The Germans made no attempt to close in. On the contrary, they began to give way and then fled.

I have seen many marvelous sights of troops in action and on parade, but I have never seen, or expect to see, a more glorious sight than our infantry advancing toward us, rifles at high port, bayonets up. The Five of Hearts and her crew had done their job, and as Major Patton had commanded, we never struck our colors.

Because of their wounds, the crew was evacuated and never returned to the 344th. A Signal Corps photographer, who happened by, took a picture of the crippled tank, and that photo is now in the National Archives in Washington. The caption states: the tank had "almost a hundred holes in it and . . . the interior was splattered with blood. The whereabouts of the crew is unknown."

The saga of the little tank wasn't over, nor was that of its valiant commander. The tank, with its prominent battle scars, now sits in a place of honor at Ft. Meade, Maryland. Arthur Snyder, who'd stayed in the service and in tanks through the long dry years between wars, commanded a tank battalion in Sicily and up the length of Italy, again serving under General Patton.

SGT. CARL ROSENHAGEN
September 29, 1918, Near Le Catelet,
North of the Salient

While the light tanks chewed on the Germans in the southern reaches of the St.-Mihiel Salient, the 301st Heavy Tank Battalion was part of a major push on its northern flank, up on the Belgian border. The assault was to take place nearly 100 miles northwest of the Exermont battle, but it was halfway up the length of Belgium, as European distances go. British General Haig had identified a weak spot in the Hindenburg Line and, in his attempt to nip the salient out of the German positions in France, was trying a two-pronged attack. The assault in the south, of which Snyder and the Five of Hearts were one small part, was only half of the pincer movement.

The other half was to consist of the Australian Corps and the American 2nd Corps, with the American 301st Heavy Tank Battalion and the British 4th Tank Brigade in support. The heavy tankers had been hearing somewhat inflated reports of the exploits of the little two-man light tanks and were eager to find their own part of the war. Events would soon oblige them. The British general in charge of the northern assault, Henry Rawlinson, decided to give control of the American troops over to an Australian general, Sir John Monash. Probably he considered both colonial units to be out of his hair, and better suited to working with each other than with regular British units.

The American units were fresh, scarcely blooded, and full of vigor, while the Australian troops had been in constant battle for months and were worn down to nubbins. With this in his mind, Monash decided to use the American 27th and 30th Divisions, supported by the 301st tanks, in the initial assault. Since breaking the Hindenburg Line would turn the German flank and effectively force them out of France and on the defensive, this was to be the last great

45

push of the war. The great defensive works here were based on the Quenton Canal, which was effectively tank-proof. Except for one stretch where the canal went through a tunnel, an assault could be carried out *over* it, on dry land. The Germans, after their first few encounters with tanks, had figured that out, too, and they were getting ready.

The 301st Battalion, with about 40 tanks (the number varied from day to day, depending on state of maintenance) was to support the 27th Division, and was commanded by Colonel Ralph I. Sasse. They'd been training in Britain for months, and this was to be their first battle. Since these were some of the first heavy tanks and much larger than the little six-ton French Renaults, a quick look at their basic characteristics would be helpful.

The tanks were roughly rhombic in shape, resembling a squashed parallelogram with a crude caterpillar track like that of a modern bulldozer wrapped completely around the hull. Their water-cooled engines developed only 150 horsepower and could drive the 30-ton hulls at about five miles per hour . . . on a good day on level ground. There were two basic models with the Americans, the MkV and the MkV*. The MkV was 26 feet long and the star version was a bit over 32 feet long, having been stretched to improve its ability to span trenches. Their armament varied considerably, depending on the sex of the tank.

Sex??? Yes, the peculiar British mind-set of the day had decided that an all-machine-gun tank would be called a female and that a cannon-armed tank would be a male. Not wanting to leave anyone out, they also came up with a cannon/machine-gun version called a "hermaphrodite." The armament, instead of being mounted in a turret as in the little Renaults, was carried in two sponsons that bulged out from the middle of the hull on each side. Each tank carried a crew of eight men, divided into a front, or fighting crew, and a rear, or mechanical crew. This, then, was the crude vehicle in which American crews put their faith and lives on the morning of September 27, 1918.

General Haig's original plan was for the light infantry to assault right up to the wire, and then let the tanks break the defenses so that the infantry and the horse cavalry could exploit the resultant breaches. Unfortunately, the exhausted British divisions that the 27th was to pass through hadn't been able to push up to the front row of German trenches. As a result, the American 106th Infantry Regiment along with a few British tanks drew that unpleasant chore. The predictable result was the traditional WWI-style series of inconclusive small unit actions with no ground gained for the casualties incurred. On September 29, the American heavy tankers were turned loose. There were, however, problems.

The infantry, to whom the armored vehicles were a doubtful novelty, didn't seem to grasp the idea of tank-infantry cooperation and tended to stay clear of the steel bullet magnets. Further, the ground had been churned into the usual quagmire by a 60-hour artillery "preparation," culminating in a rolling barrage at H hour. Several of the 301st's officers and surveyors had been injured in the attempt to install white tape from the lying-up area, or "Tankodrome," to the tank's individual jump-off points. Especially seeing that the jump-off points were, in many cases, still in German hands.

On Saturday, September 28, at 10 P.M., the tanks moved out of the lying-up area and into history. They had refueled, using two-gallon tin cans, and were about as ready as they would get. There had been several casualties, as the Germans were shelling the area with a mixture of high-explosive and mustard-gas shells. On top of this was the usual pre-radio lack of coordination. As a result, the battle, instead of operating as a well-orchestrated plan, slid forward in broken chunks, under no single command.

Charlie Company of the 301st was to have been accompanied by the 108th Infantry, but at the last minute there was a change of plan that resulted in the tankers having to move out one hour earlier than the doughboys. The tanks were expected to have rough traveling in the shell-torn ground, and the infantry and cavalry were thought to be able to easily catch up with them. They never did, and the tankers fought all day alone. Tank number 13 of Charlie Company was commanded by Lt. Dunning and Sgt. Rosenhagen of Dayton, Ohio.

Friday evening, it was still daylight; three of our boys from the 13th crew, "C" Company, took a walk through the woods where our tank was camouflaged. In a little while, they came back, one of them carrying a black cat that they had come upon in the woods. Jokingly, the remark was "Well, a black cat on a Friday night for the 13th crew sure portended good luck for the 13th crew."

The next day we started out to take our place in the battle lineup. We stopped at a tank park, or repair center, and the English mechanics mounted large fascines, or large octagon squirrel cages about eight feet in height, made of very heavy timbers and metal facings, on our 29-foot-long tanks being used in this engagement. These tanks could not cross the 12-foot-by-12-foot antitank trench the Germans had dug at the point where we would go over the top.

The 35-foot tanks could not be stopped by any trench; but the 29-foot tanks would nose down into the trench or against the other side of the trench, and there was no way for it to crawl out. By dropping this large fascine, or squirrel cage, into the trench, the front end of the tank would not get below ground level and could get across any trench.

I drove the tank after we left the repair center, and after dark we got into a couple of bad mustard-gas attacks. It was sure a hardship driving a tank with a mask on. The manual labor required to drive a tank over rough territory with the heat of the motor and confined space inside made you perspire profusely. With both hands and feet working, it was next to impossible to keep the nose clips from slipping off, and the gas burned terribly around your face and eyes; and to breathe through the mouthpiece and see where you were going was really brutal punishment. It was impossible for the driver not to breathe in some of the gas.

We finally came to a halt to load up with gasoline, or *petrol* as it was called. Aviation gas was used, and it was passed in two-gallon tins from man to man down the line to the back end of the tank. It was put in the outside armored fuel tanks, which were divided into three compartments. The refueling area was just a short distance from the front lines and was well-illuminated by German flares. Artillery and machine-gun fire was heavy, causing several deaths and injuries in our battalion. After refueling, we were briefed; then it was time to go.

Zero hour was 5:55 A.M. The artillery of both sides sounded as though the end of the world was here, and the chattering of machine guns sounded like thousands of crickets. We had a hermaphrodite tank; that is, machine guns on one side and a six-pounder (about 2.25 inches bore diameter) Hotchkiss gun on the left side. I had turned the driving over to Sergeant Barnard of Kokomo, Indiana, and I was in the observation tower, standing on a platform over the transmission, taking care of anything that might happen and picking out targets for the gunners.

Before we came to the antitank trench, we ran into about 20 machine guns coraled together, firing against the right side of the tank. The whole inside of the tank seemed to be on fire from the sparks of the armor-piercing bullets around the gun slots, and through the other slots our gunners had to see their targets. It was so intense that one gunner had to back away from his gun, and I jumped down and took his place. Private Adams, "Wooden Shoe Adams," as he was called, from Indianapolis, I believe, looked up from the gun he was on, and his face was a mass of blood.

Seeing we could not cope with these machine guns, I pounded on the motor cowling, which was how we attracted the driver's attention, and put up my fist for a left turn. Instead he turned to the right and must have had his window flap wide open because he turned right into those machine guns and was badly hit. They hollered for first aid, and I jumped to him and said, "For God's sake, Barney, keep on driving until we get through this mess." And brave Barney did, turning the tank around where we were able to knock out those machine guns with the cannon. Our six-pounder gun was manned by Corporal Gagnon and Private Evans. They had made short work of the machine-gun nest, firing case shot out of the muzzle of the gun at the Germans who were not over 30 or 40 feet away from us.

We got Barney out of the driver's seat and I resumed driving. This happened, I believe, in the first 30 or 40 minutes, or shortly after 6 A.M. We were in a bad fog and smoke screen, and I remember seeing a fascine on one of our tanks get knocked off and fly to pieces from a direct hit, and I thought, *Those boys are in a bad way for that antitank trench.*

The artillery fire on both sides was terrific, and from what some English officers told us, it was the worst since the first battle of the Somme, which was the world's greatest artillery engagement on record, up until then.

By this time the smoke screen and the fog had worsened. There were some dummy tanks made of papier-mâché and wood, which had donkeys inside of them. These were used to draw fire so that our observers could spot enemy antitank guns. We had come to the antitank ditch, and I crawled out on the hull and removed the nuts on the chains holding the fascine. Then I got back in the driver's seat and teetered the tank on the edge of the ditch. I teetered it plenty, but the chains had snagged somehow and the fascine would not drop. I headed the tank into the trench at an angle, and we bogged into the side of the trench. I worked and worked, stabbing into the side of the trench while dirt and stones and everything just kept rolling on top, making it seem that getting the tank out would be an impossible job. The German infantry made it even tougher on our right side since we had no six-pounder gun there. Being down in the trench though, saved us from their artillery while we tore that trench up from the bottom. Having torn so much of the trench away, we finally came out on a bias. I swear that we were tilted sideways at a 45-degree angle. I was looking for the tank to turn over on its side, but we lurched out. How, I don't know.

Before we had gotten to the antitank trench, we had trouble with our own infantrymen of the American 27th Division, who were running in front of our tank cutting us off from helping them against the German machine guns. Smoke and fog were so heavy now that we could not even see any of our own infantry anymore; but as we had a timetable to get to Le Catelet, we continued on.

We got to the outskirts of Le Catelet, and it was lighter here, but we saw no supporting infantry. We stopped at the edge of the crossroads, and the boys opened the doors to let in some fresh air. Lieutenant Dunning and I were looking at the map we had spread between us when I looked up and, in the gloom, I could make out some men running toward us. I thought they might be our own men, and when Lt. Dunning grabbed the machine gun between us, I grabbed his hand saying, "Don't fire, they are Englishmen," but I was mistaken.

When Dunning went to fire the gun, it was jammed, not even a shot came out. A German pushed his rifle into the front window on Dunning's side and shot a piece out of his nostril. I dropped into gear and gave the tank a leap as Dunning used his Colt automatic on the German. I had, in the meantime, hollered to the men in the back to close the doors. We had a little commotion for a few minutes swinging the tank violently to throw off the Germans who were clinging to the side machine guns so that the six-pounder could get to them with case shot. Our six-pounder crew was really good and made short work of them.

After this, we drove back the way we had come, steering by compass. We were now taking a southwesterly course, hoping and watching for our infantry, who should have been catching up to us by now. We came to an abrupt drop-off and thought that it must be a stream or gully. Visibility was nil, and after talking with Lt. Dunning, I teetered the tank again, and that old fascine that I had cussed dropped off. I remember seeing it drop straight down. How far I don't know. We backed away from there, and followed along the bank until the terrain changed.

Then a shell hit us on the right rear and tore a hole in our back end, busting our main water line running up to the motor. In no time, steam filled the tank so bad I don't know how any of the rear crew lived through it. We had our front windows open, gasping for air. We came to the bottom of a ridge 10 or 15 feet high and tried to climb it, but the motor conked out and knocked so bad and would not pull anything, even in the lowest gear. I shoved the gear into reverse and backed onto the level.

There were two terrific explosions outside of the tank and

51

then a shell hit us on top. I believe the motor casing saved us; there was a large plopping noise inside, and then we were on fire all through the tank. I climbed through Lt. Dunning's seat, the only way I could get out, and came along the motor, by the six-pounder, over the transmission. Then I saw the lower door open on the right side, and I slid out. In the smoke and fog I could see two of our boys running away. I hollered to them, and they came back. Lieutenant Dunning got his face burned getting through and out of the tank. I was lucky, as I kept my head buried in my arms and only lost some excess hair off my head.

The four of us ran for some small trenches we could see ahead. German machine guns were firing a barrage, and we laid there concealed by the fog and smoke, seeing only the fire and smoke coming out of the barrels of the machine guns. We crawled on, and suddenly, about 11 o'clock, the fog and the smoke screen started to lift. We jumped into some shell holes to hide from enemy observation. We could then make out our tank about 800 or 900 feet away. Lieutenant Dunning and I were in the same small shell hole, but didn't see the other two boys until later that night. Our tank was burning and blowing up all afternoon with smoke and flame belching out. German planes were flying low right over our heads, but they must not have seen us lying below. I think that the Germans figured we never got out of the tank.

NOTE: For this particular action on the Hindenburg Line, September 29, 1918, Lieutenant Dunning received the British Military Cross and Sergeant Rosenhagen received the British Military Medal.

This battle went on until nightfall of the next day, and then the exhausted tankers went into a period of RR&R (rest, recuperation, and repair; infantry rests, tankers work on their mounts and then rest). Then, worn down to two companies totalling 25 running cripples between them, they entered the last big tank campaign of the war, in pursuit of the Germans who, on that front, still had some fight left.

This was a steady grinding assault that used up men and tanks, but taught many lessons on the subject of tank-infantry cooperation. At the end of that assault, the 301st Heavy Tank Battalion was down to just one dozen running tanks, which Col. Sasse organized into a provisional company of battered, almost exhausted men and rattletrap tanks.

They had just one more assault left in them, and at 1:20 A.M. on the morning of October 23, they launched it on a cold, clear winter night. Their objective was a German defensive works around the French towns of Bazuel, Ors, and Catillon. The mission, British in planning and, in the opinion of Col. Sasse, overly complex, was to support separate large units of the British striking force with a dozen tanks. They were to support two flanking battalions of the British 1st and 6th Divisions. . . . With two platoons of three tanks each! The remaining two platoons of tanks were to support a brigade of infantry each. (It can be done, and this writer has done it as a tank commander in Vietnam, but it ain't easy and it does wear out men and tanks.) Fortunately, the commanders who made the plans had learned a bit about handling tanks.

There was no long preparatory artillery barrage to warn the enemy, and the tanks caught the Germans by surprise. As they rolled through the wire, the artillery dropped a creeping barrage just ahead of them. With the tanks nosing ahead slowly, just behind the fall of gunfire, shell fragments tinkling on their bows, the Tommies of the British 71st and 18th Infantry Brigades trotted along behind, taking only light casualties. The two platoons supporting the flanks of the British divisions found a bit heavier going, one encountering a heavy German artillery barrage, but, nonetheless, the operation was judged a success and by midafternoon, the provisional company, less one tank trapped in a ditch, was back in its rallying area. Their war was over.

A hundred-odd miles south of them, the light tankers were still in contact, however fleeting, with retreating Germans who had had enough of Americans in tanks. Sgt. Snyder and his gallant driver had been evacuated out on the morning of October 5, but the light tanks continued on the assault, especially after George Patton got out of the hospital. He'd been wounded on the first day of that assault, but his men, independent Americans who'd been trained by a natural leader, carried on without him. George Patton had created and launched a potent weapon, and it helped in large measure to end the senseless slaughter.

From Exermont, the light tanks carried on until October 16. In many small unit actions, tanks simply went free-lance attaching themselves to roving infantry companies in a way that wouldn't be seen again until the 1940s. When tanks got knocked out though, the bloodthirsty crews simply took their weapons and joined the infantry, leaving the tanks for salvage and repair crews to find. It got so bad that Patton, when he returned, had to threaten court-martial of any crew that abandoned their tanks. Finally, on October 16, the assault ran out of steam . . . and tanks. From then till November 1, they spent their time digging lost and abandoned Renault FT17 tanks out of ditches, barns, hedgerows, trenches, and rivers, and returning them to some semblance of combat-worthiness. They'd been at it for three weeks, and the tankers weren't the only ones who were exhausted. The American Expeditionary Force had had almost 120,000 casualties in that period.

November 1, 1918: The tanks rolled, and so did everyone else, the last great offensive of the war was under way. The light tank brigade had been working feverishly, tankers alongside maintenance men, to get back into action, but again only 15 Renaults, organized into yet another provisional company, were available for the main assault. Somerance, St. Georges, Landrevill, Bayonville, Hill 289—all fell to the rushing Americans, who indeed had trouble keeping up with the retreating Germans. Supposedly first-line German divisions were taking to their heels and outrunning the pursuing tanks. A Renault, after all, could only make five miles per hour. A panicked infantryman can easily double that. Perhaps that factor was what was influencing the German leadership.

On the 11th hour of the 11th day of the 11th month of the year of our Lord of Providence 1918, the Germans had finally had enough. They surrendered under humiliating terms, which were forced on them by the outraged Allies. There was revolution in Germany, and the kaiser fled into exile in Holland. Finally, after four years and *13,700,830 deaths,* the "war to end all wars" was over . . . for a little while. The old ghosts that haunt the nations of Europe date back past the fall of Troy and will not be fully exorcised until Judgment Day . . . if then.

5

BETWEEN THE WARS

A good case could be made for the belief that the entry of Americans into the conflict was what broke the heart of the proud German army. The Yanks took to the fighting tank like ducks take to water and made it their own. The independence of American tankers and their bred-in-the-bone gift for machinery gave them the ability to keep more tanks running and to use them more aggressively than the European soldiers. J.E.B. Stuart's "ride to the sound of the guns" dictum on tactics is burned into the American gene pool. Time and again it has been seen that if a firefight starts within the hearing of an American tanker, he will go poke his turret into it. Germany simply did not want those men loose on German soil, especially after the atrocities they themselves had committed in France. Judging Allied intentions by their own conduct, they surrendered to prevent invasion by a fresh unwearied army.

Unfortunately, the terms of that surrender so saddled the Germans with limitations and reparations that their economy, already shattered by the costs of the dreams of empire, went completely down the tubes. Forbidden the possession of the means of war, such as tanks, combat aircraft, and submarines, the nation was helpless. When the Weimar

Republican government began to print worthless paper money to buy its way out of the problem, the stage was set for the arrival of a demagogue. With astounding speed, Adolf Schicklgrüber seized the reins of power, changed his name to Hitler, and began to rebuild the German war machine.

One more time, the old Roman Eagles would march on standards at the head of conquering legions, this time carried by thundering engines and clattering steel treads. While Germany rebuilt its war machinery, the rest of the world mostly disarmed and went about the business of peace, blissfully unaware of the howling madness to come.

In the United States, the National Defense Act of 1920 gutted our army worse than any downsizing in its history. Our constitution makes the funding of a standing army very difficult, in order to protect the public from the kind of military oppression that nations like Russia, China, Cuba, and Haiti have had to live with. Consequently, after almost every war, we have shut our armed forces down to a mere cadre. The army that fought the Indian Wars, for instance, only totalled 20,000 men, and at one time almost half of them were chasing one Indian named Geronimo.

As a result of this force-paring, the tank force was trimmed from 20,000 tankers to an authorized limit of 5,000 men and 300 officers. At Camp Colt, Major Eisenhower discharged all but 250 men. The CO at Camp Polk was allowed to keep only 200 tankers. By the time Congress was done stripping out the military, the U.S. had an army about the same size as that of Portugal. At that, though, it may have been a good thing. Other armies, such as the British and French, invested large portions of their military budgets in hardware that would become obsolete in 1939 when the Panzers overawed the Czechs, crushed Poland, and gutted France. In this country, there was a considerable amount of theorizing and inventing going on. Gradually, over a period of years, the fledgling Tank Corps migrated to Ft. Knox, where the experimentation and training would be done between the wars.

While the old generals went back to somnolence, retired,

or entered politics, the young firebrands of the technical branches worked feverishly and fought for funding for their brainchildren. In Britain, J.F.C. Fuller and his cohorts developed the one thing lacking from the great tank assault at Cambrai, radio control of the tank force. And the Germans watched and took notes. In France, Charles de Gaulle advocated the use of "all-tank" units that could be used as mobile strike forces. And the Germans watched and took notes. In the U.S., J. Walter Christie developed a new suspension system that allowed tanks to leap from the WWI speed of five or ten miles per hour to speeds approaching that of motor cars. And the Germans, and the Russians, and the Japanese, and the British watched, took notes, and wrote checks. The big-wheel, torsion-bar suspension that all tanks in our army use today was in existence in the 1920s!

All through that decade of celebration and decadence, while flappers danced and the stock markets bloated themselves, the military was in a state of flux. The old horse cavalrymen experimented desperately with motorization and actually accomplished something useful. It was found that a squad of eight cavalrymen, with their horses and tack, would fit handily in a commercial articulated cattle truck and could keep up with mechanized forces on road marches. They actually maneuvered with the then evolving light tanks in the later Louisiana maneuvers and, when WWII started, went into combat alongside a regiment of M-3 Stuart tanks in the Philippines.

Through those evolutionary years, the experimental tanks steadily increased in size, speed, and power. The crude unsprung suspension of the old MkVs was replaced with a highly evolved set of bogie wheels mounted in pairs. The limited-horsepower automotive engines were supplanted by the Liberty aircraft engine out of the old Curtiss "Jenny" that Charles Lindbergh used to deliver the airmail. The all-steel tracks that would last only a hundred miles or so were replaced with double-pin, rubber-bushed tracks that would run for thousands of miles before needing replacement.

The change in armament replaced the British six-pounder (about 2-inch bore) with ever larger cannons, and the race between gun and armor was on. Ever increasing weights of armor required larger engines to move it, which made the carrying of bigger guns possible. Some of the artillery pieces of 1918, such as the old French 75mm gun, wound up in the turrets of the new tanks . . . and machine guns sprouted everywhere.

Due to Congressional micromanaging, the cavalry were restricted to "combat cars," to escort their mounted units while the infantry were supposed to be the only ones with tanks for strong-point reduction. This, as would be expected, resulted in some weird and wonderful machines, such as tracked "cars," and tanks that could remove their treads and run on wheels.

Everything had to be tried, though, and gradually the more unworkable mechanical innovations, such as flying tanks and hundred-ton monsters, were eliminated. Meanwhile, the world was becoming a more dangerous place to study the pursuits of peace.

Russia, stabilizing after the throes of the Bolshevik Revolution, began building the Red Army, under the guidance of Leon Trotsky, and adopted the new iron cavalry with zest and enthusiasm. Mating the American Christie suspension with crude but reliable diesel engines and hand-cranked turrets, they began to manufacture tanks by the thousands. It has been said that from an outsider's viewpoint, there was no visible change between the expansionism of the czar and that of the communists. Certainly, neither the Manchurians nor the hapless nations of Central Asia could tell the difference as hordes of tanks spread across their lands in the 1920s and 1930s. By 1939, Bolshevik Russia owned *25,000* tanks of varying capabilities. Hardly the armament of a peaceful nation.

After the financial crises of the late 1920s and early 1930s, the viability of international capitalism and democracy were in some doubt, and in vulnerable nations, such as Germany and Italy, demagogues began to reach for the levers of power. Germany, bound by ruinous treaties, fell to the siren nationalism of Adolf Hitler and began again to dream of world hegemony under the Aryan "Master Race."

RALPH ZUMBRO

Old von Ludendorff, who'd seen the error of his ways in the first half of the world war, now counseled Hitler to listen to his new generals of armor, Guderian and Rommel.

The Panzer officers were now agitating for a greatly expanded role for the armored corps, and after looking at a few test models, such as the Pzkf I and II, Hitler agreed. Still bound by a treaty that he could not quite yet abrogate, Hitler needed a place to train his new tank corps, and he finally found the perfect, hidden place—Russia. In a secret pact with Stalin, Hitler gained access to training areas in exchange for German technical expertise. Deep in the Russian hinterland, almost 500 miles *east* of Moscow, at Kazan and Lipetsk, near the Kama River, "experimental stations" were established. Here, as early as 1926, future leaders of both German and Russian tank corps trained and experimented in perfect secrecy from the rest of the world. This was the land, it should be remembered, from which Attila and Genghis and Tamerlane issued. This was the land once dominated by the Golden Horde, and their genes are still there . . . graduating from the Frunze War College.

While the leaders trained in seclusion, spies permeated the western democracies, gaining technological insight. Students of military lore read with great interest the books of J.F.C. Fuller, de Gaulle, and others. Test models of tanks were built both in Russia and Germany, and in the middle 1930s, both future adversaries sent first "advisors" and then combat troops to aid in the Spanish Civil War. General von Thoma, who would later lead the 4th Panzer Army, went from Kazan to Spain to command the Condor Legion, which fought for Franco. There, he polished his skill with light tanks and Stuka dive-bombers. The art of dive-bombing had been learned from the U.S. Marines, who'd invented it in Nicaragua in the 1920s.

Slowly, all over the world, the weapons of Armageddon were being forged. In the U.S., the army was still experimenting with motorizing horse cavalry and supporting them with "combat cars." The military designers of the era, however, were not idle, and the ancestors of the Sherman, Grant, and Stuart tanks were already being built, experi-

60

mented with, and shown to interested international buyers, such as the British, whose internal tank design process had become something of a national embarrassment.

All across the world, flashpoints were warming up, and it would be only a matter of time before the armored hordes would roll. Italy, now under the iron rule of "Il Duce," Benito Mussolini, still had dreams of world empire. In 1935, they invaded Abyssinia, or modern Ethiopia, destroyed its primitive army with crude tanks and poison gas, unseated its ancient emperor, Haile Selassie, and proclaimed it a protectorate. In the meanwhile, Hitler, who'd finally gotten enough tanks and planes built, totally repudiated the Treaty of Versailles and began to gobble up Europe for "Lebensraum."

First, without warning, his troops moved into the Sudetenland, the ancient contested borderland between Czechoslovakia and Germany, and began to build the Siegfried Line to face against France's Maginot Line. Two impotent lines of immobile fortresses were to face against each other while the mobile forces changed the face of Europe. Like a schoolyard bully, Hitler continued to test the will of the fast-crumbling League of Nations. Declaring that all Germans everywhere should live under a German government, Hitler next conned the League into allowing him to occupy the eastern mountains of Czechoslovakia—an act that made the rest of that nation militarily indefensible. As soon as his troops marched into Prague, which he declared as his last territorial claim on Europe, Hitler began shifting his Panzers north, to the borders of Poland, which had a mutual defense pact with both England and France. German scientists also gained unlimited access to the Curie Lode, the uranium source that the Curies used in their researches. Germany was on the trail of the atom bomb and had already started rocket research!

While the tanks were lining up and the Stukas were being loaded with bombs, the toothless League of Nations breathed its last worthless promulgation. In starry-eyed triumph, Neville Chamberlain landed at Heathrow airport waving a single sheet of paper declaring, "Peace in our time," words destined to live, if not in infamy, then as dire warning of the danger of treaties with dictators. Scant weeks later, the Panzer divisions rolled into Poland, on September 1, 1939. Poland had been admonished by the would-be Allies to refrain from mobilizing its army to avoid "provoking" a madman.

The result, in the words of Polish Captain Szacherski, was: "The telephone rang at precisely 4:55 A.M., and I heard the voice of General Wlad, saying, 'Good morning, Captain. The Germans have just crossed our frontier along its entire length. There's already fighting at the frontier posts and among the advanced units. Your orders are that it is up to the regiment to do its duty.'" The captain was the adjutant of the Polish 7th Regiment of mounted light infantry; horse-riflemen against a thundering horde of tanks!

Szacherski continues: "I immediately telephoned Major Kalwas. On the line came the voice of the duty NCO. 'Wake the major and tell him that the Germans have crossed our frontier,' I told him. 'The regiment has been ordered to do its duty.' 'What was that again, sir,' he mumbled, 'I didn't quite catch.' I repeated the message, but he still failed to grasp my meaning. 'It's war, you idiot, WAR—Don't you understand?' Finally the message penetrated. 'I see, Captain, so we really are at war.'"

September 1, 1939, 2:00 P.M.: The assault was in full swing, and the German 20th Motorized Division (truck-mounted infantry with a regiment of light tanks) had cut the so-called Polish corridor, Poland's access to the sea, through Germany and was working through light forest and meadow toward the town of Chojnice. The German lead elements were fighting the Polish 18th Uhlan (light cavalry) Regiment along a railway line that led from Chojnice to Naklo. The Polish infantry were in full retreat, and the horsemen had been ordered to attack to give the foot troops time to "disengage." In a small woods near the town of Drojanty, they lined up and prepared to attack. Grown men have shed honest tears over what happened next.

The 1st Squadron of the regiment of Uhlans charged out of those woods onto the flank of the German formation of infantry at the order of their commander, Colonel Mastalerz, who had just told his adjutant, Captain Godlewski, "Young man, I'm quite aware what it is like to carry out an impossible order," in response to the younger officer's doubts as to the wisdom of the charge. At about 5 P.M., the squadron's commander, Major Maleki raised his saber and the first cavalry charge of WWII began, right into the machine guns of German infantry.

Even at that, 250 rushing horsemen made a formidable foe, and the Germans began to pull back, dealing death as they retreated. Bent low over their horses' necks, heavy sabers held at the thrust, the cavalry rushed into modern war. As they moved at a gallop out of the sparse cover of the forest, the first men and horses fell dead, the mounts tumbling over the bodies of their riders as the guns cut them to ribbons. Still, many a German rifleman died that sunny afternoon as the riders got in among them on plunging animals, and just too close for rifle work, cut them down. The outmoded cavalrymen looked to being the winners of that skirmish until a column of tanks rattle-clattered around a bend of the road and opened up.

At first the gallant Uhlans, enmeshed in the sound and fury of battle, didn't notice, until 20mm tank cannons began blowing their mounts out from under them. As they were turning their horses to pit sabers and pistols against this new menace, their animals, still brave and willing, died under them. Horses reared and crashed onto already dead riders. Others bolted, dragging wounded cavalrymen to their deaths by the stirrups. A faint bugle sounded recall but few were left to hear it. In a few horrible moments, half of a proud regiment had died.

Riderless horses, stirrups swinging wildly, ran, panicked, to and fro across the carnage. Captain Swiesciak, who'd led the charge, was blown to the ground by a tank cannon and Colonel Masatlerz was killed by a burst of machine-gun fire as he rushed to help the captain. Here, at Drojanty was born the legend of Polish cavalry who tried to charge tanks with sabers. Time and time again, the Polish charges against infantry would be broken as a spearhead of tanks ripped them from the pages of history . . . for a while. The blitz-krieg form of war that the Germans had unwillingly learned at Cambrai and Arras had come rushing back to Europe, and there was hell to pay. Only weeks later, Poland, invaded by Germany and stabbed in the back by Russia, with whom Hitler had a secret pact, fell to the victorious Axis powers, which now included Italy and Japan.

History calls the next period the "Phony War," because there were no battles while the world recoiled in shock and the Germans regrouped. Using the autobahns that had been built for the purpose and the Reich's excellent railway system, the Panzers were moved swiftly east and north. The Low Countries, Holland and Belgium and Luxembourg, would be next, followed by France.

Holland fell first, taken by aerial bombing, paratroopers, and a sudden ground assault. Next, while the BEF (British Expeditionary Force) was getting its act together, Belgium was taken in a rush, and then across land where American tankers had fought only one generation earlier, the Panzers rushed into France. Through Cambrai, where the Germans had first faced "tank terror," the Panzers rolled. They ground on through the Ardennes, where the Americans had first proved that tanks could operate in forests, and came out in a rush, under a bold and innovative young General Erwin Rommel. The French tank corps, larger and more powerful than the German, was ill-led, parceled out in ineffective packets, and left to die on the vine. For a while France's only hope was the BEF, mounted in outdated, careworn tanks from the experimental decades. Now, though, we must look through the eyes of a British tanker, for they were the only ones who were there.

SECTION SGT. MAJOR W. R. ARMIT
France/Belgium, Spring 1940

Our battalion was lucky enough to be stationed in France long enough to get to know the country and the people of the north of France. For nearly nine months we spent some happy times in the vicinity of Arras, Lille, and Lens, and, of course, we did our share of trench-digging in back areas. The local people used to scoff at our efforts and assured us that their traditional enemies would not set foot in their country.

We did quite a lot of training with our Mark I tank, but all the time we needed a heavier weapon than the Vickers .303-cal machine gun with which they were armed. After many suggestions, we at last had a .50 Browning machine gun fitted to at least the troop leaders' tanks, and though this reduced the firepower of the troops, it made the troop leaders a bit more confident as to the outcome of any future engagements with enemy tanks.

The two-man tank was really a supreme test for the crew commanders, for in the restricted space one had to fire the gun, direct the tank, work on the radio, and if one was a troop leader, one had to look to the tactical handling of the troop. However, in the eight months we spent in France, we all worked hard, and we found that by practice we could do all the jobs and that the tank had lots of room inside it.

Just before Hitler walked into Belgium, we had been shifted south to another training area and were looking forward to lots of hard training and some pleasant hours in the nearby town of Vernon. The surrounding country was lovely and a change of the flat expanses we had been used to in the north.

Once the invasion was under way, our battalion went up north, and we found ourselves on our way to Belgium. The road party had quite a hectic time on the move, but reached our appointed place in the defensive plan without any mishaps. The tanks came by rail, and the unloading took place at a station called Athe, which was only a few miles southwest of Brussels. We had our first of the power of the enemy air force, for, in the middle of our unloading party, with the "C" Squadron still on the trucks, we had a visit from 15 bombers.

They were flying at a height of about 500 feet, and though all the small arms in the vicinity were brought to bear on them, they carried out a raid on the railway bridge near the station. Two of the flight came back to the station, and just as we prepared to take cover, they were both hit and crashed on the outskirts of the town.

We got off the train and moved our tanks up to a wood on the historic ground where the battle of Waterloo was fought. The route we followed was dive-bombed, but none of the 50-odd bombs dropped exploded. Still, it was tricky work picking our way with tanks past the bombs, and each tank crew breathed more freely after they had left them behind.

That night saw the battalion harbored in a wood so close to Jerry that no sleep was possible owing to the whistle of our own shells and the lighter German ones. We were troubled a lot by the passage of so many refugees through the wood and guarding the tanks was quite a difficult job. We settled down in the dark to get as much rest as possible, but a hurried order to move spoiled this intention. "B" Squadron was unlucky in that a plane was shot down near their harboring area and set fire to their petrol dump, severely reducing their supplies. We reached a safe harbor area just as dawn broke, and it says a lot for the intelligence work of our staff when we learned that our previous harbor had been shelled heavily just as we got clear.

Our expectations of action were very high, but we were disappointed, for the order came that we had to move back. The battalion commander gave out his orders, and it was a grave party afterward. We were told that there was a strong possibility of our being surrounded, and we received instructions that we must be prepared to fight our way out and to sell our lives as dearly as possible.

The road party moved off, followed by the tanks, which were to be put back on railcars, but as we reached the station, we learned that the Jerry air force had been there before us. There was nothing else but to go on to the next station, but each time we found the station a mass of flame. We came up against this difficulty all the way back to France, and so our tanks, which were only meant to do short journeys by road, had to march from Brussels to Arras, only turning back once in a while, to act in support roles, giving others a chance to get clear of the advancing enemy. The air seemed to be filled with Jerry planes, and several times during the march, they gave us special attention. Our chief difficulty, though, was the refugees, and it was only possible to move at night or when the roads were being machine-gunned from the air.

We duly arrived back at the Lord Gort defense line between Tourney and Orchies and had to take up positions in front of the block houses as mobile pillboxes. This work needed quite a high standard of cooperation between troops, owing to the wide area over which our tanks were dispersed. We stuck to this work for two days while the Jerries were making progress towards Arras in their breakthrough. We then received orders to move once more in the direction of Arras, and it took us about 24 hours to reach Petite Vimy, arriving there about 2300 hours.

We refueled and were led to a harbor by night just on the reverse slope of Vimy Ridge. We spent most of the night covering our track marks from the road to the harbor and camouflaging our tanks. The dawn brought a Jerry reconnaissance plane over, but our camouflage was good and we had no trouble from the air. This was fortunate as the whole battalion was parked in a small strip of wood with a distance of five yards between tanks. We would have been an inviting target from the air.

The squadron received orders about 10 o'clock that they were to be on the right flank of the battalion in an attack to the southeast of Arras. My troop was the extreme right flank of the battalion, and I was detailed to keep in touch with another battalion of tanks on our right. The orders given were of the sketchy type as we only had three maps in the squadron. So we all had a good look at the squadron commander's map and picked out various objects to help us on to the final objective.

We were timed to go into action at 1400 hours, so we started to move up at 1115 hours. We took the main road from Lens to Arras until we came to a right fork which led up to the Vimy memorial and crossed the ridge in the direction of Mount St. Elloy through Neville St. Vast. We then turned left, and this brought us round to the south of Arras. We did not expect any heavy opposition as there were not supposed to be any heavy guns up front.

We had expected our infantry to start with us, but we did not see any and so kept going. I had not had any time to put my tank commanders in the picture, so the obvious plan was to lead with my tank, and I gave orders that they should maintain a distance of approximately 75 yards on each side of me with my tank as the troop center line. Our advance was over very flat country with very little cover, and the first indication of the enemy was given by fire from what appeared to be light field guns firing on fixed lines.

Several of these shells burst near my troop, but I made up my mind that they had no observation on the tanks; this was proved by the fact that the bursts walked on behind us. I led my troop up a slight ridge, and we came in sight of a road along which were moving several German lorries filled with troops. The utter surprise on the faces of those troops soon turned to alarm when we got our machine guns going, and it was definitely first blood to us. We crossed this road and then had to converge on a crossing of a railway. I led my troop across and was fanning out again when I received a signal from Major Fernie, who was in his tank on the same side of the railway.

I took my tank up close to him and he gave me fresh orders for a special task. He told me there was a battery of field guns in action about 2,000 yards to the battalion flank, and one of them had hit the commanding officer's tank. He ordered me to take my troop over to them and destroy them or at least neutralize their fire. I signaled to my two other tanks and told them the job on hand, and off we went. On the move to the gun position we struck a sunken road, and my driver managed a crossing but my other two tanks got stuck and would have to be pulled out. I radioed my squadron commander and told him about the job I had to do and asked for support for my tank.

The squadron had become scattered by this time, and we were under troop control so he promised to support me himself. I advanced over the crest of a small ridge and ran smack into six antitank guns. They were not camouflaged, and their only cover was a fold in the ground. Before they realized that I was on them, I got two of them with the .50 Browning—the range was just over 200 yards and I could see them swinging their guns.

The other guns started on me, and one hit my turret right on the gun housing. This caused the cocking pin of my gun to snap and shook the gun back in the turret, jamming me between the shoulder piece and the back of the turret and incidentally causing a jam in the gun's feed mechanism. I forced the gun back forward in its mount and pressed the triggers for my two smoke mortars, which would shield me from enemy sights for a few minutes. They did not fire as, I later found out, they'd been shot straight off the turret. During this time, which was only the space of a minute, the Jerries hit my tank about ten times, but none of the hits did any damage.

They were now picking their shots to hit, and one shot carried away a spoke in my track adjusting wheel. I quickly made up my mind that the best way out was to back over the crest until I could get my gun cleared and back into action. I gave my driver the order, and we slowly zigzagged back a distance of about a hundred yards. I had four spare smoke generators in my tank, so the best plan was to light one and chuck it out the top with the hope that it would give some measure of cover. Of course, after lighting the smoke bomb, I found that my turret flap had jammed shut.

It was quite a shock to have a burning smoke generator in one's hand with the turret flap jammed, but after a few second's struggle I managed to get the flap open and chucked two of the generators out in front. Then, relatively safe and out of sight of those gunners, I had a few anxious moments with that damaged track adjusting wheel, but finally persuaded it to behave with the "special" tool, the sledgehammer.

I got the .50 going again and, thirsting for revenge, returned to the attack. They must have thought I was finished, for I caught that battery of guns limbered up and ready for movement to another position, and revenge was sweet. They were incapable of shooting, and I had a full belt of 200 rounds in the Browning.

During this time I had lost contact with the rest of the battalion and had a discussion with my driver as to our immediate plans. The field guns supplied the answer, so I decided to collect my troop before having a go at them. It took me about ten minutes to join up with the remains of the squadron, and I received orders to proceed with my task against the field guns, who by this time had unlimbered and were firing again; they were getting quite near with their shells!

I collected two more Mark I tanks and a Matilda tank with a two-pounder gun (about 1.5-inch bore), and we had a conference under the shelter of a railway bridge. The bulk of the battalion tanks had gone on ahead, so I decided to cover the flank to prevent the Germans from coming straight down the road and getting in between our tanks and our infantry. By now my radio mast had been shot away, and I was in doubt of the situation. As we were in the middle of making up a plan, an attack developed down the road with infantry and tanks, and though they were coming straight down the road, their guns were pointing to a flank away from us.

My gun had been pointing in the other direction, but I don't think I ever cranked that turret faster in my life. I got on the first tank while it was still firing in the other direction. A belt of .50s stopped him, and flames started to come out of this tank, the gun stopped firing, and the remains of the crew scuttled out.

The second tank was hit by the two-pounder from the Matilda, and it met the same fate as the first one. After that, no more tanks came down the road, and the infantry had faded from sight. This incident proved to me how dangerous that unsecured flank was, and I had my driver move up to the commanding officer whose tank was stationary about 700 yards away. I found out when I got up to the CO's tank that it was out of action. The side had been blown in, and I saw that the CO and his gunner were both dead.

This left us with no command, and I returned to my composite troop, and we had quite an exciting time waylaying Jerry mechanized troops, who seemed to be unaware that this road was covered. I kept up fire on the gun positions, and eventually they ceased firing. By evening things were more stable, and the rally flag was flying from the adjutant's light tank. We rallied in a hollow, and after an hour we could only muster eight tanks and about six crews who'd had their tanks knocked out. We put out our guard tanks, and as I'd managed to scrounge six bottles of rum earlier in the day, I became quite popular.

As we were getting ready to move, a reconnaissance plane came over and spotted us so we had to move with Jerry artillery shells following us. The Germans were attacking again, and we moved up in support of the infantry, the first we'd seen all day. We managed to scrounge some petrol off them and spent some time dividing up our ammunition and attending to repairs on the tanks. Later that evening, we received orders that we had to stand by to counterattack a woods about 800 yards away.

During this period, we tried to get information as to the position but it was all very vague. The officer in charge was now Major Fernie, and he left us to do some personal reconnaissance—and that was the last we saw of him. He was captured by the Germans, escaped, swam the river Somme by night, and made his own way to Dunkirk. Some weeks later he rejoined the regiment in England.

By now it was getting dark, and we heard the rumble of a heavy tank, which we took to be one of ours looking for us. Captain Cracroft approached it, and put his map case over the driver's vision slit. The tank stopped, the door opened, and out popped a Jerry officer! The surprise was mutual, and Captain Cracroft lost no time in rejoining his tank. The Germans fired their heavy turret gun at him as he doubled back, and the shell hit my tank. It did no damage, and the captain was able to regain the safety of his tank.

All hell broke loose then—several bright 37mm flares lit up the road, and the Germans rushed another tank down, supported by infantry fire, but the surprise was on our side and the firepower of our eight surviving tanks soon had its effect. The distance between us and the attacking party was only about 150 yards, and all we could do in the dark was choose the center of the bursts of tracers and fire down the lines that they made in the darkness. We had two tanks armed with Browning .50s and their bigger muzzle flashes made them come in for a lot of attention. My tank was hit four times by their heavier guns but it did not have too much effect—then.

After about 10 minutes of this battle, a German lorry caught fire and this blaze enabled us to see better, but, of course, it also showed us up, and as I was nearest to it, I ordered my driver to reverse slowly out of the light of this fire. This encounter lasted about 15 minutes, and it stopped as suddenly as it started. Their tanks were put out of action, and their infantry withdrew, leaving us in full possession of the battle-field.

None of our tanks had more than a belt of ammo left, so the captain ordered us to follow him back to our headquarters. This proved to be a very tricky business, as we had no maps and were not sure of our position. The situation wasn't very clear and, judging by the number and location of parachute flares, we seemed to be surrounded. We stuck to the road, which was a nerve-racking business as each roadblock meant either friend or foe, and we could not be sure until we were close to them. We had to take to cross-country work once more, and it was only through brilliant leading by Captain Cracroft that we finally managed to report to our headquarters on Vimy Ridge.

I shall never forget how, when we were moving down a valley to a larger road, a column of French tanks passed. In the night, we could not be sure of their nationality, and we held our breath, expecting every minute to receive a burst of fire, but they passed and left us to wend our way home. During this march, we were always in danger of being mistaken for German tanks trying a sneak attack, and it did so happen that someone in our headquarters did mistake us and let off a Bren gun. Luckily, the mistake was rectified before any damage was done.

So ended a perfect day, but there was to be no sleep for us, for after taking cover in a wood on the reverse slope of Vimy Ridge, we were ordered to another "safe harbor," and as my driver was dog-tired, I had to sit on the front of the tank and slap his face to keep him awake. Next day came an inspection of the tanks to determine battle-worthiness. In all, my tank had been hit 36 times by assorted calibers, but true to its name, it had stood up to it.

The tank was named Dauntless, and it lived up to the tradition, dauntless by name and dauntless by nature. It was, however, more than somewhat battered. The squadron commander decided that it had to be condemned as unfit for further hostilities, so it went on the list as a pool tank for spares. It continued to move with the column, and when the two battalions were combined, it joined them. The crew commander brought it nearly back to Dunkirk, but the combat and the cobbled streets had their combined effect, and the turret suddenly split right down a line made by eight antitank shell hits.

The Dunkirk evacuation, of course, is part of well-known history. The BEF lost all its hardware, save a few fighter aircraft, but most importantly, the now battle-hardened tankers and infantrymen went on to become the famed jungle tankers of Burma and the indomitable "Desert Rats" of the British 8th Army. They were, however, quite short of tanks, and while America wasn't officially in the war quite yet, we were in the tank business and wherever the Brits fought their gallant holding action, there would always be found a few American tankers on "Makee Learnee." Not too long after Erwin Rommel gave the British a good thrashing and captured General O'Connor, the first of the Yankee tanks began to make their appearance on the deserts of North Africa.

The general plan, it seemed, was for the Americans to learn modern tanking from the British, and then begin entering the war quite gradually—political developments allowing, that is. What actually happened was the attack at Pearl Harbor on December 7, 1941. Only days after that, American tanks were in action against Japanese tanks on the island of Luzon in the Philippines. What saved General MacArthur and slowed the Japanese General Homma down by four months, was a savage battle in the jungles of Bataan, by the 192nd and 194th Light Tank Battalions and the 26th Regiment of horse cavalry, Philippine scouts.

6

LUZON

Philippine Islands, 1941

Japan's brilliant but dastardly attack on the American fleet at Pearl Harbor was what one could call only a qualified military success. True, they sank seven obsolete battleships, which were, in the parlance of the time, all old enough to vote. What they missed made all the difference. Admiral Halsey's carrier task force was still at sea, and the Japanese strategists arrogantly ignored the 54 modern submarines that we had scattered about the Pacific. Indeed, the Japanese foreign minister, Baron Kijuro Shidehara once stated, "The number of submarines possessed by the United States is of no concern to the Japanese inasmuch as Japan can never be attacked by submarines." Strange attitude for a nation surrounded by water and utterly dependent on shipping for survival.

The plan for the "Greater East Asia Co-prosperity Sphere" wasn't hatched out overnight. Much like Germany, Japan had been dreaming of conquest for a long time. During WWI, Premier Shigenobu Okuma had said, "In the middle of the twentieth century, Japan will meet Europe on the plains of Asia and wrest from her the mastery of the world." Their war plan, finalized at a supreme council, was as follows:

First, without a declaration of war, destroy the U.S. Pacific Fleet and both the British and American air forces on the Malay Peninsula. Second, while the British and Americans were disorganized by the results of sneak attacks, they planned a quick conquest of the Philippines, Guam, Wake, Hong Kong, Borneo, British Malaya, Singapore, and Sumatra. Third, they wanted the richest prize of all—Java and the rest of the Dutch-held Indonesian islands, which were rich in several commodities that Japan lacked, and one that they wanted desperately. There was oil aplenty in Dutch Indonesia and uranium in the Malay peninsula. Fourth, they would establish a defensive perimeter running from the Kurile Islands through Wake, the Marshall Islands, and the western edges of the Malay Barrier to the India-Burma border. Finally, they would completely subjugate China, putting fully half the world's population under the control of Emperor Hirohito. They almost made it.

Admiral Yamamoto, who had studied America, had warned the Imperial staff that he could only guarantee a six-month run of conquests before the Americans would be able to send reinforcements to Australia. That defensive barrier had to be in place, and the Indonesian oil fields producing for Japan before then, or the war would be long and costly. Also, Japan needed to get uranium out of Malay and into the hands of the scientists at the University of Tokyo as quickly as possible.

Uranium? Yes, Japan also knew how to build an atomic bomb and worked steadily at it all through the war. The chief Japanese scientist involved was one Yoshio Nishina, who, before the war, had been a close colleague of Niels Bohr. Bunsaku Arakatsu, another nuclear physicist, was a student and friend of Albert Einstein. They knew all right, and their project had been started as early as 1939. On July 19, 1942, a code intercept of German communications traffic stated that in the Ishikawajima Dockyards, a cyclotron as large as the one at the University of California at Berkeley was under construction! The Japanese had bought a 200-ton cyclotron magnet from General Electric as early as 1937, years before the attack on Pearl Harbor.

Both Germany and Japan were working feverishly on an atom bomb, and the Japanese were actually gaining. That defensive barrier had to be put in place quickly, to allow the military time to consolidate and for the scientists to continue their nuclear efforts. What threw them off by almost four months were two battalions of outdated light tanks and a regiment of horse cavalry on the island of Luzon.

They came from Rock County, Wisconsin, and they called themselves the "Janesville 99," for there were 99 of them in that tank company. During the 1920s, a tank company had been formed in Janesville as part of the Wisconsin National Guard, the 32nd Infantry Division. Nationally, there were supposed to be just 12 tank companies in the whole National Guard, each one equipped with WWI Renault tanks. Eventually, the Guard wound up with 18 tank companies that, in time of war, would be consolidated into four independent battalions for their divisions. At least that was the plan.

Throughout the 1920s and 1930s, young men were lured to drill and to train by the promise of actually being allowed to sit at the controls of a battle tank and bring the beast to rumbling life. The Janesville company had just eight American-made Renault FT six-ton light tanks, four with machine guns and four with 37mm cannons. There were usually between 60 and 70 young men in the unit, each vying for driving and gunnery experience. The tanks spent most of the year in storage at the Rock County Fairgrounds, but for a few months each summer, they'd be shipped by rail down to Camp Grant, just south of Rockford, Illinois, for gunnery training and maneuver practice. The assigned mission of that tank company was classic WWI technique. They were to accompany the infantry and add firepower and close support to the attacking doughboys, and then rush forward to crush enemy artillery.

Newer, more modern tanks were added to the company during the 1930s but they were armed only with machine guns, not cannons. The old Renaults with their bunker smashing cannons were still the favorite on the gunnery range. They had their limitations, though—a two-man crew and a top speed of just five miles per hour. The old photos from summer camp at places like Camp Wilson and Camp Grant show young men looking proudly out from under the brims of their campaign hats and shapely young ladies perched on the hulls of the tanks—fresh from the company's annual Charleston contest.

As in all organizations, a social life had evolved. There was the Idle Hours Club where the ladies of the company organized holiday banquets, dances, and other events. Then, there was the Scorpion Club, whose only requirement was that a man be able to hold his liquor well without getting mean. The tank company lived as a social organization as well as a military unit, but history was about to catch up with the Janesville 99.

During the summer of 1940, with the Germans on the rampage and Europe being smothered under jack-booted hordes, the National Guard was quietly mobilized. On November 25, 1940, the unit was sworn into the U.S. Army as Company "A" of the 192nd Tank Battalion and given orders to report to Ft. Knox, Kentucky. Two of the tankers were barely into their junior year of high school. The other three line companies of the battalion came from Maywood, Illinois; Port Clinton, Ohio; and Harrodsburg, Kentucky.

Since late in the last war, visionaries like General Adna Chaffee and George Patton had been insisting that the U.S. needed a great new armored force to protect its worldwide interests in time of war. This was now about to happen. At that time, though, there were barely 400 tanks in the whole army. Everything we were building was being shipped through U-boat infested waters to North Africa, where the British army was being unwillingly modernized by Erwin Rommel.

Adolf Hitler was now the master of Europe and was beginning to plan the invasion of Russia. North Africa was, to him, only one leg of a thrust that should capture the vital oil fields around Baku, on the Caspian sea. Therefore

Rommel could count on only half the supplies that would have been needed for victory. In the resulting cut-and-thrust battles, the industry that produced the U.S. tank force was born. Without an existing, obsolete tank fleet, the U.S. was free to utilize its excellent designs, have the British test them against the best the Germans had, and then redesign and rebuild.

In this way, the M-3 Stuart light tank evolved to the M-5, and the cumbersome Grant medium tank evolved into the superlative Sherman series, all before the first shot was fired in anger by an American tanker. First, though, the 192nd had to be trained and equipped with "modern" tanks, like the M2A2, which had two turrets and was naturally nicknamed the "Mae West." Here in the words of Forrest Knox, of Janesville, is how to drive a light tank of that vintage:

"These things had an old sliding transmission, like on a tractor. As you went up in gears, you went up in speed. To shift, you had to overwind it, like up to 2400 rpms. There was a tachometer, but basically you learned to do it by sound. Once you got the hang of it, synchronizing the speed, you could just flip the stick and there was nothing to it. There was a hell of a roar from the aircraft engine. It was a seven-cylinder Continental radial. There was a great big propeller in front of the engine that sucked air through the engine compartment. We did everything with a simplified hand signal or touch system. There was no speech whatsoever when you drove one of those things.

"In front of you was a peep slot. Your crash helmet had a rubber pad on it. You'd shove that right up against the steel and that anchored your head. You could see straight ahead, but you couldn't see either track. There were no brakes. You had to downshift in order to brake. There were also steering clutches. Any time you started to turn, you had to pour the coal on because the slack in the track would automatically wind up at the trailing idler if you let off on the gas. If you kept the power on, the front driving sprocket would pull all the slack right up front, so if you kept the power on any time you were turning, you were fine. You kept your track snug.

But if you jerked your foot off the gas, all the slack lashed to the back and off she popped."

Throughout the remainder of 1940 and into 1941, the 192nd trained and maneuvered in the rolling hills of Kentucky. The usual three squares and a shower became distant memories as they lived and moved in a nomadic community of tanks, half-tracks, and lighter vehicles. They lived in a world of dust, scrub pines, and red dust. Home was sun-baked steel, sweat, gasoline trucks, and the drone of tank engines. Gradually, they learned their new skills, as far as anyone was able to teach, and in later 1941, they found themselves in the largest "peacetime" maneuver the U.S. Army had ever operated, at Camp Polk, Louisiana. After that, they were about as ready as they could get.

In the Philippines, General Douglas MacArthur was appointed to the top slot in the U.S. Army Forces Far East Command, and hope began to replace fear. MacArthur, son of another famous general, was quite a controversial personality, but he knew his business. He apparently knew something about tanks, and he had requested the 192nd and the 194th independent tank battalions for the Far East. He'd also arranged to have the U.S. Army Air Force station almost three dozen of the new B-17 bombers in the islands. What had once been a hopelessly outdated, vulnerable nineteenth-century colonial army was about to be upgraded . . . if there was time.

On October 27, 1941, the 588 men of what was being called the Kentucky Battalion went through a final roll call and loaded aboard the transport, U.S.S. *Hugh L. Scott*. After zigzagging across the Pacific, the transport arrived at Manila on Thanksgiving Day, November 20.

After unloading their tanks and parading through the streets of Manila, they drove north and began to set up at Fort Stotsenburg, 65 miles north of Manila. Located next to Clark Field, the camp was what one soldier called "pure Hollywood." It contained a small parade ground, hospital, PX, and a few tropical barracks constructed by native labor of bamboo with thatched grass roofs. Also in residence was the 26th Cavalry, Philippine scouts, the last horse-mounted

79

unit in the U.S. Army. As tension built, the tanks were spread around both the fort and Clark Field to guard against enemy airborne attacks. Finally, on December 7, General Jonathan Wainwright announced, "The cat has jumped," and the garrison in the Philippines went to full alert. Uselessly.

Because of the international date line, December 7 at Pearl Harbor was December 8 at Clark Field and Fort Stotsenburg. The Japanese plan included as many simultaneous attacks as possible, but since the air attack on the Philippines was to come from Formosa, the weather delayed their strike somewhat. This worked to their advantage as, upon notification from Pearl, the commanders at Manila had launched an intensive air search, which, because of the delay, found nothing. The U.S. war plan had included a strike by B-17 flying fortresses on Formosa in case of war, but because of foot-dragging and general unpreparedness, the strike was delayed. That contretemps has never been resolved satisfactorily, but there is no doubt that the commanders involved knew we were at war.

The naval commander, Admiral Hart, got the message from Pearl at 0230 on December 8. MacArthur got the word about an hour later, and official confirmation arrived from Washington at 0530. At dawn, a flight of planes from carrier *Ryujo* attacked U.S. seaplane tender *William B. Preston* in Davao Gulf. At 0930, two flights of bombers from Formosa struck Baguio and the Tugugarao airfield in northern Luzon. In the face of all this, the Army Air Corps general and one of MacArthur's staffers were still bickering over what to do when a flight of 108 bombers and 34 fighters struck Clark, Nichols, and Iba Fields, around Fort Stotsenburg at 1230 on the 8th.

There were 35 B-17s being armed for the flight to bomb Formosa and a squadron of pursuit planes taking off, when the bombers came in at 22,000 feet in perfect V formation. The ground crews were still loading fuel, ammunition, and bombs into the giant planes, and the pilots and air crews were at lunch. To the delighted Japanese pilots, the American bombers were lined up like sitting ducks, and they took their sweet time to get their aim right, as our antiquated three-inch AA guns couldn't even reach that high. Down below, the tankers, horror-struck and helpless, had to sit and watch the destruction of their air force.

Following the deadly precision bombing, the fighters came howling down to strafe . . . down to where a tanker could get at them.

The scene was a perfect hell of exploding bombs, burning, exploding aircraft, shattered buildings, bomb-pocked runways, and running, bleeding men and panicked horses as the Zero fighters roared in at treetop level. One tank crew from Company "B" rolled their tank past the burning bombers, out onto the airfield, right in front of a flight of strafing fighters, and shot one down. Small consolation, given the price in dead and wounded, burned supplies, and smashed bombers. Of 35 B-17s, 18 were smashed hulks; the pursuit squadron had lost all but two of its P-40s. The enemy lost only nine planes, one to a tank's gunner.

For almost two weeks, the Japanese bombers raided almost at will, and the tankers waited and prepared, until midnight of December 22. Orders came down sending three companies of the 192nd north to meet the Japanese landing at Lingayen. The Janesville company took the lead, and in the darkness, drivers drove by blue running lights as tank commanders pored over Shell Oil Company road maps. Convoy point man was Private Orvis E. Rinehart, who wove his motorcycle carefully around potholes while a column of half-blind tanks followed in the dark tropic night. A tragicomedy of errors was about to unfold. Company "B," sent along another route to meet the invaders, never got there. Companies "A" and "C" were to be refueled, but their gas trucks were sent to the wrong town by mistake. The M-3 could only make sixty-odd miles on one filling of gas, so the column should have been accompanied by fuel trucks, but there'd been fear of air attack. As a result, enough fuel to fill the tanks of a platoon was siphoned from the fuel supplies of the rest of the company.

From a potential of over 50 tanks, only five were actually able to meet the enemy's assault. There was no time for reconnaissance, and they met the invaders head on. In the encounter that followed, all five tanks were hit and disabled—the 37mm shells of the M-3 couldn't break the sloping frontal armor of the Japanese tanks, but the enemy's 47mm cannons could pierce the thin unsloped armor of the little Stuart tanks. One driver, peering anxiously through his vision slit into the morning light, was completely decapitated. This was not a particularly encouraging beginning for the campaign.

MacArthur's Plan Orange called for first, a holding action on the beach, which didn't happen, and then a series of holding actions down the length of the Bataan Peninsula, which worked brilliantly. Japanese General Homma had assumed that MacArthur would try to hold his headquarters at Manila and had launched a two-pronged invasion to surround the city. Wrong. MacArthur was already in Corregidor, leaving General Wainwright as field commander. Technically the plan was what is known as a "retrograde movement," buying time by retreating, leapfrog-style, behind a series of ambushes. And as the Japanese had no knowledge of Plan Orange nor any plan to counter it, this would slow their advance across the Pacific to Australia by four months, if it could be pulled off.

MacArthur, confident of his own skill, had chosen to pull off a double retrograde, using the 192nd on one side of the peninsula and its sister battalion, the 194th, on the west side of Bataan. Screening them would be the 26th Cavalry Regiment. Essentially, the tanks would be leapfrogging down the peninsula as the horsemen scouted and manned roadblocks. Some wild and wonderful things were about to happen. General Wainwright commanded the Northern and Eastern Area of Operations (AO), and General Albert Jones commanded the Southern Luzon Force. The tactics were, like many things in war, basically simple and basically hard. "Stand and fight, then pull back and dynamite" were the orders of the day, and they worked.

General Masaharu Homma had intended to simply capture Manila and that should have been the end of it. Instead he now had to face five defensive lines that had been surveyed by MacArthur many years before. The key to Plan Orange was the Calumpit Bridge, and the key to getting as many men across that bridge were the tanks . . . and the light horse cavalry that scouted out ahead of them, 26th Regiment of Philippine scouts.

Typical of the tankers was Captain Walter Write, commander of the Janesville company, and in civilian life, part owner of a feed store in town. He was, in the words of Forrest Knox, "too brave for his own good and wouldn't order a man to do anything that he wouldn't do himself." On Christmas Eve he was laying mines to seal off a road and deny the Japanese its use. Those mines were strictly Rube Goldberg affairs made by local ordnance people with what was at hand. A few sticks of dynamite, a battery, and a homemade detonator. A sudden explosion stunned Knox and his buddy Carl Nickols. The little bomb had gone off in Captain Write's hands, killing him instantly. The news of his death reached his wife on January 21 as she lay on a sickbed.

On that same day, other women, wives, sisters—even some daughters of the older men—were holding a baby shower for Mrs. John Bushaw, wife of one of the tank company's lieutenants. The Idle Hours Club had become a tank company auxiliary that endures to this day.

The withdrawal into Bataan was a hard, grueling job for the tankers. By day they manned roadblocks and ambushes, sniping at advancing Japanese and protecting refugees. By night, they shielded withdrawing infantry from infiltrating Japanese. The Philippine army was a separate unit from the scouts and not nearly as professional; they tended to bunch up and traveled in civilian buses from one line of resistance to another. Most accounts agree that, without the tanks, they would have been lost.

The following account comes from the *Journal of the United States Cavalry*, which was in the process of becoming *Armor Magazine*:

"Reconnoitering for the northern force, five tanks took a narrow road running in the direction of Japanese lines, staying in sight of each other. As they rounded a curve, the second tank lost the leader. Its driver accelerated to close the gap, but just then a shell exploded behind the tank. The tankers realized they were trapped by an antitank gun. There was no room to turn around in the dense jungle cover. The tankers simply followed an old cavalry rule: 'If you are trapped, charge.' At full throttle the four light M-3s charged down the road, smashing Japanese gun units right and left, grinding terrified gunners under the tracks and scattering the survivors with machine-gun fire.

"After that wild rush, they found a place wide enough to turn around and then came back at high speed again, to finish the job, running through gun nests and over the completely disorganized gunners. When they got to the lead tank, it had been hit several times, and the crew was dead. Then the rest of the tanks started being hit by concealed 47mm guns, and most of that brave platoon were killed.

"The men of the second tank were trapped inside a smoldering hulk, unable to move for fear of Japanese infantry, who were filtering into the area; they had only one chance, play dead. They survived the heat of the burning fuel, several Japanese inspections, and an attack by our own artillery. Finally the invaders moved out of the area, and the three surviving crewmen slipped out of their tank and began a three-day walk back to American/Filipino lines. With some help from Filipino civilians, they finally reached Manila. There were only five survivors of that platoon and after a brief rest on Corregidor, they went back to Bataan and rejoined their tank group, which had been whittled down to about company size."

Oddly, the lack of a cohesive command was one of the things that contributed to General Homma's confusion. One of Murphy's laws of war states that "professional soldiers are predictable. . . . Wars are full of unpredictable amateurs."

The two tank battalions had been combined into a provisional tank group under Colonel (later General) Weaver, but there were command difficulties. Any general officer, including General Wainwright, would commandeer the nearest group of tanks, claiming "immediate battle commander's rights" anytime the Japanese attacked. This resulted in sometimes aimless, helter-skelter movements of tanks. The enemy found this very confusing and seriously overestimated the number of American tankers in the peninsula. Robert Stewart, one of the Janesville group, now a retired mail carrier, said, "The enemy figured we must have had 2,000 tanks. It was because we shifted them back and forth. What puzzled them was the way we'd have them sitting along a road, we played leapfrog."

Lewis Wallish, a retired General Motors employee, describes the strategy: "On the retreat, we slowly moved back, usually at night. In the morning, we'd set up again. Skirmishes would happen. We took a lot of shelling, artillery fire, and bombing."

Carl Nickols said that the tank group assisted. "Any outfit that needed us, they used our tanks as pillboxes." On one occasion when the unit ran out of ammunition after firing off 90,000 rounds, he asked a supply officer for more and was told he couldn't have any. "He asked us how we'd use the ammunition, and I told him 'Against the Japs.' He refused to give us more and I told him, 'If we don't get more they'll get your ass.' . . . We got more."

The lines that they had to defend were usually natural terrain lines such as a ridge or stream. The crews would post themselves along likely lines of approach, camouflage the hopelessly tall and blocky shape of the M-3, and wait for trouble. They'd always try to work in pairs to provide covering fire for each other until the invaders came. If they'd stayed buttoned up inside the tanks they could have been snuck up on, so they became their own infantry, scouting around outside their positions, along the roads. Filipino soldiers would come retreating, riding "Pambusco Buses," trucks with fancy wooden bodies and frilly jitney roofs. Still the tankers waited in the hot stifling confines of their hulls, fingers on the triggers of their weapons as the Japanese approached.

Sometimes it would be a cluster of scouts on bicycles, sometimes a clattering Japanese tank, which they'd now learned to handle. First, they'd fire rifles or a machine gun to make the enemy deploy into combat formation, then the other, better hidden tank would open up, doing slaughter. Then when in danger of being flanked, they'd peel off and fade back to the next position, to do it all over again.

"We moved out in pairs," Knox recalls. "You'd go down a road and set up a block, and count the tanks through. When you were the last one, you gave the others half an hour headstart and then you started down the road yourself." Most of their movement was done at night because Japanese dive-bombers owned the air during the day.

"The dive-bombers were working these roads continually," Knox recalled years later, "so the chow truck didn't come. About the only truck you could depend on was the gas truck. The gas and ammo truck would make it during the night. I never ran out of gas. Carl Nickols drove ours. He was about the only gas truck left, so he had to gas the whole battalion. If the dive-bombers came, he had to stop and crawl underneath his load of gas and ammo. Some of the damnedest things happened. I saw a Jap tank come growling down a jungle road, and suddenly one of the cavalrymen, on horseback, came out of the jungle, shot the tank commander, stuffed a hand grenade down the turret hatch, and left smartly."

In among the swirl of tanks, infantry, and refugees were the cavalry, sometimes fighting their own war. Captain John Wheeler, 26th Cavalry, Philippine scouts, reports:

"After the battle of Damortis, our cavalry was assigned to cover the withdrawal of the infantry to the south. The enemy was in pursuit, and there was barbed wire on both sides of the roads so we couldn't deploy. If a man was knocked off his horse, he was trampled. The rest of the regiment went galloping down the road with bullets going by on both sides. I heard Major T.J.H. Trapnell calling my outfit and found him by a bridge. He wanted to defend the bridge, but we seemed to be the only ones left. At that moment, Lieutenant Clayton Michelson came up with the veterinary truck. Why it wasn't blasted off the road I will never know. I helped them push it down and pour gas on it and the bridge and light it. The fire just barely stopped the Japanese tanks from crossing the bridge and getting at our infantry.

"On the way back, we had to go through Damortis. Japanese patrols had slipped back into Damortis on a flank, and effected a mild encirclement. There they were in our rear. The regiment went through Damortis fast—through mortar rifle and machine-gun fire, even shells from Jap 47mm tank guns. There was no sleep that night of December 22. The following morning, about dawn, they attacked, throwing fire from long range. Machine guns chattered on both sides and then we withdrew the troops to Pozzorubio and spent the rest of the day in foxholes.

"That evening, we were ordered to withdraw again, about 15 miles, to Binalonan. Everything imaginable was on the road . . . trucks, infantry, tanks, all mixed up in the pitch darkness that concealed us from the planes. At Binalonan, we managed to get a few hours of rest for the first time in four days. By dawn we heard firing from the outposts and were hurriedly called into dismounted action to hold against what appeared to be an unknown number of Jap tanks and a superior force of Jap infantry who had ridden down in confiscated red buses . . . After this fight, we dropped back again to Tayug. On Christmas Eve, we ate for the first time in 48 hours. Canned corn beef, asparagus tips, hardtack, and coffee. All this time, other divisions and regiments were pouring into Bataan behind us. During Christmas night we withdrew south of Tayug and reached Umingan after a 13-mile march, which is pretty rough in this country. Some of us fell asleep in our saddles on the way.

"The Philippine scouts were absolutely splendid. Again and again when we came in so tired we couldn't see straight, I would watch them going miles away to find some sort of hay for the horses. We kept up the daily withdrawals till about December 28 when our last position covered the final closing of the 'Gate to Bataan,' the Calumpit Bridge, which crossed the unfordable Pampanga River."

The key to MacArthur's Plan Orange was the Calumpit

Bridge, and the key to a successful crossing of the bridge was the tanks. The bridge was a twin-spanned structure, one side for a two-lane road and the other for a railroad. The two bridges were the main funnel through which all the troops in Luzon would have to pass. The tanks would have to guard both the northern and southern Luzon forces across before crossing themselves and blowing the bridge in the face of the onrushing Japanese.

The tank units were the last to reach Bataan. At dawn of December 31, with the war only 24 days old, the main spans of the Calumpit Bridge were blown, and the north and south Luzon forces were reorganized as the Army of Bataan. On January 6, the bridge at Layac was blown, and 80,000 troops and almost 30,000 refugees were now "safe," on Bataan. There was a smaller bridge over the Pampanga at Culis, and the remains of two tank battalions were still on the other side. On the night of January 6, the tanks also crossed into Bataan and the bridge was blown. Plan Orange, the retrograde maneuver, was now complete. It was understood, however, that the Philippines had been written off as unsaveable and that there would be no succor. The troops would fight on, some as guerrillas, until MacArthur returned.

Captain John Wheeler continues his narrative: "We were cut off and forced to take to the hilly country between the Maraviles Mountains and Bataan Peak as the only way out. For three days we wandered over mountain trails, eating what little food there was left in our saddlebags. Finally we emerged on the coast of the China Sea at the town of Bagac. There we had a chance to rest up and feed the horses while our survivors wandered in."

On January 15, it was learned that the Japanese, stalled at the blown bridges, were working their way down the coast and that the Philippine army garrison at Moron, north of Bagac, had been evicted from the town. Troop "G," 26th Cavalry, was given the mission of retaking the town. Captain Wheeler ordered his now rested and refreshed troop out and a Lieutenant (now Colonel) Edwin Ramsey volunteered to lead the advance party into the village.

Captain Wheeler: "As we neared the town our artillery barrage lifted and left an unearthly quiet. Riding in between the houses with our pistols raised, we did not know what was going to hit us, but knew that something would. Halfway to the town square, I heard Jap machine-gun fire, a distinctive snapping sound caused by high-velocity and smaller bullets than ours and unmistakable. I rode at the head of the party as we moved up. When we were fired on, we turned around, rode back, and went into dismounted action. We tied our horses between the thatched huts, then moved forward down the road with men in each gutter alongside the houses."

Just then a messenger came galloping back from Lieutenant Ramsey, saying that he had been ambushed by machine-gun fire and had taken casualties and wanted support immediately. Ramsey, it turned out, had been fired on by emplaced machine guns, charged over them, losing several men and horses in the process, and then gone to ground in a ditch behind some coconut trees. Lieutenant Edwin Ramsey and "G" Troop, 26th Cavalry, had just gone into history as the last mounted charge of the old horse cavalry. Capt. Wheeler's report continues:

"From there on it was simply a matter of cautiously moving up under heavy rifle fire to Lieutenant Ramsey and his men. They had taken cover as best they could in a ditch. One was dead and three wounded in a small area. It looked like more.

"Pedro Euperio, private first class, a 19-year-old raw recruit by scout standards, saw three soldiers ahead wearing Philippine army uniforms. He moved forward, until they fired, then shot quickly. They were Japanese disguised as Philippine officers. Despite his wound, Euperio crept on up until ordered to lie down. About the first thing I saw was Euperio drenched in blood, propped up against the house—a pistol in his one good hand, directing us how to move up, indicating points under enemy fire.

"We attacked straight through to the beach. We fired where we heard fire and were happy to see when we went through the bushes that there were dead Japanese. We got straight through to the water, reorganized and attacked around Ramsey. Using him as a pivot, we swept south and killed all the Japs under houses, in trees, and under bushes. About 20 broke and threw down all equipment—even guns in the high grass. I was surprised to see two of my men with bullet holes through their helmets, yet unscathed."

That battle went on for the rest of the day, and after that action, it was determined, regretfully, by General Wainwright, that horses had no further place in a jungle-tank war and the 26th was dismounted, forever. They were the last of the American horsed cavalry, and they passed the tradition on to their sons and grandsons, who carried it on to places such as North Africa, Korea, Vietnam, and Persia. The horses did serve the defenders of Bataan one more time though . . . as rations. With the tanks out of fuel and the crews eating horse meat, their war had passed into history.

On April 8, 1942, four long months after the war began, it was over for the "Battling Bastards of Bataan." Word came down to destroy weapons and surrender. Anxiously the tankers and cavalrymen debated on what to do. Many of the Filipinos simply melted into the jungle to become resistance fighters who'd harass the conquerors for three more years . . . Until Douglas MacArthur came stalking ashore at the head of a column of amphibious tanks and several divisions of case-hardened infantry.

Lieutenant Ramsey eventually wound up leading a force of almost 40,000 men and had a price on his head, as did many other Americans who'd gone into the jungles. Most, however, were too weak to survive in those jungles. *Perhaps the worst is over,* they thought, but it was just beginning.

Of the 99 tankers who left Janesville, Wisconsin, in 1940, only 35 survived the battles, the death march, and the long years of brutal slavery—some in Japanese mines, some in factories, some simply murdered by callous guards. Not quite three dozen made it home to Wisconsin, but they live there still. They had their moments of glory, and their place in history is assured. They were the ones who tripped up the Imperial juggernaut and bought the time the nation needed.

7

THE PACIFIC

While the tankers and cavalrymen and a gallant remnant of U.S. and Filipino forces fought their desperate delaying action, the Japanese octopus slithered into the central Pacific. England, the Netherlands, and what was left of the American fleet would have to fight to hold the Japanese back from what was then called the Malay Barrier, which was a name that applied to a string of big islands stretching from the tip of the Malay Peninsula to New Guinea. If Japan was allowed to collect these mineral-, oil-, and rubber-rich lands into the Co-prosperity Sphere, she would be well-nigh self-sufficient. Worse, once in control of those vital sea gates, the straits of Malacca, Sunda, and Lombok, they would be able to pour into the Indian Ocean to threaten British India and Australia.

Things did not look too good for the Allies that bleak spring and summer of 1942. In rapid succession the tentacles of the Imperial octopus curled around the lands of the old colonial powers. One such invasion force worked its way down the South China Sea to North Borneo and Sumatra. Another task force struck at East Borneo, the Celebes, Ambon, Timor, and Bali. A third, the most dangerous, lanced straight down the Solomons. In rapid succession the

Japanese avalanche took the Admiralties, New Britain, New Ireland, and the northern shore of New Guinea. From Rabaul in New Ireland, they started down the Solomons chain. They easily took Buka, Bougainville, Vella Lavella, New Georgia, and, finally, Guadalcanal, Florida, and Tulagi. The Pacific was going to be their oyster, and they were in the process of prying it open to extract its pearls.

Guadalcanal was the real prize, for its flat northern plain was an ideal site for an airfield, which they quickly proceeded to build. That had been the secret of their success—the rapid construction of air bases from which to pound the next objective into submission. Not that there had been much resistance to their virtual walk-over of an under-defended region. After Pearl Harbor and the disastrous battle of the Java Sea, about all we had working in the way of long-range offensive forces were three aircraft carriers and 50 submarines of varying capabilities.

Forced to utter desperation, the U.S. could do few things, but would have to do them well. We did. Very well indeed. The first thing would be to start preparing a ground force to take and hold airfields for the long road to Tokyo. Japan had built those airfields for conquest, but that game could be played both ways. That chain of airfields would turn out to be an arrow aimed directly at Tokyo, Hiroshima, and Nagasaki. But, before any Allied aircraft could land on one of those runways, the tracks of tanks would claw up it and grind the Japanese defenders into raw meat.

Next, the Japanese navy, its single greatest striking force, would have to be neutralized. While the U.S. Army and Marines were frantically training troops and getting ready to fight, the U.S. Navy launched an unrestricted submarine campaign that made the efforts of Hitler's U-boats seem tame by comparison. Those garrison islands were cut off from Japan and starved in order to soften them up for the U.S. Marines and their tanks. Savage sea and air battles gradually began to put the brakes on Imperial dreams, but wars are won on the ground, not in the air or on the sea. The greatest warship and the fastest bomber are only support mechanisms to put a young man with a rifle in the enemy's palace . . . or a tank in his front yard, and that was exactly what was about to happen.

All during the time of the Philippine delaying action, American industry had been getting into gear, producing ships, planes, and tanks. The whole economy had shifted to a war footing with, to the rest of the world, shocking speed. Rapidly now, our first production tank, the little M-3, began to come off the assembly line. The British got some, the Australians got a few, and the U.S. Marines got even fewer. On the morning of August 6, 1942, only two months after the surrender of Corregidor, a U.S. Marine landing force hit the beaches on islands north of Guadalcanal, the first offensive effort of U.S. ground troops in the war, and their few ancient tanks went right in with them. A new era of warfare was beginning.

GUADALCANAL

The island of Guadalcanal is shaped like a sweet potato with a deeply curved northern shore which faces a body of water known as Sealark Channel. Across this channel is the island of Florida and inside its southern bay are two small garrison islands, Tulagi and Tanambogo/Gavutu. The 1st Marine Division was given the mission of invading the main island of Guadalcanal at Lunga Point while its reinforcing element, units of the 2nd Division, drew the secondary objective of Florida and its satellite islands. That secondary objective, however, was the first to be hit, and it was hit by Marines with a long tradition of battle esprit, all the way back to Belleau Wood. Who were these young men, and what was the tradition that made them fight so ferociously? Perhaps this quote from their official history will identify them:

"When the 2nd Marine Division was formally activated on February 1941, its keystone unit was the old 6th Regiment. Nearly a year before, the 6th had detached a battalion to found the reactivated 8th Regiment and these two regiments with the 10th Marines (artillery) had been joined in the 2nd Marine Brigade. Now the brigade became the division.

"The historic 6th was an ideal father for the new regiments. It not only provided them with a core of seasoned troopers, on duty since 1937, but it brought the division the traditions of Château-Thierry and Belleau Wood. At Château-Thierry, in WWI, the French lines were collapsing under savage German attacks when the 6th and 5th Marines, organized as a brigade, arrived on the front. A frightened French officer, his eyes hollowed by fatigue and terror, appealed to a young U.S. Marine captain to join in the retreat. The captain's answer still rings in the records and memories—and the character—of the 2nd Marine Division.

" 'Retreat hell!' he said, 'We just got here!' "

"Less than a week later, the U.S. Marines fought for and secured Belleau Wood. It was a battle of unquestioned ferocity. The American forces drove forward into massed machine guns, and in a frightful 24 hours, the U.S. Marines saw 31 officers and 1,056 men killed or wounded. In the midst of the battle, the American attack faltered. For an eternal moment the issue was in doubt. Suddenly, through the awful noise of battle came the battle cry of an immortal sergeant of the 6th Marines as he plunged forward at the head of his squad.

" 'Come on, you sons of bitches! Do you want to live forever?' "

"That squad and other squads swept forward into the terrible woods, the woods that were to be renamed 'Le Bois de Brigade de Marine,' by the grateful French. Even in peacetime, the gaudy 6th had an affinity for trouble. In 1924 it turned up in the Dominican Republic and at Guantanamo Bay. In 1927, it was rushed to Shanghai, under the command of Major General Smedley D. Butler to defend the International Settlement from the warring factions of the Chinese Revolution. That was also the first U.S. Marine combat use of tanks, as they took a provisional company of tanks with them, mounted in WWI-vintage Renaults."

Now, they would always be known as the Americans who were first to fight on enemy soil, when they stormed ashore on Tulagi, Gavutu, and Tanambogo. But, how would they fight, these young men of a newer generation? Would they match up to their fathers' performance at Belleau Wood? Would they carry on the tradition of the old international marines of the 1920s and 1930s?

At 0600 hours, August 6, 1942, Col. R. E. Hill led his 1st Battalion down the nets and into the swaying plywood Higgins boats to find out. Behind them in the wan dawn light, ship cranes were lifting light tanks out of their holds and putting them onto tank lighters. These tanks weren't even as new as the M-3s that had fought on Bataan; they were even older models, the M2A4 that their crews referred to as "armored eggshells."

By noon of D-Day, there was little developed fighting on either of the large islands, Guadalcanal or Florida, but the action on the twin dumbbell-shaped islands of Gavutu/Tanambogo had become savage. Initially, the 1st Marine Paratroop Battalion had drawn the Gavutu assignment, but on D+1 had been reinforced by the 3rd Battalion, 2nd Marines, under Col. Robert Hunt.

The two islands were separated by a narrow causeway that was swept by Japanese fire, and Col. Hunt decided to try something new. He ordered Captain Tinsley, a tough, lanky Kentuckian, to take his "I" Company, in Higgins boats, around to the north end of Tanambogo, accompanied by two tanks under Lieutenant Robert Sweeny, from Illinois, in tank lighters. This would be the first recorded combat amphibious landing of tanks in history. At 1620 hours on D+2, they beached on the oil- and blood-soaked sands of the island, and the Japanese went absolutely mad. One tank was already ashore, working with the infantry when Sweeny's lighter beached and he opened the ramp with his treads, ramming the tank ashore and into the first armored beach assault in history.

No Imperial soldier expected to survive, and they fought as if they did not want to. As Sweeny guided his two tanks inland, screaming soldiers ran at them with pipes, crowbars, even small logs, in an attempt to jam the treads. At the same time all the tanks' guns were going, and each of those tanks had four .30-cal machine guns beside its 37mm cannon. Unfortunately, the little tank had outrun its infantry and was now alone. Sweeny lifted his body in the TC hatch to get a better view and took a bullet through the head, which took the top of his skull off. The old radial engine stalled, and the crew, smothered with hostile Japanese, tried to fight their way out. They'd not yet learned the trick of scratching each other's back with MG fire, which had saved so many lives on Luzon. The Japanese ran an iron bar into the tracks, poured gasoline on the tank, and set it and the crew on fire. Only one man survived.

Accounts vary as to what happened next, but apparently the other tank stuck with its infantry, and the war's first bayonet attack drove the hostiles from the battlefield. The counterattack was broken, the new beachhead held, and the next morning 42 dead Japanese soldiers were counted within the sweep of Sweeny's guns. At that point, however, things began to come unglued.

During the disastrous naval battle off Savo Island, the Japanese navy had sunk the American cruisers, *Astoria,* *Vicennes,* and *Quincy,* and seriously damaged cruiser *Chicago.* The Australian cruiser *Canberra* was so badly damaged that she had to be sunk by an American torpedo. At that point, the only thing that saved the Solomons campaign was the hesitance of one admiral, Gunichi Mikawa. He didn't know just where our carriers were and decided to return to his base at Rabaul. He received commendations for his sea action . . . and a chewing out from Admiral Yamamoto for not pressing an attack of the landing force at Guadalcanal.

Unfortunately, the American squadron that was protecting the supply ships upon which the U.S. Marines were dependent, didn't know that. Rear Admiral Kelly Turner, the officer in command of amphibious forces, only knew that he was low on fuel and ammunition and had to resupply . . . and when he took the remainder of his savagely mauled task force to safer waters, the supply ships went with him.

In the almost palpable tropic darkness, Sunday, August 9, the navy up-anchored and set a course for Espíritu Santo, 557 miles south of Guadalcanal, leaving the bulk of the 1st and 2nd Marine Divisions literally "high and dry."

The next morning the U.S. Marines felt like the lost "Battling Bastards of Bataan." No mama, no papa, and no Uncle Sam. The only tanks ashore were those of "C" company of the 2nd Tank Battalion; and one lone U.S. Marine was heard to say, "By God, they've hauled ass," as he looked unbelievingly out over the empty sea. The U.S. Marines never quite forgave Kelly Turner for that one. After the shock wore off though, they got busy. There were enough tank lighters and landing craft, including the famed Amtracks, to do some shuffling, and it was found that tank engines would run quite happily on captured gasoline.

The Marines were bone weary from battle, wearing blood- and grime-stiffened uniforms, and were critically short of rations, so they ate liberated canned fish and rice. For two long weeks they subsisted on captured rations, lived with rotting corpses, scrounged Japanese weapons and shovels and sandbags, and fought . . . and won. They fished with hand grenades, ate fish and crab and canned pineapple, and smoked barbarously rank Japanese cigarettes. The tobacco burned so fast that a paper spacer had to be used to prevent lip burns.

Flies and mosquitos became an airborne plague, carrying malaria and the germs of dysentery and dengue fever from the rotting corpses of Japanese and Americans alike. Still the digging, fortifying, and flushing of armed, hostile remnants went on. On Guadalcanal itself, the unfinished Japanese airstrip was completed by Americans, using captured grading equipment to finish the Lunga Point Airfield. They named it Henderson Field after a pilot lost at Midway, and even before the ships returned, it was in business.

On August 12, a U.S. Navy PBY-5 Catalina amphibian

bomber landed with Admiral McCain aboard. The navy officer pronounced the field fit for fighter use and took off with a load of wounded marines, the first of almost 3,000 to be evacuated from Guadalcanal. On August 20, Grumman Wildcat fighters and 12 Dauntless dive-bombers from the carrier *Long Island* (CVE-1, the first of the little escort carriers) landed at Henderson, and the Cactus Air Force was in business.

Around the shores of the islands surrounding Guadalcanal, a new sea weapon was invented. A tank lighter is a slightly more sophisticated landing barge, and when a tank is aboard, it can fight and was used as a gunboat. Time after time, the 37mm guns of the little M-3 tanks blasted enemy patrols and ambuscades into dog meat. Like Civil War Monitors, the tank-boat combination prowled the little islands around Tanambogo, Gavutu, and Florida, mopping up little pockets of resistance.

On Guadalcanal itself, the landings, at first almost unopposed, were now meeting rapidly stiffening resistance, although the Japanese command was still under the impression that this was only a "strong reconnaissance." On August 21, a wild banzai attack stormed the U.S. Marines' lines at the mouth of the Ilu River, a 50-foot-wide sluggish tropical stream . . . right into the faces of a platoon of light tanks and a section of 37mm AT guns that had been hauled into place by muscle power.

The guns murdered them, despite the display of "spiritual strength" that was supposed to drive the Americans into the sea. Then the marines flanked the Japanese, hit them in the face with tank cannons, and strafed them with fighters from Henderson. By 1700, it was over, and the Japanese commander, Colonel Kiyono Ichiki, disgraced in his own mind, burned his regimental colors and shot himself. Almost 800 of his men had joined him in death, and the few survivors fled eastward. To quote Admiral Tanaka: "This tragedy should have taught us the hopelessness of bamboo spear tactics."

It was becoming more and more obvious, however, that the little M-3 Stuart was just a bit light in the butt for the rigors of jungle busting and close combat. They barely survived on Guadalcanal, but valuable lessons were learned, such as the need for close infantry support. The M-3 was simply too fast in the gearing, and continued slow-speed work tended to fry the clutches. There would be other, newer models of the little Stuart, and it would also find fame as the first of the flamethrower tanks, when a genius mounted a normal handheld flamethrower in the bow gun position.

Something bigger and slower, with thicker armor and a bigger gun, was needed, and it was on the way. The 38-ton, diesel-powered version of the Sherman, the famed M4A2. This tank, the natural partner of the marine infantryman, would make its debut on bloody Tarawa. And it would save the day . . . after they finally got a few ashore. Assault landings against heavily fortified beaches were a wholly new concept.

The first of the Sherman series, along with its predecessor, the Grant medium tank, had been fighting in North Africa since January 1942. They'd given the Germans a nasty shock when they assaulted the Gazala Line in May of that year. Erwin Rommel's diary records that "A new American tank had torn great holes in our lines." During the period of British usage of the Grant tank, there were several teams of Americans embedded in the British tank regiments, first as technician instructors who went into combat, and then as crews on "makee learnee," to transmit their knowledge to the divisions training up in our southwestern deserts. Then they would go ashore in North Africa.

8

NORTH AFRICA

November 8, 1942

The Italians, who had been one of the last of the European
nations to consolidate, finally decided to get into the
international colonization business and snapped up Ethiopia, then fought a war with Turkey, just to extract Libya
from the rotting corpse of the old Ottoman Turkish Empire.
There the matter rested until an almost bankrupt Italy fell
under the sway of "Il Duce," Benito Mussolini, and decided, probably at Adolf Hitler's instigation, to evict the
British from Egypt. This was a mistake, and it set the desert
tanks rolling.

On September 13, 1940, Marshal Graziani sent his 10th
Army across the border from Libya into Egypt, with six
infantry divisions and eight armored battalions. The outnumbered British forces, consisting of three battalions of
infantry, one of tanks, and a couple of platoons of armored
cars, together with three gun batteries, retreated in good
order—but very swiftly, from Fort Capuzzo. At this time,
the British army in Egypt consisted of about 36,000 men,
and General Wavell, who was expecting the Italian offensive, just let them come on and let the desert chew on them

while he built his defenses. By September 16, the Italian offensive had about run out of steam, and they began to dig in around the city of Sidi Barrâni to "organize supplies for the next stage." In other words, a garrison army couldn't even live in the desert, let alone fight the British, who'd been there for quite a few decades.

On December 9, 1940, the world heard the sound of British artillery opening up their offensive against Sofafi, Nibeiwa, east and west Tummar, Maktila, and Sidi Barrâni. Within two days the British had captured 38,300 soldiers including four generals, 400 guns, and 50 tanks. Several days later, on the 15th, a Sunday, the Brits roared through the Halfaya Pass on the Egyptian-Libyan border and put the Italian 10th Army into full retreat. By Tuesday, the 17th, the British were in the Italian town of Sollum and were looking hungrily at Tobruk.

History was winding up rather tightly back then. On Wednesday, the 18th, Adolf Hitler had just signed the infamous directive 21, the invasion of Russia, known as Operation Barbarossa. The very next day, the Italian high command appealed to the German high command to send a German armored division to North Africa as soon as possible. Right then, they lost control of their war, because the Germans sent Erwin Rommel and the Afrika Korps, whose mission was to cross the Suez and link up with the Japanese at Baku, as well as to flank Russia and take the oil fields at Baku.

Behind the scenes, pressure was building up, because like Japan, Germany had an atomic bomb program, and it was at that time, just as far along as our own Manhattan Project.

During this time, at Tokyo University, a Japanese nuclear physicist, one Goro Miyamoto had converted their cyclotron into a mass spectrograph, which could separate the fissionable U-235 from U-238. Following this lead, Ryokichi Sagane, at the Rikken Institute for Physics and Chemistry, converted their cyclotron into a mass spectrograph and began to produce U-235. In California, at Berkeley, Sagane's old teacher Ernest O. Lawrence was producing about an ounce of U-235 per day.

These slow laboratory methods would never produce the amount of nuclear material that Professor Bunsaku knew would be needed, and several methods were being experimented with. Finally the Japanese settled on a thermal diffusion process, which relied on using heat to separate gaseous U-235 from U-238. This method had the added advantage that the Japanese had access to the inventors of the process . . . in Germany!

On June 26, 1940, a Professor Harteck had sent the following plea for support to the German War Office:

> As is well known, two methods can be adopted for building a uranium reactor.
>
> Reactor type I consists of natural uranium and about five tons of heavy water.
>
> Reactor type II consists of uranium metal enriched in uranium 235 and consequently smaller in quantity, together with smaller quantities of heavy water or even ordinary water.
>
> The German research group has been following the first method while the Americans will probably have adopted the second. Only experience will show which of the two is more practical in the long run. In any event, the second method will result in significantly smaller reactor units, which might possibly be usable for driving army vehicles.
>
> THIS LATTER METHOD IS, FURTHERMORE, MORE AKIN TO THE MANUFACTURE OF EXPLOSIVES. [Author's emphasis.]

The race was on. The contestants were, at that time, roughly equal, but Harteck had an ace up his sleeve, the low-temperature reactor.

While all this scientific experimentation was going on, however, out in the real world, in North Africa, the Pacific, and Russia, a war was going on and we were losing. Erwin Rommel soon put an end to the rampages of General Wavell with his superior generalship and much better tanks. The old slow Matilda and Valentine tanks of the British were soon outmaneuvered by the swifter Panzer MkIIIs and outgunned by the Panzer IVs. In desperation the Brits put in an order to the American war plants, which in the late 1940s had yet to get into high gear.

What they got was the little M-3, which was so much better than what they had to work with that they immediately dubbed it the "Honey." The little tank was a bit undergunned and short-ranged, though, and required some modifications to make it desert-worthy. Its automotive excellence was what made such a difference. At that time, a tank that could run over 2,000 miles without needing new tracks was a military miracle. Its gun was adequate, barely, but the aircraft engine that drove it was reliable and simple, and it saved the day. For the first time in history, a commander could count on all of his tanks reaching the assault line at the appointed time. Not only was the American tank more reliable, it was about 10 mph faster than its German equivalent, which gave it a tactical advantage.

All through 1940 and 1941, American tanks were shipped to North Africa, modified and experimented with, and the information was sent back to American factories. Several models of the Honey became even more suitable for desert combat, and then the first of the big M-3 mediums began to arrive, along with a few American crews who needed the experience. There'd been technical experts sent along with the tanks, of course, but what was needed were combat crews. Eventually, three crews of tankers were sent. They got their experience, and the story was written by their commanding officer—a horse cavalry officer.

THE ENEMY IN AFRICA
MAJOR HENRY CABOT LODGE, JR., CAVALRY RESERVE
As told to the Editorial Staff of the Cavalry Journal

The British 8th Army is now pursuing the fleeing German Afrika Korps back over the route along which we saw it advance last summer. Simultaneously, American expeditionary troops have landed in force on the western coast of Africa to allay any possible retreat into French North African territory. With these two recent developments in mind, the strategic importance of Africa and the Middle East is again limelighted.

During the past two years, our enemy in Africa has seen fit to keep a considerable army in Italian Libya and, more recently, in Egypt. In addition, Germany has maintained even more divisions in the Balkans and Italy. Undoubtedly, the Axis has an envious eye on the Middle East, control of which would mean possession of the Suez, as well as the rich oil fields of the Tigris-Euphrates and the Persian Gulf.

The loss to the Allies of the Middle East would have been the greatest shock that they would have yet sustained. It would have seriously imperiled the British Empire and reduced their war effort to a defensive role in the UK. It would have isolated, if not eliminated, both China and Russia from major participation in the war. It would have aligned the Moslem world with the Axis, consigned Africa to Axis exploitation, and enabled Hitler and the Japanese to join hands.

For two years, the British forces in the Middle East have fought against an enemy formidably trained and equipped and often in superior strength. At last the tide of war has turned in Africa, and the Germans are suffering their first major defeat. But the war is still far from over, and other German armies remain to be conquered. The job ahead is still not an easy one, and our enemy, whenever and wherever we meet him, is *not* a weakling.

This I learned while serving with other American tankmen during the German advance in Libya last summer. We were shelled, bombed, and machine-gunned. We saw the German army in action, saw it work with precision and efficiency, saw it push back British forces and seriously endanger the Allied lifeline in the Middle East. Although our small American tank force "took it" and struck back with a final score that did credit to both men and machines, we acquired a healthy respect for the Nazi fighting machine.

I was serving on active duty with the 2nd Armored Division

last spring when I learned that a small group of volunteer tankmen were to be sent to Libya to observe and participate in the fighting then going on. I was fortunately among those who were selected to go. Several days after our departure from the States, we arrived in Cairo and reported for duty. The next day we moved up to the front in a train crowded with British, Free French, Indian, and Australian soldiers.

At Capuzzo on the Libyan-Egyptian frontier, most of the party of Americans went on to Bardia for a week's training with British units. I went forward to make an overall observation of the combat area where Field Marshal Rommel was just beginning his push, which eventually took him to within 40 miles of Alexandria.

One day we were driving a command car when the Stuka dive-bombers arrived. We jumped out of the car and dived headlong for a slit trench just about the time they dived. They were after a line of British supply trucks en route to the front. After the Stukas blasted the entire line of trucks, they swept back in graceful arcs and started strafing us with machine guns.

Back in Bardia, I learned that our men had made rapid progress and were ready for combat. They went into action on June 11, 1941, near the town of Acoma, swung their tanks alongside British manned tanks, and were promptly attacked by German tanks at a range of about 4,000 yards. The main engagement started at about 0300 in the morning. All day the American crews kept up a withering fire that held the Germans some 700 yards away. Although it is difficult to keep an accurate score in a tank battle, the American crew knocked out at least eight German Panzers before the Germans brought up their 88mm guns and the British gave the order to retreat. The American men and machines acquitted themselves well. The next day the men turned in their M-3s and prepared to report what they had learned.

One of the important conclusions drawn from our observations and brief experience was that the remarkably efficient organization, drive, and timing of the German army should not be underestimated. Nor should it be forgotten that German equipment is on a par with their aggressiveness.

A man would have to be blind not to see that the German soldiers were superbly equipped for the particular rigors of desert fighting. German civilians have had to content themselves with ersatz makeshifts, but not their fighting men. One afternoon I talked with a German prisoner who was calmly confident that his side would win. "Because our equipment and organization are better." I did not remind him that America had not yet delivered her first punch.

As we left Africa last summer, one man remarked, "It seems a damned shame to clear out after our first crack at 'em."

"Yeah," said another, "but we'll be back, here or in France—or somewhere."

Adapted, with permission, from Armor Magazine. *Note: It is from this period that the inspiration for the Humphrey Bogart movie* Sahara *was drawn.*

NORTH AFRICA
NOVEMBER 8–12, 1942
OPERATION TORCH

The Allied landings in North Africa on November 8, 1942, were a hodgepodge of political expediency that got the tankers in serious trouble. Joseph Stalin was pressing for an Allied second front, but the Allies weren't about to take on "Festung Europa," yet, and Rommel had to be stopped, so the decision was made to conduct Operation Torch and land in North Africa.

The problem was the French. They weren't full allies yet and were divided into many factions, some on the Allied side. Some, the Vichy segment, were somehow loyal to the Germans. Then there were the Free French who were divided into the DeGaullists and the Darlanists, none of whom would cooperate with the British, who'd had to sink a part of the French navy to keep it out of German hands. Into this mess strode one of the most brilliant figures in history, George Patton.

On November 8 through 12, the landings were accomplished at Safi, Casablanca, Oran, and Algiers, against French resistance of varying intensity. Through a mixture of force and diplomacy, the various French factions were made to see reason. At Casablanca, for instance, the Americans reasoned with tanks.

On the west end of the landing site at Cap de Fedala, a hostile gun battery held out against the landing force, firing barrage after barrage at the cruisers *Augusta* and *Brooklyn*. Aboard the *Augusta,* George Patton seethed in frustration at French resistance and sent his personal representative, Colonel William Wilbur, ashore to break something loose. Going ashore with the second wave of troops, Wilbur commandeered a jeep and ordered the driver to head south. Braving both trigger-happy sentries and the language barrier, he arrived at Casablanca before dawn and delivered a personal letter from Patton to the French commander, suggesting a cease-fire.

Returning to American lines, hours later, the colonel came upon the stalemate at Cap de Fedala. Commandeering a platoon of Shermans from the 756th Tank Battalion and a company of infantry from 2/7 Infantry, he stormed the gun battery, rendered it useless, and forced the Vichy French garrison to surrender, earning the Congressional Medal of Honor in the process. Now the way was clear for General Patton and his staff to land, and the invasion could spread south. The American tankers, relatively inexperienced, were just about to run into the German first team, Erwin Rommel's Afrika Korps.

THE TANK "TEXAS"
TUNISIA, JANUARY 1943
LTC LOUIS HIGHTOWER

We pulled out about 1700 that morning, in response to a call that 30 German tanks were attacking a hill called Djebel

Lessoude, not far from the town of Faid. When we got there, 15 German MkIV tanks, 26-ton tanks with a 75mm gun like our own, were ahead of us on the eastern crest. To our left, there seemed to be 22 more German tanks of varying Marks. My battalion pulled up in a rough line, and we began to slug it out. In the first engagement, we lost three Shermans, knocked out while we took down five or six of theirs. Then the 22 tanks came over the hill at us, and turned out to be about 50 MkIVs and at least four of their new MkVIs, the awesome Tiger 1. This, as far as I know, was the first battle test of the Tiger and its 88mm main gun.

Our battalion, seriously outnumbered to begin with, began to pull back as the Germans tried their usual trick of envelopment. They sent out a long pincer on each side of us, trying to get behind us from both sides. We kept pivoting and shooting at first one German pincer and then the other. We kept from being surrounded, but at a heavy cost. We were losing tanks, knocked out but not killed, just disabled, when their dive-bombers caught us and came in wave after wave.

They didn't hurt us much, as the TCs could see the bombs falling and have their drivers dodge them, but they smoked us up so bad that we couldn't see. I had my artillery FO call in some 105 barrages while we pulled across two miles of open field into Sidi Bou Zid. The front line here was very fluid, and the town had changed hands several times. Now we'd gotten back to our artillery, self-propelled 105s, and they covered us by using their guns direct fire, shooting straight at the Germans. They were now hitting Krauts with every pop, and I saw three MkIVs flame up with just three shots.

We reorganized in the town, but after about two hours, they began another huge double envelopment, and we had to pull back again. We got our artillery and supply trains safely on the road and then started down the road back to Gafsa ourselves. After getting all our tanks under way, except my HQ section, which was two light tanks and two mediums, my TEXAS, and one other, we took out across country, very cautiously as we were outnumbered and, considering the existence of those Tigers, seriously outgunned. We'd meant to cover ground more quickly than a road-bound column, and it was fortunate that we had. Suddenly we heard gunfire and, coming over a rise, came upon a debacle.

Nine MkIVs and a Tiger were shooting up one of our columns of half-tracks and light vehicles, which were completely helpless before them. The guns on the other medium tank were jammed, and since the two M-3 light tanks were too thinly armored for the task before us, I sent them away and signaled the column of our light vehicles to swing in behind us as my driver raced to put TEXAS between them and the Germans.

As the Germans turned for what they thought would be a picnic, we let go and struck their commander's tank with our third shot. He stopped cold, as if he'd hit a tree. We got a second tank with one more shot, and the Nazi tanks braked to a halt and began to fire at us in earnest. We could fire on the move, though, and kept going at about 15 miles per hour. We put three more shots into another Nazi before discovering that it was the Tiger. I saw the shells burst against him, but don't know if he was disabled. However, he didn't shoot at us again, so we must have done some damage.

Another MkIV came up to him, and we got that one with one shot, still moving ourselves. He flamed up like a flower. Then another MkIV approached the Tiger and the burning tank, which was stupid because all my gunner had to do was move his sight over a hair, and that tank also flamed up with the first shot. Then our gun overheated and jammed, and we were in serious trouble as the remaining MkIVs really opened up on us. We could actually see the shells coming along close to the ground, like a ricocheting stone on the water. One shell fragment came straight down our gun tube, rattled around the turret but caused no serious damage.

Another shell went through the bogie wheels, under the tank, and out the other side like a rabbit, bouncing off across the desert. Then, with a sound like a giant bell, a shell hit our turret, but didn't penetrate. Another hit made our ears ring, but we kept on working on that jammed breechblock. As soon as our gun was unjammed, we began firing again, but now a German 75mm shell smashed the bottom of our left rear gas tank, and blazing gasoline spurted out over the back of the tank, the tracks, and on the ground around us. Heavy black smoke began to roil up from our hull. I shouted to my boys, "Now is the time to git," and we boiled out like peas from a hot pod from the burning hulk of old TEXAS.

We took what little we could carry with us, ducked behind the burning hull, and cut out across country. After walking a couple of miles, keeping a wary eye out behind us, we came upon an abandoned half-track and loaded up on it. A few miles farther on, we found a soldier with a broken back, lying on the ground, and picked him up too. After laying him out on blankets and trying to ease his pain, we continued until we came on another Sherman whose crew were about to destroy it because it had been broken down and they didn't want the Krauts to get it. We put it back in shape, got it running, tucked the half-track in behind us, picked up our convoy, and came on home.

Adapted from Armor Magazine, *November–December 1942.*

HILL 609
NORTH AFRICA
APRIL 30, 1943

By spring 1943, the Axis powers in North Africa were on the run, but there was still a *lot* of fight left in the Germans. The Americans and British, aided by the Free French, who'd buried their hatchets in order to gain access to American equipment, were pushing the Wermacht up into Tunisia, while the British 8th Army compressed the Afrika Korps from the east. The main German line of resistance at that time was a row of fortified hills running east and west, south of the city of Mateur. The main fortress was the top of Djebel Tahent, known by its map reference as Hill 609.

This hill wasn't what one would call tank country, and the Germans knew it. The slope was so steep that tanks couldn't climb it. At least not German tanks. Throughout the war, the Jerries kept making that same mistake, hanging one of their flanks on an impassable terrain feature . . . only to wake up one morning to find a company of Shermans sitting up there shooting up their HQ and supply trains. The Sherman would climb till it fell over backward, pulling infantry uphill along with it.

Hill 609 had wall-like cliffs at many points, but there were places where the slope was "only" 45 degrees. On April 29, Captain Gwinn, CO of "I" Company, 1st Tank Regiment received a warning order from his battalion CO. He was going up 609, the hard way. For several days previously, the infantry had been working their way forward to a jump-off point at the base of the hill, and artillery had been pounding the Germans incessantly. Just as incessantly, the Germans had been showering mortar rounds down on the besiegers and calling their own artillery down on the Americans. Things had just about reached an impasse, so General Ryder, of the 34th Division, decided to call in the tanks. Captain Gwinn and his officers made the traditional commander's recon, studied the problem, and made their plans. Here is Capt. Gwinn's story:

"April 30: Company 'I' arrived at an assembly area behind Djebel el Kerh, southwest of Djebel Tahent, at 0230 hours. In order to get to our defiladed positions, we had to descend a very steep hill, running cross-country in the dark and cross a wadi at the bottom. This would have been very difficult but Jerry obligingly shot up a flare, which made our task easier.

"We got to our assembly area, behind the hill and arranged for a stand-to at 0400 hours, and then the men got some sleep. At 0415 hours, after picking up our infantry, we jumped off. Lieutenant Adams, with five tanks, was to move his 1st Platoon forward and gain a position on a rimrock to the company's left, from which he could cover the entire by fire. On reaching his primary objective, however, he found it to be inaccessible. He switched to an alternate position and was able to get a sufficient field of fire to cover our advance with his tank guns."

The other platoons then advanced rapidly, up the slope, with their accompanying infantry. When the slope became too steep for the infantry to keep up, one infantryman would grab each rear fender of the laboring Sherman and the rest of his squad would tail behind, each man holding on to the webbing of the one ahead of him. Capt. Gwinn continues:

"Quite near the hill, the terrain narrowed so that there was maneuver room for only one platoon at a time, and Lieutenant Riggsby led the 2nd Platoon into a defilade position while Lieutenant Rupert, under heavy antitank fire, took his 3rd Platoon up the slope. Once he had cleared the narrow area, 2nd Platoon and its infantry followed. The infantry tried to designate targets for the tankers, but the noise of incoming mortar and artillery shells made this almost impossible.

"The tank company CP was just forward of the 1st Platoon's gun position and suddenly came under direct antitank fire from the right. Before any damage was done, though, Lieutenant Adams located the gun, a ground-mount 75mm, and knocked it out with his own tank's cannon.

"The 2nd Platoon then began to run into difficulties, and Lieutenant Riggsby's tank was knocked out by antitank fire from a concealed gun. Platoon Sergeant Neal then took charge of the platoon and covered Lieutenant Riggsby. At this time one of 3rd Platoon's tanks, that of Sergeant Kaschak, was knocked out and set afire by a 50mm antitank gun, which scored five penetrations out of six shots at 300 yards.

"Lieutenant Rupert then withdrew his remaining three tanks about ten yards to a defiladed position and began to rake the enemy infantry and gun positions. Our infantry went up over the crest of the hill and tore into the Germans in a wild bayonet charge. The mission was accomplished and, as our infantry took possession of the hill, we were ordered to withdraw to our assembly area. Our losses were two tanks completely inoperative and two which were repaired and put back into operation a few days later."

The official report continues: "It is worthy of note that when his tank was knocked out, Lieutenant Riggsby and his crew remained in it and fired until his ammunition was exhausted, materially assisting the advance of the other tanks and infantry."

The attack had started at first light, and by 0930 hours, the tanks had reached their objective. Because of the hill's rimrock, 20 feet high in places, the summit of the hill was inaccessible to the tanks, but they stayed close up and beat down the enemy defenders with cannon fire and allowed the infantry to get over the crest.

The job wasn't over, though. The Jerries wanted that hill back, badly, and the next dawn there was an infantry attack that was beaten off, only by getting to the bayonet and hand-grenade stage. There were other, lower hills in the area, and that same morning, the enemy tried to regain the crest of Hill 531 just south of 609. This time, though, "I" Company had gotten some tanks up there, and that attack was crushed by cannon and machine-gun fire from the tanks. By May 2, there was heavy motor traffic on the road to Mateur. The Germans were withdrawing.

It is worth noting here that, during the period of Operation Torch, the Germans, after several tries, made the first successful long-range flight of the V-2 rocket, which could lift a 3/4-ton cargo about 200 miles, and that in both Germany and Japan, atomic research was continuing, desperately. At this point in time the more rational thinkers among the Axis powers *had* to know that they were in trouble. On January 30, in Russia, Field Marshal von Paulus had surrendered an army of 285,000 men, after Stalingrad. On May 12, the last of the Axis in North Africa surrendered another 240,000, and in the Pacific, the Allies were on the offensive, island-hopping north toward the Land of the Rising Sun.

In every case, one of the prime tools had been the Sherman tank. In the hands of the British and Americans, the sturdy beast had broken the Afrika Korps; under Russian commanders, it was more reliable than the T-34 . . . and in the capable hands of the U.S. Marines, it had broken the defenses of bloody Tarawa. Suddenly the Axis leaders discovered that they *needed* a miracle weapon.

At Nordhausen, the Germans built an underground V-2 factory, using nearby Buchenwald as a source of slave labor. During three years, an estimated 17,000 slaves died in those tunnels building "Vengeance" weapons. The V-weapons never made any sense as deliverers of Amatol explosives, but as carriers of nerve gas or irradiated material, they would have worked, and very nearly did. In northern France, the "V"-series intercontinental launching sites exist to this day . . . as tourist attractions.

The Allies knew about the German atomic research, and in February 1943, they took out the heavy-water plant at Norsk Hydro in Norway. Unfortunately, there was another plant . . . in Korea. That was one reason for the high-speed island-hopping campaign, to get bombers close enough to stop the Japanese atomic program. As it turned out, the only thing that would break the island defenses was the Sherman tank . . . and the crews that would learn to wear it like a second skin.

9

TARAWA

November 20, 1943

THE SECOND MARINE DIVISION
OPERATION GALVANIC

There had to be a Tarawa. All the landings to date had been against lightly defended beaches, with most of the fighting inland. The Japanese, however, had been watching and learning, and they'd had time to dig in. We'd caught them just at the farthest reach of their expansion on Guadalcanal, before they'd had time to consolidate. They'd been on Tarawa Atoll since September 1942, and in 11 months they'd done a lot of digging. They even had the big eight-inch shore defense cannons that they'd filched from Singapore Harbor.

Tarawa Atoll is shaped like a large upright triangle, mostly made up of small islets of an acre or two. The biggest and most fortified piece of land was the island of Betio, at the southwest corner of the triangle. The problems were three fold. First, the emperor's engineers had done some serious work on field fortifications. Second, there were ship-tearing coral reefs all around Betio. Third, there were insufficient data on the tides and that could make all the difference. The plan was for the landing craft and the still-new LVTs (landing vehicle, tracked) to carry the U.S. Marines and their tanks right up to the beach. Things didn't quite work that way.

Betio is only two and one-quarter miles long and about one-half mile wide. It is shaped something like a pork chop, with the convex side to the north, inside the lagoon. At the time, the troops on the island were the best the Japanese had—5,000 Imperial Marines—and they'd been digging for most of a year. They had 8-inch cannons, 4.7-inch dual purpose guns, 37mm and 47mm guns, and the island simply bristled with machine-gun nests and rifle pits. What made the island strategically important was a recently completed airstrip that would support bombers that could attack the next island objective, 800 miles closer to Tokyo.

The assault plan was ingenious and audacious. The Navy would pound 2,700 tons of assorted ordnance on the island while the amphibious force motored into the entrance to the inner lagoon and beached on the supposedly ill-defended "back door." There was a long pier jutting out into the lagoon, and the Marines intended to make full use of it. This was to be the first use of the Amtrac in a combat assault, and, while they'd already been used in such places as North Africa and even up in the Aleutians, no one knew how they'd function on coral and against heavy defensive fires.

The light Stuart tanks having proved not quite adequate for assault work and jungle crushing, the 2nd Marine Tank Battalion had been equipped with one company of brand-new, diesel-powered M4A2 Sherman tanks. These had much heavier armor, powered turrets with a 75mm cannon, and could run in deeper water than the Stuarts. They were to be put ashore from their own special landing craft and make the assault along with the infantry. The 14 tanks were also being brought along in a new type of ship, the dock landing ship (LSD), which would launch them directly into the sea on their special lighters.

The Marines themselves were only too eager and spoiling for a fight. Major Herbert W. Amey, Jr., of Pennsylvania, told his men, "We are very fortunate, this the first time a landing has been made by American troops against a well-defended beach, the first time over a coral reef, the first time against any force to speak of. And the first time the Japs have had the hell kicked out of them in a hurry." This attitude prevailed from the top brass down to the lowest riflemen. When asked by a correspondent if he was afraid, one young private answered, "Hell no, I'm a Marine." Nobody in all of history had ever done what the American Marines and their tanks were about to try. We were on the short end of a "learning curve" that would lead straight to Normandy. Somebody had to do it the first time.

Right away, things started to come unglued. The attack wasn't a surprise. The Japanese actually fired the first shot—a flare. Then they opened up with the big 8-inch Singapore guns, hitting a few transports which were in the process of putting Marines into lightweight Higgins plywood assault craft. Then battleships *Maryland* and *Colorado* opened up and suppressed the Japanese gunners. All this time, the marines in the little plywood boats had been circling outside the lagoon while two minesweepers cleared the channel so the boats and the Amtracs could get into the "lightly defended" northern shore of Betio.

Out at sea the big LSD, U.S.S. *Ashland,* had squatted in the water. Below its waterline, large valves had opened, letting saltwater into specially designed ballast tanks. In the ship's stern, a pair of huge doors opened, letting the sea into the cargo well. As the water surged in, it began to float the landing craft that held the tanks of "C" Company, 2nd Marine Tank Battalion. As they felt their small craft begin to float, the coxswains started their GM diesels and began to back the clumsy craft out of the hold into the bright, thundering tropic dawn.

The lagoon was a raging volcano. The splintered palm trees stood like broken teeth. From the center of the island, a swirling mass of dark smoke rose like a Kansas tornado. At the base, this cloud was shot with large orange, white, and red infernos as an ammo dump went off. Now the landing craft were in through the pass in the reef, but the smoke was blowing straight toward them, and they couldn't see the defenses, nor could they see the condition of the reef. Then the battleships and the cruisers lifted their fires, waiting for the promised air strike . . . which didn't come. Now the Marines were going ashore against hostile fire that was building by the second as the Imperial gunners found the range.

The first party in, under Lt. William Deane Hawkins, was the scout/sniper platoon and they headed straight for that long pier . . . until their boats ran aground. The tide had gone out and stayed out. The reef was almost bare and wouldn't even float the Higgins boats, let alone the tank lighters. Instead of the normal fall neap tide, which had been figured in, there was also a "dodging tide," which came only a few times a year, and which the marines didn't know about. Now the only way to reach the shore was across the reef. Only two things could move, the untried Amtracs and the tanks. This was on-the-job training with a vengeance.

The first wave of Marines was cut by more than half because most of them were in the boats. Only the few in the Amtracs could make the shore, and they went in. On the outer edge of the reef the tank lighters circled, probed, and at last found a place to drop their ramps and let the eager Shermans of Charlie Company out onto the reef . . . a full *mile* offshore. While the Amtracs clattered and struggled over the reef and through the potholes, the heavy tanks would have to pick their way cautiously over coral that could drop out from under them with no warning.

The Japanese commander, Admiral Shibasaki had once boasted, "A million men could not take Fortress Tarawa." Well, maybe, but the little boats that approached the shore shocked the Japanese, because they just climbed out on the reef and kept coming. Eight hundred yards out, the Amtracs hit the reefs and enemy fire, and began to take casualties. The Tracs were the only way to the beach, and as the Higgins boats circled at the edge of deep water, they began to shuttle back and forth over the jagged coral, putting the marines ashore in drops and driblets. At 0910, the first wave of Amtracs, all hit but none out of action, waddled out onto the sand and dropped their infantrymen. Far out on the reef, the tanks, with their own scouts probing ahead of them on foot, carefully worked their 36-ton hulks across the jagged coral. Every once in a while, one would spot a gun position on shore and take a shot at it, but they weren't doing much good . . . yet.

In some places, the Japanese had strung enough wire and post obstacles across the coral to stop or disable the Amtracs, and then the marines had to jump out into a sleet-storm of lead and stumble through the wire to the beach. And as soon as they got to the beach, they hit a four-foot high seawall that stopped the Amtracs, and would stop the tanks when they got there. Now the Tracs themselves were in range of the antiboat guns and the 4.7-inch DP guns and were being taken out. Some, hit by 8-inch shells, vanished in smoke, fire, scrap metal, and shredded flesh. There would be some hundreds of Marines unaccounted for, simply blown to crab food.

Somehow, the Amtracs made trip after trip, getting three waves of Marines across that fire-swept reef. The promised air strike came, one-half hour late. During the time it should have been hitting, the Tracs and the marines took an awful hammering from the defender's guns. Out of 87 that started from the line of departure, eight were wrecked on the way in, leaving the Marines to swim, and many, overburdened with gear and weapons, simply sank and drowned. More Tracs were disabled on the reef, but the rest turned back to pick up more men from the circling plywood boats. Fifteen sank due to bullet holes when they launched into deep water. But return they did, time after time, bringing load after load of precious guns and supplies. Then two Japanese tanks came rumbling down to the beach.

The Marines had found a harried refuge at the base of the seawall, under the Japanese guns, but now those two tanks could destroy even this scant haven. A 37mm gun had made it to the beach, but it weighed almost half a ton. "Give us a hand," the gun crews yelled, and willing hands literally threw the little cannon over the seawall. Japanese tanks were never stoutly armored, and the 37mm quickly knocked out one tank, forcing the other to clear out. Meanwhile, the Shermans of "C" Company were picking their delicate way across the reefs. No one had ever expected a tank to have to do this kind of work, but they were learning.

Now the fourth, fifth, and sixth waves were coming in on foot as the supply of Amtracs was diminishing. Slowly, sluggishly they were now coming through waist-deep water, many just dying and sinking in a bloody swirl into the now gray, surging, and pink-stained water. The battle was an hour old and only 2,000 Marines had gotten ashore. Only one of the assigned landing team leaders, Major Crowe of 2/8th Marines, had gotten ashore so far, the rest having been killed in the assault wave. Overhead, the observation plane from the old battleship *Maryland* circled, and the pilot could see wave after wave walking bravely into death. "I wanted to cry," the pilot said later. On the shore, stopped cold, burned, battered Marines pounded the sand with their fists in frustration. They'd gotten this far but were stopped by certain death. They'd go till they dropped but now they were low on ammo and plasma. Something had to be done.

Third Battalion, 2nd Marines had gotten ashore, barely, on the western tip of the island, but had taken 35 percent casualties. They were pinned down but still full of fight when their CO, Major Mike Ryan, heard the most welcome sound in his life, the clatter of tracks, the throaty rumble of a GM twin diesel engine, and the confident chatter of armored machine guns. Turning back to the sea, he saw two sleek armored hulls heaving out of the gentle bloodstained surf like a pair of prehistoric monsters. Originally, there had been six Shermans slated for this beach, but, in trying to avoid running over dead and wounded Marines, four had dropped into reef holes and were stalled, engines flooded, or tracks hung up in flesh-eating coral.

Only two, one of them named China Gal, commanded by Lt. Ed Bale of Texas, and a running mate, had made it ashore. They were enough. The Marines had had no artillery and no bunker breaking capability because their pack howitzers were still awaiting transport. China Gal heaved herself past a hole blown in the seawall by naval fire from destroyer *Ringgold,* which had won a duel with a Japanese shore battery. With her bow gun hammering a way clear for her, China Gal began to take out bunkers, one after another, clearing the way for the riflemen. Suddenly she was hit by a Japanese tank, the shell damaging her suspension.

Bale swung his gun and gave his gunner the command, "FIRE!!" A 75mm shell ended that menace. Later on that day, his running mate, another Sherman, was hit by something heavy and was burned, but at sunset, China Gal, though damaged, was still operating. Some tanks seem to lead a charmed existence. China Gal and one other seemed to be unkillable. The rest weren't so lucky. While the Japanese didn't seem to have dedicated AT weapons, they did have some 4.7-inch DP guns that could, and did, kill a Sherman.

On the western end of the island, the other two platoons of Charlie Company got ashore, after two hours of hole-dodging on the reef, sometimes in water up to their turrets. Second Platoon was almost up to the beach when one tank dropped into a pothole and had to be abandoned, temporarily. The other three climbed through a hole in the log wall and turned west, toward the center of the assault. Linking up with 2/2 Marines, they made tracks for their objective, the airstrip.

Third Platoon, with another four Shermans, had crawled up on the easternmost beach, received their orders, and moved out south, across the island. Both platoons had been given a kind of "generic order," to "knock out all enemy positions encountered." This they did, more or less, but they were operating buttoned up, half blind, and without any close-in infantry. Two tanks ran afoul of a 4.7-inch DP gun and were knocked out. Another was destroyed by forces unknown. By nightfall, the only tank operating on the eastern beach was a battered survivor named Colorado. Two others were under repair by their crews, and there was some cannibalizing going on.

All during that day, the scout/sniper platoon, under Lieutenant Hawkins had been performing yeoman service. He'd linked up with a Lieutenant Leslie of the engineers, who had both demolitions people and flamethrowers, and they began to burn the Nipponese out of their holes. At one side of that long pier, which was so desperately needed, was a fortified area, and the scouts and engineers used their rifles, grenades, and flamethrowers to burn and blast that area clear. But there was still another difficulty, the long stone pier was honeycombed with MG nests that were raking the assault teams from the sides.

That little problem was solved by a Higgins boat coxswain named Stokes. He loaded a flamethrower team with plenty of spare bottles into his boat, and when the tide had come in far enough to float his little plywood craft, he idled it down the pier while the flamethrower team fried the gunners in their holes. Tarawa was the laboratory from which all other assaults sprang. From now on, vehicle-mounted flamethrowers both on tanks and landing craft would be a permanent part of the Marine inventory. They also found out that they needed tanks that could swim.

The lessons, however, did not come cheaply. By the end of the first day, the assault forces had come only 200 yards inland from the beaches. Most of their tanks were temporarily knocked out and on the seawalls. Lines of desperately wounded Marines, out of morphine and plasma, suffered silently, not even able to cry out in pain, lest they draw hostile fire on their comrades. Of the 135 Amtracs that had taxied them across the reef, barely three dozen were still mobile. All along that 200-yard strip, barely one-tenth of a square mile, desperately exhausted Marines were digging in as the sun went down in a golden haze. No one had ever fought a battle like that before, against more fortifications than many small nations owned, manned by an enemy who seemed to be not only willing but eager to die for Emperor Hirohito, the living god of Japan. Slowly, one by one, they set their guards and dropped off to a fitful sleep.

All night long, tired working parties carried and rafted out the wounded and brought in water, ammunition, and rations. The Higgins boats were shuttling from the supply ships to the thousand-yard-long pier, and the Japanese knew exactly where it was. From sunset to the bloody dawn, they kept intermittent shell fire on the pier, but somehow they forgot about the Marines on the beachhead. For their part, the Marines snuggled down for the night, except when tapped for a working party. They did suffer a few more casualties from a lone bomber they nicknamed Washing Machine Charlie—probably a cousin to the one that made their lives miserable on Guadalcanal. Every island seemed to have one.

During the evening, some of their 75mm pack howitzers managed to get ashore. Those little guns could be broken down into small, mule- or man-sized loads, and some came ashore in Amtracs, others in rubber rafts that smuggled out the wounded. Others were simply dumped in the water off the end of the pier, and the gun crews picked them up and waded to the beach, carrying their cannons on their backs. Shouldering aside the floating bodies of their mates and slipping past the burned-out machine-gun pits under the pier, they got their guns ashore. As the Amtracs thinned out due to combat damage or mechanical attrition, the marines floated their weapons on their packs and swam them ashore, many dying in the process and sinking, lost, yet mourned, into the surf. No nation in all of history has sent better men out to defend its causes.

War correspondent Robert Sherrod wrote this in his notebook: "The machine guns continue to tear into the oncoming Marines. Within minutes I see six men killed. But the others keep coming. One rifleman walks slowly by, his left arm a bloody mess from the shoulder down. The casualties become heavier. Within a few minutes I can count at least a hundred young Marines lying on the flats. The Marines continue unloading from the Higgins boats, but fewer of them are making the shore now. Later—there are at least 200 bodies which do not move on the dry flats or in the shallow water that partially covers them. This is worse, far worse, than yesterday."

Some of the fire was coming from the rusting hulk of a

ship some 700 yards offshore. During the night the Japanese must have swum and waded out to it, and now it was full of machine guns and riflemen, all with plenty of ammunition. First the U.S. Navy tried dive-bombers from the aircraft carrier offshore, but that didn't silence the gunners. Finally the Marine engineers and a platoon of riflemen simply waded out, blew the ship up with TNT, and finished off the survivors with rifle and bayonet.

Ashore, the hammering and clanking and cursing finally ceased, and there was a welcome rumble. China Gal was back in business, and her ammo racks were full. Then with a cough and several ominous creaks, another repaired Sherman kicked itself into life. Mike Ryan's two enforcers were rolling and shooting. By noon Ryan's Marines were around the southern curve of the island, hitting the defenders of the western side in the back, easing the way for the force attacking from the sea.

On the far eastern beach, the crew of tank Colorado, after checking lube levels and eating C rations cooked over a can of sand and gasoline, fired up their battered mount and set off to aid Jim Crowe's infantrymen. They were jam-up against the fiercely defended Japanese command bunker and were making very little headway, tank or no tank. As late as 11:40 of the second day, the shore commander, Colonel Shoup, radioed division HQ out on the ships: "Situation ashore uncertain." Then word arrived of Ryan's tank-backed success, and everyone worried a bit less. Ryan and his men and tanks had evicted some Japanese marines from their fortress and were now *inside* the works and were holding against fierce counterattacks. Suddenly, we were winning. More Japanese were committing honorable hara-kiri, and some were being spotted wading across the shallow lagoon to the next islets. Those would have to be tracked down and killed.

Now it was decided to land the 6th Marine Regiment in two places to hasten things up. One battalion would be landed on the eastern end of Betio to attack west toward the long tail of the island. Another battalion would be sent north in rubber boats up to the island of Barikiri to trap any survivors who had managed to set up there. At the same time, "D" Company of the tank battalion landed—all light tanks, since the invasion had no more Shermans. At this time, there were only three Shermans running on Betio.

Heroism was the usual trait on that battered island. There was the rifleman from Texas who calmly picked off six Japanese snipers, then stood up and stalked through a hail of fire, snarling, "Go ahead and shoot me down you son of a bitch." There was the sergeant who volunteered to walk between China Gal and her running mate, spotting bunkers for them.

"They asked for an intelligent Marine," he said. "I ain't very smart, but I went." The tanks, firing delay-fuse shells, could pierce most of the smaller bunkers, and gradually, still bleeding casualties, the Marines took over the larger part of the island.

Toward evening the Marines were finding more and more suicided Japanese soldiers who had blown their heads off with a toe-fired rifle or blown their guts out with a grenade. The second night was relatively peaceful, but the island was beginning to stink of death. By the dawn of the third day, the stench was overpowering. No one had had time to do anything with the corpses, both Marine and Japanese. The bodies were crawling with maggots, and the yellow ropes of intestines were swelling with trapped gas and bursting with nauseating puffs of rotten moisture. It got into a man's hair and clothing and became part of him. In the heat and moisture, Betio/Tarawa had become a living charnel house.

Now the Marines were ready to finish the defenders off. They shifted some artillery up north to Barikiri to fire back down on Betio's long curving tail. All over the island, groups of men and machines were beginning to move eastward, pushing the defenders before them or causing them to die in place. The three Shermans were still working, and the light tanks were each now surrounded by an appreciative cluster of infantrymen. The tanks would move slowly ahead taking out strong points while the riflemen came along behind them, banging away at anything that looked like it could hurt a tank. By now the danger of some fanatic with a magnetic mine was fully understood. Marine snipers kept a careful watch over their tanks. The tank-infantry team was being born.

Now the amazed Marines heard the clatter of yet another set of tracks. Even before the battle was over, the Seabees were driving bulldozers out on the airstrip, leveling it, and preparing it for American use. Lieutenant Hawkins had died that morning, clearing bunkers, and now, even as the last Japanese were being cleared, their airstrip had been renamed "Hawkins Field."

On the north side of the island, Major Crowe had a problem. There was a network of bunkers surrounding an absolutely huge bombproof installation that was the Japanese command center and power station. *Take this out,* he must have reasoned, *and it'll break their backs.* To get at the defending bunkers, he had tank Colorado, still functional and ready to go. Lou Largey had his driver maneuver the tank into position and was getting ready to fire, when Marine 81mm mortars scored a catastrophic direct on one of the bunkers. There was an earthshaking blast, which was felt all over the island. The mortar bombs had been delay-fused, to penetrate the log bunker, and they'd found an ammunition storehouse. When the dust settled, Largey put a few 75mm HE shells into the surviving bunkers, and that phase was over.

Taking the command bunker was like taking a small hill, but with the tank to keep the defenders' heads down and using flamethrowers and satchel charges, the Marines got to the top. The Japanese went hysterical and came out in a wild banzai charge—Right into the welcoming arms of the regimental weapons company that was waiting for them with everything they had. Besides Colorado, there were 75mms on half-tracks, 37mm AT guns firing canisters, grenades, machine guns, and rifles. When it was over, a Seabee drove an unarmored dozer into the fray and buttoned up that command bunker, permanently, with a plug of dirt, sand, and rock.

On the south side of the island, by noon, the assault of the 6th Marines had been brought to a sudden halt by a network of guns and machine guns mounted in steel turrets on cement foundations. The turrets had 360-degree traverse and could fire in any direction. There was, of course, just one recourse—China Gal. The old girl was busy elsewhere, so the Marines adjusted their lines and then dug in for the night. Morning would be time enough.

During the night, there were several more desperate banzai charges, but, with the aid of a couple of destroyers anchored in the lagoon to act as floating batteries, they were pushed back or destroyed in place. The two Marine pack howitzer batteries also fired almost incessantly, breaking up one Japanese assembly area after another. At dawn, one tired Marine stood with his rifle hanging from slack hands and said, "They told us to hold, and, by God, we held."

By dawn of the fourth day, it was time for the *coup de grâce*. There were exactly two Sherman tanks left running on the whole island: Colorado and China Gal. At 0700, the carrier fighters, followed by dive-bombers, came in and really worked the tail of the island over. Then the Marine artillery, then the Navy again. There couldn't possibly be anything left alive, could there? At 0800, the Marines pushed off to find out, flame gunners right alongside the riflemen, two battered, durable, impossible Shermans right along with them. On the flanks were seven M-3 light tanks, hopefully staying out of trouble.

Company "I", 3/6 Marines, under a Captain MacLeod, hit a bunker complex and simply called up Colorado. As the flame gunners assaulted one bunker after another, the tank beat the defender's fire down. Then the defenders broke from the biggest bunker in a wild rush, out an escape channel. An infantryman rapped hard on Colorado's side with a rifle butt and pointed in near panic. Largey swung his turret into a tanker's dream shot. He caught the whole lot of them end on with no place to duck and let go with the 75, round after round. Asked later, he guessed that he might have nailed as many as 75 troops, but nobody was matching up the body parts to check.

China Gal, too, was having a field day, blasting out dugouts, trenches, and pillboxes, wandering happily back and forth across the battlefield under the watchful eyes of her infantry guardians. They were learning. The light tanks, supporting the Shermans, were also finding plenty of work to do and staying out of trouble, as the Shermans weren't leaving anything alive that could hurt the smaller tanks.

A little past noon, on the fourth day, a U.S. Navy carrier plane landed, apparently just to check out the strip. Fishtailing wildly around the working dozers, the pilot brought the plane to a smoking halt. The young pilot hung around for about an hour, talking with the Marines and Seabees and then took off to a nice clean ship with clean sheets. Hawkins Field was in business. Courtesy of the United States Marine Corps . . . and 14 Sherman tanks, only two of which survived.

That rather expensive airstrip had cost the lives of 1,085 Marines, 727 sailors and airmen . . . and about 5,000 Imperial marines. Of them, let it always be said: They knew how to fight and how to die.

Above the Marine graveyard on Betio stands a white plaque with these words by Captain Donald L. Jackson of California, inscribed on it in epitaph:

I

To you who lie within this coral sand
We, who remain, pay tribute of a pledge
That dying, thou shalt surely not
Have died in vain

That when again bright morning dyes the sky
And waving fronds above shall touch the rain,
We give you this, that in those times,
We will remember.

II

We lived and fought together, thou and we
And sought to keep the flickering torch alive,
That all our loved ones might forever know
The blessed warmth exceeding flame
The everlasting scourge of bondsman's chains
Liberty and light.

III

When we with loving hands laid back the earth
That was for moments short to couch thy form,
We did not bid a last and sad farewell,
But only "rest ye well."
Then with this humble, heartfelt epitaph
That pays thy many virtues sad acclaim
We marked this spot and, murm'ring requiem,
Moved on westward.

10

KWAJALEIN ATOLL

February 1, 1944

FOURTH TANK BATTALION, USMC

The farthest reach of Japanese imperial ambitions was stopped at Guadalcanal. Bloody Tarawa was the sharp end of the learning curve, and the lessons were duly sent back to the States and included in the training of the 4th Marine Division . . . to be applied at Kwajalein.

The 4th Division holds several "firsts" in its unit history, one of which is that it was the first Marine unit deployed directly from the States into combat. The division had trained at Camp Pendleton, California, and, between practice landings on the beaches of the Golden State, bunker assaults in Windmill Canyon at Pendleton, and rubber boat practice on the Santa Margarita River, the new Marines had had time for some serious partying in L.A. and "Dago." One of their favorite watering holes was the bar of the Biltmore Hotel in Los Angeles, which will be heard of later.

Finally, the training and the partying were over and on January 6, 1944, the division loaded onto LSDs and LSTs for the long trip across the Pacific and down into the tropics.

"Operation Flintlock" was under way, and it was hoped that by this time, the amphibious forces had been able to absorb the lessons learned on Guadalcanal and bloody Tarawa. The 4th had several new pieces of hardware in its inventory and a whole list of new doctrines to try out. The most important of which was "Get the tanks on the beach with the infantry."

The main problem facing the tankers was that tanks don't float very well. The partial solution at Tarawa had been to at least partly waterproof the Shermans so that they could run in fairly deep water. It had also been found out that the Amtracs could climb over coral as well as float, and someone had asked, "Well, why don't we put a tank turret on an Amtrac?" Thus was born the LVT(A)1, or simply *Amtank*. They were armed with the turrets of the old M-3 light tank, crewed by six men, and they turned out to be surprisingly seaworthy.

Right up in the bow were the driver and beside him an assistant driver/machine gunner. To the rear, where the cargo bay had once been, the hull was decked over and had a turret with a 37mm cannon and another machine gun mounted. The turret crew was two men, the TC/gunner and the loader/observer.

Behind the turret were a pair of gun tubs, which each had room for a gunner with a .30-cal machine gun and a steel gun shield. The vehicle itself was powered by an aircraft engine that nestled in the rear of the hull. It would do about six knots in water and 27 mph on land. It turned out to be a potent weapon indeed, but we lost the concept during too many years of peace. History seems to repeat itself, if we let ourselves forget our lessons. From 1953 to about 1964, the Amtank disappeared from history, only to have to be reborn as the ACAV in South Vietnam. Ironically, it was the Viets themselves who reinvented the concept.

The other items in the inventory were two specialized landing craft that had been missing at Tarawa. The vulnerable plywood Higgins boat had been replaced by the far more rugged LCI, or landing craft, infantry, which had a steel hull and bow ramp, and could ram right up on the beach.

Next, the tank lighters that had failed to reach the beach on Tarawa were replaced with an LCM (landing craft, medium) that could do two very important things. They were shallow draft and could run in some very thin water. Also, they could carry a Sherman tank right up to the beach and land it right in the face of a Japanese gunner. This was an improvement of no small value.

The changes in doctrine were very simple—pound, pound, pound, with ships, guns, and planes. This time they wouldn't just keep the defenders' heads down till the Marines got ashore, they would blow them out of their holes in the coral with everything they could bring to bear. In 1944, that was beginning to be a considerable tonnage of hot metal and TNT. Even old battleships from the 1920s were on the gun line, and one Marine described the sound of their shells as "like a freight train coming in to land."

The Kwajalein Atoll had been picked for several reasons, the most important of which was its airfield. Boeing Aircraft Company was building the B-29, which would be able to bomb the Japanese home islands *if* it could be based within a thousand miles of the center of the Japanese empire. We needed another stepping-stone, and on the north rim of the atoll were two islands, one with a nice shiny new 5,000-foot airstrip. Throughout the war, the Nipponese engineers unwittingly provided us with ready-made airstrips for our bombers, but, unfortunately, the price they charged was payable only in blood.

Roi-Namur is shaped like a giant butterfly with the airstrip spread out on the left wing, and all the housing and administrative buildings on the brushy right wing. It is within easy bomber and fighter range from Hawkins Field on Tarawa. Two days before the island's own personal D-Day, the old battleships *Tennessee, Maryland, Idaho,* and *Colorado* accompanied by five cruisers and 19 destroyers, arrived and began to put the first of 2,655 tons of steel on the beaches of Roi-Namur and the namesake island of Kwajalein, on the south rim of the atoll. Considering that there were about 9,000 defenders, only half of them combat troops, every Japanese soldier on the islands had a shell with his name on it coming his way. To quote one of the official histories: "The island looked as if it had been picked up 20,000 feet and dropped." This was where the term "beach conditioning" was invented.

While this was going on, the Marines in the north, and the Army's 7th Division down south on Kwajalein itself were doing something new, a trick they had learned on Tarawa. They took the nearby small islands, some only a few hundred yards across, by putting tank-infantry teams ashore and killing off or capturing the small garrisons. Then they'd install artillery batteries to support the main attacks. They were learning. Some of those islands were so small that one whole platoon of tanks actually crowded them. The little M-3s were unable to penetrate bunkers, so this job fell to the Shermans, which could roll right up to a bunker, insert the muzzle of a 75 and blow the defenders to kingdom come . . . or whatever paradise awaits the followers of Shinto. This was probably where the G.I. phrase "Tough Shinto" was coined.

Then came the main invasion of Roi and Namur, actually two separate islands joined by a little spit of land and a causeway. Dive-bombers came straight down on the defenders with half-ton blockbusters as the tanks rolled off the LCMs and the infantry trotted alongside the thundering Shermans. It all seemed too good to be true, and once the airfield on Roi was secured, the commanding officer radioed, "This is a pip. Give us the word and we'll take the island." Right about then, things started to get a bit hairy.

The infantry had run into several pillboxes that had escaped the initial bombardment and called back for tanks and demolition equipment. Right then somebody unknown, but probably an over-inquisitive tanker, put a shell into the biggest Japanese ordnance storehouse on the island and set off a torpedo warhead. That one-ton charge set off the torpedo/bomb dump and at 1400 hours, there was a "huge, shattering explosion that blotted out the sun." From the picture, a modern Marine would have thought that someone had set off a tactical nuke.

A dirty gray mushrooming cloud heaved thousands of

feet into the air, and the day became, for a while, as black as night. Smoke, rubble, bombs, and torpedo warheads were flung into the air, and right there 2nd Battalion, 4th Marines, took half their casualties for the island of Namur. Two more large, but lesser explosions kept the Marines' heads down until about 1630, when the advance continued.

Marine Pfc. C. B. Ash was having a rough day. He'd been what is called "spare parts" in a tank company and had been assigned as a bow gunner (BOG) in a tank named KICKAPOO at the last minute. This was his first taste of combat, as he relates the heavy action in his own words:

"February 1944, Charlie Company hit the beach. Each crewman had to memorize the beach area, and at the last briefing, they gave a test. If you flunked, you had to walk ashore with the infantry. The Navy delivery was very good; we didn't even get the tracks wet. The entire island was a huge bomber strip, and the infantry was along the edge of the runway. The Jap infantry were hiding in the storm drains, using them for foxholes. At this point in time, in this outfit, tank-infantry tactics were nonexistent.

"The company moved through the infantry, passing between the aircraft rivetments, which were designed to shield parked aircraft from nearby bomb bursts. We didn't pick up any infantry, just formed up into assault formation and moved out.

"Burt Nave, in tank 3-2 KNAVE, hit a mine and blew a track. T. J. Taylor, driver in the command tank, ran the CO's tank into a huge shell hole, and Sergeant Owens in KAPU had to pull them out. Then we got into a half-assed line and started a charge for the north end of the island. Along the way we machine-gunned the Japs in the storm drains, which they were using for communications trenches.

"The company set up between two map points in a bent line at the edge of runway Charlie, overlooking Jap gun emplacements, trenches, etc. Our platoon sergeant Joe Bruno, blew up a Jap fighter plane . . . and got chewed up for blowing up a usable Zero that the brass desperately wanted to inspect. He always figured that if he got five, that would make him an ace. Japs were running all over the place, and we fired at anything that moved.

"In KICKAPOO crew, Joe Ramos, TC; McCue, gunner; Krauland, loader; Pete, driver; and myself, Ash, BOG were on the far left of the company line, shooting all kinds of things. . . . Then I thought I heard water running. I looked at the water cans strapped down on the right sponson and neither was leaking, nor had I pissed myself. Looking over at the driver, I saw a sheet of blood running down the turret from the TC hatch between us!

"The turret was turned 90 degrees to the right and the blood was pouring from Joe Ramos's head. 'Head for the beach,' I yelled at Pete, and he asked, 'Where is it?'

"'You're the driver, you're supposed to keep up with shit,' I yelled back. I finally got him moving in the right direction, and moments later, we homed in on the tank retriever and the aid station.

"McCue and I pulled Joe out of the turret, and everybody was yelling. *'Easy* take it easy.' With half a bullet sticking out of his head, you could see he wasn't feeling anything. We laid him next to a growing line of dead Marines and said our goodbyes. Nobody had seen us leave the company line, and we needed to get back. After a bit of back and forth, I elected myself TC, grabbed a somewhat reluctant live body off the retriever, and we took off into the wild blue."

So ended Pfc. Ash's first half hour of combat. He survived to fight yet again in Korea and spend a full career in the USMC in tanks. Over on the right half of the twin islands, Namur, things were thickening up, too. The infantry had run into several pillboxes that had escaped the initial bombardment and had had to call back for tanks and demolition equipment. The operation had ceased to be a "pip."

A tank commanded by Captain James Denig poked its nose down a dusty jungle track, and suddenly five Japanese swarmed aboard it. One of them threw a grenade into the turret, setting the tank on fire. A nearby automatic rifleman, Howard E. Smith, pumped two magazines through his

BAR, and four of the hostiles rolled off the tank, dead. Another Marine got the last one with his rifle. Then, disregarding the snipers, Corporal Smith jumped up on the now burning tank and began to pull wounded crewmen out of it. Captain Denig later died, but two other men lived. And Corporal Smith received the Navy Cross.

The Japanese were beginning to see the end, and they reacted in typical fashion. When the invasion forces got to the north side of Roi, they found a trench full of enemy soldiers who had commited hara-kiri by putting the muzzles of their rifles in their mouths and pulling the triggers with their toes. Some, in their desperation, even tried to take on tanks with grenades, sometimes successfully, most times not.

Corporal Michael Giba said, "We rolled the tank up to the edge of a huge shell crater, stopped, and all of a sudden we were swarming with Japs and had to button up. I looked out the periscope, and a soldier was laying on the turret looking back at me. He looked me right in the eye. He seemed kind of puzzled about just what to do. Then he rose to a squatting position, removed a grenade from his pocket, held it against the periscope, pulled the pin, and lay down on top of it. The periscope was broken but none of us was hurt. The Jap was killed. Then another tank opened up on us with its machine gun and cleared the turret of remaining Japs."

After the islands of Roi-Namur and Kwajalein were cleared, the Marines swept south, down the length of the atoll, while the U.S. Army began to work north, mopping up pockets of resistance and meeting the Marshallese natives. These people, descendants of Micronesian sea rovers who'd come west by canoe thousands of years ago, had been semi-Christianized by German missionaries back before WWI, and church-style music was now part of their culture, adapted to island instruments of course.

The official division history reports that as the Americans helped them back to their shattered homes, there was a certain amount of unavoidable fraternization and that some of the Marines began to go native, adopting tribal dress as they joined the songfests. The mind conjures up a picture of a battle-hardened Marine tanker wearing a breechcloth made of his pistol belt and a towel marked "Biltmore Hotel, Los Angeles," while a topless native beauty sits on his knee singing "Onward Christian Soldiers," to the beat of a native drum and a harmonica.

So ended the battle for Kwajalein Atoll. The Japanese garrisons on Mille, Wotje, Yap, Truk, and Jaluit had been bypassed. We now had a 60-mile-long fleet anchorage and another stepping-stone 600 miles closer to Hiroshima. And at the Rikken Institute in Tokyo, Professors Takeuchi and Nishina had just generated uranium hexafluoride and tested a separator that would filter out the pure isotopes of U-235.

Professor Yoshio Nishina, it should be remembered, had worked so closely with Niels Bohr in Denmark that Bohr's children called him "Uncle Nishina." In early 1944, Nishina's budget was 20 million yen, or about $35 million at today's equivalent. There were now at least three running cyclotrons in Japan, and as the Allies closed in, the Japanese Imperial staff had seen the calligraphy on the wall. Their atom bomb program suddenly went into high gear.

In Korea, the giant Noguchi works was creating heavy water and mining uranium at a place called Konan. Niels Bohr had once estimated that it would take 250,000 kilowatts to produce an atomic bomb, and a Mr. Jun Noguchi had over one million kilowatts coming out of the Chosin Reservoir. The time would come, when the B-29s began to bomb Tokyo, that the entire program, code-named F-go, would have to come to Korea.

In America, the giant B-29 had finally become operational, and it was now feasible to consider bombing the Japanese home islands. First, however, there would have to be a few more stepping-stones, named Saipan, Tinian, and Guam, and they would not come cheap. Wherever the giant superfortress landed, its wheels would roll across the treadmarks of the tanks that had captured the real estate the aircrews needed. In many cases, the fighting would still be going on when the planes landed.

As the fighting for the Marshalls wound down, halfway

around the globe, the main event was just beginning—the Allied invasion of Normandy. There, the hard-won lessons of Guadalcanal, Tarawa, and the rest of the Pacific beaches would be put to work against Hitler's "Festung Europa."

Pfc. Ash's story was adapted from Marine Corps Tankers Association, issue 4-93, November 1993. Capt. Denig's story came from the official journal of the 4th Division.

11

D-DAY

April 6, 1944

In the spring of 1944, the whole world seemed to be trembling to the heavy clatter of tank tracks—mostly American. The iron monsters had clawed their way across the Pacific and, even as D-Day approached, were still hammering away on Iwo Jima and Okinawa. They'd evicted the Germans from North Africa, Sicily, and Italy, and were now about to cross the English Channel.

In just a few years this nation's industrial might had created an army the likes of which the world had never seen. Hitler's "Thousand-Year Reich" was about to be terminated with extreme prejudice. From all over the United States and Europe, vengeful warriors were gathering in England, which seemed to be carrying enough armor, men, and material to sink the island. Before the invasion, though, there would have to be training, and this can be seen through the eyes of the men that participated in the invasion and its preparations.

DEAN ROCKWELL
LCT SKIPPER, OMAHA BEACH

My name is Dean L. Rockwell and I was born on a farm in Case County, Michigan, May 25, 1912. I graduated from Three Rivers High School in 1930, attended Eastern Michigan University, graduating in 1935. At the time of my enlistment in the U.S. Navy in 1942, I was a high school teacher and coach. I spent the early summer training at the Naval Station in Norfolk, Virginia. Late in July, I was assigned to the training ship, *William P. Biddle,* for schooling in the use of landing craft. We trained on various small craft such as the LVP and the LCM, during which time I was spot-promoted to ensign, given a crew of ten men, and sent to the navy base in Philadelphia to pick up an LCT (landing craft, tank), a 105-foot vessel which none of us had ever seen before. In late November of 1943, I was promoted to lieutenant (JG), and selected as a group commander in LCT Flotilla 12. On January 12, 1944, we set sail for the United Kingdom. Fourteen days later, we landed at Swansea, Wales.

From March 9 to May 24, I worked with the 741st, 743rd, and 70th Army Tank Battalions on Slapton Sands training area, just outside of Dartmouth Harbor. My LCTs would anchor each night up the Dart River, and each morning, go out to work with the Army on special exercises. Of the three tank battalions, only one, the 70th, had had any combat experience, having fought in North Africa and Sicily. The others, seasoned by a few veterans, would be going into combat for the first time.

All the Army men loved to come aboard the LCTs for the good food and coffee. And after eating in Army mess later on, I understood why. I only thank God that I joined the Navy instead of the Army.

The mission of my LCTs was to carry and launch 96 specially outfitted Sherman tanks. These tanks were equipped with the "duplex drive." In back, between the treads, were a pair of propellers to drive them in water. The flotation was supposed to come from an extensible canvas hull, which would, barely, provide enough buoyancy to support the 36-ton

Shermans in calm water. Unfortunately, there were only about nine inches of freeboard from the top of the shroud to the water, and the English Channel has always had a reputation for unpredictability.

The mission of these tankers was to launch, via special equipment, 5,000 yards, about 2.8 miles out from the beach, and swim ashore to a point where their treads could pull them up on the beach. This whole plan and equipment was highly secret, and the whole area around Slapton Sands had been cleared of civilians. Further, each of us was told, by order of General Eisenhower, that even mentioning this in a letter home would bring a general court-martial.

We left Dartmouth on May 25 for the D-Day assembly points. Sixteen LCTs carrying the tanks of the 741st and 743rd Battalions were destined for Omaha Beach, and the other eight were carrying the 70th Battalion and were slated for Utah Beach. I and the rest of my skippers spent the next few days being briefed on Operation Overlord, the name for the invasion plan. Each day, we looked at film strips of the invasion beaches which had been made up of overlapping photographs taken by scouting fighter planes.

Everyone knows that there was one false start which was canceled by foul weather, but finally in the early A.M. of June 5, we sailed for France. We proceeded eastward for most of the morning and early afternoon, linking up with other forces or units to form the vast armada. The sun came out briefly, and I can still see in my mind's eye the hundreds of ships, as far as the eye can see, coming together in man's greatest assembly of military force in history. Since our LCTs were the slowest craft in the invasion, the whole armada was held down to our pace of about five knots. Right through the night of June 5–6 until we were 5,200 yards off Omaha Beach at 0400, right on schedule.

The original plan was for our landing craft to turn toward the beach and then launch the DD tanks over the somewhat delicate launching gear for their swim to the shore. Unfortunately, a heavier than predicted sea was running, and the hapless tankers began, one by one, to sink to the bottom of the channel.

The decision whether or not to launch the DD tanks to swim was absolutely critical. But how to communicate? We'd been under radio silence all the way across the channel, but I was in communication with my other craft by low-power tank radio and decided to break radio silence. The Germans by now *had* to know we were here. I got in touch with a Captain Elder of the 743rd Tank Battalion, and we made the joint decision to cease launching. The signal was sent out over the tank radios that all the LCTs were to go straight in to Omaha Beach and put the tanks ashore. At 0600 minus 30 seconds, my LCT 535, from which I commanded the flotilla, put the first tanks ashore on Omaha, right into the sights of an 88mm gun. As soon as the ramps were down, the battle was joined, and as soon as the tanks were ashore, we pulled that famous naval maneuver, known as "getting the hell out of here." By 0630 those tanks were firing directly into the gun slits of the concrete bunkers.

CAPTAIN JOHN AHEARN
"C" Company Commander, 70th Tank Battalion
UTAH BEACH

I was born on November 30, 1914, and was drafted into the U.S. Army on November 7, 1941. Our group was sent from Governor's Island to Ft. Knox, Kentucky, for basic training, and while there, I heard of an opportunity to go to Officer's Candidate School. Graduating from there, I was assigned to the 70th Tank Battalion, where I stayed for the rest of my army career. I spent some time in Africa, schooling the French in the use of American equipment, and then participated in the Sicilian invasion as the assault gun commander of our company. In November 1943, we sailed for the British Isles, arriving in Liverpool a few days after Thanksgiving.

We had been a light tank battalion, but now we were to become a medium tank battalion with the M-4 Sherman. We originally camped at a British army barracks near Swindon, then moved to Barton Stacy, a camp near Andover. In January 1944, I was made company commander of "C" Company. In April 1944, we participated with the Navy in the "Tiger" landing exercises at Slapton Sands near Dartmouth.

During this period, my company of 16 tanks was temporarily increased to 21 tanks by the addition of five bulldozer tanks, all of which would eventually revert to engineer control after the drive to Cherbourg. The plan was for the dozer tanks to help clear the seawall on Utah Beach and to aid in breaking out of the hedgerows inland.

Those five tanks were manned with 15 combat engineers. From somewhere in "C" Company, we had to find the additional 10 tankers. This necessitated that I find within my own company everybody who had any experience with tanks at all and reassign them to the new vehicles as drivers and tank commanders. Then we revamped the rest of the company.

In the weeks before the invasion, I was very busy supervising all this activity, and as company commander, was constantly under the surveillance of the battalion commander and his staff. By this time we were the only company left at Lupton Camp, because "A" and "B" Companies had been sent off to be equipped with the dual drive tanks for the landings. These DD tanks were in other parts of the United Kingdom.

Our battalion was assigned to support the 8th Infantry Regiment of the 4th Division under the command of Colonel James Van Fleet, and I recall that in his briefings, he used a lot of football metaphors to explain our mission. Company "C" would be engaged even before we hit the beach at H-Hour + 15 minutes. Our mission was to provide, if necessary, the initial overhead artillery support in front of the first wave of the assaulting infantry. On the beach and afterward, we were to provide flank protection of the 8th Regimental Combat Team. Then we were further ordered by General Barton, who commanded the 4th Division, to break out of the beachhead and make every effort to contact and assist the 101st Airborne Division, which would be dropped in during the early morning hours.

On June 3, we proceeded to a pier near Dartmouth where we loaded our normal complement of tanks, plus those five extra dozer tanks, onto our LCTs. The loading plan for those

21 tanks was developed a few days earlier by a British naval lieutenant, two of his staff, Lt. B. J. Riley, and myself. Because of our orders to fire in support of the assaulting infantry, we limited each craft to three tanks. On five of the LCTs we placed the dozer tank in front and a straight tank on either side of it to achieve maximum traverse for their guns. On the other two LCTs, all three vehicles were straight tanks, but in the same firing positions.

After we had returned to port when the June 5 landing was aborted because of bad weather and heavy seas, we again set sail in the early morning hours of June 6. During the delay, I made better acquaintance with the British officer who commanded my LCT and visited with my own men. Because of the revamping of my crews, I had several new tank commanders, and one sticks out in my mind.

He was a 19-year-old boy by the name of Owen Gavigan, who had joined the battalion in Sicily. He was a very bright individual, and I thought that he would make a good tank commander. When we were assigned the extra dozer tanks, I made a tank commander out of this young PFC.

Around 0300 or 0400 on the invasion crossing morning, I went up on deck. It was inky black, and several times I heard the commander of our boat yelling by megaphone with some of the control boats trying to determine our position. At this time, we mounted our tanks and began our final checks. About 0540, we heard the tremendous roar of the bombers going overhead to hit the beaches and then, south of our position, we saw the big flashes of light as the battleship *Nevada* and other capital ships opened up. Then there were fighters in the sky as dawn began to break, and we could see the whole stunning panorama.

As dawn broke, we were enveloped in smoke and dust from shell bursts. Antiaircraft fire could be seen rising from the beach where we were headed. Landing craft armed with 4.7-inch guns and others fitted with rocket launchers began bombarding the sandy beach and the dunes beyond.

We began to get a clearer picture of where everybody was, and it became evident that there'd been some problem with the DD tanks of our battalion and that we were not going to come in as planned at H-Hour + 15 minutes behind them. They weren't to be seen, and we were going to be the first tanks in on Utah Beach!

About this time, with all the noise and fire from the ships, there was a terrific explosion to my right, to the north, which turned out to be one of the LCTs carrying four of our battalion's DD tanks hitting a sea mine. This vessel immediately sank and of the 20 tankers and the British crew, only tanker SSgt. Glenn Gibson, the LCT commander Sam Grundfast, and one of his sailors survived.

The British landing commander did an excellent job bringing us as close to the shore as possible, and we disembarked in five to seven feet of water. We didn't have the canvas flotation screens but we'd been weatherized and had shrouds over our engine grilles that allowed us to run in deep water. As it turned out, Pfc. Owen Gavigan, commanding dozer tank #5, was the first tank out on Utah Beach! My tank was directly behind Gavigan's.

Then it became evident that this was not the part of the beach that we'd expected to land on; we were 1700 yards south of our planned beaching point. Not only this, but not all of my tanks had arrived. One LCT had had to return to England because of difficulties at sea, and another had been sunk. Because of the radio silence, I'd not known of this. We waded ashore and took stock. Of the 16 straight tanks assigned to "C" Company, including my own, only 11 were ashore.

Suddenly I recognized General Teddy Roosevelt, Jr., on the beach, and dismounted and walked over and reported to him. I told him who I was and what my mission was. He told me to go ahead and sweep both to the north and south ends of the beach, and try to find a way off and to get inland as fast as possible and to be "generally supportive."

I directed my exec, Lt. Yeoman, to take half of the tanks and proceed north while I took the other half and headed south. As I had landed at Red Beach, I immediately assumed command of the Third Platoon, which was normally under Lt. Thomas Tighe. After the shrouds had been removed from the tanks, I led our six tanks southward, looking for an opening. At this time, heavy shell and mortar fire were falling on the beach, and many soldiers were becoming casualties.

We had not gone far before I spotted a narrow opening that had apparently been used by enemy vehicles. We quickly moved to exploit this, but at the opening, I discovered a sinister looking object that looked like a miniature WWI tank about three feet long, just sitting there, not moving. This had not been in any of my briefings but we had to get through.

Still concerned about this German infernal device but cognizant of our mission to establish a beachhead "at all costs," I told my driver, Tony Zampiello, to "gun it," and we sped through the opening, with Lieutenant Tighe's platoon streaming on behind us. We were off the beach and in Normandy. Later on we found out that our little menace had been a radio-controlled, tracked bomb that carried 175 pounds of TNT. Luckily for us, either the bombing or the naval gunnery had destroyed its control point.

Once we'd gotten inside the seawall, we moved out between the seawall and the road where we joined some infantrymen from the 2nd Battalion of the 8th Division who were working their way southward. As soon as we turned left across the field between the road and the seawall, we discovered a large German fortification which jutted back from the seawall. Instinctively, I set our tanks to firing on it, and with this, a number of Germans came out with their hands in the air and yelling at us. As it turned out, these weren't German nationals but impressed soldiers from another nation. As I dismounted, they began yelling "Achtung, Minen" to me and gesturing me to stay still. I directed them to move toward the road, and we delivered the 30 or so prisoners to the infantry. Then I very carefully retraced my steps, out of those mines and back to my tank.

I have since become aware that my tanks had silenced the German beach stronghold at Beau Guillot. I have been told that our capture of the soldiers controlling this strong point helped considerably in relieving the congestion of men and material at Exit 2 and generally helped speed up the assault on Utah Beach.

After this, we again moved out southward and came to a large crossroads leading to the little village of Pouppeville. At this juncture, I told Lt. Tighe to go on inland while I took two tanks to continue exploring this same road. I was looking for any strong points or bunkers that we might assault. Suddenly the tank hit a land mine that broke the track and blew the left front bogie off. I radioed this information to Lt. Tighe, told him to assume command of his platoon and continue inland toward Pouppeville, and then set about scouting on foot.

After placing our machine guns for defensive purposes and while the crew worked on the track, I decided to reconnoiter toward the beach in order to locate the next German strong point. Since the hedgerows made it difficult to see, I climbed to the top of the nearest one to gain a vantage point.

At this time, I heard calls for help and, looking toward the beach, saw three men whom I surmised were injured paratroopers. I moved along the hedgerow in their direction until it became so thick and impassable that I could no longer continue. At this point I was faced with a dilemma. I could back away or I could try to get closer and better analyze the situation. I decided to move cautiously down from the hedgerow to the field. I did so and then decided that I was near enough to be able to sling the tank's first-aid kit to them. As I turned to retrace my steps to the tank for the first-aid kit, an antipersonnel mine blew up under me, throwing me into the bank of the hedgerow. I was unconscious for a while, but when I came to, I began yelling "Zamp, Zamp" loud enough to be heard, and Zampiello and my loader, Private Felix Beard, came and found me badly wounded in the lower legs.

I warned them about the mines and told them to throw me a rope. Because they had no rope long enough, they came down anyway, picked me up, and carried me back to the tank. While part of the crew put a tourniquet on my leg and got morphine and hot coffee into me, the rest went looking for the medics. Because we had outrun our infantry, this took them several hours, but finally two medics and a jeep appeared, and I was taken to a field hospital.

The hospital had been set up in tents just inland from the beachhead, and they immediately gave me six bottles of plasma. Then the decision was made to perform an amputation of only one of my legs at a time so that my system could recover from the shock. That evening they amputated my right leg. The wounded were supposed to be shipped back to England, but because ships were hitting sea mines and sinking in the harbor, our evacuation was delayed. The next morning, while a number of us who had been severely wounded were laying on stretchers outside the hospital tent, we were strafed by what turned out to be the last gasp of the Luftwaffe over Normandy.

The next day we were taken by Navy ship to an evacuation hospital near Plymouth, England. I then began a long series of operations including the amputation of my left leg.

Later on I heard from our battalion maintenance officer that there were some 15,000 mines in the Utah Beach area and 1,100 in the fields where we'd hit that land mine. So my odds against injury hadn't been too good. Later on I was most pleased to learn that the commanding general of the 4th Infantry Division, General Barton, and General Collins, the commanding general of VII Corps, had recommended me for the Congressional Medal of Honor. I eventually received the Distinguished Service Cross and a battlefield promotion to the rank of captain.

12

EUROPE, 1944–45

Near Marthille, France
November 13, 1944

This is the personal story of LTC Albin F. Irzyk, now a
retired general, who commanded a battalion across France
and into Germany, leading from the turret of his own tank.

By now everyone was living in the vehicles, eating, sleeping,
shaving . . . calls of nature posed some problems. Regardless
of how exhausting the days were, a man was alert in the turret
of each fighting machine all night long to keep from being
surprised by infiltrating infantry or Germans with the Panzer-
faust, their version of our bazooka. Staying awake was no
problem, as the coldest place in the world is a tank turret in the
wintertime. Frostbite and trench foot caused by wet cold feet
were beginning to take their toll.

Our mission this day would be to take the towns of Oron,
Villers sur Nied, and, hopefully, Marthille. I had a meeting of
the advance guard commanders at 0730, ordering my light
tanks to lead and probe for the enemy while the medium
Shermans would act as a reaction force, if the little M-5

Stuarts got into trouble as they so often did. At 0830 the force moved out. It started out as any other combat day on the move, in the attack. There was simply no inkling at this early hour of what a significant, memorable day this would turn out to be.

The force moved directly east, and the troops entered the Bois de Serres with some trepidation, but since they received no fire, they picked up speed and moved smartly through the width of the forest. Apparently this was not the place the Germans had chosen to fight. As they emerged from the woods, they saw Oron only a kilometer away and continued their rapid advance. The aggressiveness of the advance guard must have surprised the defenders for they overran Oron against only slight resistance and grabbed a bag of prisoners in the process. These were quickly hustled back into the custody of the 35th Infantry Division, so that progress would be unhampered. The last thing a tanker needs is POWs on foot to baby-sit.

The enemy was now awake and fighting, so it became slower going. The advance guard had to do considerable fighting along the four kilometers to Villers sur Nied, but ultimately seized the town. Now it was on to Marthille, which appeared to be a quick three kilometers away in this densely populated land. I was just about to order the advance to continue when I began to become slightly nervous. *Whoa, I thought to myself, let's just think about this a bit. This has been a bit too easy, and the Germans are due to react.* I'd noticed that the ground to the left, north of the road to the village, rose rather sharply to a kind of ridge topped by a forest, the Bois Communal de Lesse. This ridge dominated the road below and being higher ground, would be drier than the muddy fields in front of us. I decided to utilize the tanks' mobility and get off the road. Many times before, we'd used that mobility to our advantage, and now I ordered my tanks to get off the road and up the slopes of the ridge.

I really had no way of knowing just how momentous this decision was to be. I told my tankers to "ride the ridge," and reconnoiter by fire. This tactic is used when the enemy is strongly believed to be out there, even though one can see nothing at all. The purpose is to keep from being surprised by provoking the enemy into fire before they are ready, thus revealing themselves. The .30 coaxial machine gun, which is mounted parallel to the tank cannon, is used to shoot up suspected enemy locations. If the enemy is flushed from concealment, the tank cannon goes into action. An advancing tank unit sometimes sounds like a much larger unit in a desperate battle for survival, but it is simply looking for trouble.

In this attack formation, the light tanks were leading to feel out the enemy, followed closely by the Sherman medium tanks. The first light tank to reach the crest of the ridgeline was commanded by SSgt. Ellsworth Ranson of "D" Company. He opened fire at the first suspected location and *bingo!* The tracers from his co-ax began to ricochet off something in that clump of brush. Instantly his gunner fired the 37mm cannon, and the hit blew the camouflage off a pair of antitank guns which were immediately fired by their crews. The guns had been loaded in preparation for our arrival but were pointed in the wrong direction—down the road we had been about to take.

The light tank slid back into a bit of cover, and the Shermans, with their 75mm cannons, made short work of those two guns. It was late in the fall and most of the leaves were off the trees, but the Germans had cleverly used every bit of available cover to conceal their weapons and equipment. Recon by fire from the first tank had successfully laid bare their presence, and like a pack of hounds the tanks broadened their formation and moved forward, shooting at every suspicious location and object. Almost every suspicious object turned out to be an antitank gun pointed the wrong way! The guns were uncovered one moment, destroyed the next.

Almost immediately after the action began, hordes of Germans came streaking out of Marthille, breaking up into small groups and heading for their guns. Apparently these were the relief crews, the ones off-duty, who had been keeping warm in the cluster of nearby homes. Each group of men ran for its own gun to help in the fight, but most were simply too late.

Worse, by their direction, they sometimes inadvertently gave the gun's position away. Many were mowed down as they ran, and those who survived were totally winded by the time they reached their guns. It was too late anyway; those guns were already gone.

For the tankers it was better than Coney Island, better than any target practice they had ever had. They advanced swiftly, firing furiously and super-effectively. Incredibly, in a period of 30 to 40 minutes, it was all over. This short savage action would turn out to be the biggest "catch" of the entire war. This hornet's nest would prove to have had one of the largest concentrations of antitank guns ever encountered in such a limited area.

The tally was staggering. There were 21 antitank guns destroyed. And what guns those were. Ten of them were the vaunted, vicious 88s and the other 11 were the high-velocity, lethal 75s, the same one mounted in the Panther tank. Also destroyed were six mortars, seven half-tracks, and three trucks. More than 100 enemy soldiers were killed and 50 were taken prisoner, and two or three hundred went streaking back east toward the fatherland as fast as their legs could carry them. They were accompanied by two Panther tanks that had appeared out of nowhere, fired hastily and ineffectively at the Shermans, and then, met by a hail of cannon fire, disappeared.

This was a triumph of tremendous proportions. Our only casualty was one Sherman damaged when it hit a stray mine. The enemy had very cleverly concealed their guns in bushes and hedges with their fields of fire fixed on the road, *which the tanks did not take.* Coming from a totally unexpected direction, the inadvertent flank attack surprised and completely undid the enemy. American tankers are naturally trigger-happy, and everything within a radius of half a mile that could hide a man or gun had been hit by the tankers.

After the tankers had swept the area to ensure that there were no Germans left behind, we assembled on the dominating ground and bivouacked there for the night. As soon as they were positioned and had cut their engines, the crews hopped down from the tanks, and like a bunch of kids, which many of them still were, they jumped around on the ground in excitement and jubilation, clapping one another on the backs. What a fantastic, incredible, incomparable performance. Nothing up to this time could even come close to touching this, not even a World Series no-hitter. It was a classic, a one-of-a-kind.

As they savored their victory, the short day began to end, as the crews heated their rations and began to secure themselves for the night in case the enemy counterattacked. The battalion command post moved closer to Marthille, and as night fell, so did more snow. The pitch-black night and the softly falling snow had a lulling effect on me, and I had trouble believing that so much destruction and violence had visited in this area such a short time ago. Gradually, though, my mood shifted from one of self-congratulation and elation to a sobering feeling of almost shock. But for one almost intuitive, possibly divinely inspired decision, we would have been massacred.

The enemy had set up an absolutely perfect ambush. They had lined up cleverly, using the cover and concealment all along the base of the dominant ridge, an amazingly large number of antitank guns. The murderous 88s and the 75s with their armor-piercing rounds were zeroed in on the road below. The range, only three kilometers at maximum, was close enough so that these weapons would zap through the Stuarts, and even the Shermans, like hot knives through butter.

By letting the lead tank almost reach Marthille, the enemy would have had our entire battalion strung out all along the road like ducks lined up in a shooting gallery at Coney Island. Once they opened up, there would have been no place to go. We'd have been trapped between soft muddy fields on one side of the road, and a boggy streambed on the other. The 8th Tank Battalion would have been murdered, blown to smithereens. For me, inside a light tank that day, the war would have ended. This time, though, the so-called fickle finger of fate was definitely on our side. That and a kindly hand from the Man Upstairs. With a silent, fervent prayer of thanksgiving, I "pulled the shade" on this memorable, unforgettable day.

The foregoing is adapted with permission from the book, He Rode up Front for Patton, *by Brigadier General Albin Irzyk,*

USA Ret. Published by Pentland Press, Inc., 5124 Bur Oak Circle, Raleigh, NC 27612.

LIEUTENANT JAMES TURNER
Company A, 37th Tank Bn.
September 19, 1944, Near Arracourt, Eastern France

Combat Command A (CCA) of the 4th Armored Division was headquartered at Arracourt, eastern France in the early fall of 1944. Arracourt is 15 miles east of the city of Nancy and 75 miles from the German border on the Rhine River. To the west of CCA HQ, several task forces were operating. A task force made up of Baker Company, 37th Armor, and Charlie Company, 10th Infantry, was operating in the Chambery area. Another TF made up of Able Company of the 37th and Able Company of the 53rd Infantry was in the Luneville area. I was the platoon leader of Able Company's 1st Platoon. A battery of the 94th Artillery was available to both task forces. This was the situation at 0600, September 19, 1944.

At 0800, we were in bivouac, preparing for the day's sweeps when the 37th's HQ bivouac area was attacked by a German Panzer brigade, equipped with the MkV Panther tank (75mm gun) and accompanied by Panzer grenadiers, the infantrymen trained to fight alongside tanks. Since Charlie Company was in the bivouac area, the attack was repulsed, forcing the Germans to back off and regroup. This they did, and then they began to advance on Arracourt. B/37 was recalled and rushed eastward toward Arracourt. They reached the area at about 1100 hours and set up a defensive position one-half mile east of the town. The company was in defilade, invisible to the advancing Germans, but able to see and shoot out of their little valley. To a keen observer, only the tops of their turrets might have been visible. Able Company was released from its operations around Luneville and sped back to aid "B" Co. One platoon, the 3rd, was split off from the company to aid in the protection of CCB HQ. I was in command of the 1st Platoon, and just as we approached "B" Company's area, my tank broke down, and I took my platoon sergeant's tank and the remainder of the platoon.

We pulled into the same defilade position as Baker Company, but to their left. My platoon was on our extreme left flank, and the Germans had now become aware of us. They fired a few shots from a range of about 2,000 yards, but would come no closer. Those long 75s that the Panther carried could hit hard, and one of Baker Company's tanks was hit, knocking the gun and hatch covers out of the turret.

Now the Germans withdrew about 1,500 yards to look the situation over, and our CO, Major Hunter, advanced our little task force about two miles to relieve a composite unit made up of tanks from C/37 and a few tank destroyers from the 702nd TD Bn. One German tank was exposed on a hilltop about 1,500 yards away with its crew on the ground, working on it. Since solid AP shot wouldn't pierce a Panther's armor at this distance, I had my gunner, Sgt. Emhardt, put an HE shell into it, hoping to wound some of the crewmen. The tank answered, firing one AP shell, which did no damage. My original gunner had been wounded in a night skirmish with the Germans four days earlier, and as would be expected, I looked with some misgivings on this new individual. My concern was unfounded, and as will be seen, he did a superlative job.

At 1600, Major Hunter decided to sweep forward with both companies (15 tanks total, due to detachments and attrition). "A" Company was on the left, and "B" Company was on the right. I was on the extreme left flank of the line, and as we proceeded I saw a MkV being worked on with most of the crew busily engaged in the engine compartment behind the turret. I had Emhardt put one round of AP into that engine compartment and the crew fled, hurriedly. We then came on some German infantrymen who had gotten separated from their tanks. Peeling off from the formation, which was still advancing, I began to chase them down a shallow valley. This led me to a German bivouac area that consisted of a line of five German tanks sitting across the valley. Their turrets were not pointed at me, and I immediately opened fire, two rounds to each of them, one in the engine room, and one in the turret. We hit each of these tanks.

As we engaged, while Emhardt and the loader, Pfc. Moore, worked on those tanks, I tried to contact our company commander, Captain Spencer, but could not contact him as his tank had been hit by German fire and was burning. My gunner had killed four of those five tanks, but the fifth, even with two hits in him, was moving off slowly. We moved forward to finish off this cripple, when three more Panthers blocked our path—possibly they were the ones who had set Capt. Spencer's tank on fire.

I laid the turret on the new menace, and my Emhardt and Moore went to work furiously. The big 76mm gun in the Sherman was now too hot to touch, and the turret was filled with acrid fumes. I could barely see my loader as he worked in the dim combat lighting inside the turret. Aiming and firing as soon as he heard the breech close, Emhardt got two shots each into the first two of those tanks, but now our turret was too jammed with shell casings and our ready racks were empty. We'd have to pull back to clean house and dig some more ammunition out of the racks, which were behind the driver and under the turret—a tedious process.

German turrets were always slower than ours, but now the last Panther in that line had us in his sights. He put two rounds through our turret, killing Moore instantly and breaking both of Emhardt's legs. The bow gunner, Harold McIver, and my driver, Al Rylak, were burned and took some shrapnel from the shattering of our own armor. I took 14 wounds, in the left leg, foot, my left side and chest, plus a partially severed Achilles tendon. The first shot knocked me to my knees in the turret, and the second ejected me from the turret and out onto the hull, from where I rolled off to the ground!

Darkness was falling fast, and as I looked up I saw Major Hunter's tank approaching, and somehow I managed to stand up and climb up onto his tank. I tried to tell him of the danger and also about KO-ing nine tanks, but I don't think he could understand what I was trying to say. We started to approach my KO'd tank, but another tank was already there, helping the crew. It was now close to full dark, and Major Hunter recalled the units to an assembly area. We later found out that after Capt. Spencer's tank had been hit, Captain Leach, the CO of

Baker Company, had taken his tanks and circled to the right, flanking the Germans and putting the remains of the German task force to rout.

I later learned at the hospital that our 2nd Platoon, under Lt. DeCreane, had been alongside Capt. Spencer and had taken the brunt of the assault of the second group of Germans. He had been hit, recovered, and ordered his platoon to advance. He was immediately hit, and DeCreane and three of his crew were killed. When I talked to his bow gunner in the hospital he was not physically hurt, but was still in shock. It still amazes me that from the first shot fired in that action to the time we were hit, only seven minutes had elapsed.

That was the way the war was going then, hundreds of little unreported firefights between tanks. Six days later, on September 25, the 3rd Platoon leader, Lt. Donelly, was killed in another of these battles, and the exec, Lt. Shea, had been injured in a freak accident. This left the company with only one officer, Captain Spencer, and it was pulled back into CCR (combat command reserve).

Adapted by author from material submitted by James Turner for this book.

LTC ALBIN IRZYK
East of Mainz, Germany
March 18, 1945

In World War II usage, the 4th Armored Division had been divided into three combat elements known as combat commands; they were designated as CCA, CCB, and CCR, or reserve. As we moved toward Mainz, which was itself the gateway to Frankfurt, my battalion had been working back and forth across the land, seeking a crossing of the Rhine River. On this day our objective was the town of St. Johann, which dominated an important crossroads. We were part of CCA and my Able Company moved out quickly, boldly at 0600 on that fateful day.

We'd been bivouacked about 13 kilometers south of Bingen, and were only 3 kilometers from the largish town of Sprendlingen, which "A" Company took with no resistance, being in control of the town by a little after 0730. This was an auspicious, heady beginning. The lead elements were now on the road to St. Johann when we received a message from CCA commander Col. Sears, to hold in place. CCB, it turned out, had been attacked by 13 enemy tanks and some self-propelled guns. They had moved to break through the positions of CCB at Hackenheim, which was only eight kilometers southwest of our position at Sprendlingen. Our "C" Company had made contact with CCB the day before, so we knew where they were. Colonel Sears explained that CCB had had to send tanks and infantry *back* to Bad Kreuznach to help clear out that large city, as there was still organized German resistance in it.

Colonel Sears further explained that because of the uncertain situation in CCB, division did not want CCA to advance farther. Our hearts sank at this news. We'd just begun to roll and hated to stop now. It was a beautiful, clear day, perfect for offensive operations, and if the enemy had not defended the large, important town of Sprendlingen, in all likelihood, he would not defend the smaller, lesser towns of St. Johann and Wolfsheim. If we moved now, it would be clear sailing all the way to the objectives.

After an hour had passed, with no further word, I began to worry. If there *were* enemy out there, we'd already tipped our hand, and they could sense where we'd be headed. We were now, because of the enforced wait, providing them with ample time to make preparations for a stand. I took my own tank and moved east of Sprendlingen for a personal reconnaissance. From where we sat, I could look straight down into the innocent-looking town of St. Johann. The road into that town was all downhill and a straight shot through open terrain covered with vineyards. This was the heart of the famous Rhine wine country.

After consulting with my staff, I decided to give "A" Company a breather and let Charlie Company take this objective. Due to the narrowness of the valley, only one company could find room to get into an assault formation so "C" could assault while the others supported by fire. We, still restricted from attacking, began to juggle our companies for the best supporting positions.

Almost directly south of the town, at a distance of about three kilometers, was a tall, steep hill, the top of which would accommodate most of a tank company. We decided to use the old military maxim and "seize the dominating terrain." I ordered Len Kielly's Able Company to climb to the top of Hill 271 (elevation in meters). We did not realize just how rough it was until we watched "A" tanks climbing like goats. Suddenly we're not looking at the backs of advancing tanks, we're looking at the *tops* of their turrets. The Sherman had the reputation of being the best climber of the war, but we were still amazed that they were able to weave their way through the steep woods to the open top. Soon they were looking down on the world and could cover Charlie Company's advance and pot-shoot any antitank gun that showed its presence. . . . We thought.

We also decided to make a "lateral advance." We were prohibited from advancing east, but there had been no statement about improving our situation, so I ordered Baker Company to make one hop, south and a bit east to the town of Glau-Bickelheim. "B" Company was soon positioned to use a narrow road over Hill 271 to St. Johann or to sweep around the hill to Wolfsheim and come in from the rear if the "C" team needed help.

With "A" and "B" in place to back up "C" Company, we figured that we'd created the best battle plan possible. We thought that the Armor School back at Ft. Knox would have given us an "E" for excellent. Theory and reality are vastly different things, however, and you also could never quite predict how the enemy would react to your carefully laid plans. "The best laid plans of mice and men go oft awry." We were poised to attack, but still no orders came. Another hour passed, and then another. The best hours of the day were vanishing. This was March—it got dark early. Soon it was midafternoon. Still sitting, still no word. Now I began to be afraid that we'd get the word with very little daylight remaining.

Sure enough, that's exactly what happened. It was almost 1600 when Colonel Sears finally got the go-ahead from division and passed it to us. "C," like the rest of us, had been literally pawing the ground, chomping on the bit, to use an old cavalryman's terminology. Now they had the word and cranked up and moved out aggressively, hoping to cover as much of the open ground as possible before darkness closed in. In an open, deployed formation they moved down the slope.

There was a subtle ridge, just a roll in the land, before the ground dipped sharply down into St. Johann, and as the lead platoon reached it, surprisingly, shockingly, came the loud screeching, booming, trademarks of the 88. Suddenly, unbelievably, there were five Shermans hit and burning. The Germans must have had that spot zeroed in, for they wasted neither time nor ammunition—they were right on. We watched, horror-stricken at the rapidity with which a promising attack had turned into a disaster. For a few moments we were stunned at the loss of five tanks in one fell swoop. The attack had come to an abrupt halt as the remaining tanks of "C" scurried for cover from those guns. Suddenly, it was very quiet. What to do now? Lieutenant Rubin's 1st Platoon had been virtually wiped out.

I quickly radioed "A" Company sitting on top of Hill 271. Surely they must have seen the enemy guns, why didn't they fire on them? Len Kielly, in great frustration, answered the question. He said that the Germans were tucked in snugly between St. Johann and the foothill of 271. His tanks were so high up that they couldn't depress their guns far enough to reach the antitank guns sitting down at their feet.

Talk about frustration. So much for taking the dominating terrain. However, there was a way out. Our ever-alert artillery observer, Bob Parker of the 94th Field Artillery began to rain 105mm shells down on that gun position, with some helpful guidance from the tankers up on that hill. Hopefully that would rattle the gunners on those 88s enough to get some tanks into the town. We still had a mission, to get to St. Johann, Wolfsheim, and beyond. We had to advance, but how?

"C" was badly hurt and reorganizing. It would soon be pitch-dark. There was not time for "A" to climb back down from Hill

271 or for "B" to retrace its steps from Glau-Bickelheim to take over the lead. The situation was what is called "volatile." I could not order "C" back into the attack and expose them to guns that could kill a Sherman with one shot. That would cause still more losses. Yet, the advance must not bog down. Something had to be done quickly and dramatically. The task was now fully in the lap of the leader, one Albin Irzyk.

I remembered two things. One, Colonel Sears had once said, "You can't push cooked spaghetti." Two, my personal philosophy of not asking any of my men to do something hazardous that I personally was not prepared to do. So I, not too enthusiastically, had the decision forced on me. My crew and I would make the rush past those guns while the artillery was keeping their heads down. We hoped. Once in the town, I could order, "I'm in the town, close on me." The charge by a lone, extremely fast-moving tank should work as it would be a radical surprise for the Germans.

We had a short, intense staff meeting between myself, the battalion exec, Bert Ezell, and our S-3 Sam Diuguid. We quickly reviewed the battalion's mission in case I got hit. When I told the crew what we were up to, they looked stricken, but their eyes said, "If you can do it, we can, too." I told the driver to floorboard the accelerator and the bow gunner and turret gunner to keep all machine guns firing and that I would be working the one in front of me, too. We all took a deep breath, and then I said, "Let's go!"

We edged out of cover and then, with all guns blazing, simply flew down the sharply descending, almost straight road. This was not a moving tank, it was a flying tank. That Sherman was probably going faster than any tank had ever gone before. Four hundred horsepower was getting a 32-ton gravity assist. *It worked!* We were halfway home before the startled German gunners reacted, and their shots were hopelessly behind our zooming Sherman. We got through the kill zone faster than those guns could traverse.

As we got near the first building, knowing that we were safe for the moment, we were astonished to find a lone tank tucked up close to the side of the house, out of sight of the German gunners. And there, with his head out of the turret was Lt.

Mandel Rubin, a platoon leader who, with his platoon shot out from around him in the first assault, had somehow slipped through. He looked lonely, puzzled, and now dumbfounded. Logically, we should both have stayed in the lee of that building and waited for the rest of the battalion, but we were on a "high" and kept rolling. We were exhilarated, we were invincible. We kept on up the darkening street at full throttle. The whole town was dark, windows boarded up, nothing stirring, a seeming ghost town.

Somebody'd been there, though. Right in the center of the town was a roadblock, huge logs stacked one upon another. It was not manned, there was no enemy fire, so we tore it apart with the tank's cannon, alternating AP and HE shells. At close range we splintered the huge logs, and then the driver pushed through the debris. Again we picked up speed and then at the far end of the town, on the outskirts, another identical roadblock. We used the same destructive procedure and moved on.

We were now out of town, and the road between St. Johann and Wolfsheim looked open in the early darkness. Why stop now? Wolfsheim next—it was not far away—then the road intersection, and it would be over. It was utterly foolhardy for a tank battalion commander to be charging ahead alone in the dark, but we picked up speed. It was now halfway to the town, and it looked like clear sailing.

Suddenly there was a soft explosion, and the tank came to an abrupt, jolting halt. It felt as if we'd hit a wall. I heard screams in the turret, felt pain in my right leg, and knew that we'd been hit by a Panzerfaust (German bazooka). I climbed out of the turret to survey the damage and was astonished to see my turret crew already on the ground, severely wounded. How they got past me without my seeing it, we never did figure out. The pain must have driven them to heroic speed, like a man who, during a crisis, can lift a car off a loved one.

We took inventory and found out that the tank had been hit from the left side. Metal fragments had bounced around the turret, and that was what had wounded us. I'd been standing mostly out of the turret hatch, so only my legs had been hit. They were bleeding, but it was not a serious wound. I now had to find out how badly damaged the tank was. Climbing back inside, I found out that the turret was jammed and that for the moment, it was a useless tank.

The driver and bow gunner, being below the ricocheting metal, had been unhurt, and we all five clustered in the ditch at the roadside to figure out what to do next. Except for the low moaning of my wounded turret crew, it was eerily quiet with only a sliver of moon illuminating the scene. Then the silence was broken by the sound of a tank approaching at a pretty fast clip.

Aha, I thought, *it worked, they're closing up. That ought to be Lieutenant Rubin's tank.* Sure enough, out of St. Johann came a tank, moving at good speed. It was closing rapidly, without slackening speed, but since we could see it, we were convinced that they could see our hulk sitting in the middle of the road. But why weren't they slowing down?

Crash! The loud reverberating clank of heavy metal hitting equally heavy metal reverberated through the night air. The blow was so sudden, so violent that it had not only bounced around the occupants of the tank but injured them as well. From out of the turret came the tank commander, obviously hurting, but also puzzled, embarrassed, and angry. But it was not Lt. Rubin. The man was Lt. Joe Ike, another "C" Company platoon leader. He threw up his hands as if to say, "I can't explain it," and we both charged up to the driver's hatch for an explanation. To our great horror, he was dead. As they came out of the village, the tank had been hit by a Panzerfaust, maybe the same one which killed the driver. For many yards, that had been a runaway tank. Instead of reinforcements, we now had two crippled tanks with their crews crouched in the ditch and several wounded and hurt men.

As we talked nervously, our eyes darted in all directions. Then I thought I saw movement back toward the village. Sure enough, as we stared a big object eased slowly out of town. It was a huge tracked personnel carrier jammed with Germans. They seemed to be in no hurry. Slowly, but inexorably, the carrier rumbled down the road, steadily getting closer. Unfortunately, many of those in the ditch couldn't get up and flee into the woods. This could easily be *it.* Something had to be

RALPH ZUMBRO

done quickly. In desperation, an idea hit. Right in front of my TC hatch, I'd just recently had a .30-caliber machine gun mounted. I'd used the weapon on the charge into St. Johann, and there was still most of a belt of ammunition in it.

Jumping back into the turret, I let off a quick burst and then, aiming with the aid of the tracers, pulled tightly down onto the target. Still it kept coming, but I could see bodies slumping. Then, to our great relief, the carrier, now out of control, turned off the road and into the woods. Saved by a whisker. Now all we needed were medics and reinforcements, and that was still my job. I knew the situation and could lead the relief force straight in.

Right now, I was not in command or control of the battalion. I was only a lone individual searching for help. Back there, they didn't know where we were or what had happened to us, and I could only hope that the chain of command was working. After quickly briefing Lt. Ike, I slipped my .45 out and slid into the dark woods, moving parallel to the road. Almost back to town, I heard voices and worked my way closer to the road.

Eureka! There, moving out of St. Johann, was a body of men led by Sam Diuguid. Behind him was the "B" team which had been recalled from Glau-Bickelheim and had taken over the fight from the badly battered "C" Company. Sam halted the force, and we had a quick consultation. We got medics up to the wounded, and then I left Sam to continue the mission while I went back with the wounded to get patched up.

Back at HQ, I was told that Bert Ezell, in my stead, was at a meeting of unit commanders at CCA. Yes, the chain of command was working. Then I went to the aid station where the wound was quickly cleaned and treated. What had happened was that fragments had penetrated the right boot and leg above the ankle. Painful, yes, but it could have been far worse. All in all, I felt like a mighty lucky man. Close calls? I'd lost count.

When I'd limped back to HQ, Bert had returned from CCA and greeted me with considerable relief. He reported that he'd brought Col. Sears completely up to date and that Sears had told him that the original order to attack toward Mainz was canceled, as it had been learned that the bridge there over the

164

Rhine had been blown. While we were talking, a message was received from Sam reporting that he and the "B" team were sitting astride the road intersection east of Wolfsheim. *Mission accomplished.*

Adapted with permission from the book He Rode up Front for Patton, *by Brigadier General Albin F. (Al) Irzyk. Published by Pentland Press, Inc., 5124 Bur Oak Circle, Raleigh, NC 27612.*

TENTH ARMORED DIVISION
June 9, 1945, North of the
Town of Crailsheim, Germany

The town of Crailsheim is a small, picture postcard town in southwestern Germany, on the Jagst River. In the early days of June 1945, with the end of the war only a month away, the German army was thought to be on the ropes, with most of the stuffing knocked out of it. That belief wouldn't be quite accurate, for with the American tankers moving so fast the walking infantry simply couldn't keep up. There were many pockets of well-armed Germans embedded in our rear areas. Some were eager to surrender and get the war over with. Others, particularly the SS, weren't, and sometimes battle was joined far from the front lines. As a result, many little combats missed historical record, like this one, from an article in *Military* magazine.

CAPTAIN HERBERT SAMUEL ROTH
93rd Armored Field Artillery

The 93rd was a troubleshooting artillery unit. It was unusual in that it wasn't an official part of any division. Controlled at corps level, it was sent where necessary to add to the firepower of any unit that needed it. They got tough assignments because of their expertise, and their battle stars included North Africa, Naples-Fogia, Rome-Arno, southern

France, Rhineland, Ardennes-Alsace, and central Europe. Sam Roth had been with them from the beginning, at Fort Sill, and he had held most of the lower-level officer positions in the unit. At the present time, he was the battalion S-4, or supply officer, and was looking forward to the end of a long war.

He'd been out in a jeep with his driver, attending to the affairs of his battalion, and was heading back to his HQ in Satteldorf, when he came upon a roadblock. Apparently the Germans were still active here in a so-called safe area. A tank company captain from the 10th Armored Division was having an intense discussion with one of his TCs. The captain had just been ambushed in a little woods about 600 yards south of the roadblock. That supposedly safe woods was full of Panzer-faust launchers and machine guns.

The captain, looking pretty excited, said that he and his driver narrowly escaped. Then the captain told the sergeant TC that his mission was to clear this road with his tank machine gun. The sergeant protested that this would be sheer suicide because of the cover afforded the enemy by the woods. During the discussion, Sam managed to ease his way up to the side of the tank captain. Although there was no doubt in his mind that he was capable of delivering the artillery support the tankers obviously needed, he intervened almost tentatively, saying, "If you want, I can put some artillery fire in those woods."

The tankers didn't know who Sam was or what unit he was from, except that they assumed that he was from their task force, named Richardson after its CO. He wasn't; the 93rd was freelance. For a long moment, nobody said anything. The tankers, acting puzzled just stood there, staring at this boyish-looking artillery officer whose serious brown eyes were squinting at them.

The tank captain was probably wondering if it was worth taking a chance on this hotshot artillery kid who might accidentally succeed in having a couple of rounds dropped right where nobody needed them—on their own position. But with a touch of Patton bravado, he said, "Sure, Captain, give us your best shot."

Sam swung up on the sergeant's tank, switched its radio

over to the 93rd's working frequency and called up the fire direction center (FDC) of one of its batteries. To prevent his fire from falling on friendly troops who might be using the road from the south, he first called in an order for another roadblock to isolate the pocket of Germans. He then described the enemy ambush with exact grid coordinates from his own map and called for artillery fire.

In almost no time, the rounds were on their way, whistling over the startled tankers. At the FDC, plotters had simply noted Sam's location on their plotting boards, marked the position of his target, along with their own position. Using that information, along with esoteric factors such as weather conditions and powder temperature, they'd computed elevation and azimuth, and somebody'd picked up a field phone and yelled, "FIRE MISSION!" Scant minutes later the marker round landed.

Sam's adjustment was by a single gun. He observed that the initial smoke round had landed exactly as ordered. Exactly 200 yards short of the target so that he could adjust by it. The next two rounds were also exactly as ordered, bracketing the target. He then ordered, "Fire for effect," and the six-gun battery began pounding the targeted area with ladder fire, a rolling barrage that started from the bracketing rounds and walked through the woods with a rolling barrage. *Not bad,* Sam thought to himself, *just like at Fort Sill.*

The tankers, especially their captain, had watched all this with amazement. Never before had any of them seen firsthand how artillery fire could be called in to assist them—personally. They had seen many artillery barrages before, but never one quite so made to order. So when this weird quirk of fate began to dawn on these combat-hardened men, they looked on Sam as though he were a kind of magician. Especially appreciative and respectful was the expression on the face of the sergeant who moments before was being ordered to take his tank down the road to clear those woods, where he was sure destructive fire from Panzerfausts, the German bazooka, awaited him and his men.

The enemy bazookas and small arms were silenced now, the road was cleared again for friendly traffic, Sam wore a pretty big grin as he waved "so long" to the tankers, and he and his driver went on about their own business. For Sam it was just a routine mission.

RIDING A TANK IS SIMILIAR TO RIDING A HORSE
Northern Ireland, August 11, 1944
Ernie Pyle
Scripps News Service

I have been bunking in lately with an armored unit; one of the outfits that have tanks and fast armored troop carriers. Such troops are scattered all over one portion of Northern Ireland. These are the boys who will become the battering ram when the Second Front finally opens. After airplanes have blasted out the initial path, the Armored Corps will bore open a way for the invasion troops to follow. This is the newest branch of the U.S. Army. I am impressed with it, not so much with the weapons, for I know nothing about the various types of arms, but with the men themselves.

There is an esprit de corps about the tank troops that corresponds somewhat with the spirit of the submarine service. It is based, I think, on two things. The fact that these men are destined for dangerous action and the fact that the officers are so close to the men. Visit any tank field and you'll find all the officers in coveralls. You can hardly distinguish them from the enlisted men. They ride their own motorcycles. They are young and alive. The gap between them and their men is smaller than elsewhere in the Army. I had thought that all tanker commanders were officers, but this isn't true. An officer commands a platoon, or whatever they call it, of five tanks. He rides in the turret of one tank and directs them all, but the others are commanded by noncoms.

One of them showed me through his tank. It is a monstrous thing, and the firepower it carries is shocking. The men are fitted in so tightly they barely move, yet they have as much to do as an airplane pilot. Everything is intricately mechanized with gyroscopes, automatic switches, and all kinds of devices.

168

TANK ACES

The tank is padded with soft rubber inside, yet in just climbing around the tank while it was standing still, I bumped my head half a dozen times on cold hard steel.

The boys say that riding a tank is much like riding a horse. If you try to hold yourself rigid against the bumps, you wind up bruised and bleeding. You have to learn to go limp and just go with the tank as the rider goes with a horse. The space within the tank is so cramped that even I had to squeeze in in order to move around. I asked if the Tank Corps made a point of getting small men, but apparently it's just the opposite. This particular tank doesn't have a crew member under six feet, and there is one driver who weighs 200 pounds.

You have to be a real man to be in the Tank Corps. You don't have to be big, but you have to be strong and tough. The vibration and bouncing and jiggling inside the tank are exhausting. You need terrific stamina. One tank commander said they drove more than 200 miles in one day, he and the others taking turns at the controls. The commander who showed me through his tank was Sgt. Herbert Hatcher of Glasgow, Kentucky. He has been in the Army two years. He was a farmer before joining up. Practically the whole Tank Corps seemed to me to be made up of Midwesterners, most of them farmers.

The Tank Corps needs two things: a cheerleader for inside, and one for outside. If the exclusiveness of the service could be drummed into the men the way the Marines drum it into their men and if somebody outside would dramatize and popularize the tank service to the public, the Tank Corps might soon steal some glory . . . even from the Marines.

13

PACIFIC ASSAULT

With the war in Europe well under way and the Allies ashore and contributing their share of blood and steel, America was free to commit her vast resources to the final crushing of the "Greater East Asian Co-prosperity Sphere." With the giant B-29s coming off the assembly line, it was now possible to think of doing serious damage to the Japanese home islands. The plane could carry nine tons of bombs for an average radius of 2,000 miles. With the taking of the Mariana island chain, the Japanese inner ring of defenses was broken, and the whole of the home islands were within range of the flying Superfortress.

There was still a seaborne link with Germany though, and giant cargo-carrying submarines were making the long risky voyage halfway around the world. They took some raw materials to Germany and brought much technology back. The plans for jet aircraft, for instance, were brought, as well as updates on Professor Paul Harteck's low-temperature reactor. The Axis powers, lulled into a false sense of security by their early successes, had allowed their scientific research to lag behind, and now it was time to play catch-up. . . . If their defenses could hold out long enough.

Saipan and Tinian had fallen, and even as the Marines

battled the die-hard Japanese troops, the planes were land-ing on the newly captured airfields. The last big battle in the Marianas was Guam, and it got a bit hairy for the tankers.

THE BLACK WIDOW
Sgt. Lou Spiller, Tank Commander
1st Platoon, "B" Company, 3rd Tank Bn.
GUAM, July 25, 1944

On the day of the 25th, our tank, named the Black Widow, was in support of the 21st Marine Infantry Regiment, taking out enemy positions along the Mt. Fonte/Mt. Tenjo road. My platoon leader, Lt. Warden, had to leave our tank to converse with the infantry company commander. On his way to the command post, he was struck by enemy mortar fire and had to be evacuated. As often happens in the tropics, night came upon us suddenly, and it became too dark to negotiate the narrow twisting road back down to our company command post. We were temporarily stuck on a little shelf with a ridge to one side and a steep drop-off on the other.

The tank crew was now made up of Pfc. Smith, bow gunner; Cpl. Herbert Parmenter, loader/radioman; Pfc. Schaeffer, gun-ner; and myself, as the tank commander. With the loss of our officer, we were temporarily assigned to Lt. Charley Kirkham's 2nd Platoon. This made up a total of seven tanks, which we formed into a semicircle with our backs to the ridge. It was a new experience for us as tankers to get stuck out by ourselves in hostile territory without any infantry dug in around us. It's the nature of tanks to not be very good at defending them-selves from an enemy that gets in too close. We can't depress our guns to fire at the ground next to us. The enemy had a nasty habit of throwing gasoline fire bombs at us, and, without infantry to screen out the tank killers, we were in trouble. We'd have to dismount some crewmen for security.

Realizing this, we were prepared for a long night. Things were quiet for the first few hours, but then about 2330, some flares started to fall in between our own flares that had been fired intermittently. We began to see Japanese silhouetted against the skyline. I checked with the platoon commander to see what our next move would be, and he radioed back to commence firing. We fired our .30-caliber machine guns and the 75mm cannons at anything that moved, knowing that our own Marines would not be out moving around in the situation.

Some hostiles had slipped around our flanks where our own Marine infantrymen should have been and came up from our rear. Two of them set up a machine gun nest right under the rear of the tank. We could hear them talking excitedly and firing their machine gun in short bursts at other tanks. About this time, as I was moving about in the tank, wondering what to do about these fellows, I looked out of the driver's periscope and saw an unbelievable sight. Illuminated by the flares and star shells was the vision of soldiers charging the tanks with drawn sabers. They'd fired off the star shells to signal their own attack, but the shells lit them up, too.

Suddenly it got quiet . . . for a few seconds . . . and then an artillery high-explosive shell went off on the front slope, about a foot from my periscope. We weren't penetrated, but another shell hit and shattered the periscope, temporarily blinding me. The shock of the explosion jarred the escape hatch loose, and it fell down on the ground behind where the bow gunner sat. So there I was, half blinded, not able to see, with the hatch out and a machine-gun crew under the Black Widow. I had to figure some way to eliminate them before one of them threw a hand grenade through our open hatch or threw in a firebomb or demolition charge.

I knew that moving the tank in the dark would be dangerous, as I wasn't sure how much distance lay between the rear of the tank and the cliff that dropped several hundred feet to the gully below. Knowing that something had to be done in a hurry, I fired up the engine, pulled the tank forward a few yards, then put it in reverse with one track locked and gunned the engine. The tank spun halfway around, crushing the two soldiers and their machine gun.

According to reports issued later by division HQ, this had been a coordinated attack by the Japanese defenders of Guam to drive the Marines from our beachhead. There were an estimated 3,500 Japanese killed within the division area that night. All night long they came at us, but we held our positions, even though some of them penetrated as far back as regimental headquarters.

When daylight finally came, we picked our way back through hundreds of fresh corpses back to our company headquarters to refuel and replenish our dwindling supply of ammunition. Thus ended the longest night of my life. Although it was 50 years ago, I still remember the events of that night in vivid detail.

Adapted from Marine Corps Tanker's Association Newsletter, *Vol. 4-94, November 1994.*

CENTRAL PACIFIC
GUAM, 1944
TANK vs. TANK
Sgt. John Chapman, Combat Correspondent

Stateside movie fans have never seen a Western adventure or a gang thriller with a chase sequence that will surpass the one First Lt. George R. Cavender starred in during the taking of Guam. The lieutenant's experience, spontaneous though it was, embodied all the planned elements that go to make up a rip-roaring Saturday matinee serial: Surprise, suspense, and the eventual triumph of good forces over evil. Moreover, it outmoded the horse, the careening car, and the runaway train as factors for the chase, for the Michigan Marine went after his man in a Sherman tank.

The drama got its opening cue from a Japanese officer, playing the part of the villain who unwittingly directed his lost tank through the line of the 21st Marine Regiment and past Lt. Cavender's platoon of tanks as they stood idle, waiting for a mission. Resting on the ground near the road, the Marine tank men had heard the high-pitched giveaway whine of the enemy vehicle as it approached. They were alert but unbelieving, until the hostile tank rolled by and they saw the tank commander, his head bloody from a wound, staring straight at them. "I can't understand why the Jap didn't rake us with machine-gun fire," the lieutenant mused later. "I guess he was just as confused as we were."

Recovering from their bemusement, the leathernecks raced for their tank, revving the two-cycle diesel engines to an ear-splitting roar and taking off in hot pursuit of the fleeing villain. The bow gunner in the pursuing tank that day was Pfc. Paul E. Stewart, who declares he will never forget the mile-long dash in fifth gear down the coral highway, the heavy steel tracks calibrating the road as if it were a long ruler. "We were gaining on the Jap and had our 75mm gun loaded and zeroed in on his rear," the lieutenant related, "but we held our fire. We were heading toward our own rear, and there was a danger of hitting Marines bivouacked down there."

Soon the Sherman was passing hundreds of Marine infantrymen who also had been attracted by the screaming engine of the enemy tank and were lined up on either side of the road. They were pointing after the enemy tank and cheering on the chasers. Lt. Cavender confesses that it occurred to him that the event had all the earmarks of a Hollywood scene. "I don't think that I fully realized that we were heading for a fight to the death with the enemy," he averred. "It seemed more like a game."

The Japanese TC set the stage for the final act. Turning off the main road, he churned down a smaller one, which led out into a field and formed the stem of a "T" with a sixty-foot strip of high brush. When the Marine tank arrived in the field, the fleeing machine had disappeared. Was the enemy lying in wait behind the left-hand corner of the "T" crossbar or the right? That was the ticklish question that Lt. Cavender had to make up his mind about, and quickly. Moving slowly, cautiously, every crewman in her tense as piano wire, the Sherman swung around the starboard corner of the strip of bush.

Lucky guess. For there at the other end of the patch, his guns trained on the wrong corner, sat the villain. Hollywood script writers are prone to end their celluloid narratives with a kiss, and this one concludes that way too, after a fashion. "We kissed the Jap with two 75s," Lt. Cavender related. "The last I saw of that tank, it was rocking with inner explosions."

Adapted from MCTA Newsletter, *Vol. 1-95, January 1995.*

All during the time that the Marines had been working their way up the central Pacific, the Army under General MacArthur had been working its way up through the northern Solomons, the Bismarcks, and Papua/New Guinea. Their objective was, of course, the retaking of the Philippines. Midway between the Marianas and the Philippines was the island of Peleliu, which the U.S. Navy and Air Force both wanted as a staging area for the invasion of the islands. Also, the big Japanese base there needed to be reduced to eliminate any interference in U.S. operations.

The original plan had been to take the islands of Yap, Ulithi, and Morotai as well, but when it was found out just how weak the garrisons on those islands were, the decision was to take Peleliu first and leave the others to die on the vine. Once Peleliu was reduced, then Ulithi, the best fleet anchorage in the central Pacific, could be used to stage the invasion of Luzon, and MacArthur would have his "Return." The Japanese commander on Peleliu had changed his tactics from the normal beach defenses to a hideously effective system of defense in depth that would take as many American lives as Omaha Beach. He just let the invasion troops come ashore into his prelaid fields of fire and slaughtered them—except for the tanks, whose stubborn effectiveness made it all possible.

PELELIU, WESTERN PACIFIC
Sgt. Walter Wood, USMC Combat Correspondent

Liz was hit before she made the beach, but she was the kind of tank that's hard to stop. On D-day, in Peleliu, she was the second Sherman in a column of five, grinding across a coral shelf toward Peleliu through water that was almost turret deep. The Japanese in hill positions ashore walked their mortar barrage on the column from front to rear. The lead tank staggered under a direct hit. Oily black smoke almost obscured the column as the Sherman brewed up. Then Liz got it on the nose—a mortar shell smack dab on the muzzle of her turret gun. The hole in the gun muzzle was no longer round. It was egg-shaped, and it made her fighting mad.

Liz was madder even than she had been at Arawe, New Britain, so she didn't need any prodding by Sgt. Stanley "Pete" Piotrowski of Dearborn, Michigan, to lunge forward and make the beach. Besides the tank commander "Pete" Piotrowski, there were Sgt. Theodore Belgarde of Whitefish, Montana, the driver; Cpl. Anthony "Pat" Flaherty of St. Paul, Minnesota, the gunner; Cpl. Evan M. Knott of Chelsea, Michigan, bow gunner; and Cpl. Anthony Vranich of Buffalo, New York. Liz was proud of them all.

They drove Liz to a notch on the perimeter of the beachhead and parked there to work on her. It was a hot spot to work, but Liz's armor could take it, and the sweating Marines would jump in the ditch whenever the Japanese guns threw heavy stuff their way. For five hours they took turns hacksawing the oval muzzle off her 75mm cannon so that she could shoot again.

The crewmen were in and out of the ditch more than a few times, and many sniper bullets pinged off Liz's thick skin as they sawed on the barrel. Pete was afraid they wouldn't make it, and he was mad, too. When he wasn't sawing, he was yelling, "Hurry up, hurry up." He thought Liz and he were going to miss all the action. It was 0900 when they started and soon other Marine tankmen came over to help. Platoon Sgt. Bernard Rosoff of Brooklyn took charge of the working party and they all took turns sawing. All told, they used up 22 hacksaw blades on the tough gun steel. Rosoff was hit in the arm by mortar shrapnel even though he jumped in the ditch when they heard the shell coming in. It was that close. He kept on working and didn't think much about the sore arm, until seven days later they evacuated him to a hospital ship with blood poisoning, his arm all purple and swollen.

By noon, the day was hotter than the well-known hinges, and all the available water was rust-colored and tasted like the oil can from which it was poured. They sawed on Liz until 1400 hours that hot day, and when there was only a half-inch of steel to go, Sgt. Piotrowski got impatient and smashed the end off the barrel with one swing of a heavy tanker's sledge-hammer.

Snub-nosed Liz was ready to avenge her humiliation. When Sgt. Belgarde opened the throttle, she rolled up to within a few yards of a concrete reinforced pillbox filled with enemy and let herself go. She knocked out the emplacement with 45 rounds of shells fired from her sawed-off gun and cut down the men who tried to escape with her .30-caliber machine guns. Liz felt better about the day and dropped back to the airstrip to refuel, re-ammo, and be a lady-in-waiting for a while.

She didn't have to wait long. At 1630 the Japanese tanks came out, and Liz selected one and went in and made the kill.

Liz's number was 13, but it's plain to see that it wasn't up. She spent 35 days in Peleliu.

When she got back to her home base, Liz was scrapped, or as Sgt. Piotrowski put it, "retired, undefeated."

Adapted from MCTA Newsletter, *Vol. 2-94, April 1994.*

The way was now clear for the invasion of the Philippines, and here, the Amtank, a unique marriage of the Amtrac and a tank gun turret, would play a critical part. Some of these floating tanks had been armed with the 37mm turret of the old M-3 light tank, but there was a newer model, armed with a 75mm howitzer. The later versions of this vehicle, the LVT(A)4, had gyrostabilized guns and could fire accurately on to the land, even from ocean swells. The gun's hydraulic stabilizer was linked to a gyroscope spinning quietly away down under the turret, and, while the little floating tank pitched and rolled with the seas, the gun remained stable. The capability gave a whole new meaning to the term *assault fire*. The seagoing function gave the army a whole fleet of little gunboats that could bounce the enemy out of coastal caves by firing from the sea.

14

THE AMTANKERS

PHILIPPINE CAMPAIGN
1944–45

The Army's first amphibian tank battalion wasn't even on the books when it went into battle for the first time. It just seemed to evolve to fit the situation in which it found itself, but this is a typical American trait. The outfit had been dismounted from the old 2nd Horse Cavalry Regiment only 15 months before it was converted to Amtanks. First, they'd been organized into a light tank battalion and gotten mechanical training. Then, due to the success of the Marines with the first models of the Amtank, the U.S. Army, which would be doing much of the unpublicized fighting in the Pacific, decided that it, too, needed an amphibous tank battalion. The powers that be took one of the battalions of the 2nd Cavalry (mechanized) and designated it to be the 776th Amtank Battalion.

To quote Major John Collier, who wrote several articles on the unit, "The tactics came from the cavalry and artillery, the seagoing equipment was contributed by the Navy, and the weapon, the 75mm howitzer, came off the back of an Army mule." Most of the men who went into combat with that outfit had been horse soldiers, and that is where its tradition of slash and raid came from. They carried out combined arms, Panzer-style, at sea far behind Japanese lines, making long sea marches and bivouacking on remote beaches and islands at night. They sailed like buccaneers and fought like cavalry.

In June 1944, when the battalion was in Hawaii, they received their complement of the new LVT(A)4, armed with the 75mm howitzer in what was known as the M8 turret. They were still organized as a tank battalion but they received intensive artillery training to fit them for their new role. Since there were no artillery specialists in the unit, men had to be taken from other duties and trained, causing some drastic liberties to be taken with the table of organization.

When the 7th Infantry Division stormed ashore on the flaming eastern beaches of Leyte, they were carried in Amtracs of the 536th and 718th Amphibious Tractor Battalions and led by the thundering guns of the 776th, which poured accurate fire in from the little floating tanks. Though the guns were only 75mm, there were as many of them as there were 105s and 155s in the whole division artillery regiment. And they were on the beach, where they needed to be, not aboard ships several miles out to sea. Nothing like them had ever been seen before. Those little cannons could lob HE and white phosphorus over the back sides of enemy hills into places that even naval guns couldn't hit, blowing up enemy troop concentrations before they could get into battle formation.

As soon as their tracks hit the beaches, they set up as an artillery park and went to work for 7th Division FOs, until the big guns could be gotten ashore. They broke up Japanese counterattacks with the massed fire of over 50 guns. A normal artillery battery has six guns, but each platoon of the 776th had five, and there were three companies of three platoons each, plus the HQ vehicles. Soon, however, the infantry got too far inland for the little 75s, and since the mountains of Leyte fall right into impassable swamps, the Amtanks had to stay on the beaches. Their steel-cleated swimming tracks would have destroyed what few roads existed. Eventually, though, they found a way to get back into the war.

The 7th Division still needed artillery support, and a new plan was devised: Send the tanks by sea, all the way around the island. There were still plenty of hostile warships in the surrounding seas though, so they'd have to stick close to shore. The battalion split off a task force, which was combined with cargo-carrying tractors from the 536th and 718th Amtrac battalions, under the command of Major Ottoman of the 776th. The first seagoing cavalry raid in history was about to be launched. The total complement of the new unit was 46 LVTs from the 536th, 34 LVTs from the 718th, and 20 Amtanks from the 776th.

Under cover of darkness, several LSTs carried the provisional battalion down the east coast of Leyte, and put them into the sea off the southern tip of the island. As they said their farewells to the sailors, there must have been some doubt in the minds of these seagoing cavalrymen as they launched straight into "Injun country." Those western seas off Leyte were still enemy-controlled. The 7th Division had come overland from Leyte Gulf and was trying to cut the island in two, but the Nipponese were still full of fight. The mission of the task force was pure cavalry: distract, demoralize, and destroy.

They launched at sea in the dark of night and beached temporarily on the island of Panoan at the mouth of the straits of Panoan. The plan was for this to be a maintenance break, but the beach was so strewn with boulders that it caused some track damage, which also had to be repaired. The grousers that drove the hulls like paddle wheels had to be repaired, and all the cap screws that held the tracks together had to be checked. Fuel had to be topped off from 55-gallon drums and all lube levels checked. And all this under total blackout conditions as the enemy situation was none too clear.

After first light the next day, the provisional battalion left the beach and entered the swiftly running Panoan Straits. One tractor had a dead battery and had to be towed offshore and jump-started. Another began to overheat and the maintenance track took it under tow while a mechanic traced the problem to a faulty oil-cooler. The maintenance track was named "Miss Fixit" and had the prettiest pinup in the battalion on its side. Its commander was motor sergeant Tonzola. The crippled Amtrac was repaired under way and took up its station as the battalion worked its way through the straits and up the coast of Leyte. An LCM was the control boat and led three columns of Amtanks, followed by the cargo carrying Amtracs and another LCM, which was the safety boat that would assist any stragglers. Needless to say, every vessel was loaded down with fuel, food, supplies, and ammunition. On their sides were names like Popeye, Donald Duck, Battling Bitch, and Barracuda, with pictures to match.

By noon, the formation had passed the southwestern tip of the island, still undetected. They beached for a half-hour maintenance break to check tracks and lube levels and top off the fuel tanks from the drums, then back into the water, swimming at five knots speed. The big radial engines that drove the churning tracks were a comforting sound as the day wore on, but every eye was scanning the horizon and searching the clear blue skies. All it would take was one prowling aircraft to spot them.

That night they again beached in formation, with the Amtanks facing the jungled interior and the Amtracs facing out to sea. The Japanese still had aircraft patroling, so fires had to be forbidden and the meals prepared inside the hot, smoky hulls over gasoline-burning squad stoves. During the night, two bad sprockets were discovered and repaired before dawn. Then they were out to sea again, in a series of beach-hopping runs interspersed with maintenance breaks. On the third day, November 30, they reached the vicinity of St. Augustin and set up a perimeter defense. They'd just made a 97-mile run by sea and established a raiding base in the enemy rear.

The first raid was on December 5, 1944, when the

Amtanks made a night strike. They moved out quietly by water from their beach camp. At Balogo, a false attack was made to draw as many Japanese soldiers in as possible. Getting in close enough for direct fire, they shelled the town with the howitzers and raked it with machine-gun fire. Once sufficient reinforcements had been brought by the defenders, the little tank fleet wheeled north, shelled the town of Tabgas and put an infantry raiding party ashore at the mouth of the Tabgas River. The beach defenders fled in consternation at this new tactic, leaving the Americans in control of the area. Once the raiding party was ashore and could look around in relative peace, they found lots of things for the tanks to shoot at. By dawn most of the enemy installations were thoroughly shot up.

On December 7, 1944, to mark Pearl Harbor Day, the provisional battalion shelled the town of Albuera from the water, again hoaxing the Japanese defenders into thinking that a raid was coming. As soon as there was movement along the shore, the other half of the battalion launched from LSTs, escorting a new unit, the 77th Division, which landed at the town of Ormoc. This time the Amtanks not only supported by fire from the sea, but finding firm ground, rolled right out of the water and into the town of Ormoc, acting just like conventional tanks.

The Ormoc assault group, TF 78.3, under Rear Admiral Arthur Struble, had the protection of 12 destroyers, two subchasers, and air cover from the 5th Air Force. Unfortunately, the Japanese air force was still functional and blitzed the attacking force with an air raid that sank one destroyer and an attack transport. The Sons of Nippon sent in about 45 planes and lost 36 in a battle that went on far into the night. Underneath all this, the Amtanks and Amtracs went steadily about their business.

They were again the only heavy-caliber support that could be gotten there, and the American beach commander made a lucky decision. He assigned most of the Amtanks to beach defense, suspecting that the Japanese might just try something. Sure enough, late that night, a lookout on one of the floating tanks spotted a large dark shape approaching

Picture of LTC George S. Patton standing in front of a
Renault tank, near Langres, France, July 15, 1918.
(Armor Magazine)

Two tank crews composing a light section. One tank is
armed with a 37mm cannon and the other with a Hotchkiss
machine gun. *(Armor Magazine)*

American light tank and infantry in firefight somewhere in western France, 1918. Notice the four of diamonds painted on the turret and the deceased German on the ground. This tank is working for a living. *(Armor Magazine)*

American soldiers learning tank skills in the school at Langres. *(Armor Magazine)*

American manned tanks going forward into action in Argonne, near Boureuilles, Meuse, September 26, 1918. The spade painted on the second tank identifies it as the unit Arthur Snyder was in. Notice the drums of extra fuel carried on the ditching skids; these were used for the approach march and then dropped for the assault. *(Armor Magazine)*

USMC tanks advancing on Munda airfield in the Pacific in 1943. This was the M-3 light tank that fought on Bataan and Guadalcanal. It did good service but was too small for the brutal work required of tanks in the jungle. *(Armor Magazine)*

Korean-American tank-infantry team moving cautiously through devastated village. This is one of the last models of a Sherman; so many changes had been made, it was designated the M4A3E8. *(Armor Magazine)*

Soldiers of two units—the 55th Armored Infantry Battalion and the 22nd Tank Battalion—going into what can be described only as the mouth of Hades, a burning town set on fire by bombardment but still holding hostile forces. *(Armor Magazine)*

American tank crossing the Elbe River with Russian troops watching. *(Armor Magazine)*

France, August 21, 1944. Assault on the Marne River bridges. Heavily camouflaged tank is engaging enemy, trying to get to the bridges before the German engineers succeed in blowing them up. *(Armor Magazine)*

Tank crew resting in France. Notice that although the tarp is spread, their gear is rolled up and ready to go at a moment's notice. This was part of the 37th Tank Battalion, commanded by Creighton Abrams, the namesake of the current Abrams tank. *(Armor Magazine)*

The M26 Pershing tank, named after the WWI commander of the AEF, was our best tank of the war but entered combat very late. It could face the vaunted Tiger on almost even terms. This tank model liberated the V-2 factory in Nordhausen. *(Armor Magazine)*

Tank working through devastated village in Binh Dinh province. The TC is Sgt. Robert Urban. *(Ralph Zumbro)*

Sp4 Robert Holt and SFC Hazelip on bow of tank 3-4, the ''Apache.'' *(Ralph Zumbro)*

3-73 airborne armor tanks in Saudi Arabia, with the 82nd Division, ready to go in the assault to Kuwait. Most of these tanks are older than their crews. This model fought in Vietnam, and some of the men are running their fathers' old tanks. *(Armor Magazine)*

Iraqi T-72 terminated by Marine M-60 tank using SABOT ammunition. Notice the inevitable G.I. humor. *(Jason Walker)*

from the sea, blacking out some of the western stars. Several Amtanks began to fire their stubby 75mm guns at the looming menace, and it caught fire and was revealed as a transport ship trying to land desperately needed reinforcements. The ship was shot full of holes and forced to go back out to sea, still burning.

The next day, the Amtanks that were still working with the 7th Division again attacked Albuera, while the infantry assaulted overland, having been put on a good firm beach by the Amtracs from the 536th, which had been escorted by a few Amtanks. This time they not only assaulted from the sea, they rolled right out of the water and shot up a large supply installation by direct cannon fire and machine-gun work. Some of the Amtanks now had over 300 miles of water travel behind them, and they were still running and fighting, every single one of them.

It went on for days, and the Japanese were just as determined by night as by day. Tech 4 Olin Blair was on guard in his Amtrac, which was parked at the edge of the water, when he began to hear suspicious sounds.

"I heard some small marine engines. I called a major in the 77th Regimental Combat Team HQ and told him what I had heard. I suggested that they fire a star shell out to sea to see what was out there. The major replied, 'Can't do that, we'll illuminate the beach.' I said, 'Well I can hear some marine engines out there. If you don't know anything about them, then they aren't out there.' It wasn't 10 minutes later that I heard a scraping sound out front toward the water, right in front of my Trac. As soon as I heard that scraping sound, a 40mm gun of an antiaircraft outfit opened up and hit that barge with the first shot, then we all opened up."

The first shot from the 40mm hit several drums of fuel on the barge, and the resultant illumination revealed two Japanese landing craft trying to land tanks on the beach, right in the middle of the perimeter. By then the whole beach was alight with gunfire and there was a *lot* of firepower there. The Japanese only got the one tank off and it was immediately destroyed, along with the others still on the barge.

The provisional battalion quickly developed a flair for

independent operations, many tanks and Tracs going free-lance, getting fuel and ammunition and rations wherever they could. Sgt. John Masoner reports:

"We operated as independents, just outlaws, six or seven of us operating pretty much alone, often as volunteers and in those situations doing just about what we wanted to do. Our orders would usually give us the general direction of our mission and a fair estimate of the distance—sometimes a mile or two off. In this type of action, however, Sgt. Rex Byrd was like a homing pigeon—he could find anything.

"We were always in trouble out there. The Japanese had been broken up into little groups by pressure on three sides by the Americans. They would infiltrate in little pockets or were trying to break through for food, so we could always expect to run into Japs, if they wanted to give their position away. We captured some of their mortars in the hills above Ormoc and fired theirs and ours back at them. Their mortars made a different sound than ours, and it just tore the Japanese up when we fired their own mortars back at them. There were places above Ormoc where we could walk on dead Jap bodies toward Valencia, as if they had been laid out like a boardwalk."

On December 18, the provisional battalion received orders to take a platoon of Amtanks and 10 carriers, and carry a reinforced company of infantry to that portion of Leyte closest to Cebu Island. By 2200 hours that night, the force was assembled and moved out up the west coast of Ormoc Bay, bound for the town of Merida. No opposition was met, and the task force moved up the coast to check the town of Quiot for enemy occupation.

En route, they were signaled by two large native sailing craft who begged for medical help. The convoy of tanks and Amtracs was halted at sea, lying easily on the gentle swells, and the medical officer and two of his men were transferred to one of the native craft, which had dropped its sails and been paddled alongside the Amtracs. There they were greeted by a horrible sight. Several natives, some of them less than six years old, had been bayonetted and horribly mutilated by the Japanese soldiers on Ponson Island. One child was already dead, but all others were treated. Those outlying islands were eventually going to have to be sanitized.

The 6th Army command wanted to end the Leyte campaign as quickly as possible so as to get on to other projects, like Okinawa, and decided to run an end play around the now-cut-off Japanese General Suzuki, who was in command of what was left of his forces. Rapidly, they forced their way up the Ormoc valley, north alongside Ormoc Bay, and took the city of Valencia. From there, the divisional artillery of the 77th Division could reach the city of Palompon, which was the last Japanese-held port on Leyte.

The generals came up with the idea of sending the amphibian force from Ormoc around the end of the peninsula on a sea voyage to assault the city from the ocean. The only problem was naval escort for the raid. The U.S. Navy was stretched a bit thin right then and couldn't come up with any destroyers. Admiral Kinkaid said that he could provide a PT escort that should do the job because his big ships were in the process of neutralizing the Japanese navy in the area.

There was some urgency because the Japanese in the area were turning brutal and could be expected to implement a scorched-earth policy, which eventually destroyed the Philippine capital of Manila. Even now, groups of natives were coming to American commanders with horror stories of murder, rape, and all the usual atrocities. The PT boat skippers were always involved in small actions around Ormoc Bay, as the Japanese seemed to be going absolutely insane with suicidal and murderous fury. This tendency made the sealing of the harbor at Palompon urgent.

The longest single open-water run by Amtanks came on Christmas Eve, 1944, when almost the entire force, escorted by PT boats, which were idling along on one engine, set sail westward out of Ormoc Bay and around the tip of the peninsula to the town of Palompon, a 45-mile voyage in the open sea. At dawn on Christmas day, the tractors put a large force from the 77th Infantry Division on the beaches, and the last Japanese bolt hole from the Leyte area was closed.

Now, the enemy could no longer land supplies or escape to fight again. Here, as usual, the 75mm howitzers of the Amtank company provided the close-in artillery support. From the town of Valencia, only 12 miles away overland but over 45 by sea, the 155mm "Long Toms" of the 531st Field Artillery Battalion were giving the port a good going-over.

The Amtanks of the 776th were the assault wave, followed by the infantry in the tractors of the 536th and the 718th. These three battalions fought together as if they were a regiment (and most of the veterans are still in contact, sometimes holding common reunions). On Christmas morning, 1944, they put a small army ashore at Palompon and then began digging themselves in. There was little resistance, then. An infantry chaplain came around with a little pedal-powered organ, and the men gathered around him singing Christmas carols. On the same day, General MacArthur formally announced that the Leyte campaign was over—except for "minor mopping-up operations." Those three islands off the western side of Ormoc Bay still needed attention.

By the end of December, the rumors were flying that the next project was going to be the taking of the Camotes group of islands that shielded the western boundaries of Ormoc Bay. By this time, though, the Amtanks and Amtracs were beginning to show serious signs of wear, and all operations had to be called off for a few days to run the necessary 100-hour checks, which included removing and inspecting the aircraft engines that drove the vehicles. This was accomplished by lashing a coconut log between two palm trees, hanging a chain hoist from it, and driving the vehicles under the hoist, one at a time.

One set of tracks had to be completely rebuilt, and bogie wheels had to be replaced on many of the vehicles. Two transmissions had gone out for various reasons and had to be replaced. The steering bands were worn, and several driving sprockets had to be replaced as the studs that held them on the final drives were shearing, one by one. But, by January 14, all 80 tractors and all 20 Amtanks were up and running. Those islands were going to be deloused—by tanks, from the sea, escorted by PT boats!

The names of the PTs operating in the area were *Little Butch, Impatient Virgin, Eight Ball, Little Lulu,* and *Green Harlot.*

At 2400 hours, January 15, 1945, Task Force SWEET POTATO, commanded by a LTC Walker, with Major Bullock in command of the infantry contingent, set off from Ormoc. They were escorted by the PTs, which began shelling the island of Ponson at dawn, just as the Amtanks went in again, for about their tenth amphibious landing in three months. The natives had told the Americans that there were over 200 Japanese on the island, but there was no military resistance . . . and almost no natives.

In the little village of Dapdad on the west coast of Ponson, the men of the 776th found 300 mutilated bodies of the Filipino natives in their own church. Most were sprawled on the floor, but many were hanging from the rafters and many of the women had been violated with bayonets. Only one family out of the whole village had survived, by hiding out while all their friends and relatives were massacred.

Since there had been no opposition on Ponson, the TF reloaded on the Tracs and motored over to the next island, Poro, where they finally found the Japanese garrison, which had just walked across the shallows between the two islands at low tide, the night after their final atrocity. The villagers at the little hamlet of Tudela told the Americans where the Japanese defenders were, and slowly, painfully, with the help of the 75mms of the Amtanks, they were dug out and killed. The Japanese engineers had dug and blasted escapes and sally ports in the coral that opened onto the sea and beaches and couldn't easily be reached from the land. The solution was to launch some of the Amtanks back out to sea to act as gunboats. The floating tanks would sail right up to a coral embrasure and lob 75mm HE into it with a delayed fuse. The shells would actually ricochet around before they went off, way down inside the tunnel. Finally, on the morning of January 31, it was over. The Japanese launched their, by now, entirely predictable "banzai" charge and went out in a blaze of glory. The score? 488 KIA.

At that point in history, on the scientific front, several things were happening. The Germans, now almost on the ropes, had succeeded in producing not an atomic bomb, but irradiated uranium oxide that, if dispersed by conventional explosive, could still kill a city . . . in about two weeks. The Japanese, whose atom bomb project was still under way, were actually ahead of the Germans, and the U.S. had Japanese-born Americans on the ground in Japan and knew what was going on. The weather over that country is usually just cloudy enough to make high-altitude precision bombing difficult, so the great, low-level firebomb raids commenced and among the targets, were Osaka University and the Rikken Institute, which had been working on the Japanese A-bomb since almost before the war. As a result, the research was gradually moved to Konan, in Korea, to avoid the bombing.

Japan's air force was still in the fight, though, and their dispersed factories were turning out aircraft parts. The fighters that were hurting the big silver bombers were coming from two major islands: Okinawa and Iwo Jima. Their turn would be next, and the job would be hard and messy.

15

IWO JIMA

Western Pacific
February 19, 1945

Make no mistake about this. We had to have Iwo Jima if we were to take Okinawa and, if necessary, invade Japan. True, we already had the bases in the Marianas from which to launch the B-29s on their gigantic raids, but we were losing too many of the big silver ships. There were radars on Iwo that could see them, and three airfields that could send patrol fighters out to intercept and harass the bombers. From Iwo Jima came the warnings to the Japanese home islands that allowed them to put defensive fighters in the air.

The most important thing, though, was the combat range of our best escort fighter plane, the P-51 Mustang. When flown from Iwo Jima, it could pick up the bombers from Tinian and provide protection all the way to Japan from outside the range of any existing Japanese fighter. No less important was the existence of Iwo Jima as an emergency landing field for crippled bombers. So, how to take the island? We now had bombers and battleships like no other nation in history, so simply bomb the defenders into oblivion. Right?

The 7th Army Air Force under General Willis H. Hale

tried first. They raided Iwo 10 times in August 1944, 22 times in September, and 16 times in October, just for a warm-up. On December 8, while the Amtankers were still fighting off Leyte, the Air Force began hitting Iwo Jima on a daily basis. For 72 days they kept it up, with aid from five separate naval task forces, from cruiser to battleship size. The first of these was led by heavy cruiser U.S.S. *Chester*. Before the invasion, some 6,800 tons of bombs and 22,000 assorted naval shells up to 16-inch caliber were deposited on Iwo, before the first Marine stepped ashore.

Unfortunately, the Japanese, too, knew the strategic value of the little pork-chop-shaped island and had been busy. They had been digging caves and tunnels, pouring cement and importing ordnance from as far away as Germany. Japanese General Tadamichi Kuribayashi was one of Japan's best military engineers and had been working steadily since September, adding to the island's already formidable defenses.

On February 16 and 17, 1945, eight battleships, five cruisers, and a flock of destroyers opened up on the island, which was already denuded of vegetation, and kept it up all day while frogmen checked the sea approaches for underwater mines, finding none. On the 18th, more of the same. On the 19th, Admiral Kelly Turner, who had commanded the amphibious force since that fateful morning on Guadalcanal, gave the fateful order: "Land the landing force."

What happened next was the single bloodiest engagement of WWII for the Marines. By sundown of the first day, 566 Marines lay dead or dying on the black sand beaches of Iwo Jima. Combat correspondent Robert Sherrod wrote: "The first night on Iwo Jima can only be described as a nightmare in hell." By the time the struggle was over, 6,281 Marines and Navy personnel would be dead, and another 19,217 wounded. That means that roughly one third of the whole landing force became casualties. Another way of looking at it is to note that the Marines lost 17 battalion commanders in that battle; the fighting was that close.

From the very beginning, the tankers and Amtankers got

an unwelcome surprise. Their tracks wouldn't pull well in the soft black volcanic ash from Mount Suribachi. The amphibians, because of their narrow treads, were almost helpless. Finally, though, the Shermans clawed their way up the beach, aided by naval gunfire, which breached General Kuribayashi's barrier wall. By this point in history, the battleship captains had realized that, for the most part, their time of glory had been taken over by the big aircraft carriers and had begun to specialize in direct-fire gunnery, or "forcible entry," a role they still fill today.

One ship in particular, U.S.S. *Nevada*, which had been launched in 1916 and sunk at Pearl Harbor, had come back for revenge. Her commander, Captain H. L. (Pop) Grosskopf, had made her the most accurate close support ship in the navy, and wherever a tanker could put a white phosphorus marker shell, *Nevada* would follow it with 14-inch armor-piercing shells. This was how the tankers got off the beach and how they broke the giant bunkers that were too big for their 75mm cannons.

The naval shell fire had suppressed the Japanese on the beach and driven the rest to ground temporarily, but they came out fighting and shooting. As soon as the Americans were on the beach, they began to take casualties. Until the end of the 19th, there was more than a little doubt as to the success of the beachhead. The days and weeks of bombardment had been soaked up by the soft black sand, which had hidden the bunkers and MG nests, and very few of the defenders had been killed. Now their tactic was to hold the Marines in as tight an area as possible so as to let their own artillery break the invasion. It almost worked.

The island itself seemed to aid the Japanese. For the most part, wheeled vehicles couldn't operate at all, and the Amtracs were severely limited. Here, as usual, it was up to the tankers and their Shermans. By the afternoon of the first day, the assault battalions had made it only to the base of Motoyama airfield number 1. There, they got pinned down by heavy machine-gun fire and called for a tank. Marine tanker, Wilson McClendon answered the call.

"I went in with the third wave and my platoon was attached to the 23rd Marine Regiment. The Japs had some big antitank weapons, 47mm and some German 88s like we had to face on Saipan. What happened was that they let us come on in and then opened up. We could only go so far because we had to wait for the navy to lift their fires. When the Navy quit, about 1100 hours, the Nips came out of their caves and blew us to smithereens.

"The mines were the biggest problem. We mostly had to have an infantryman to guide us where we could go, but we had specialists for that job, dismounted tankers. The infantry wanted to get across the airfield but they couldn't because of the machine-gun fire, so I took my tank there and that's where I got into trouble. We got out in the middle of the airstrip, looking out for mines, and then got hit by an antitank gun. It went in one side but didn't have enough velocity to go out the other, so we just rang like a giant bell when the slug hit the other side of the hull. The next one hit the engine compartment, killing the engine and setting us on fire. The third one went through just beside the driver, and we got out of there.

"The Japs had set the mines to immobilize the tanks, and then they'd swarm aboard and try to blow you up with magnetic mines that would stick to the sides of the hull, except that by that time we'd put wooden sides on the tanks and the mines wouldn't stick. Also, our infantry was pretty good at keeping them off us. They liked us, you see, but sometimes they didn't like us because we attracted fire wherever we went."

They delivered fire, too, wherever they went. A sergeant named James Haddix, finding a cluster of Marines pinned down in a shell hole not far past the barrier wall, calmly stationed his tank right in front of them and went to work. The big-shouldered hull of the Sherman took everything that the machine-gunners could hand out, and for four hours, Haddix and his crew sheltered the riflemen and methodically smashed everything that threatened them with his turret cannon. Any Japanese who attempted to sneak up on the tank with a mine was killed by the infantrymen.

The Sherman was also the only battle ambulance that they had on the island, and CWO Robert Swackhamer, who was the tank maintenance officer on Iwo Jima, came up with a modification for the escape hatch. This is his explanation of the change, given in a taped interview.

"The escape hatch was right under the bow gunner, and if you pulled the lever, it just dropped right out of the hull. It wasn't attached to a hinge or anything. We begged, borrowed, and stole stock from the Seabees, used our own welders, and made hinges for them.

"It was a little tube welded to the hull and a bolt welded to the hatch. That way, we could drop the hatch only a couple of inches and then swing it out of the way. Once we had that hinge, we could roll right over a wounded Marine, haul him in, and run him back to the aid station. Some tanks came back with as many as six Marines stacked in them. I had one rifleman stick his head up through the hatch and ask, 'Say, where do you hide in here?'"

By the evening of the first day, the aid stations were doing more business than they had expected, and due to the accuracy of the Japanese gunners, many of their supplies were shot up and they were short of many things, including plasma. Corpsman Ray Crowder was there when the first wounded tankers came in and recognized one that he'd met on shipboard.

"It began to get dark, and the casualties began to come into the aid station fairly rapidly. I took down the names, ranks, diagnoses, and all the other necessary information, as well as I could without any light that would draw hostile fire. One of the casualties that came in was a guy that I'd met on the Dutch ship *Bloemvontein,* on the way from the States to Guam. He was in the 3rd Tank Battalion, but I'd not seen him since we left the ship. I will relate the details leading up to this incident as they were told to me later.

"Several tanks were in an assault on a position near Motoyama airfield number 2 during an attack. Three of them were knocked out by antitank guns as they tried to advance across an airstrip. Several of the tank men were wounded, but all of them escaped from the tanks except for two. This friend of mine was one of them. He had started to leave his tank, but a mortar shell landed nearby him, leaving him temporarily blinded due to sand and blood in his eyes. He decided to stay in his tank and wait for rescue.

"He didn't dare attempt another escape from the tank as he couldn't see where he was going, and the area was swept by fire anyway. He was also afraid that he might accidentally walk right into some Japs instead of Americans. He stayed in the tank all afternoon with his pistol loaded and ready to shoot. After dark, some of the men from "B" Company decided to go up to the knocked out tanks and get the Tommy guns, pistols, and ammunition from them. They didn't know that he was still inside until they opened the hatch and he threatened to shoot them. They had a bit of a difficult time convincing him that they were Americans and not Japanese speaking English.

"The other man that was trapped in the other tank had to be left there till the next day as his leg was crushed and pinned by metal, and the rescuers had to fight to clear the area around the tank so that an acetylene torch could be brought up to cut him loose.

"When the blinded man was brought into the aid station, he had his eyes bandaged, and we didn't bother to rebandage them, as we knew that there was nothing we could do here, and we were also short of bandages. As I was taking his clinical data, he recognized my voice. I hadn't recognized his name but he knew my voice. After I had asked him a couple of questions, he burst out, 'What's your name?'

" 'Crowder,' I said, continuing to write down his diagnosis. 'Then you are the corpsman I met on the Dutch ship going to Guam. I recognized your voice.' He was elated over meeting me and held my arm very firmly. I could see that the expression on his face had changed from a solemn expressionless mask to one that was happy and smiling. I talked with him for a few minutes and then explained that I had to to take care of the other men. Still he held on to my arm with a firm grip and would not let go. I finally persuaded him to let go by promising that I would try to get down to the hospital to see him. I knew that I probably couldn't, and never saw that young man again.

"That night seemed to be a terribly long one, but I suppose it was because I had quite a bit of trouble getting to sleep. I think that it was because I was seeing so many of my buddies coming back from the front lines wounded or shell-shocked, and I wanted to be up and helping them out. Mortar shells kept hitting around our position, and some of the shrapnel peppered around us. I kept thinking that I would never fall asleep, but after turning and twisting in my foxhole for some time, I fell into a deep exhausted sleep. One big mortar hit in our area and wounded several men, but I didn't even awaken for that impact." So ended the first day of the invasion of Iwo Jima.

Sleep would be hard to come by for 24 more grim days, the period that it took to finally capture the island from its fanatical defenders. Iwo Jima, it turned out, was considered to be part of Japan proper, and as far as General Kuribayashi and his men were concerned, the invasion of Japan had already begun. To quote from the official history of the 4th Marine Division:

"There was no cover from enemy fire. Japs deep in reinforced concrete pillboxes laid down interlocking bands of fire that cut whole companies to ribbons. Camouflage hid all the enemy installations. The high ground on every side was honeycombed with layer after layer of Jap emplacements, blockhouses, dugouts, and observation posts. Their observation was perfect. Whenever the Marines made a move, the Japs watched every step, and when the moment came, rockets, mortars, machine guns, and artillery—long ago zeroed in—would smother the area in a murderous blanket of fire. The counterbattery fire and preparatory barrages of Marine artillery and Naval gunfire were often ineffective, for the Japs would merely retire to a lower level or inner cave and wait until the storm had passed. Then they would emerge and blast the advancing Marines."

Many times, the only weapon that could dig the stubborn, crafty defenders out was a tank on the spot. The Japanese engineers had cleverly hidden cannons on rails behind camouflaged iron or concrete doors that couldn't be seen, even from very close up. Wilson McClendon remembers:

"We were working up north of Motoyama number 2, helping a battalion of infantry, just a platoon of five tanks, and out of the corner of my eye, I saw a flash up on this hillside and a movement as one of those guns—I think it was a six-inch—went back on its rails and the door closed. So I marked that spot in my mind, took the override control, and put my gunner on it. I told him to mark the setting of his elevation and traverse indicator so he could get back to it in a hurry. I told him to watch that location while I looked over the rest of the hill. It wasn't but a little while till I saw that damn door open and that cannon start coming out. 'Okay, Johnny,' I said, 'get him,' and he swung the gun back to that setting and fired a round of HE into that hole. There was this long rumbling explosion, and the gun came rolling and tumbling down the hillside. The door, the gun, and everything came down that hillside. Only tanks could do that. You had to be right there with a cannon.

"A lot of the time, though, we would use the flame-throwers mounted in the BOG position. We had these adaptors that let the assistant driver pull the Browning machine gun out of the ball socket and replace it with a normal man-pack flamethrower, and we always carried a few spare sets of napalm tanks, all charged up and ready to go. Later on, we had a flame gun as an extra co-ax that mounted where the telescope sight used to be."

While flamethrowers go back to WWI and were used by both sides, the Marine use of flame-throwing tanks began in late 1943, when the Army Chemical Ordnance people demonstrated a man-pack flame gun to the Marines on Goodenough Island in the western Pacific. The almost instantaneous reaction was to install the new infernal device in a light tank. The little M-3s and M-5s could not stand up to antitank weapons and their 37mm guns weren't much use against heavy bunkers, so they were a natural candidate for the conversion.

A battalion maintenance tech, named Ed Huckly, did the first conversion by making an adaptor out of an aircraft propeller hub and the bung from a 55-gallon drum, which would fit the flamethrower where the bow gun used to fit. Presto, instant flame tank, and now the little M-5s could reach far down into a bunker. If the occupants weren't burned alive, they were suffocated when the napalm or flame oil consumed their oxygen. Given the fanatical nature of the Japanese army and marines, the threat of a flame weapon was about the only thing that could bring about a voluntary surrender.

By the time of the Iwo Jima invasion, the flamethrower tank was a proven and valuable concept, and while there were now dedicated flame tanks, the conversion mount continued to be used, and as would be expected, a lot of jury-rigging was required. This got the tank repairmen out into combat with the line crews, as Robert Swackhamer recounts:

"This tank here," he said, showing a picture of a pretty well beat-up Sherman, "was under repair, when a sniper went to work on us. He was firing out of a little crevasse and couldn't see down to the hull, but if you got up to turret level, he'd pop off with one of those little 6.5mm Nambu machine guns, the one with the hopper feed. If we'd opened the turret hatch as we wanted to, he'd have been able to wiggle a few down in there. About that time a flamethrower tank came along, and we pointed out where we thought he was shooting from, and they gave it a good squirt and out came that machine gun.

"We were always out in the field repairing mine damage. There was one tank, for instance, that ran over an aerial torpedo warhead—that's about a ton of explosive—that'd been rigged as a mine, and the only way we could identify the driver was that there was a little patch of curly brown hair on the inside of the hatch, otherwise he was gone. One man survived the blast, though, and the driver of the tank behind this one eeled out of one of our trick belly hatches and dragged him back. He's alive and living in Michigan now."

The battle for Iwo Jima was long and hard, and there is a misconception that it ended with the raising of the flag on Mt. Suribachi. It did not. The famous flag-raising was the result of a determined assault on February 23, just four days after the initial assault, and there were still 20 more days of bloody hand-to-hand combat to go. Even in the flag raising on Suribachi, though, the tankers were represented. History recounts that the first flag was too small to be seen all over the island, so another was hastily provided—the battle ensign of LST 779, which had put the first of the tankers ashore to breach the seawall.

The battles continued unabated. Charlie-Dog Ridge, the amphitheater, Turkey Knob, all fell to the deadly tank-infantry teams, but it was not easy. Lieutenant Jim Lucas wrote:

"It takes courage to stay at the front on Iwo Jima. It takes something which we can't tag or classify to push ahead of those lines against an unseen enemy who has survived two months of shell and shock, who lives beneath the rocks of the island. An enemy capable of suddenly appearing on your flanks or even in your rear, and of disappearing back into his hole.

"It takes courage for officers to send their men ahead when many they've known since the division came into existence are already gone. It takes courage to crawl ahead 100 yards a day and get up next morning, count losses, and do it again. . . . But that's the only way it can be done."

The Japanese general wrote the following: "Above all else we shall dedicate ourselves and our entire strength to the defense of this island. We shall grasp bombs and charge the enemy tanks and destroy them. We shall infiltrate into the midst of the enemy and annihilate them. With every salvo, we shall without fail kill the enemy. Each man will make it his duty to kill 10 of the enemy before dying. Until we are destroyed to the last man, we shall harass the enemy by guerrilla tactics."

These are not the words of defeatists, on either side. Regardless of the wishes of the faithful, however, God seems to favor the side with the most firepower, and with the Imperial Fleet broken, there was no way that Japan could resupply that island. Worse yet, from their viewpoint, was the fact that from the moment the Marines landed, no longer could their radar locate the B-29s that were headed for their homeland, nor could patrol planes land for refueling while scouting for the American Fleet. The fighter squadrons that had been intercepting the bombers were gone, now basing out of Okinawa. By February 25, small American spotting planes were already using Motoyama number 1 airfield, and on March 4, the Marines could watch the first crippled B-29 land on Motoyama number 1 with pardonable pride. Robert Swackhamer was there.

"I'd been up north around number one airfield working on a crippled tank when I saw this big plane coming in over Suribachi. I didn't know they *made* airplanes that big. He came in with two fans running and two smoking, and I thought he'd never make it. He hit the ground and bounced and swung sideways and stirred up a huge pall of lava dust that we thought was going to catch up with him and smother his engines. I thought he'd never get it stopped, but he swung it sideways and shut her down. . . . Turned out that one of the crewmembers was a brother to one of our "A" Company tankers, name of Grapevine. . . . Lives in Wisconsin, I believe."

For the record, let it be graven in stone that the crippled bomber landed on fresh tank tracks, which had clawed that airfield out of Japanese hands and made it available to the Air Force. Within a few months, the Army Air Corps could announce that 1,449 Superfortresses and 15,938 crewmen had made emergency landings on Iwo Jima. The real estate had been worth the sacrifice.

By March 9, the situation had stabilized to the point where the chaplains thought it safe enough to hold religious services. Combat correspondent Robert Cooke described one service at the front.

"The Catholic altar was a pile of water cans, the Protestant, the radiator of a jeep, and the Jewish, a stack of ammo crates. The communion rail was a mound of black volcanic gravel . . . yet not in any of the world's great cathedrals or churches was there a more sincere reverence. Men ignored heavy shells overhead. The chaplain's words were interrupted by the roar of planes. Clouds of dust from tanks swept the area, but the chaplain's vestments, the altar cloth, and cross gleamed through the pall of the battlefield."

Forty years later, a few of the survivors of that horrendous struggle met in peace and healed old wounds. Their monument now stands on the shore of Iwo Jima. Inscribed in Japanese on the landward side and in English on the seaward side are these words:

REUNION OF HONOR

ON THE 40TH ANNIVERSARY OF THE BATTLE OF IWO JIMA, AMERICAN AND JAPANESE VETERANS MET AGAIN ON THESE SAME SANDS, THIS TIME IN PEACE AND FRIENDSHIP. WE COMMEMORATE OUR COMRADES, LIVING AND DEAD, WHO FOUGHT HERE WITH BRAVERY AND HONOR, AND WE PRAY TOGETHER THAT OUR SACRIFICES ON IWO JIMA WILL ALWAYS BE REMEMBERED AND NEVER REPEATED. FEBRUARY 19TH, 1985, 3RD, 4TH, 5TH ASSOCIATIONS, USMC AND THE ASSOCIATION OF IWO JIMA, JAPAN

The battle wasn't over until March 26, though, and there was a lot of fighting to be done while the big bombers landed for repairs and the long-range Mustang fighters escorted their silver brothers to the flaming cities of Imperial Japan. The new Japanese fighters could still base out of Okinawa, for a little while. History, in the form of the B-29, was closing in on Japan. The bomber that landed in front of Robert Swackhamer was probably a survivor of the first of the great fire-bombing raids that destroyed most of Japan's larger cities, long before the Hiroshima and Nagasaki bombs were dropped. One after another, the big cities and industrial centers were razed.

The Japanese atomic research center, however, had already been moved to Korea, which was now putting out almost half of the Japanese industrial production. That situation was going to have to be dealt with, one way or another, as was the invasion of the Emperor's home islands. First, however, we needed a large solid base island as close to Japan as possible. Okinawa was next . . . and just at this time, a submarine loaded with the fruits of German technical research was putting out to sea. Its cargo would seal the fate of two cities.

On March 26, the battle for Iwo Jima was finally over, and so, almost, was the war with Germany. The Axis, however, had one last dastardly bolt to launch. Professor Paul Harteck's low-temperature reactor had produced—something—that had to be stored in thick, heavy lead containers. On the same day the battle for Iwo Jima ended, one of Germany's few remaining big cargo submarines, the U-234, slid out to sea, under command of Captain Johann Fehler. "Dynamite" Fehler, although new to the U-boats, was an old Asia hand, having been demolition officer on the surface raider *Atlantis* under Captain Rogge. He knew eastern waters well, and was the obvious choice to deliver a cargo to hard-pressed Japan. Before Germany surrendered, *all* its atomic and other hi-tech research was to be bequeathed to Japan.

Fehler's big 2000-ton minelayer had been converted to a submersible cargo vessel, and foremost on its cargo list were 50 lead boxes, each one containing radioactive material destined for the Imperial navy. The total was supposed to have been 540 kilograms, or over one-half ton. One of Japan's military attachés, a Captain Tomonaga, who would make the trip with the material, carefully marked each one with the symbol U-235 and stowed it in one of the converted mine shafts. Research and calculation had shown that one didn't have to have a nuclear explosion to cause widespread death; simple irradiation of a city would do.

The radioactive material was to be mixed with fine sand and spread by a conventional explosive. A city could be caused to die slowly, by ghastly radiation poisoning.

Fehler was delayed by a collision, however, and finally set sail on May 5, 1945, after repairing his fuel tanks. On the other side of the world, on that same day, one of the big Japanese submarines released a load-carrying balloon that crossed the coast of Oregon and exploded far inland, on Gearhart Mountain, killing six people. The experiment worked. It proved conclusively that Japan could get a weapon through America's 1945 air defenses. They'd been testing those defenses for over a year with balloons, some of which were big enough to carry several hundred pounds of cargo.

Luck was with America and the Allies right then, because on May 8, the surrender of Germany was announced, and all German submarines were ordered to surface and reveal themselves. At that point in time, Captain Fehler and his boat, the U-234, were in the North Atlantic, heading south for the tip of Africa. Their voyage track would have taken them to the super secret German U-boat base at Panang, on the Malay peninsula. Instead, Fehler surrendered to a destroyer, the U.S.S. *Sutton*.

When the big U-boat docked at Portsmouth, New Hampshire, she was met by a collection of high-ranking military officers and scientists. What was in those lead containers is *still* an official secret, but the scientists took elaborate radiation precautions. The question that was obviously on the minds of the military men was, "If this one submarine made it, how many others have gotten through?" German technology and weapons had shown up in the Pacific already. If something as large as an 88mm cannon was killing tanks on Saipan as early as June 1944, what else was loose in Japanese hands? There was even a complete, disassembled Me 262 jet fighter in that submarine, along with thousands of pages of technical and scientific data. Suddenly the need to invade Japan and shut down those weapons factories had become most urgent.

With the docking and examination of the cargo of that

U-boat, the fates of Hiroshima and Nagasaki were sealed. One more time only would the tanks have to claw their way across coral and into danger, but the stakes had just gotten quite a bit higher.

Crowder story adapted from MCTA Newsletter, Vol. 4-92, November 1992–January 1993; Swackhamer and McClendon from taped interview with Zumbro; and Haddix excerpted from official history.

16

OKINAWA

April 1, 1945
South of Japan

Okinawa was going to be the biggest Pacific invasion so far, nearly as big, in terms of men, as the Normandy invasion. We had to have that island as a base for the next two operations—Olympic and Coronet—which were going to be the invasion of Japan proper. April 1, 1945, was known by several names. It is called April Fools' Day, and in that year, it was also Easter Sunday. On Okinawa, it was Love Day. Love being the letter of the phonetic alphabet chosen to designate this invasion, to keep it separate from other invasions.

The biggest difference from all the other battles, however, was that here the Japanese went mad, absolutely mad, as they have always considered this island to be theirs. Its populace and culture are much the same as the home islands. As far as the Imperial High Command were concerned, Operation Olympic had already started, and they put their own version of it into operation. Code named Ketsu-Go, it contained the operational instructions for the divine wind, the kamikazes. Ironically, some of their first victims were tankers.

The first target of a kamikaze strike was the U.S.S. *Hinsdale,* an attack transport. The second one was LST 884, which carried "I" Company of the 3/2 Marines and a complement of Amtracs and Amtanks. The airplane was a Zero fighter, and it went straight into the side of LST 884. The light wooden structure of the plane splattered, but the engine, still running and flaming went straight through the hull, setting off the fuel and ammunition stored in the tracked vehicles that were getting ready to launch, cooking and burning the tankers and infantrymen terribly. The worst shellacking the U.S. Navy had ever taken was starting. The kamikazes were essentially living, sentient cruise missiles, and they killed 39 ships and almost 4,000 sailors off the island of Okinawa.

The landings themselves went surprisingly well, due to the new Japanese tactic of letting their opponents get ashore and into the range of mortars and light artillery before opening up. The kamikazes killed more Americans than their soldiers did that first day. The lack of resistance was at first puzzling, but it was finally determined that their tactic was simply to hold our fleet in place by allowing men to get ashore so that they would have to be supported. Then the divine wind would blow their ships away. It almost worked.

The army Amtanks and Amtracs of the 776th and the 536th were here, from the Philippines, as were the 2nd Marines from Tarawa and Saipan. Ed Bale, who'd fought so gallantly in a tank named China Gal, now commanded a company of his own Shermans. But where was the enemy? The whole northern half of the island seemed to have been abandoned to the invaders as the men and tanks came ashore. There was a seawall, no more than five feet high behind many of the landing beaches, but naval gunfire had blown great holes in it. Some of the great 16-inch shells, however, had blown craters in the reef that were just big enough to trap a tank or Amtank if the driver wasn't wary enough.

EXCERPTS FROM THE COMBAT DIARY OF COMPANY "A" 6TH MARINE TANKS

2 APRIL 1945, LOVE PLUS ONE: At 1200 hours this company received orders to land on Beach Green One, but received no orders where to report on landing. All three LSTs beached at about one-half-hour intervals. In absence of orders, the company commander reported to the tank battalion HQ. We were told to bivouac at 7993 Yoke, where our tank dozer, having come ashore the day previous, was waiting.

LOVE PLUS TWO: The company less one platoon moved with the 29th Marines and set up a company perimeter at 8292 Xray and 8291 Dog. Remained in reserve and saw no action.

First platoon reinforced with two tanks from Charlie Company and a tank dozer from H&S company moved out at 0800 to Division reconnaissance company CP where a Major Walker was contacted. A patrol was organized and at 1230 moved along the coast to Naka-Domari. Then SE to reconnoiter Ishikawa. . . . Did not make it to the village, tanks returned at 1900 hours.

And so it went for 12 days, until the Americans found the Japanese who'd simply been lying doggo, waiting. While they were doing their recon homework, though, the tankers were busy armorizing the area. It was during this type of work that they began to make contact.

LOVE PLUS ELEVEN: A culvert was carried into the field on the back of one tank and placed in a stream-bed at 7674 Nan, while a blade tank from H&S company filled in over it. Then the tanks supported from stationary hull defiladed positions as the infantry advanced. At 1600 hours, three platoons with two command tanks moved out in a tank-infantry attack with George Company, 22nd Marines. They got to within 200 yards of a hill named Sugarloaf, before taking fire so heavy that the infantry had to withdraw, the tanks then pulled ahead and shielded the infantry from withering machine-gun fire. Then, firing into caves and at muzzle flashes, the tankers proceeded to sanitize the area. The wounded were loaded onto the tanks and a withdrawal was effected by 1915. The commander reported expending 652 main gun rounds and sealing many caves and destroying many automatic weapons, but no count could be made.

LOVE PLUS FOURTEEN: Working with 3rd Bn. 29th Marine Regiment. Providing overhead supporting fire into caves. Two ammo dumps in caves were destroyed in catastrophic explosions, all tanks serviceable in action. Tank retriever crew even got into the action, firing their bazooka into a tomb, killing 7 enemy and knocking out a MG. Opened two caves with camouflaged steel doors and destroyed several camouflaged pillboxes.

And so it went, in a steady grinding operation, one or two caves, 2 to 30 soldiers at a time, beating down a steady defense in depth that at one time reduced "A" Company to only four running tanks. Of course, with 10 or 12 tanks knocked out and dragged back to a safe area, that meant that there were a lot of crews, all mechanics, to work on them. The number of tanks in service could jump from 6 one day to 11 or 12 the next . . . and then back down to 4. The tank-dozers fought as well as excavated, and the tank retriever crews were in the thick of action, using their bazooka. The damage done by one tank company that usually had about half its strength knocked out and being worked on is impressive.

This list is from their diary at the end of June 22, 1945.

Enemy killed, 616, captured, none.
Enemy equipment destroyed.
  12 heavy machine guns
  4 ammunition dumps
  6-47mm guns
  1-105mm gun
  1-77mm gun
  45 knee mortars
  1-90mm mortar
  2 DP guns
  9-20mm guns
  5 searchlights
  1-60mm mortar
  6 fuel dumps
  3 QM dumps, 1-6" gun
  18 assorted light automatic weapons
  2 caves with steel doors
  2 caves containing ammo dumps
Our own loses were 3 KIA, 3 DOW, 44 WIA, none
missing

Captain Philip C. Morrell, CO, Co. "A," 6th Tank Bn., 6th Marine Division, April 30, 1945, in the field, Okinawa Shima. (Author's note: Capt. Morrell is now retired as Colonel Morrell and is the current president of the Marine Corps Tanker's Association, which has graciously provided many of the stories included in this volume.)

The 6th Marines and their tanks had a steady grind, after coming ashore, but the 7th Regiment ran into the Japanese main force and had to get really creative in order to get their infantry across ground that was being swept by a leaden broom of death.

June 11, 1945, 1st Marine Tank Bn.
Col. Arthur J. "Jeb" Stuart, Commanding

As the 7th Marine Regiment hammered its way down the length of Okinawa, they ran into an obstacle composed of the Kunishi Ridge, north of the town of Kunishi, and Japanese General Mitsuru Ushijima's veteran 24th Division. The ridge was a coral honeycomb of antitank weapons, bunkers, pillboxes, minefields, caves, and reverse slope defenses. The fanatical suicide-prone defenders and the general's "no quarter" policy had slowed the 7th Marines almost to a stop, and their CO, Col. Snedecker, had come up with a solution, which would quickly involve the tankers.

Since daylight attacks across open ground were decimating the regiment, Snedecker eventually decided on a night attack to take the high ground after probing the Japanese defenses and being bloodily repulsed. Even 47 years later, he hasn't forgotten the look of that land. "The unobstructed fields of fire, concealment, and observation were all in their favor. In essence, the enemy was literally looking down our throats," Colonel Snedeker said in a recent interview.

Shortly after noon on June 11, strong infantry patrols from the 1st and 2nd Battalions of the 7th Marines moved out with tank support from "C" Company, 1st Marines, under First Lieutenant George Jerue, to probe the enemy defenses. After two hours of tough going, the Japanese defenses stopped the 7th Marines roughly halfway to the objective. At 1447 hours, the heavy casualties forced Col. Snedecker to order the withdrawal of the patrol to regroup. It was soon apparent that a daylight attack across this open ground was a costly affair.

According to Col. Snedecker, the critical situation demanded unusual measures. Consequently, after completing a personal commander's reconnaissance of the Kunishi Ridge, he ordered a night attack to seize it under the cover of darkness. At 0225, June 12, two rifle companies—C/1/7 under Capt. Rohr and F/2/7 under First Lt. Huff—crossed the valley quickly and quietly. They climbed the ridge and boldly seized a 300-yard section of its topographic crest. "C" and "F" Companies' night assault caught the enemy by complete surprise, and they started digging in immediately. They knew what would be coming in the morning.

The original plan called for the rest of their battalions, the 1st and 2nd of the 7th Regiment, to quickly reinforce the two companies the next morning, but at first light, the enemy discovered the Marines in their midst and launched a violent counterattack on what Snedecker called a "ridge-head." Since they still controlled the adjacent sections of the ridge, the enemy still had the advantage. Their fields of fire and other defenses were still intact, and just as on the day before, could make any unarmored assault too costly to succeed. The rest of 1/7, under LTC Gormley, tried three times to cross the open ground to join their comrades on Kunishi Ridge . . . to no avail.

The situation in 2/7 Battalion, under LTC Berger, was no better. Up on the ridge, mounting casualties among Huff and Rohr's troops precipitated calls to battalion HQ for help, water, ammunition, and medical support. Grazing bands of Japanese machine-gun fire cut through the smoke and haze, causing more casualties or immobilizing the infantry in a prone position. Tanks went into open fields shepherding the stretcher bearers carrying the wounded to the rear. The tanks carefully moved above the wounded men, pulling them up through the escape hatch to safety. The tank commanders made full use of the recently installed 2-inch smoke mortars mounted in the turrets and fired from the inside. These little mortars firing smoke bombs, coupled with WP smoke from the 75mm cannons, helped conceal the litter bearers from hostile eyes. During this part of the action, several "C" Company tanks were temporarily immobilized by direct hits from Japanese large-caliber artillery coming from Yuza Dake Ridge to their southeast.

Col. Snedecker and his battalion commanders, Berger

and Gormley, soon realized that drastic measures were in order to relieve the pressure on Kunishi Ridge, and turned to the tankers for solutions. They got them. Tank company commander Jerry Jerue got with his platoon leaders, Charley Nelson, Jerry Atkinson, and Tom Duddleston, and their TCs. Several of the tank commanders devised a plan to employ tanks in a ferry system to haul the infantry up to the crest. Col. Snedecker and "Jeb" Stuart quickly approved this unorthodox idea because it was late in the day, and there was no time to waste.

This tank force consisted of nine 75mm gun tanks and a dozer tank. Six of "C" Company's tanks were earmarked as troop/supply carriers for the operation, and another three were tasked to cover the movement forward to Kunishi Ridge.

In order to maximize the number of troops that could be carried, the crews of the tanks were reduced from the normal five to the irreducible minimum, the driver and the TC; this left room for six fully equipped infantrymen in the hull and turret areas. That would be: one in the bow gunner's seat, one squatting behind him, one in the gunner's seat, and three standing where the loader usually operated. In order to get them out, the tank would have to face the enemy, open the escape hatch, and ease the Marines out, one by one.

What made all this possible was a tanker's modification developed on Iwo Jima by CWO Robert Swackhamer, who ran the maintenance operation there. The normal operation of the escape hatch was for that 100-pound piece of metal to drop completely out of the hull when its catch was released. Swackhamer had devised a new mount that allowed the hatch to drop only a few inches and then pivot out of the way, still attached to the tank. After some experimentation, this became standard on many Marine tanks.

Using the doubtful concealment of Tera village, 1,000 yards north of the ridge, the tanks were lashed all-round with supplies, water cans, ammo, wire, and medical supplies, including blood plasma. Then the tankers literally stuffed the six Marines into their hulls for the run forward. The first ferry trip to Kunishi was slow and dangerous. The column used the same narrow track that Huff's and Rohr's commands had used earlier that morning. The tank dozer carefully led the way, using the blade to widen and strengthen the road shoulders . . . under constant harassing fire from the defenders.

The gun tanks covering the movement kept shooting at the weapons emplacements on the northern slopes of Kunishi, which were shooting at the armored convoy. A suicide team tossed two satchel charges at the dozer tank at the base of the ridge. Fortunately, they missed their mark and the convoy continued on. The tanks stopped in a road cut near the top of Kunishi, and the infantry quickly crawled out, via the bottom escape hatches. Then wounded Marines were gently slid in through those same hatches, and the tanks headed back for the village of Tera.

Depending on the gravity of their wounds, as many as six men could be evacuated inside the hot cramped hulls; those whose wounds prevented them from crawling into the tank were placed on top of the engine compartment behind the scant cover afforded by the gun turret. These Marines were strapped in place and protected by sandbags. Sadly, several men were hit again on the return trip. It had taken over one hour to make the first round trip, but subsequent runs were accomplished in as little as 45 minutes, depending on enemy fire.

On the second trip, Dr. Eddie Hagen, USNR (MC), sent a doctor and several medical corpsmen to succor the seriously wounded up on the ridge. Before nightfall, "C" Company 1st Tank Bn., had carried all the critical supplies, plus nine tank loads in three runs for a total of 54 men, equivalent to a reinforced rifle platoon, across the fire-beaten valley to the top of the ridge. The wild idea had been an instant success and was soon copied by the 1st Marine Regiment to get to the top of the eastern end of Kunishi Ridge, carried by tanks. An excerpt from "Jeb" Stuart's report tells the story:

"During the seven-day Kunishi Ridge battle, June 10–18,

1945, the 1st Tank Battalion provided large-scale medical evacuation and ferried reinforcements to Kunishi Ridge. In daylight hours, most vehicle traffic from Kunishi south to rear areas was denied, except for tanks. For example, on June 16, tanks carried 160 troops to and from the ridge. In other words, Marine tankers ensured the success of infantry attacks and rendered Kunishi Ridge tenable."

For the 7th Regiment, the fighting was much like the battle they had fought for the Dakeshi and Wana Ridges the month before, but without the tank ferry service. Kunishi was far from cleared of the dug-in enemy, and the open cane fields were dangerous to cross. Tanks continued to evacuate the wounded. The Marines in the more inaccessible parts of the ridge were supplied by airdrop on a daily basis, once most of the antiaircraft guns had been taken out by tank-supported infantry. No further advance was possible until the combined-arms team had completed their task.

Flame tanks of "B" Company, 713th U.S. Army Tank Bn., covered by the USMC gun tanks working in pairs, "processed," the area, clearing it of the enemy. Col. "Jeb" Stuart of the Marine Tank Battalion, who coined the term, "processing the objective by fire," likened this method to a corkscrew, forcing the enemy into submission and pulling him out of the caves. Finally, the job was done, and the regiment could proceed on to the next ridge, named Mezado, and start all over again.

The official statistics reflect the critical contribution made by tanks in this seven-day battle for Kunishi Ridge.

The final totals: reinforcing troops with equipment carried forward to the ridge . . . 550.

Wounded evacuated from Kunishi . . . 600, including some nonwounded observers, etc.

Supplies, plasma, ammo, rations, barbed wire, water, commo wire and telephones . . . 90 tons (est.).

The foregoing is adapted from an unpublished planned manuscript: Tank Operations During the Battle for Okinawa, *by Walter Moore.*

* * *

On June 22, the senior Imperial officer on Okinawa, Lieutenant General Ushijima, committed hara-kiri, and the Americans took his stronghold and raised Old Glory. The battle for Okinawa was officially over. That, however, did not mean that the fighting stopped. All the Japanese, obviously, had not received the word or preferred to run their own war, stealing food from the natives or the Americans and living the bandit life. The Americans, who were in the process of getting ready for the invasion of Japan proper, were forced to run "antitermite patrols."

They set up more permanent camps of tent cities and homemade shacks, went scrounging for necessities, and in the process they kept running patrols and killing die-hard Nipponese holdouts. The Amtrac and Amtank crews especially were used as dismounted patrols because of their experience on Leyte. Since almost every vehicle had a man or two who could be dismounted without stripping too many men out of the vehicle, they'd learned to be as good as infantry as they were tankers. This now began to pay dividends. The men of the 536th, particularly, were singled out by the local G.I. newspaper, the *Gunto Graphic*, and called the "Post Campaign Commandos."

Sergeant Goacher, who'd fought on Leyte, said, "We went out twice a day, once in the morning to make sure the Japs had not collected during the night, and once in the evening, to make sure they had not collected during the day." Another sergeant said, "It didn't make any difference when we went out because we always ran into them." The patrols usually consisted of five to eight men armed with a collection of weapons. One patrol went out in the morning to find the Japanese who had set off a trip flare at their spring, and found and killed 13.

On July 12, Sgt. Lynn "Buster" Bullen, of Mason, Michigan, led a patrol on what they all thought would be a routine mission in hilly country near Nakagusuku Castle. Tec.5 "Mousy" Hammond was out on point when he saw two or maybe three holdouts and came back to tell Bullen, who took another man up and shot one Japanese who was hiding in the tall grass at the edge of a field. The patrol then reformed and began to work their way around a huge boulder that was about 8 feet high and 20 feet across. Moving as quietly as woodsmen, which many of them were, they came upon nine more hostiles and killed six of them immediately.

"We were above the Japanese," Bullen explained, "and had them pinned in the rocks. To get out, they had to expose themselves." Then they opened up with knee mortars, light machine-gun fire, and small arms, some of it American made, as they pilfered weapons off our dead. By now the patrol had used up all their grenades, and using their walkie-talkie radio, they called back for reinforcements.

First Lieutenant Anthony Bogards and eight more soldiers rushed to the contact point with more ammunition and grenades. They soon overwhelmed the Japanese firepower with automatic weapons and grenades, including incendiaries. One soldier's pants were set afire, and he took off running but was put out by several bullets. It was, as one soldier said, "Just tough luck." In this case, those two or three Japanese reported by Hammond had turned out to be thirty, including six officers, who could be identified by their swords. It was estimated that only six escaped.

Corporal Clarence Palmbus remembers when he got shot. "We thought we had cleaned them out and went forward to inspect the area. I was standing on a little hill. All of a sudden, I saw this Jap, who I thought was dead, raise a pistol and point it toward me. He had to turn slightly; I shot and he shot. I was wounded in the rib-cage area, and he was killed. The fellows called for the stretcher team and took me to the hospital. Two days later they gave me the pistol that the man shot me with."

As the Japanese soldiers on Okinawa demilitarized and turned to banditry, there were a lot of tough times for them. "Hand Grenade" Grenead and Mousy Hammond were on a patrol and walked up on a group of sleeping Japanese. An officer woke up and saw that they were completely surrounded with no chance whatever but went for his pistol anyway and got shot down before he could draw. As Grenead remarked, "There wasn't much battle to that."

In another instance a patrol snuck up on a group who were eating, right out in daylight, and surprised them. They instantly dropped their rice bowls and went for weapons—they all died. Sgt. Bullen, on patrol, surprised one who was hanging out his laundry and called on him to surrender. As automatic as clockwork, the Japanese went for his gun and just as automatically, died. "He never should have done that," Bullen said later.

All during this time, as they were patroling, the men were working on their Tracs—repairing, rebuilding, and over-hauling. They now knew the name of their next operation. It was to be called Olympic, and it was the invasion of the southern main island of Japan. As originally planned, Operations Olympic and Coronet would have used about half the U.S. Army, most of the Air Force and *all* of the Marine Corps.

The invasion forces would have had to fight over twenty million armed Japanese on their home ground, and American losses alone were calculated to be over one million. The campaign was figured to last until 1948, at least, with no guarantee of complete success even then. Worse, the Russians would have been in on the northern invasion, after taking all of Korea. That would have left Japan as divided as Germany was.

This was not a good situation, especially as, even with their cities in flames, the militarists had refused requests to surrender and just stop causing deaths. On August 6, 1945, the first atomic bomb was dropped; on August 9, the second. Even then, Emperor Hirohito had to override the militarists and order his military forces to lay down their arms. When the U.S.S. *Missouri* entered Tokyo Bay, Prince Takamatsu had to personally restrain a kamikaze unit from crashing her number one turret. He ordered them to remove their propellers. If any man deserves a peace medal for his actions, Prince Takamatsu does, for a kamikaze strike on the *Missouri* would have triggered an almost unstoppable chain of events.

It was later revealed that the Japanese had slightly over 5,000 planes slated for kamikaze duty, with willing pilots in training; the bloodbath would have been the worst in human history. Japan would probably have been wiped from history for a while, and the hatred would never have been erased. As it turned out, Harry Truman on September 2 could issue a proclamation.

". . . As President of the United States of America, I proclaim this day, 2 September 1945, to be V-J Day . . . a day of victory over Japan. We shall not forget Pearl Harbor, and the Japanese militarists can never forget the battleship *Missouri.* . . . Japan's power to destroy and kill has been taken from them."

When the victorious Allies began investigating the scientific progress inside Japan and Germany, they found things that would curl the hair on a billiard ball. In northern France, they found missile-launching silos that were designed for something much larger than a V-2—complete with long-range guidance radars that could see past Britain.

At the V-2 factory at Nordhausen, Col. Jack Welborn rode a brand-new M-26 tank through the gate of the underground works and found a magician's cave. When that installation was investigated, it revealed V-2s with cargo bays designed into them. At Erfurt, about 43 miles from Nordhausen, one of Prof. Harteck's "Uranbrunners," or uranium burners, had been installed in the basement of a schoolhouse, using slave labor. The Germans could easily have thrown either radioactive contaminants or nerve gas, of which they had 15,000 tons, into Britain.

In both Japan and Germany, research into a microwave shooter or death ray was being pursued with feverish intensity. Japan, however, sheltered the real kicker. Their atomic research was vaguely known, but they possessed no intercontinental aircraft equivalent to the B-29. Or did they? In Tokyo Bay, there were two freshly commissioned super subs that were as large as our modern attack submarines. They were I-400 (Lt. Commander Nambu) and I-401 (Commander Kusaka) of 6,500 tons displacement each. With a range of 30,000 miles, each of them carried three airplanes that could be catapult-launched and could carry a

1,760-pound bomb load for 750 miles at 300 mph. In addition, they could carry manned torpedoes. Those manned torps, or Kaitens, could move a 2,000-pound warhead for several miles, enough to get far inside any harbor in the world.

Strangely enough, these two were fully fueled and crewed. And this was at a time when even their giant battleship, *Yamato,* had been sent out against the American fleet off Okinawa on a one-way suicide mission, undermanned and with not enough fuel for a return trip. What was so important that those two subs, less than a year old each, were given top priority for crews and fuel? Possibly the radioactive cargo of the U-234? Or was it something much worse, a real atomic bomb?

In Korea, the Russians, who were rapidly coming down the peninsula, ran into Japanese who refused to surrender and who fought fanatically for two months, trying to buy time for the scientists and technicians inside the great works at Konan. What were they protecting? As things turned out, those scientists had everything needed for an atomic weapon. Everything except enough time.

Probably no one will ever know just how close to a viable atomic bomb Professor Nishina's technicians were, but Russia exploded her first atomic bomb years before they should have been able to . . . and suddenly started throwing her weight around—more than usual, that is. If Harry Truman hadn't ordered those two bombs to be dropped, the ground assault on fortress Japan would have taken until late 1948 before the last fanatic warrior was driven up the steps of the sacred shrine that sits in the middle of Tokyo.

If that had happened, the first two cities to go under the atomic bomb might have been San Francisco and Seattle, instead of Hiroshima and Nagasaki, and the name of World War II would have been . . . Armageddon.

We needed those Pacific islands from which to base the bombers, and we couldn't have evicted the invaders from them without the tanks. Nor could we have driven across the countries of Europe and breached Hitler's "Festung

Europa" without the armored divisions. For all its admitted flaws, the Sherman tank was one of the most important political tools of all time. But by 1950, it was getting a bit long in the tooth. It was time for a new tank, and that one, like the Sherman before it, would have to get its debugging in battle . . . on a little peninsula named Korea.

17

TASK FORCE SMITH AND THE PUSAN BREAKOUT

Korea, June 25, 1950

At 0400, on a rainy Sunday morning, June 25, 1950, with neither warning nor provocation, 100,000 well-armed, highly motivated North Korean troops with tanks and MiGs crashed across the 38th parallel into the southern half of their nation, carrying all before them. How did this happen, and why? How had we gotten this lax, to let a little half-nation almost throw us off the peninsula?

The roots of this debacle go back to August 1945, when the Russians came howling down the peninsula in search of the Japanese nuclear research plant at Konan. It had been decided that the Americans approaching from the south would disarm the Japanese as they worked their way north and that the Russians would do the same as they came south. The decision to use the 38th parallel of latitude was a purely arbitrary one, and the Russians were probably quite happy that the line was set so far south of their new item of booty—the research/industrial centers at Konan and Hungnam, which depended on the electrical power supply at Chosin Reservoir. Those centers had been producing, among other things, uranium and heavy water.

The border was supposed to be a purely administrative one, but the Russians, as usual, needed secrecy for their nefarious undertakings and slammed down the first "Bamboo Curtain." They desperately needed time to work on that Japanese nuclear works at Konan (Hungnam). They tore up all the north–south railroad tracks, blocked all the roads, and put patrols of armed guards across the countryside. They cut families, districts, even the whole nation in two. There were supposed to have been elections to allow the people of Korea to choose their own government, and in the south, Syngman Rhee was elected. In the north, the elections were a sham, and a Russian-trained, Chinese-backed despot named Kim Il Sung was installed in the city of Pyongyang.

Seemingly, that was that. In 1947, however, Russia exploded its first A-bomb, years ahead of predictions, and from then on had the confidence to act as a superpower. At that point in time, the aggressions of 1950 were assured. In 1949, as agreed, the superpowers withdrew from the Korean peninsula. The Americans left behind what could euphemistically be called a police army of some 65,000 ill-trained troops with leftover weapons, some Japanese, some American, all old. They had neither tanks nor aircraft, and about 100 heavy guns.

The Russians, on the other hand, had bequeathed to their northern puppets a well-trained, handsomely equipped tool for aggression. The NKPA, or North Korean People's Army, had heavy assault artillery, battalions of T-34 tanks, and about 200 combat planes. It was 135,000 strong and had been inculcated with the belief that the *south* had been the one to close the border and that their life's mission was to reunite their shattered nation. When the U.S. presence in the south had been reduced to about 500 advisors, the plum was ready to be picked.

Worse yet, America itself, as after every other war in history, was happily shutting down its gigantic military establishment and going about the business of peace and wealth. With the Marshall Plan putting shattered Europe back together, we had put the Orient on the back burner. At that time in history, we did not even have a single intact, functioning *company* of tanks. The Shermans had all been turned in to Rock Island Arsenal, the M-26 Pershings were going up on pedestals as monuments, and Ordnance at Abderdeen and other places was busily engineering the new main battle tank, the M-47, or Patton tank. Just about then, Douglas MacArthur, who was in the process of reinventing Japan, woke up one dismal morning with a small war in his backyard.

By the fourth day of the invasion, the southern capital, Seoul, had fallen, and the Korean army was in full retreat, along with its American advisors. They were all homing in on the southern port city of Pusan. On June 30, at Camp Wood, Japan, LTC Charles Smith, commanding officer of an understrength infantry battalion of the 34th Infantry Regiment, part of the 24th Division, had just collapsed into bed after a grueling period on alert duty. Suddenly he was shaken awake by his wife, who told him that his immediate superior, Col. Stephens, was on the phone and wanted to talk with him, *now*. Putting the receiver to his ear, he heard his regimental commander snap:

"The lid has blown off! Get on your clothes and report to the regimental CP!" Smith looked down at his watch. He'd had just an hour and a half of sleep and was being sent off to war.

A Sergeant Meninger of that battalion remembers: "When the invasion came, of course, everyone was interested but it never occurred to us that Americans serving in Japan would ever get involved. For me, it was a typical Sunday night in Japan. I was at home with my family. It had rained all day. My wife was giving the kids a bath, prior to putting them to bed, and I was reading a book and nursing a drink when the call came for me to report to headquarters. My wife wanted to know what the call was about. 'Something must be wrong with next week's schedule,' I answered. 'I'll be back as soon as I can.'" Eleven months later, he was. What would go into the history books as Task Force Smith (TF Smith) was on its way to its rendezvous with destiny.

Because of budgetary cuts, all the units in Japan were at two-thirds strength, and Smith's CO, Col. Stephens, had to strip officers and men out of his other battalions to at least try to get Smith's battalion up to strength. By 0300 on July 1, the TF was on its way to an airfield where the only six C-54 aircraft in Japan were waiting to take them to Korea. General Dean, the commander of the 24th Division, had short, succinct orders for Smith.

"When you get to Pusan, head for Taejon. We want to stop the North Koreans as far from Pusan as we can. Block the main road as far north as possible. Contact Brigadier General John Church. If you can't locate him, go to Taejon and beyond if you can. Sorry I can't give you more information. That's all I have. Good luck to you, and God bless you and your men." Smith had just 440 men with him at that point in time. By 0845, July 1, the first plane was airborne.

Because of the foggy conditions over the Korean airstrip at Pusan, the landing of even these few was spread out over the whole day. Fortunately, the Korean Military Advisory Group, KMAG, had laid on transportation, about a hundred assorted vehicles that ranged from military trucks to civilian buses. All along the route from the airport to the railroad station, they were greeted by ecstatically happy Koreans waving flags and cheering. A Lieutenant Philip Day remembered it this way:

"The city wasn't very big in those days. We got all our gear and climbed onto the flatcars. As we waited to pull out, a train from up north came in. It was covered with human beings—troops, officers, old men, women, children, and, most important, at least to me, wounded. *My God*, I thought, *maybe there was a real war going on.* Hysteria and panic traveled with this train. I heard a gunshot. Someone learned that a South Korean army officer had committed suicide; we were told his family had been captured in Seoul. We didn't have time to think much about that because it was then that our train moved out of the station."

This was not exactly the best organized war this nation has ever fought. The next morning, the men of TF Smith got a frightening demonstration of the destructiveness of air power. A South Korean ammunition train had pulled into the station at P'yong t'aek, and Australian aircraft from God only knows where strafed it, demolishing the train, station, and a large portion of the town. That afternoon, a South Korean truck column was strafed, and ROK rifle fire forced the plane down. The KMAG captured one very embarrassed American pilot.

TF Smith stayed the night at P'yong t'aek and then moved on to Ansong, where they met up with their artillery. It was the Fourth of July, 1950, and the task force was now moving into their first blocking position. The official history proclaims that all went well and smoothly, but Lt. Day remembers otherwise.

"We moved at night, arriving around 0300. Everyone was tired. Then it began to drizzle—a cold wet penetrating drizzle. The men began digging foxholes on the hill east of the highway. Guys went down to bring up ammunition, and because of the conditions, the hill became muddy and slippery. Time went by. It was raining now. Everyone was tired, wet, cold—and a little pissed off. The feeling was, why not wait for daylight to do all this climbing and digging."

Eventually, they got into a position about one mile long, straddling the main road through Ansong. Their only anti-tank defenses were two 75mm recoilless rifles, one 105mm howitzer with six rounds of antitank ammo, and a few WWII-vintage bazookas with doubtful ammunition. And the tanks were coming, Lt. Day recalls.

"'Hey, look over there, Lieutenant,' Sgt. Chambers yelled. 'Can you believe it?' Looking down, I made out a column of tanks. Seems like there were eight of them. I couldn't believe my eyes. 'What are those?' I asked, and Chambers answered. 'Those are T-34 tanks, sir, and I don't think they are going to be very friendly toward us.' The company commander was called, and everybody got real excited about them. The day was beginning in earnest."

Lt. Day was with one of the recoilless rifle teams that took the tanks under fire. "We picked up the gun and moved it to where we could get a clean shot. I don't know if we were poorly trained or just not thinking, but we set up the gun on the forward slope of the hill, and when it fired, the back blast blew a hole in the hill, which instantly covered us in mud and dirt.

"The effect wasn't nearly as bad on us as it was on the gun, which had to be cleaned before it would fire again. When we had it clean, we moved the gun to a better position and began banging away. I swear we had some hits, but the tanks never slowed down. . . . More of the tanks began shooting at us. . . . I don't know what happened to the other two guys with me, but one blast knocked me and the gun over backward. I began bleeding from my ears. I wasn't unconscious, just stunned."

Then they tried the bazookas, the old 2.36-inch models that had been outdated since WWII. A Lieutenant Ollie Conner took one of the weapons to close range, crawling down a slope and into a ditch that led him to the rear of one of the T-34s, where the armor was supposed to be the thinnest. He fired at a range of about 15 yards, and the little rocket just burned itself out against the tough Russian steel. Again and again he tried, firing some 22 rounds against the tanks. Some of the rockets were so old they failed to explode at all. By 0900 more than 30 tanks had rumbled through TF Smith, which was impotent against them. Sgt. Chambers then tried to get some artillery fire with tragicomic results. The first tank through had cut the wire to the 105mm artillery battery, so Chambers tried a sound-powered field phone to get some 60mm mortar fire on the tanks. The answer came back.

"They won't reach that far."

"Well, how about the 81mm mortars?"

"They didn't come over with us."

"How about the 4.2s?"

"The 4.2s can't fire yet."

"How about the artillery?"

"No communications."

"What about the Air Force?"

"They don't know where we are."

"Call the Navy."

"They can't reach this far."

"Well, then send me a camera, I want to take a picture of this."

Then the tanks were in among the guns of the artillery battery, one of which, stationed alongside the road, had just six rounds of antitank HEAT ammo. It damaged two tanks, which pulled off the road to allow their running mates through. One of them began to burn, and its crew abandoned it. Two were captured but a third began firing a burp gun into a machine-gun position, killing the first American of that war.

The six rounds of HEAT were soon expended, and the hapless cannoneers switched to regular HE shells, which only knocked the tanks around, not stopping them at all. TF Smith had no tanks of its own and was getting a real mauling. The next wave of tanks panicked the already-shaken men, and they fled the guns, which were then manned by NCOs with the officers handling the shells for them. Eventually, Lieutenant Perry, who'd been wounded, shot in the right leg, talked the men into coming back to the guns, but without HEAT ammo, they only managed to knock out four tanks out of 33, and slightly damage three more. The tanks moved on, and the task force could only dig in and wait for the next onslaught.

Slowly, painfully, TF Smith leapfrogged its way back through Ansong, then back down the road, 80 miles, back to Pusan, where they were compressed into the infamous "Pusan Perimeter," while reinforcements were rushed in from Japan and the States. But, where *were* the American tanks?

The U.S. Army, short on funds as always after winning a war, was in the process of designing a new tank, the M-47, and had just one tank battalion more or less ready. The 70th Tank Battalion at Ft. Knox, Kentucky, was a demonstration outfit that had two companies of old Shermans from WWII and was supposed to be getting a heavy company of M-26s, also dating from the last war. Suddenly, the battalion commander, LTC William Rogers, got orders to be ready to move to Korea within 96 hours. The 70th was told that they were the best prepared tank unit in the army at that time.

Panic calls went out across the country for tank parts and engines that dated back to the end of World War II. Col. Rogers remembers it this way: "It was nothing more than a paper outfit, consisting of about two hundred men. We did not have a single item of equipment. . . . Nothing! The most urgent matter was to *find* the tanks for our companies. We took Pershings (M-26s) off the concrete pedestals where they'd been serving as monuments and used them to equip one company. We drew Shermans from the Rock Island Arsenal. Meanwhile, they were sending me tankers from all over. Nobody knew anybody else." They were, however, tankers, and by working day and night, the deadline was met.

At San Francisco, the 70th was loaded on board the transport, U.S.S. *General Brewster,* and shipped to Korea. By August 14, the tanks were committed to battle in the Taegu sector of the Pusan Perimeter. Author T. R. Fehrenbach, in his book, *This Kind of War,* tells it best: "When the armor growled and roared up to the Naktong, front line troops ran forward to meet them, many of them openly sobbing in relief. They crowded around the ugly steel monsters, and patted them as if they were blooded horses." By dint of heroism that shall always be remembered, the defenders of the Pusan Perimeter had kept a port open and bought the time . . . and the heavies were here.

On July 10, the first elements of the 78th Tank Battalion had entered the war, but they had proved to be no match for the T-34. Listed as a "heavy" battalion, the 78th was nonetheless equipped with the little 15-ton M-24, which the 85mm gun of a T-34 could pierce with frightening ease. Worse, the 75mm gun of the little tank, named after General Adna Chaffee, couldn't break the frontal armor of the bigger Russian vehicle. There would have to be more heavies brought in, and quickly—Shermans, Pershings, and some hasty improvisations that were designated as an M-46; they carried a new, experimental turret on the hull of the old M-26.

In Japan, yet another tank battalion was coming to life, made up totally from scratch out of WWII veteran Shermans that had been rebuilt by the Japanese. In fact, the support of the Korean War was the single biggest contributing factor in the restarting of Japan's heavy industry. In July and August of 1950, the Tokyo Ordnance Depot managed to get *8000* various wheeled and tracked vehicles refitted, even as tankers were being found all around the Army and recalled from civilian life.

Equipped with revamped, so-called Easy Eight Shermans (M-4A3E8), the 8072nd provisional Medium Tank Battalion bootstrapped itself into existence and went off to war. The first element of the unit into action was its "A" Company, which reached Pusan on the last day of July and was in action less than a day later. Three days later, the unit, now designated the 89th Medium Tank Battalion, was complete and part of a growing fleet of American armor. They would be heard from again. By the third week in August, there were about 500 assorted armored vehicles in the Pusan Perimeter, and Gen. MacArthur was planning his amphibious landing at Inchon. Something had to give.

Adapted by the author from Military *magazine, Vol. VII #1, July 1990; Vol. VII #2, July 1990; and Vol. IX #12, May 1993. Used with permission of the editors.*

PUSAN BREAKOUT
TASK FORCE LYNCH
KOREA, September 26, 1950

What was now known as the U.S. 8th Army had filled the Pusan Perimeter to overflowing, and it was time to go on the offensive. General MacArthur had created the X Corps out of the 1st Marine Division and the 7th Infantry Division, and sent it ashore at Inchon in one of his brilliant but risky counterstrokes. One officer is quoted as saying that if the Japanese had been holding that beach, we never would have taken it that easily—if at all. After the invasion force was ashore and out of danger, MacArthur directed the 8th Army to launch an offensive to link up with X Corps. What happened was the wildest ride the old 7th Cavalry had been on since George Armstrong Custer led the regiment into the valley of the Little Bighorn.

The 3rd Battalion, 7th Cavalry, which was part of the 1st Cavalry Division, would lead the breakout, and their objective was to be the village of Osan, nearly 102 miles away. Nobody'd ever attempted an armored raid of that distance before. Commanding the raid was LTC James H. Lynch, CO of the 3rd Bn., 7th Cav. TF LYNCH would have the backup of 2nd and 3rd Platoons of "C" Company, 70th Medium Tank Battalion. Backing them would be TF WITHERSPOON, named for its CO and comprising another battalion of the 7th and the regimental HQ under Col. William A. Harris. They moved out at 1130 hours with the scout platoon in the lead, followed by Lt. Robert Baker and his three-tank platoon of Shermans. Following the point was an engineer unit, three companies of infantry in trucks, and a battery of artillery. Bringing up the rear was the other platoon of tanks, just in case.

For miles, the only reaction to their audacious march was the cheering of liberated South Koreans. Through Taegu and Sangju they rolled—with no opposition whatsoever. At Chongju, a larger town, Lynch got cautious and put the tankers in the lead, replacing the unarmored scout jeeps. Lt. Baker found the two deserted, except for a few old women and, with the jeeps back in the lead, TF LYNCH rolled off again. So far, it was turning out to be a joyride . . . until they ran out of fuel.

A gasoline-burning Sherman can only make about 100 miles (on level ground) before it needs another 175-gallon fill-up. The TF had come just over 64 miles over hilly roads at high speed, and it was time to top them off for the rest of the run—at night. To Col. Lynch's great dismay, he found that, somehow, the refuelling truck for the tanks hadn't come along. They were trapped in enemy country with their tank force about to run out of fuel. LTC Lynch and Col.

Harris boldly decided that, considering the absence of organized enemy resistance, they could run the risk of running with their headlights on.

When Lieutenant Baker got word of this, he was already distracted by the thirst of his tanks and was working his way down the line of trucks, scrounging all the five-gallon cans that he could find. Naturally, there was a tendency for the trucks to bunch up while this was going on, and just as naturally, Colonel Harris caught Baker at it and chewed him out right and proper.

The lieutenant continued to collect gas cans for his tanks until one of the recon troops came running back in the growing dark, screaming that a North Korean tank was coming their way. The tankers were getting set for battle when the "tank" turned out to be only three NKPA trucks. The North Korean drivers panicked, bailed out of their vehicles, and left on foot. After they'd quit vibrating, the scouts and tankers plundered through the trucks and discovered that they were ex–South Korean trucks, full of gas cans! There were enough to refuel Baker's platoon, and the three tanks of the trailing platoon as well. Mentally thanking the enemy for their generosity, the TF moved out at about 2000 hours, headlights blazing into the moonlit night.

Coming out of the side roads and onto the main highway to Osan at the village of Chonan, the TF swung north to link up with X Corps. The enemy should be showing up about now, Lynch felt, and gave Baker permission to engage, if necessary. Entering Chonan from the south, tanks in the lead, Baker found it full of hostiles who didn't seem to recognize the different type of tanks and were reassured by the bright headlights. Since the streets didn't match up with his map, Baker simply stopped by a lone NKPA soldier and asked, "Osan?" The soldier automatically pointed out the right road and then, recognizing the Americans, took off in panic. Baker cut him down with machine-gun fire, and the ruse was over.

Leaving the village behind, Baker's three tanks tore into the enemy, liberally basting them with MG and cannon fire. Baker caught a full company of NKPA, and chewed them up while his other two tanks used their tracks as weapons to conserve ammunition. They simply ground up the northern invaders with their tracks, all the while heading for Osan as fast as possible. The three tanks were now completely out of Chonan, but Baker had suddenly lost radio contact with LTC Lynch. He'd lost physical contact as well, outrunning the main body of the TF. Suddenly, with Baker out of sight, Lynch found himself in an unarmored jeep, leading his main body of troops personally into "Indian Country."

Ten miles south of Osan, Lynch could hear sporadic firing and decided to go tactical again. He ordered the headlights turned off. Baker, unfortunately, didn't get the word and roared into Osan at full speed. Just north of the village, Baker stopped his three marauding Shermans as he'd spotted tank tracks in the dirt. They weren't American. More cautiously now, they moved forward, taking small-arms fire intermixed with some antitank rounds. Then, with the headlights still on, they recognized the distinctive chevron-shaped treadmarks of an M-26! Suddenly an antitank round of unknown origin exploded on the turret of the last tank, killing the TC instantly. Then a white phosphorous grenade exploded, illuminating all three tanks in its smoky white glare. An American voice came out of the dark beside Baker's tank.

"What the hell are you doing here?"

"I'm from the 1st Cavalry," Baker yelled back, and jumped from his tank to shake hands with a lieutenant from the 31st Infantry Regiment, which had come ashore at Inchon. That was at 2226 hours on the 26th of September, 116 air miles from their starting point and 196 miles by road. It was the longest single advance by an American unit through enemy country in any war. Then things began to come unstuck.

About half an hour behind Baker, LTC Lynch was bypassing a T-34 that sat by the side of the road with its gun tube pointed forlornly off to one side and looking knocked out. Suddenly its 85mm cannon belched fire and its machine guns opened up, raking the column of unarmored trucks. Then another tank opened fire from a hidden position off the road! Lynch and his passengers quickly abandoned the jeep for some cover in a ditch alongside the road!

At this time the North Koreans started their engines but did not move, and this was their fatal error. The U.S. had developed another bazooka, the 3.5-inch model that could kill a T-35, and Lynch's S-2, or intelligence officer, quickly ran forward, gathered up an infantry platoon, and had them bring their bazooka back to attack the tanks. Now the TF headquarters unit was itself engaged in combat, instead of directing other units from a safe area. One of the T-34s was destroyed by a single 3.5-inch HEAT rocket, and the other, suddenly frightened, lurched onto the road, running over two jeeps and several trucks before wandering off into a rice paddy where it got stuck. It was immobilized by a hail of 57mm and 75mm recoilless rifle fire.

Then a Sergeant William Hopkins ran up to the tank, whose crew had vanished, and threw several grenades into it. They went off, but the engine kept running, so an infantry company commander, Lt. William Woodside, jumped up on the tank and poured part of a five-gallon can of gasoline into the engine compartment. The engine still ran so the regimental S-3, Captain James Webel, also jumped on the tank, took the can from Woodside and dumped the whole five gallons into the engine compartment. A huge explosion blew Captain Webel far into the air and dropped him 30 feet from the now fiercely burning tank. Luckily, he suffered only minor cuts and burns on his hands and face.

At 0012 hours, on the 27th, Col. Harris was able to reach 1st Cavalry Division on his long-range radio and inform them that TF LYNCH was in a firefight. At that time he wasn't overly worried, but just an hour later he radioed that he was being held up eight miles south of his objective, which Baker had already reached. His message was "Send tanks forward immediately, we cannot disengage."

After the first two T-34s had been dispatched, more tanks rattle-clanked down the road . . . from the north. Somehow, Baker's tank detachment and the recon squad had bypassed a strong NKPA tank and infantry force, or more probably simply alerted them by their swift passage. Lynch, now in personal combat, ordered his driver to get in the nearest truck and block the road with it. This the driver did, and the two T-34s stopped, and the commander of the lead vehicle yelled out in Korean, "What the hell goes on here?"

He was answered by a hail of small-arms and recoilless-rifle fire that set the truck on fire and made the tankers button up. Now the fat was in the fire as *eight* more T-34s rumbled up simultaneously with the arrival of the second platoon of three Shermans, which had bulled their way up from the rear of the column. There were now just too many T-34s, and the two opposing tank units began to slug it out at point-blank range. Nearly simultaneously, one T-34 and two Shermans were hit. The lead American tank fired a HVAP (hypervelocity armor-piercing) round and penetrated a T-34 beside its gun mantelet, killing the turret crew. Then it was knocked out by another T-34. With the Shermans now helpless, one T-34 pulled out from their formation and began to savage the American column. Once again, jeeps and trucks were crushed as the tank growled its way through the column. A Captain Robert McBride, thinking that the tank was a "friendly" gone rogue, jumped out in the road and tried to yell at it to stop. A burst of fire creased his rear end and disabused him of that idea, sending him scurrying into a ditch. Sgt. Hopkins again tried his grenade attack, but was killed this time.

As the tank neared the artillery unit, the battery commander, Captain Theodore Wardlow, unlimbered one of his 105mm howitzers and with a few of his men, manhandled it into firing position astride the road. Two men jumped on the trails to ride the spades in, and the impromptu gun crew fired several rounds at the armored marauder, finally blowing the turret off of it when it was only 30 yards away from them. The North Koreans had made one fatal mistake, however; they'd gone out without their infantry into the middle of a night full of American hunting teams. One after another, the T-34s were hunted down and killed by 3.5-inch rocket-launcher teams. Seven were killed that night, and three escaped northward. That seemed to have broken the resistance of the NKPA that night, as when Lynch dismounted his infantry for an assault on Osan at 0700, only slight resistance was met.

"C" Company, 70th Tank Battalion destroyed four more T-34s on September 28, and Air Force planes spotted two more in the open and killed them while the infantry mopped up scattered pockets of resistance. The ride of Task Force LYNCH and the 7th U.S. Cavalry was over, and the chase was on, all the way to the Yalu River. Ol' George woulda been proud of them.

18

KOREAN TANK TALES

1950–51

When asked to describe a typical tank battle, most people would automatically think of Desert Storm or, if historically minded, of the great desert battles of WWII. The mind immediately conjures up pictures of massed formations dueling at long-range across North Africa or Europe. In Korea, however, there was no such thing as a typical tank battle. The patterns simply did not follow what had been taught at Fort Knox. After the landings at Inchon on September 16, 1950, ROK soldiers and American troops crossed the 38th parallel into North Korea and took the war to the enemy.

The 70th Tank Battalion, part of the 1st Cavalry Division was, as usual, right out in front and in the thick of the fighting. Resistance was fierce, as the North Koreans were now on their own home grounds. On October 13, "B" Company of the 70th was supporting a cavalry unit when it ran into a company of North Korean tanks supported by infantry a bit north of the city of Kaesong, on the road to Kumchon. On the outskirts of the little village, the lead platoon of "B" Company was leading the assault when a group of four T-34 tanks rolled out of the town and opened up on them. The 85mm Russian guns had little effect on the heavy M-26s, but the American 90s were deadly.

Two of the T-34s were spectacularly destroyed by the first two shots, at less than 100 yards. The 90mm HVAP rounds penetrated and blew their turrets clean off. The third tank burned when hit, and the fourth was abandoned by its crew after taking a hit on the front slope. That platoon was out of the tank business. Later on in the day, two more T-34s were destroyed at no loss to the Americans, but at dusk the NKPA counterattacked. The "B" Company commander had placed three tanks astride the road north out of Kumchon as part of his night defensive position, when four more T-34s rumbled out of the mist. Considering that a Russian-pattern tank company has only ten combat vehicles, that would have been the last armor that the North Korean commander had available.

The TC of the center M-26, Sgt. Marshall Drewry, saw the first enemy tank when it was only 50 yards away and screamed at his gunner to fire. Instantly the heavy tank bucked to the recoil of the 90, and an HE was on the way. By a fluke, the shell struck the T-34 directly on the gun tube, splintering it. The North Korean tank was now helpless and disarmed. Instead of panicking and abandoning the vehicle, the crew charged the American tank and rammed it, bow to bow, trying to overturn the heavier vehicle. The American tank had been sitting on night watch with its engine off, and now the 500-hp Russian diesel was turning the clawing tracks, trying desperately to overturn the heavier American tank. The muzzle of the T-34's cannon looked like a banana peel, and dirt, rocks, and sparks flew from under its treads.

The gun tubes now overlapped. Sgt. Drewry's hand on the commander's gun handle couldn't bring his gun to bear. All he could do was to club the enemy gun like a medieval knight with a lance. Even the two tanks on his flank couldn't fire without killing Drewry, who was fighting with his head and shoulders out of the turret. A hit on the enemy tank would have killed him as well; the turrets were only eight feet apart. Suddenly, Drewry's driver, who'd gotten the engine started, slammed the tank into reverse and backed up just enough to clear the gun muzzle. At a range of three feet, Drewry's gunner fired, putting a hypervelocity round into the T-34, setting it on fire.

Two more T-34s were now in the fray, and the tank on Drewry's right side killed first one, then the next; and a fourth spun in its tracks and fled the scene in obvious panic. Other than a bent fender, Sgt. Drewry's tank had sustained no damage. Just another typical tank battle in the Korean war.

Adapted by author from the January–February 1993 issue of Armor Magazine. *Used with permission.*

At this point in time, a unit advancing up the steep, rocky, sparsely populated east coast of Korea uncovered what might have been the communist's reason for starting that war.

An article in *The New York Times,* October 26, 1950, page three, reads as follows. The dateline is Hungnam, Korea.

NORTH KOREAN PLANT
HELD URANIUM WORKS

A vital Russian research-supply project, believed by United States atomic energy experts to have been a Soviet uranium processing plant, has been captured by the South Korean Army near this northern east coast port. Authoritative sources in Washington said the Atomic Energy Commission had known about the plant for a long time. They indicated it would not surprise them if a second plant like it were to be found in North Korea.

The huge factory was strongly fenced in and guarded by electric barriers. An American military advisor to the South Koreans and a United Press correspondent saw a building constructed along the lines of a Kansas City grain elevator. Behind it was a compound 100 yards long, 50 yards wide, and crowded with a great concentration of high voltage wiring which apparently powered two huge machines that seemed to be the center of the intricate set-up. Sandbags had been piled around the machines and apparently they had been unhurt by United States raids.

There is a similar article in *Newsweek* magazine for November 6, 1950, and that is just the tip of the iceberg. The Japanese name for Hungnam, is Konan, where the old Japanese atomic research plant was captured by the Russians. After the capture of that installation, Russian atomic research took a great leap forward, and they set their bomb off years ahead of predictions. As late as 1947, the year the Russians detonated their own nuclear bomb, refugees from North Korea had reported that both Japanese and German scientists were working there, and that one Japanese in particular, a Professor Tamura, regularly visited the installation from Japan.

It is also very significant that not too long after the capture of that plant, the Chinese launched their most furious assault yet, forcing the American evacuation of the whole area, including the infamous retreat from the "Frozen Chosin" Reservoir. The last vehicle out of there, by the way, was a USMC tank, firing canister over its back deck.

CHONGJU, KOREA, October 29, 1950
Company "D," 89th Tank Battalion
Tank Vs. Tank

Pyongyang had been taken, and the North Korean government driven from power. The war appeared to be over, but there was an ominous stiffening of enemy activity. The drive to the Yalu river had not yet been completed, and a UN task force was headed north on just that mission. The force was built around the British 27th Commonwealth Brigade, which consisted of the following units: a battalion each from the Royal Australian Regiment; the Argyle and Sutherland Regiment; and the Middlesex Regiment. Since these units had been rushed to Korea without their support units, the U.S. Army had attached American engineers, artillery, and the 89th Medium Tank Battalion. This was the unit that had been assembled out of spare parts in Japan three months earlier, equipped with leftover WWII Shermans and sent into battle untrained. They'd obviously not taken long to get their act together.

The tank company was in the lead on that day, with "D" Company of the 89th being the lead element. Lt. Francis Nordstrom's platoon of Shermans was second in line. Overhead, a liaison airplane, piloted by Lt. James Dickson orbited, searching the terrain ahead for signs of trouble. Dickson had already stopped the column several times that morning, while fighter planes made runs against enemy tanks. About noon, as the head of the column neared the top of a high hill, Dickson again halted them, warning of enemy tanks dug in and camouflaged on either side of a narrow pass that they'd have to use, through a low hill in the distance, which was part of the next ridgeline.

The fighters were busy supporting another battalion at the time, when Dickson spotted yet another hidden tank. He radioed the tankers to use their own guns as artillery and take the T-34 under fire. The enemy tank was dug in on the reverse, or far side, of the next ridge, and with the pilot spotting hits for them, the Shermans of Nordstrom's platoon began to send shells over the hill. The tankers didn't really expect to hit anything, but after only ten shells, heavy black smoke began to belch out of one of the positions, and Dickson called off the fire mission. Meanwhile, the two battalion commanders involved, the Australian, and LTC Welborn C. Dolvin, commander of the 89th, had come to a conclusion. Attack.

Since Nordstrom liked the point position where he could open the action and control it, the two commanders agreed to let his platoon take over the lead. He moved out quickly, with no infantrymen riding his hulls. The other two platoons, led by Lieutenants Cook and Van Der Leest, would each take aboard some of the Australian infantry and move out to the flanks of Nordstrom's five tanks. This covering force amounted to 13 tanks and 2 small companies of infantry.

The point where the enemy tanks were dug in was two miles distant and surrounded by strips of rice paddies. It was approachable only by a winding dirt road, and there was no way through the paddies around it. The only way possible was to punch straight through. The plan was for Nordstrom to move out at high speed, with Cook's and Van Der Leest's small forces following at 500-yard intervals. Each supporting platoon would, about a thousand yards short of the pass, discharge its infantry and then support their attack by gunfire . . . at least that was the plan.

Nordstrom in the lead tank was about a hundred yards from the opening of the narrow cut in the hill when he saw enemy activity: North Korean soldiers climbing the hill in a hurry. He ordered his bow gunner to open up on them, as he'd also spotted a machine-gun position. Dropping down in the turret to his own sight, he took these under fire with his 76mm cannon, blowing the crew away and also blowing some of the camouflage off a concealed T-34, which immediately fired an 85mm cannon slug at him, the round passing between Nordstrom's head and his hatch cover. "Gunner, AP, Tank!" Nordstrom yelled, and the gunner put three quick shells into the hostile tank at less than a hundred yards distance. As the third shell hit home, there was a huge explosion, diesel fuel began to burn, and ammunition began to cook off.

Nordstrom, only 70 yards from the cut, chose not to enter it as there would surely be someone set to shoot straight down into his hatches, which would have to be open to give him some visibility. With his other five tanks lined up behind him at some angle to the hill, he ordered them to probe the hillside with fire. One tank's shells tore the camouflage from another enemy tank, and Nordstrom's gunner, firing by reflex, killed that one with two shots. The second round blew the T-34's turret 50 feet into the air.

By then the other two platoons had closed up, and the Australians had dismounted and were attacking on foot. Lt. Cook's tank platoon had found firm going, and had been able to follow their infantrymen into battle, digging out MG nests and bunkers for them. At the rear of the column, Lt. Van Der Leest hadn't been able to find firm ground so he'd had to stick to the original plan, and send his infantry on while he stayed back and supported them with his guns.

Nordstrom continued to probe by shooting, until his gun jammed. Then the cannon of the tank behind him jammed, and an enemy shell came toward him from the left front, the southern half of the hill. Frantically, Nordstrom and his turret crew worked on their gun while the platoon sergeant, MSgt. Jasper Lee, covered them with his gun, firing at likely places of concealment on the hillside.

Suddenly the jammed shell came free and was heaved out of the loader's hatch. Nordstrom then began a methodical hammering of that battered slope, shooting at all places that looked like they could hide a T-34; at his sixth shot in that series, there was a terrific flash and an explosion that set fire to nearby trees and bushes. Then a cannon shell came howling across the top of Nordstrom's turret, passing between the .50 mg and the radio antenna and slamming into one of Lt. Van Der Leest's tanks and injuring four of the Australians, who were still aboard it. Immediately, Nordstrom and his tankers began to fire into the area from which the shell had come. Because of the smoke, it was impossible to detect the exact location of the hidden gun. Another green tracer came out of the smoke, and then the enemy fire stopped. By now the American tankers were having to conserve ammunition, and suddenly the hill became eerily silent, as if each side were taking stock of the situation.

Lt. Van Der Leest took this time to dismount and run to

the tank in his platoon that had been hit. Placing a pencil in the groove in the turret that the impact had made, he sighted along it, picked up a place on the hill, and passed the information along to Nordstrom by radio. The location was from the right side of the road, and Nordstrom had three tanks of his platoon begin probing the top of the ridge with their 76mm guns. With his own tank, for lack of a better target, he put a few hopeful shells into the area from which the first shell had come.

Sure enough, the third round resulted in another explosion and fuel fire. At this time enemy action began to taper off, and the Australians reported that all their objectives had been taken. When the smoke cleared from the road cut, there was an additional armored vehicle, a self-propelled gun that had not been there when the action started.

Apparently, its crew had been left to guard the western end of the pass and had become impatient with the lack of targets and come through the cut to join the fray, using the smoke from the burning tanks as a screen. After being almost killed twice that day, only Nordstrom's battle instinct saved him that third time as yet another cannon's cross hairs settled on his turret. And the enemy wasn't done yet.

The British commander of the expedition ordered the force to form a defensive perimeter for the night, and they set up with a platoon of tanks and a company of infantry on each side of the road. At 2100 hours the NKPA launched an infantry attack that seemed to be directed at the tanks more than the Australian infantry. There were so many North Koreans in among Nordstrom's platoon that the tankers had to turn on their headlights to see them and shoot the enemy off each other's hulls. Eventually it came down to pistols and grenades among the tracks, but finally it was over, and at dawn, 30 NKPA bodies were found around the tanks.

Adapted from the book Combat Actions in Korea, *by Gugeler. U.S. Army Military History.*

RIVER CROSSING OPERATION
THE HAN RIVER KOREA, 1951
Company "A," 89th Tank Battalion

On March 7, 1951, the crews of Company "A," 89th Tank Bn., crawled out of their sleeping bags. Wet heavy snowflakes dropped from a dismal sky onto muddy fields and still warm hulls of the tanks where they melted into an icy slush. The company had been bivouacked in what was left of the village of Kwirin-ni, and the tanks were parked around the perimeter of the village, each next to a battered house. They were arranged in march order so that they could simply pull out in line, ready for the day's mission, which promised to be a bit challenging. They were to cross an unsounded river in support of an infantry assault against the Chinese.

The drivers went off to their various vehicles to start engines and let the big Ford V-8 tank engines warm up while they ate breakfast. Those V-8s, designated the GAA, were five times larger than the current Ford car engine—500 horsepower and 1100 cubic inches in displacement, and they were thirsty. They would, however, run in water up to the turret, as long as the driver kept the hammer down to avoid flooding—and that feature would be tested today. Each of the first eight tanks was pulling a trailer with five plywood assault boats nested on it, and the day's operation was to support the infantry by gunfire while they paddled the boats across the Han River to assault a dug-in Chinese unit.

Company "A" was temporarily attached to the 3rd Battalion, 35th Infantry Regiment of the 25th Division, and, since the infantry unit was larger and in command of the operation, orders came from their HQ. The engineers estimated the Han River to be seven to eight feet deep at that time of year and, accordingly, no plans had been made to get the tanks across the river until a pontoon bridge had been built, later in the day. The 89th's own CO, LTC Welborn C. Dolvin, however, wasn't sure about that. It is never safe, in any situation, to tell a tanker where he can't go. He may damage something, but he'll get there.

After reconnoitering both by air and ground, putting himself in considerable personal danger, LTC Dolvin spotted the abutments of a destroyed bridge, going from the north bank of the river to a sandbar in the middle of the river, north of its junction with the Pukhan River. Possibly, just possibly, something could be arranged that would prevent a lot of unnecessary infantry deaths. Dolvin was just unsure enough of the idea that he didn't issue an order to "A" Company commander, Capt. Herbert Brannon. He did, however, make a VERY strong suggestion that Brannon investigate the terrain and the river.

Brannon went to the engineers for more information, but couldn't get more than Dolvin had given him, because the Chinese kept the river covered by machine-gun fire both day and night. After more personal reconnaissance on foot and considerable analysis of maps and aerial photographs, Brannon decided to risk one tank, with suitable precautions. His plan was to send one tank and the tank retriever, which had a long recovery cable and a powered winch, out ahead of the company. The tank would try the crossing, attached to the retriever and, if it swamped, the retriever could pull it back out . . . theoretically. Lieutenant Thomas Allie, leader of Brannon's Third Platoon, volunteered to make the attempt.

By 0430 hours on the 7th, the snow had stopped and the tanks were on the road, their big Ford engines rumbling steadily. In order to keep as quiet as possible, the column moved slowly. At the time, it was still too dark for the drivers to see more than the dim outlines of the muddy track that served as a road. Each tank carried, in addition to the 70-odd rounds of cannon ammunition stowed in its hull, 52 rounds stacked in fiber canisters on the back decks. According to plan, they would fire this off as a preparatory barrage to aid in "prepping" the objective.

TANK ACES

At 0555, four battalions of American howitzers of 18 guns each, a battalion of 155 howitzers, 18 guns, and a regiment of British guns commenced firing on the target area. They'd previously registered on the targets in earlier days so their rounds fell on known targets. At the same time, Captain Brannon's tanks opened up in direct fire against the hazy hills, shooting at the shell flashes of the artillery and at any secondary explosions that occurred. It was still too dark to make out distinct targets.

By now the infantry had arrived and unloaded their assault boats from the trailers that the tanks had dropped off at the river's edge. Since the seats and paddles for all five boats are stored in the top boat of the stack, there was a bit of clattering, bitching confusion, as usual, but the assault got off in good order. They crossed several hundred yards below the sandbar that the tankers would be using, later in the morning. The Chinese, however, hadn't been entirely squelched by the intense bombardment. They were beginning to lob artillery and mortar fire onto the south bank of the Han, and machine-gun fire was punching holes in the assault boats.

LTC James Lee, the infantry battalion commander, and Captain Brannon watched the crossing from the battalion's OP, or observation post. Lee was more than a little skeptical of the tanker's project, but knew that even a few tanks on the other side would save lives and hasten the assault. At 0740, when informed that his infantry were across and receiving heavy small-arms and mortar fire, he told Brannon, "You can try the crossing, if you wish." Brannon relayed the okay to Allie, who, leading the retriever, was already approaching the river.

Allie led the two vehicles to the river's edge, where they stopped momentarily to attach the tow cable to Allie's tank. The tow pintle of a tank is a circular clamp that can take much more strain than a normal trailer ball; it is, in fact, about as strong as the fifth wheel of a small semitractor. At 0800, Allie's driver took the tank into the water even with the downstream end of the sandy island. At that point, the water was only about a yard deep, but the driver and the bow gunner were buttoned up, and directions were coming from Lt. Allie, who was standing erect in the TC hatch, talking to the driver over the intercom system. At that point in time, the only limiting factor was the speed at which the winch cable could be payed out of the winch.

Suddenly, the winch caught, almost stopping the tank, whose driver simply applied the full 500 hp, pulling the attached tank retriever toward the river! Then the tow pintle snapped out of the Sherman's hull, leaving a six-inch hole through which the Han river proceeded to rush, threatening to swamp the laboring engine. Relieved to be free to move, the driver, Sgt. Guillory Johnson speeded up and heaved the tank up onto the south bank of the island. Originally, Lt. Allie had intended to proceed straight across, but spotting the footings of the old war-damaged bridge, decided to try crossing there. Running up the length of the island, he ordered Johnson to enter the water downstream of the old earthen mounds.

Straight down into seven feet of water, over the driver's hatch the heavy Sherman plunged. Now water was not only rushing in through the pintle hole, it was coming in past the gaskets of the driver's and bow gunner's hatches, up past the escape hatch in the belly and through the turret race. Johnson, an experienced driver, knew that he had only one chance to keep going. Keep the tank in low gear and floorboard the accelerator to avoid the engine getting flooded through its exhausts. At each of the three old earthen footings, the tank climbed almost out of the water and then plunged back to almost turret deep. Nonetheless, after only two hair-raising minutes of this, Allie's tank found itself high and dry on the north bank.

Wanting to have only one tank in the water at a time, Allie radioed back to his platoon sergeant, Sfc. Starling Harmon, who followed and soon was on the far bank beside his commander. The third tank, somewhat overeager, rushed into the water, only to have its unsecured belly hatch jar out and flood the hull with water, drowning the big V-8. One at a time, the other tanks of the platoon were across and soon were put to work . . . and they were needed.

The infantry had managed to make only a thousand yards of progress before becoming stalled at a road that cut across the triangular piece of land that was formed by the juncture of the two rivers. They'd gotten pinned down by enemy fire that seemed to be coming from a railroad embankment and a small hill about 600 yards west of them. Allie, now that he had a running mate to cover him, moved out while his other two tanks were still making the crossing and tore into the enemy. The first thing they did was to put HE shells from their 76mm guns into every observable enemy position on that hill.

When fire from the hill stopped, they swung their guns to the railroad embankment. There were half a dozen freight cars on the tracks, burned and shot up by an air strike, but still affording concealment and cover to three ChiCom heavy machine guns. Both tanks opened up and after several thousand machine gun bullets and 15 cannon rounds, that menace also was silenced. The infantry immediately broke cover and trotted forward, gaining 600 yards in only minutes.

Allie and Harmon ranged ahead of the infantry, spotting more enemy positions. As the infantry came over the railroad embankment, three more ChiCom machine guns opened up on them, only to be silenced by Allie and his whole platoon, as his other two tanks had now arrived. MSgt. Curtis Harrel spotted one more gun and silenced it. Then for about a half hour, the tanks raked the enemy positions with their coaxial machine guns, covering the infantry, who advanced yet another 700 yards, reaching their objective with only minimal casualties. By midafternoon, the whole of "A" Company, including the tank that had flooded out, were across the river. Once again, the tanks had served as forcible entry tools, saving American lives and speeding victory.

Adapted from the book Combat Actions in Korea, *by Gugeler.*

THE TURKEY SHOOT
KOREA, Spring, 1952
Staff Sergeant Chris Sarno, USMC

It was mid-March of 1952 and Able Company, 1st Tank Bn., 1st Marine Division, finally settled into a rear area somewhere south of the MLR (main line of resistance), on the eastern front in North Korea. We had been on the line since December 15, 1951. We were cruddy, mean, and tired, but now looked forward to being in reserve while the 1st Korean Marine Corps Regiment took up our positions atop the mountains we secured in the "Punch Bowl" sector of the MLR.

Able Company of the 1st Tank Battalion consisted of 20 M-46 Patton series tanks and a complement of 100 combat Marines, who were now about to indulge in the sybaritic pleasures of hot showers, hot chow—and maybe even a night movie. We were bivouacked on the slope of a small knoll, mired in calf-deep mud. The frigid Korean winter was slowly, reluctantly, releasing its grip on its victims.

I remember I had to take three showers to convince myself that I was finally clean. The shower unit was set up in a small tributary of the Soyang-Gang River, operated by South Korean service laborers.

Scuttlebutt had it that the entire 1st Tank Bn. was going to rally here in this region of low hilltops. Sure enough, in a couple of days our buddies in Baker, Charlie, and Dog Companies all rumbled into the tank park. It was the first time the battalion was all together since it had shoved off for the Inchon invasion some 19 months ago. It was an awesome spectacle of armed might. We'd been here only four days when the word came down that the 1st Marine Division was being reassigned to the western front for the defense against a suspected push by the Chinese Communist 65th and 63rd field armies. We were directed to take up positions 40 miles south of Seoul in relief of the 1st ROK Division. The problem was how to get there.

At present, this muddy sloppy base was 50 miles inland on the eastern coast, and it was 140 road miles to Seoul, so what to do? "That's easy," said Captain Raphael, our very capable skipper, "we go east to meet up with 'Daddy' "—the United States Navy. There'll be a tiny fishing hamlet called Soko-Ri.

Precisely at 0500 on March 27, 1952, the entire tank battalion hit the magneto and starter switches and, with Able Company on the point, shoved off for little Soko-Ri, all 105 tanks. (Due to its organization and mission back then, a Marine tank battalion was exactly double the size of an Army battalion.) It was a marvelous and forceful sight to view tanks all lined up to the far distant skyline, all winding their way down those narrow dirt roads. If all of you out there never saw USMC combat-loaded tanks, let me tell you what we looked like.

Each tank had all kinds of gear and souvenirs lashed to their turrets and hulls. There were helmets, Russian and old Jap rifles, C-ration boxes and bags of rice, tarpaulins and cammo nets, air recognition panels, ammo boxes galore, and 55-gallon fuel drums (full of gasoline). A band of gypsies would have had nothing on us, as this cutthroat band of Marines headed east, right into a raging snowstorm that hit us at 2200 hours in a narrow mountain pass.

Fortunately, Captain Raphael had told me to get some shut-eye before departure because Division projected that it would take us 24 hours of nonstop driving before reaching the beach at 1700 the next day. Sgt. Chris Sarno relieved the driver Lionel Durk at a maintenance stop. The storm was still howling, and those snowflakes seemed as big as baseballs hitting my goggles. We were snaking our tedious way down through Everson-Arrow-Mountain-type terrain. The eastern front area of operations on the Korean peninsula was similar to the back of an alligator, mountain after mountain.

Needless to say, I was wide-eyed awake and alert traversing these snow-clogged mountain passes. One slip and it was a *long* way down to the valley floor on most of this road march.

All I could think of was *I have to keep tank A-41 on the road, and I have to get my crew there safely.* Around 0600, Sgt. Bartz up in the turret said over the intercom. "What's that strange smell?" I yelled back, "It's salt air, you idiot, we made it! That's the ocean at Soko-Ri!"

Quickly, a small Army MP unit proudly escorted us a couple of miles to the rendezvous point, and the Army couldn't do enough for us. They gaped at us like we were from another world. Inwardly, I was bursting with pride at all this Army adulation. We all were shaking hands and back slapping with these soldiers. I recall one smiling soldier yelling over and over again, "It's the Marines, they saved my butt at the Yalu and here they are again."

"You're damn right, Army," the Jarheads yelled back.

With the sun coming up fast, the beach area was packed like a giant sardine can with 105 tanks side by side. It was another eye-filling sight to see the Navy steaming bigger and bigger over the horizon. Seven LSTs, two destroyers, and a cruiser would be our chauffeurs on the five-day cruise around the boot of Korea.

Marines always loved to see the Navy for we knew that we would have clean dungarees, hot damn good chow, showers, and a *DRY* sack to crap out on. While on board, we held 24-hour watch on the tank deck (20 tanks per ship, bull-dogged down by the sailors), pulled maintenance, and cleaned our weapons and ammo every day. We knew what lay ahead of us on the MLR north of Seoul, and the time was running out.

We stormed ashore at battered Inchon, said our goodbyes to the Navy, and saluted them. I can still look back in my mind's eye and envision looking back at the ships and the sea when a submarine surfaced with its speakers blaring a farewell and to "go get them." How about that, even a submarine for added security on that little cruise. We surely loved "Daddy."

In the middle of a starless black night we went roaring through devastated Seoul. It was the biggest city in Korea, and it had been overrun four times so far. Up past the railhead at Munsan-Ni, over the Freedom Gate Bridge we went. Then out into our sector of the MLR in support of the 5th Marine Regiment, who were jolting overland in six-by-sixes. By April 1, 1952, the 1st Marine Division was in position on the western front for the defense of Seoul.

The terrain on this front was far more conducive to tank mobility because of the rolling terrain dotted with rice paddies (home of the Korean King Rat). The higher mountains to the north were manned by CCF (Chinese Communist Forces) troops and not by the bedraggled remnants of the North Korean People's Army. The CCF were redoubtable adversaries well equipped with generously bestowed, excellent Russian equipment.

On April 2, 1952, just to let the Chinese know that there was a new kind of kid on the block, we were assigned to tank combat patrols. One platoon of five tanks to various companies of the 5th Marine Regiment. This particular mission, I was the bow gunner with Second Lt. Wilson as TC and Cpl. Ray Kapinsky as gunner. It was a nice, sunny spring day as we were moving slowly behind the low hills. When we got to the crest line—lo and behold—out in front of us in a little valley of paddies was a company-sized unit all shaggin' ass for cover. Lieutenant Wilson and I had our binoculars on those terror-stricken troops, who were literally sprinting for their lives.

He immediately ordered us to open up with 30s and 50s but not the 90s, yet. The five tank gunners couldn't believe the field day unfolding in front of them. It was a turkey shoot. Shortly, Lt. Wilson ordered the use of the 90s with fuses set for airburst, over the heads of the fleeing CCF. The 90mm cannon is a demoralizing weapon to be on the receiving end of, I kid you not. It was a foregone conclusion that there would be no survivors. The fresh green paddies slowly began to turn crimson as that beautiful spring day saw one enemy company perish, down to the last man.

"Well, welcome back to the Korean War," I said silently to myself. "It's the best war the Corps can find for us." We were in the asshole of the world doing what we had been diligently trained for by officers and NCOs who had vanquished the Japs in WWII. I never read battle accounts such as this because the coverage of the war was being restricted by the same politicians who were now dictating to our field commanders. Truly, Korea was the ominous harbinger of Vietnam, two decades later.

That same night, I drew watch from 0200 to 0600 with my gunner, Ray Kapinsky from Pennsylvania. Apparently we had really gotten on someone's nerves over in the CCF camp, for that whole night, heavy artillery from goony land raked the MLR for hours, but not coming too close to our position. We were talking about the day's action, and Ray told me what went through his mind as he looked through the telescope sight.

"Chris, I saw this one gook's face ever so clearly at 400 yards and here I was going to crank off a 90mm at him and I could see his face."

"So what did you do Ray?" I asked him. His reply was, "I squeezed the trigger and sent this gook to kingdom come."

This was the way it went on the MLR every day and night until I was rotated home in August 1952.

Adapted from MCTA newsletter, Vol. 6 #4-93, November 1993, and Military *magazine.*

MARILYN MONROE
KOREA, 1952
by Chris Sarno

That day of Marilyn's show, I was with about 80 Jarheads from our antitank company of the 7th Marine Regiment, some 35 miles north of Seoul. We headed south very early on a cold dreary morning to see the show at the staging railhead at Munsan-Ni.

She came on stage around noon while snow flurries swirled around. They didn't bother her, or us, at all. She wore a clinging cocktail dress, and I mean *clinging!* She moved and gyrated with animal magnetism for an hour. This set the tone immediately, to our heart's content and delight. Naturally, when she broke out singing "Diamonds Are a Girl's Best

Friend," the house came down. I swear she wore no bra or panties that day, or fooled us if she did. The entire stage was guarded by three rows of MPs that day, and it was stormed at the end of her performance.

I noticed with my binoculars that Marilyn had those bedroom eyes, but to a lonely Marine it may have been a fleeting intuition. It quickly left my mind due to the explosive performance she rendered. I enjoyed her spontaneous sex appeal that literally obliterated my defenses. Although she was not beautiful in the classical sense, she was absolutely stunning in a sensual manner, a real head-turner. On that day she played up to us, spurred on by the raucous cheers that reached crescendo proportions.

I have to admit that I was never a fanatic follower of Marilyn Monroe, but having been in Korea for two years, through savage combat and other enemy tedium, I was her slave for that one day. Where she came from or where she was going thereafter, we knew not, nor cared. We had her to ourselves for one glorious bleak and cold winter day in Korea.

Yes, there were cameras clicking all over the area, and the Marines from the 7th Antitank Battalion were busy tearing the tankers' binoculars from one another's hands, with a lot of elbowing and shoving, too. I . . . and I speak for a lot of other Marines who witnessed her show, we literally devoured her unashamedly.

In all fairness, Marilyn that day ingrained in me a deep respect for her as a person who cared about us. I'll never forget her as long as I live. Sure I felt sad about her personal life, but we all have our crosses to bear, and I never judged her upon her untimely demise. Imagine what it was like to see a beautiful girl after 22 months away from the States, living with that mortal fear of day-to-day existence in that war-torn country. All during the bumpy and dusty way back, those 80 Jarheads were in love with Marilyn. The longer we rode, the quieter we became, interrupted intermittently with a smitten reference to this sexy woman.

To the USMC, God bless us all and thanks to the Almighty

for giving us that bright, though fleeting, moment when Marilyn Monroe gave us a touch of love.

Adapted from MCTA Newsletter, *Vol. 3-93, July 1993.*

THE PRECEDENT

A war that need not have been caused us 160,000 casualties. The Republic of Korea's toll was over five times worse, at 850,000, but it seemed that the whole free world wanted to get involved. By the time we fought the ChiCom army to a standstill in the middle of 1951, there were French, British, Australian, Turkish, Dutch, Canadian, New Zealand, Filipino, Thai, Greek, South African, even Colombian and Ethiopian soldiers fighting the communists. India, Sweden, and Italy had contributed medical units. It was the first war that the United Nations fought, and it set an awful precedent. . . . The UN has *never* won a war.

Here was set the precedent of sanctuary for an aggressor. General Douglas MacArthur once recommended that 30 to 50 atomic bombs be dropped on ChiCom airfields north of the Yalu, but instead our airmen were directed to bomb only the southern ends of the bridges and forbidden, with the threat of court-martial, to cross into Manchuria, even in hot pursuit. History does not record the perpetrator of that flawed policy, but they were obviously on the side of the communists, who were its beneficiaries.

The Chinese, after less than a year of war, ran out of steam, and General Ridgeway's kill-them-all tactics were costing them more soldiers than they could train or the Russians could equip. By the middle of 1952, Ridgeway and his staff and his UN allies were dead sure that they could throw the ChiCom army out of Korea. . . . So what happened?

An American election year is what happened. The President was told by his advisors that if he gave the okay for an offensive, he would be politically dead. The experts, who wouldn't have to do the dying, were also seemingly afraid of a war that might have expanded to involve China and Russia—neither of which had long-range bombers and only one of which had a few crude A-bombs. Advice that bad could only have come from some trusted official who was in league with the enemy. It is worth noting that at that time, Senator Joseph McCarthy was involved in hunting out communists in our government. Unfortunately, the senator was a bullyragging, bombastic blowhard, who caused his whole movement to be discredited . . . long before its job was done.

American presidents are *still* getting tainted advice. As a result of that bad advice, we had to mortgage 40 years of dreams to hold back an aggressor that could have been kicked back to its kennel in 1953. That war, as every war since then, was won on the ground by the American army, Marine Corps, and our allies and given away at places like Panmunjom and Paris and Basra. When the Korean war was allowed to end with a stalemate, the die was cast for Vietnam.

Here also was set the precedent of a liberal, opinionated American Press Corps. In a book named *No Bugles, No Drums* by Rudi Tomedi, which this writer highly recommends, an Army public information officer (PIO) named Jim Holton, who was there, states:

"Part of the problem was that they (correspondents) simply didn't get around much, even to American units. They spent virtually all their time at the press billet in Seoul. There was an old Japanese-built apartment house. Every major news organization had an apartment there. They had a well-stocked bar. They had a dance hall. There were a lot of Korean women coming and going. And meanwhile the correspondents were getting virtually all their information from the daily briefings held by the Eighth Army PIO. With the war in a stalemate, they were able to get by quite well on those briefings. As much as the public wanted, they were able to do right there in Seoul."

Does this sound familiar? This writer's cousins, who were in the Korean War, in armor and infantry, saw damn few reporters, and I, who was right in the middle of Tet, 1968, in downtown Pleiku, saw none at all in a full year. This is why we allow our leaders to lose wars for us. We are not informed by those who have taken on a sacred trust to do just that. Correspondents, years after the event, have admitted, in print, that rather than believe what honest soldiers told them, they fabricated stories that would please their editors.

Several of those writers have even admitted that they preferred to believe what the *North Korean* PIOs told them about the talks at Panmunjom. Lenin once said that, "Before we can destroy the West, first there must be the long march through their institutions." If you will pardon an old soldier's bitterness, that long march seems now to be an accomplished fact, as the news coverage of Vietnam, 20 years later, proved all too well. That war, also, was one where the terrain was "unsuitable for armored vehicles." Nobody, however, had asked the tankers, who were soon up to their turrets in jungles and communists.

19

THE VIETNAM WAR

1964–75

The question is often asked, just how did we get sucked into a two-bit war halfway around the world, and how did we manage to lose it? There are several good reasons. First off, international communism was on the rise just then, and one country after another was falling to the power of Russian imperialism. All over Africa and Arabia, our mineral and petroleum sources were being threatened by the minions of Moscow. If Vietnam had fallen, two things would have been jeopardized. First, the Straits of Malacca, through which much of the East's commerce flows, could have been shut off. Second, there is about as much oil under Vietnam and the Spratly Islands as there is under Saudi Arabia.

The debacle of Dien Bien Phu is well known, as is the history of the partition of Vietnam into north and south after the end of French rule. When President Jack Kennedy began to get briefings that the communists were, as usual, not living up to their alleged promises, he sent several observers over there, to get personal information for him. One of these was a widely traveled woman journalist named Rose Wilder-Lane, who had been all over Europe after

World War I, and had seen communism in action. She had seen the horrors of Bolshevism cause untold millions of deaths, and she had met Leon Trotsky and had seen an obscure Vietnamese intellectual named Nguyen That Thanh, help Vladimir Lenin set up the original French communist party.

Of all the ex-liberal journalists in the world, Rose Lane was one of the most logical for Kennedy to send. When she came back with reports of village chiefs being kidnapped and murdered; of schoolteachers being shot and replaced with communist cadres; of children taken from buses and mutilated to keep them from schools, Kennedy knew that the Reds were again on the march and that he had to act. Unfortunately, John Fitzgerald Kennedy's only military experience was getting run over by a Japanese destroyer, which he should have been able to hear about a mile away. Worse, he had surrounded himself with a bunch of bright-eyed, bushy-tailed, empty-headed whiz kids from assorted universities who had even less experience. Already there was a recipe for disaster.

At that point in history, the new Special Forces were actually winning the war, but they were fighting three problems, not one. First, of course, were the communists, both local and the invading Northerners. Second, was micromanaging from Washington. Third, and worst, was the fact that the existing Vietnamese government was a newly established pseudo-democracy, still in the process of learning how to function. The Vietnamese soldiers, by and large, were loyal and competent, but they were led by political appointees, not professionals. We lost 58,000 men in 14 years. They lost a million or better. If their names were added to the Wall, it would stretch to the Washington monument.

The die was cast when Rose Lane came back to Washington and told Jack Kennedy that Ho Chi Minh, the man who was now running the government of Vietnam, was actually Nguyen That Thanh, the same man who had known Lenin in France during World War I. The man had gone through three name changes from 1917 to 1954 in order to hide—first from the French, and then his own people—the fact that he was a communist. He now called himself Ho Chi Minh.

Rose knew the story because she had been enamored of communism herself, having been educated in a liberal American university, and then having gone over to Europe and Asia to see the new dream system work. Suddenly, as the purges began, the lights went on behind Rose's eyes as she saw the facade of social engineering split open like an overripe melon to reveal the ancient trait of despotism. The old expression is: "I'm from Missouri, and you have got to show me." Rose Lane had been shown starving children and burned farms, and she *was* from Missouri.

Almost automatically, she returned to her roots and became an avowed enemy of the communism that she had toyed with. Rose Wilder-Lane, you see, was raised in Mansfield, Missouri. She was the daughter of Laura Ingalls-Wilder and was the real Little Rose in *The Little House on the Prairie*. She'd come a long way in 70 years. She'd come down the Illinois trail in a covered wagon and lived to see men fly to the moon. She'd also seen social engineering kill more human beings than Genghis, Attila, Tamerlane, Hitler, and Tojo combined.

Slowly, by increments, we first sent advisors who weren't supposed to even defend themselves. Then Special Forces teams, who weren't supposed to go into the privileged sanctuaries, then a few line combat troops to protect the advisors, then more advisors with more Americans to protect them. Shortly, the communists found out that they were losing and called to Uncle Ho for help. The next thing anyone knew was that the North Vietnamese army was coming down the Ho Chi Minh Trail, and the fat was in the fire. The only sure counter to masses of light infantry is hordes of light armor and skilled infantry to work with it. Something like the American tank-infantry teams of the Pacific war had to be created, and quickly. . . . And that hard-won knowledge had been lost.

The track-laying warrior/mechanics who led the way, however, weren't American, nor were they French; they were Vietnamese. They took a new American invention and put their own stamp on it, a stamp that endures to this day. The almost automatic opinion "everybody knows you can't use tanks in a place like Vietnam" merely shows how short the military memory can be. Long forgotten were the savage battles on Guam, Saipan, Leyte, and other tropic paradises. Even the ridge-running tankers of Korea had been forgotten as we prepared for the great confrontation in Europe. It's always the little things that trip us up.

Armor is speed, protection, mobility, and firepower, directed by a certain elan and dash. It ain't necessarily a heavy tank. When the French returned to Indochina after WWII, they brought with them a heterogeneous collection of American armor, which, used properly, should have done the job. They didn't and it didn't, and they were driven from power, although many of them stayed on in the newly independent pair of nations.

When Vietnam was partitioned, one of the old French armored units—now composed of all Vietnamese troops—left North Vietnam and headed south. When the 3rd Reconnaissance Squadron found out that they were going to have to live under communism, the troopers simply cranked their tanks and headed south, at speed. Once their families were clear of the new regime in the north, they placed their services at the disposal of the Saigon government, such as it was. They drew such assignments as static security, palace guard, and convoy escort, and were only half-jokingly referred to as "coup troops," and their tanks were called "voting machines"

Meanwhile, in America, a new machine was going into production, a machine that could have been expressly designed for the conditions in Vietnam. The same people who had built the world-famed Amtrac had built the M-113, an armored box on tracks that could go almost anyplace. America, unfortunately, didn't have a war going on just then, to battle test the new vehicle . . . or did we? On June

11, 1962, two experimental rifle companies mounted in M-113 APCs were turned loose in the Mekong Delta, and the war was changed forever.

The combination of the Vietnamese mentality and the armored amphibian produced a new concept, the armored cavalry assault vehicle, or ACAV. There is something in the Asian mentality that runs to bunkers, machine guns, and mortars, when confronted with a highly mobile, aggressive enemy. The original concept had been for the APC to act as a battle taxi that would deliver infantrymen to a place where they could fight on foot. What actually happened is that the Viets considered it to be a rolling bunker and used it as such.

The first time they went into combat, the infantrymen simply opened the top hatches, climbed halfway out onto the hull, and shot everything that moved, as the gunner with the big .50 Browning beat up the ambush that had sprung itself on them. Through gradual experimentation, they reduced the number of infantrymen and replaced them with wing gunners, one on each side of the now armored .50 cal. Oddly enough, they had reinvented the exact armament layout of the old Amtank that had fought on Saipan and Tinian.

By September 30 of that year, they had traded nine wounded and four dead of their own, for 502 Viet Cong dead and 184 prisoners and uncounted VC wounded. The rifle companies were then told that they were cavalry and redesignated as "troops." For the first time in Vietnam's history, armor, in the form of the ACAV, was effective off the roads—even in the rainy season. Here is one American's tribute to them.

KY BINH (CAVALRY)
Major Robert Burleigh

Mot, hai, ba, bon, di! (Crank 'em and roll 'em) the young Vietnamese cavalry lieutenant orders over his radio, and his troop of armored personnel carriers is instantly on the move. As is the case on most operations in the Republic of Vietnam, they are unaware of just exactly what awaits them as they move out across the brown dry-season rice paddies.

At the same time, several questions enter the mind of their American advisor, who is embarking on his first mission with the armored cavalry troop. How will these small slender soldiers react when they come in contact with the Viet Cong? Will they be aggressive? Can they be trusted?

As the thick dust from the now dry paddies rises from the tracks of the carriers and covers everybody and everything, the advisor, an armor captain, thinks back to the numerous editorials and articles that he's read back in the States. Wiping his forehead and leaving a muddy streak that drips down into his eyes, he remembers how the journalists had contended almost unanimously that the ARVN (Army of the Republic of Vietnam) was not contributing its fair share to the war effort. He thinks back to the claims of some prominent correspondents and politicians that the officers and men are not competent and that they are afraid to close with the VC.

Now, here he is, perched on top of an APC behind his counterpart, the Vietnamese lieutenant, still wondering how they will react. Suddenly the loud, heavy cracking of .50-cal Browning machine guns gets his full attention. He is just about to find out. The lead Vietnamese platoon leader had spotted a group of Viet Cong and opened up on them. In front of the captain, the Viet lieutenant is issuing orders to his cavalry troop at a furious rate as his own track swings into action.

As if by remote control, all 15 tracks arc around from their column formation into an assault line, so that all tracks can fire on the enemy. There are now nine ACAVs moving out on line toward a distant tree line. The American captain notes that four tracks have dropped back and worries for a minute, and then realizes that they are the mortar tracks—the little troop's artillery. In less than a minute, 81mm mortar bombs are falling into that tree line. There is a mechanical howl as the big 318 Chrysler truck engines are given their full ration of fuel, and the track lurches toward that tree line, which is now sparkling with muzzle flashes. At this point, the apprehensions of the

American disappear. "These are little tigers," he mutters to himself.

The above, of course, is an amalgam of several actions, but similar things are happening every day in Vietnam. Having served as an advisor with the 2nd Troop of the ARVN 10th Armored Cavalry Regiment, I have been shocked (and usually outraged) by many of the comments appearing in many American publications concerning these soldiers and their fight against communist aggression. Since my return from Vietnam, I have been somewhat disappointed in discovering that a large percentage of our citizens have accepted as gospel the accusations of these journalists.

It appears that the American Press, with some few exceptions, has chosen to concentrate the greatest number of column inches covering the ARVN to the bad units and the inadequate soldiers. This is a gross injustice, not only to the many honorable and competent Vietnamese soldiers but to the American people, who have a right to know the truth. The Vietnamese cavalrymen with whom I was associated are an outstanding group of soldiers and a real credit to any cavalry unit. They are most proud of the fact that they are Ky Binh (cavalry) and wear their distinctive black berets with pride, as do the advisors.

Once the advisors to the cavalry troop have established good rapport with the soldiers, they are considered part of the unit. The mutual respect is beyond belief. The advisor learns to share every joy and sorrow experienced by the soldiers. When a trooper is injured or killed, he feels the same compassion as if the men were part of his own unit. Why? Because the American advisor *is* part of that unit. He has gone into battle with them, slept beside them, pulled watch with them, and gone drinking and partying with them, on off-duty hours. Once he is adopted by a Viet unit, the men will not let him forget that he is part of them. The smiles, the pat on the back, the invitation to join a volleyball game, the visits to their homes, all weld him into the Vietnamese troop.

The Viet cavalrymen can react just as fast as Americans. At 0150, August 14, 1967, the city of Tay Ninh came under mortar fire. The target seemed to be the city's Chieu Hoi (honorable surrender) center, near the city's edge. . . . *Eight* minutes after the first mortar bomb fell, the whole troop was in motion. The troopers had been sleeping in and around their tracks, and when the drivers awoke, they just jumped aboard and cranked the big V-8 engines.

The mortars were fairly short-range types, judging from the sound of the explosions, and we knew where most of the likely mortar locations on that side of the city were. The Vietnamese troop commander headed our unit for them without any help from me; he didn't need it. We all also knew that any competent VC commander would have set up an ambush site between our known base and his mortars. That is merely military competence, and there were very few inept VC.

At 0250, we hit an ambush. It was triggered by a B-40 rocket that hit the ACAV of the platoon leader of the lead platoon. He was a recently commissioned second lieutenant and received only minor burns, cuts, and shrapnel from the blast. Now the platoon was under an intense hail of AK-47, SKS, and light automatic fire, probably from RPD machine guns. Despite the rain of fire, the lieutenant dismounted from his burning track and ran to the next in line, yelling commands to its radioman. A burst of automatic fire almost decapitated him, and he fell in front of the ACAV.

At the same time, the troop commander and the troop medic dismounted and ran to the burning track to pull the wounded from the burning vehicle and get them to safety. Meanwhile, the remainder of the troop were gaining fire superiority and crushing the ambush. Shortly after the last of the wounded were pulled from the track, it exploded as the burning gasoline got to the stored munitions aboard. After things had settled down, it turned out that the only friendly casualty that night had been the brave young platoon leader.

The VC lost four visible KIA (U.S. body count) and one RPG captured. Two weeks later, a Chieu Hoi who had been involved in the action said that about 30 of his group had been killed or died of wounds as a result of that action. For their valor that night, the troop received commendations from both the Vietnamese province chief and the American senior advisor.

These officials were of the opinion that there was a danger of the province headquarters being overrun that night and that the sudden, violent reaction of the 10th Cavalry had averted that disaster.

During my tour in Rach Kein, Long An Province, our troop also operated with an American unit, and after several combined operations, a mutual respect developed between the Viet cavalrymen and the American recon platoon of the 3rd Battalion of the 39th Infantry. After several operations, though, the CO of the American battalion decided that he should give the recon platoon a rest, and ordered a platoon from one of the line companies to go out with the Viet cav.

On hearing this, the recon platoon rebelled. The men went to their lieutenant in a body, and informed him that if anyone was going out with 2nd Troop, 10th ARVN Cavalry, it was going to be them. The op order was subsequently amended, and the reconnaissance platoon went out with their Vietnamese friends, hunting the Viet Cong.

The Vietnamese taught me as much as I taught them, if not more. Their formations and ability to react to new situations were outstanding. Every track commander was quick to respond to orders and very aggressive. The unit was well skilled in the complex art of guerrilla warfare, and many times I believed that they had developed a sixth sense about where the Cong, or their mines, would be. Granted, their methods were unorthodox, but so was their war.

They have also been criticized for their maintenance techniques by people who were never there and who were log-book-happy bureaucrats. During my one-year tour, we never had more than one track down for mechanical reasons at any one time. Almost all downtime was caused by enemy action and/or lack of spares. They maintained their tracks to the point that sometimes their wheeled vehicles went wanting, and they spent more time on the crew-served weapons than on their own weapons and personal equipment. That shows just how much the ACAVs meant to them.

The Vietnamese cavalryman has been cheated by many who do not know him. He is a proud man, proud of his country and proud of being part of the Ky Binh. He is proud of his profession and of the black beret that is the symbol of his profession. He has a right to be proud.

Adapted from Armor Magazine, *September–October, 1968.*

Slowly, as the war escalated and more Northern invading divisions were sent marching down the Ho Chi Minh Trail, more and more American troops were committed to match the communist invasion. First the air cavalry, then the 4th Division, and then the 25th "Tropic Lightning" Division was sent in from Hawaii. Since the Vietnamese had proved beyond doubt that armor could run in at least part of the country, and the U.S. Marines had brought their big M-48s ashore, General Westmoreland, with some misgivings, allowed three more heavy units to come in, the 11th Cav, the 3/4 Cav, and the 1-69th Armor, whose lineage went back to Korea. That battalion had fought in Korea, as the 89th Tank Battalion, and had covered itself with glory there.

The battalion had, however, been a pick-up unit, made out of spare parts, and had since been regularized as the 1st of the 69th—they were about to set the standards for armor use in jungles. Many of their tankers had fought in both WWII and Korea, and they brought their experience and memories to Vietnam, blended them with the advice that they received from their Vietnamese counterparts, and created something never seen before. Their battalion commander, then LTC Ronald J. Fairfield, tells the story best.

20

THE TANKS ARRIVE

Commander's Briefing

Every member of the 1st Battalion, 69th Armor had at one time raised his hand and sworn to defend the Constitution of the United States, and an opportunity to do just that was fast approaching. In late August 1965, a new lieutenant colonel assumed command of the outfit, which was stationed in Hawaii. This battalion commander had previously served as a company commander in the same battalion in the Korean War, when it was known as the 89th, so he wasn't exactly a stranger. Further, he'd gotten the word from his last assignment that 1-69 could easily be sent into a hot combat zone—the Republic of Vietnam. Ronald J. Fairfield had come home and immediately proceeded to put his house in order.

His first order was that, when moving, all tanks would be in combat order, gun tubes to the front, instead of in travel lock. This simple order caused an immediate change of attitude in the tankers, who'd gotten a bit soft with easy duty in America's tropical paradise. General Westmoreland, it turned out, had decided to let its parent unit, the

25th Infantry Division, which was already in country, keep its tanks. There'd been loose chatter on the part of West-moreland's staff and other senior infantrymen that armor in general, and tanks in particular, weren't suitable for use in Vietnam. Their idea of combat was to advance with rifles at the ready and bayonets fixed. There had been some success-ful armored combat, though, by the Vietnamese, so the go-ahead was reluctantly given.

The actual alert for preparation for overseas movement was unusual and a bit peremptory. The battalion was in the midst of its annual training cycle on the Makua Valley gunnery range, when the battalion commander was called in and told to report to General Collins, Fort Shafter, HQ, U.S. Army, Pacific. The meeting was to respond to ques-tions from General Westmoreland concerning the move-ment of 1-69 from Schofield Barracks, Hawaii, to Vietnam, combat loaded and ready for immediate deployment!

No one had briefed the battalion commander, but it wasn't really needed; he knew what was coming and had been working his companies at a furious rate. They needed new tanks, however, which were on the way, and they were due for their annual field training and live-fire exercises with the new equipment. Much discussion took place on how, where, and by whom, with General Collins relaying the answers to Westmoreland's local office, upstairs in the same building. The decision was made by Westmoreland to divert the ships carrying the battalion's rebuilt M48A3 diesel tanks to Okinawa, where the battalion could marry up with them. It could have been handled a little smoother, but that was the manner of COMUSACV (Commander U.S. Army Command Vietnam). We'd not had our annual training test, but we were to find out that the Viet Cong and the NVA were more than willing to provide one.

When the CO returned to the battalion, it hit the fan. The tables of organization and equipment (TO&E) had to be reworked. Inoculations had to be brought up to date. New equipment, such as generators and chain saws, had to be requisitioned and the combat load of the tanks had to be changed. The mix of high-explosive and armor-piercing ammo for the 90mm cannons had to be changed to high explosive, canister, and white phosphorus. Our scout M-114 vehicles had proven disastrously unreliable and had to be replaced with another model, the M-113, which was proving itself in the Mekong Delta in the capable hands of the ARVN cavalry.

The unspoken question in the minds of the troops was: "Will I be wounded, and if I am, what will happen to me?" The CO talked at length about the heritage of the unit, all the way back to WWII and Korea. The old 89th Battalion had never left a man or tank anywhere. The point was strongly made that the same philosophy would be adhered to again. No one would be left behind. Period! And they never were.

The battalion wives, led by Susan Fairfield, pitched in and got their tankers ready to travel. Families were readied for return to the continental U.S., or in the case of locally recruited soldiers, their Hawaiian homes. Where a vehicle was needed, wheels were loaned. Where muscles were needed, they were commandeered. The post commander, General Weyland, arranged with U.S. Army Pacific to allow families to stay in post housing as long as needed, easing the strain on the younger wives.

Sailing was of no great consequence, as the 69th was long used to sea duty, being transferred between the islands by LST several times a year. We were shipped on a U.S. Navy contract transport. Food was so-so, and the troops were in reasonably comfortable quarters for the relatively short voyage to the Republic of Vietnam. We were advised that the ship would have to make a fuel stop in Yokohama, and, after consultation with the company commanders, the decision was made to give the troopers one night of shore leave, with the proviso that everyone had better be back on board by sailing time. The result of this policy somewhat disrupted the Yokohama naval installation.

Picture in your mind the relatively sedate officers and enlisted men's clubs of a peacetime naval installation . . .

suddenly invaded by a battalion of hungry, thirsty, soon-to-be-shot-at tankers. Those clubs made a lot of money that day, and not just off the breakfast menu. Hamburgers, steak, omelets, beer, martinis, whatever. Next morning, they came a-running by taxi, rickshaw, and even bicycle. Every man made it back . . . to whatever lay ahead for the battalion.

On Okinawa, we were billeted in a part of the Marine base, Camp Hanson, and our tanks began arriving. We took delivery of our new mounts, familiarized ourselves with the new radios, and took turns zeroing the guns at the Marines' gunnery range. Then we began loading onboard LSTs for the run to Vietnam. To our great delight, we found out that the ships were the same squadron that we had used many times in our deployments around the Hawaiian Islands and over to the Pohakaloa training area. Thus, there was no confusion. Our crews knew the navy crews, and there was a feeling of mutual respect. When you have U.S. Army noncoms working with navy chiefs, an officer's only job is to stay out of the way and look important. Soon enough, we'd have serious work to do.

Apparently Headquarters MACV (Military Advisory Command Vietnam) was having second thoughts about the use of heavy armor. The original destination of the battalion was to have joined the 3rd Brigade of the 25th Infantry in the general area of Pleiku in the central highlands. Their thinking was that the tanks would be more effective on the firmer soil of the uplands, rather than the softer lowlands. The war situation, however, changed their minds. While en route, we learned that only Bravo Company would unload at Qui Nhon and make the long run up the Annam Cordillera to Pleiku. The rest of the battalion would offload in the vicinity of Saigon for immediate combat. Obviously, somebody'd gotten their tail in a crack, and any reservations about the use of armor were fading rapidly.

The battalion commander had preceded the unit by flying to Saigon by commercial air to meet with General Dessaure, the assistant commander of the 25th Division. Luckily, a meeting with the U.S. Navy Saigon advisor to the Vietnamese navy, a captain, was arranged, and we learned that the plan was for the tanks to be unloaded by heavy crane, a tedious three-day process. Apparently, that captain had only worked with unhurried civilian contractors and expected a rather leisurely exit from the LSTs. He was also driven by the fact that there was an extremely short period of high tide in the area at that time of year. Any delay in the disembarkment could easily leave the LSTs stranded for 24 hours, within rocket range of the mangrove swamps, known to be infested with Viet Cong.

There was much intense discussion, which was ended by the production of a cable from COMUSMACV (Commander U.S. Military Advisory Command Vietnam) to one LTC Ronald J. Fairfield, CO 1-69 Armor, directing him to move his battalion so as to arrive combat loaded for immediate deployment, signed Westmoreland—end of discussion. The Navy captain, however, wasn't convinced that we could pull this off, but it was made quite clear that this was a bad assumption and that the lead LST, once the ramp was down, would be empty in 25 minutes or less. Somewhat reluctantly, he gave his blessing to the operation, not really convinced that we could pull this off.

The engines were running when the doors opened, and when the ramp touched the sand, "A" Company's command tank roared over it, gun tube hunting for hostiles. In considerably less than the specified time, that Navy captain was staring at the rear end of a rapidly vanishing company of tanks. Behind him, the LST was backing off the beach to make room for another vessel. Because of the security situation existing in the capital area, we could not leave the navy yard until after midnight, but when we did move, it was directly into combat. We'd been in country just 12 hours.

Yogi Berra once said: "It's like *déjà vu* all over again." In some of the heaviest fighting in Korea, "A" Company, of what was then known as the 89th Tank Battalion, commanded by then Captain Fairfield, supported the 27th Infantry against an earlier generation of communists. Now, at the request of General Dessaure, "A" Company laid parallel for indirect fire, in support of the 27th, and reached out with its long 90mm guns to hammer targets that the artillery simply couldn't reach. The targets were destroyed, and many secondary fires ignited. Off the beach and into combat. The 69th was fighting again.

The French, the Japanese, and now the ARVN had never been able to evict the Viet Minh and now the Viet Cong, from the Ho Bo woods or the Filhol plantation; 1-69, however, was another matter. The general commanding the 2nd Brigade, 25th Infantry Division, had sent us in to support the 27th, also requesting that we knock down as many of the tough eucalyptus trees as possible. His engineer bulldozers had been having a tough time with both the trees and the VC. There is, however, a considerable difference between a five-ton dozer and a fifty-two-ton, 900-horsepower armored vehicle. Very shortly, a narrow-minded infantryman with a strong prejudice against tanks had his thinking changed, at least a little, and more combat was to come. Five years of it.

Adapted from material contributed by Gen. R. J. Fairfield, USA (ret.).

The cavalry unit that was the 25th Division's eyes and ears was the 3rd Squadron, 4th Cavalry, and is known throughout the Army as the "Three-Quarter Cav." It deployed to RVN at the same time as the 69th, and for the transfer was actually op-con to the 69th, until it began operations on its own. While the big blood-and-thunder operations like Cedar Falls and Junction City got all the press attention, the most important work of the Americans wasn't only the killing off of communist bandits, *it was the undoing of the damage they'd done.* Villages had to be made to live again, and the hearts and minds of the villages won back to the Southern government. Here, in the words of a man who was there, is how that was done . . . by tankers and cavalrymen. This is *why* we were there.

THE OTHER WAR
CAPTAIN JOHN P. IRVING III

As our small column moved out the main gate of the main base at Cu Chi, and down the dirt road in a swirl of fine, talcum-like dust, not a single Vietnamese was anywhere in sight. Even so, we moved cautiously through the deserted Filhol rubber plantation, which bordered the road on both sides. Not more than 1,500 meters from the relative safety of the 25th Division base camp, the four APCs of our small unit swung abruptly to the left and off the road. We entered a small hamlet of 25 mud-walled, thatch-roofed huts. The personnel carriers with their .50-cal. machine guns moved rapidly to the right and left edges of the village while the remainder of the column—two jeeps and an M-577 medical vehicle—parked in the center. Those of us in the command vehicles jumped out and began moving through the hamlet. Very cautiously. Still no sign of life. I thought, *Why bother with this place. No one lives here.* Then, picking our way along the single, wagon-rutted muddy scar of a road toward the rear of the village, we spotted some yellow fuzzy ducklings. They were swimming peacefully in a shallow muddy pool. Then I heard a baby cry, a sound instantly muffled. "Listen," I said to Captain John Claxton, "there must be someone in there!"

"Yes, I told you there're people here. They're just hiding," he answered.

Since he was the squadron S-2, knowing such things was part of his job. Soon the radio crackled out "all clear," and we relaxed enough to get down to the business of setting up the 577 track, which had brought along the squadron doctor and his team. They quickly established their mobile aid station right in the middle of the road and sent the interpreter, Ly Van Minh, to round up the villagers for "sick call."

Here was my first contact with complete abject poverty. Houses with dirt floors, mud walls, and rice straw roofs. As I stood there, unbelieving, I saw two huge black eyes staring at me out of the gloom of one of the huts. Peering closer, I saw that they belonged to one of the prettiest little girls I had ever seen. Her face was dirty and thin, and wore no smile, but it had the timeless beauty of the Orient. Then the reason of the *why* of our being here overwhelmed me. This was the reason—the children, the promise of a future, of a better life. If we could bring a smile to that little face, all of this fighting and dying would not be in vain.

Reluctantly, the people came. They came out of the holes they had dug beneath the corners of their houses, holes for protection from the war. They came out of curiosity, out of fear, and out of genuine need for the medical treatment that our "Bac Si," or doctor, could provide.

The squadron had been given responsibility for the new life Hamlet refugee village of Bac Ha#2 as part of the Civic Action Program in Vietnam. The importance of the program was emphasized as early as the summer of 1964, when the chairman of the Joint Chiefs of Staff, General Earle G. Wheeler said:

> "The problem out there is not only a military problem, it is a political problem, and I believe even a social problem. . . . The point is that the final touch out there is not going to be the achievement of a military victory. I believe parallel to our achievements in the military field there must be equal accomplishments in the political field, if you are going to obtain, in the long term, a free South Vietnam, able to pursue its own destiny."

The major part of our mission was to assist in any way possible, toward the development of the village and its people. The culmination of this development and a good measure of its value would be the election of a village chief . . . without the interference of the Viet Cong.

At this point in time, the mission of the tankers and cavalrymen split into two complementing roles. The combat forces would be out in the hills beating the bushes for

Charlie and his big brothers, the NVA, while the lighter vehicles and the medics attempted to reassemble some kind of life for the villagers who had been captive to the Shadow Government and the VC tax collectors who came in the night and murdered families. While the tanks led infantry sweeps through the Ho Bo Woods, the medics worked on the "hearts and minds" of the populace. . . .

The first MEDCAP (Medical Civil Action Patrol) visit could not be regarded as a great success. However, it served as the nucleus for an expanding program to help our adopted friends. To me, it became a concrete symbol of the value of positive action, no matter how small, in overcoming the results of man's inhumanity to man. Captain Richard Joiner, the S-5, or civil affairs officer, had primary responsibility, but ideas and help came in from everywhere in the squadron.

The S-1 provided interpreters without whom the mission would have been impossible. Initially the S-2 found the people hostile and uncommunicative. But eventually he was able to fill in many gaps in his intelligence picture. The villagers became very cooperative after seeing the positive results of our program. Many times they volunteered the exact locations of mines in the road, which we would otherwise have found the hard way.

Coordination for the protection of the team that went into the village was provided by the S-3. This normally consisted of the ground surveillance section of the HQ troop and the two APCs designated for the squadron commander and the S-3. This was the equivalent of a scout section, and it proved to be adequate. An infantry squad from one of the line troops, or the aero rifle platoon, was also used during the early stages.

My S-4 shop became a staging area for material and goods going out to the hamlet from the people of the United States, direct to the people of Bac Ha#2. Lieutenant John Barovetto was my transportation section leader, and quite often, he went out to "our" village. He then wrote to his mother of the primitive conditions and lack of clothes, soap, and little things like candy and toys. She mentioned the contents of the letter at a club meeting.

This resulted in a deluge of contributions. When the boxes finally stopped arriving in the mail, we estimated that we had received over three-quarters of a ton of generosity.

The maintenance officer, Capt. Richard Barnhart, probably provided what was to be the most ingenious form of help to our project, a portable shower. It was mounted on a one-and-a-half-ton trailer. A frame constructed of aluminum tubing and covered with canvas gave the users a degree of privacy. Although some of the people had to be taught that soap was for washing and not for eating, the shower proved to be of unlimited value. It made possible a degree of personal hygiene that was essential to the medical program. A little harder to measure, but of obvious importance, was that it served as a welcome break in the serious daily routine of a peasant village. The children, who were the best customers, thought that taking a shower was the best game they had ever played.

None of this rapport or progress would have been possible without the untiring, dedicated efforts of the squadron surgeon, Capt. Eugene Geortzen, M.C. His ability to diagnose and treat superstitious peasants made the difference between the success or failure of the program. A complicating and discouraging obstacle to be overcome was that he had to work through an interpreter. A typical treatment would begin with the doctor asking an old woman who had obvious pain written on her face:

"Where does it hurt?"

A flurry of wild gesticulating and a baffling exchange of words would follow. The answer was, "I don't know."

"Can she point to it?"

"She says hurts all places, what means point?"

Then the doctor and interpreter would fly into a pantomime to clarify the meaning of the word point. This goes on and on. Sometimes 30 minutes were required just to give two aspirin for a headache. Progress was slow and painful, but there was progress . . . during the day.

The Viet Cong were concerned over our presence and

attempted to undo at night what we had accomplished during the day. They made frequent visits designed to terrorize the peasants and disprove our ability to provide protection. One night they came to the hut of Tran Cong Vinh, who had been a member of the VC before he became disillusioned and came to live at Bac Ha#2. Vinh was an outspoken critic of the VC and their aims. On one otherwise quiet night the enemy came and discussed the matter with him. He was given a choice: "Come back with us now or die."

"Never," he spat back at them, and they killed him.

The bullet that killed Vinh also went through his little daughter's head as she clung to her father. The two of them had been dragged kicking and screaming out of their mud-walled home and into the street where we found them dead the next morning.

Only after the villagers realized that we were sincerely trying to help them were we able to influence or guide their progress. The MEDCAP team and their donations of soap and medicine were good foundations for this, but this could only be a beginning.

Within an armored cavalry regiment there is a considerable amount of construction equipment available. There is equipment that can be diverted to civic action projects when it is not needed elsewhere. We were especially fortunate in that our division had been augmented with additional engineer units. Through a great deal of judicious planning and timing, we were able to divert enough equipment usage to build a well-drained road down the center of the hamlet and provide a rudimentary drainage system.

We stayed well away from local political activities, but these also progressed under our shield, as the VC were driven off or killed by armored sweeps across the green land. The people seemed to have forgotten the assassination of Tran Cong Vinh, and were becoming more expressive. The local government realized that they were ready to take part in the upcoming election. Therefore, the inhabitants were hastily screened, issued identification cards, and registered as voters. Now they would have a village chief, someone with whom we could deal directly. Before this, all coordination had had to be done at the district level.

After this, progress came at a relatively rapid pace. In recognition of the major step forward, the government gave the refugee camp a real name. It now became the village of Tan Thoi. We gave them barrier material with which to build a protective fence around the village. Now there was a chief whom we could advise on how to organize and train a Popular Force group selected from the able-bodied men, so that they could defend themselves. Bricks were obtained through the civic action program to enable the people to build a much-needed school for their children.

Soon, too soon, the time came for me to leave, to take another assignment. They were now giving me my own troop of cavalry, and the war would again catch up with me. I made my last visit to the now bustling village of Tan Thoi with mixed emotions . . . and it was safe to go unarmed. I thought of that first day and how quiet it had been. The stillness had been broken only by curt commands, the crunch of boots, and the echoes of a firefight off to the north. *The VC had been a close and real menace, before the ACAVs and tanks and helicopters had driven them from this land.*

Now the village was filled with the laughter of children and the gossip of the people. The thought of sudden death possibly lurking in every hut had been wrapped around me like a wraith. Now only the children were wrapped around me. What used to be an ugly scar on the landscape had been transformed into a gravel road marking the center of the village. Down at the end of the road, stood a new eight-room school and meeting hall with a cement floor. Along the main street were the inevitable tin-roofed business huts that housed everything from souvenir shops to laundries.

Gone were the mosquito-breeding mud holes. Gone were the hollow-eyed looks on the faces of the children. Gone was the need to be constantly alert for the whistle of mortar bombs or the raiders in the night. These are but a few of the problems met and solved by one small armored unit in fighting the "Other War." The job goes on.

Adapted, slightly, from Armor Magazine, *May–June 1968, by author.*

Author's note: One wonders just where the TV media were during all this, especially after the area had been made safe for them?

21

THE JUNGLE TANKERS

11th Armored Cavalry, Outside Xaun Loc, RVN
November 24, 1966

The famed Blackhorse Regiment had moved to Vietnam in mid-October and had set up housekeeping on a square mile of land just 12 kilometers south of the provincial capital of Xaun Loc. To the residents of the local villages, it must have seemed like a major invasion as convoy after convoy of heavily loaded trucks rumbled past their hamlets. One major feature of this friendly invasion, though, was that for the first time in many years, the local section of National Highway QL-1 was open to civilian traffic, since the armed convoys effectively suppressed the local VC. The communists, however, weren't going to take this lying down.

Early in November, intelligence reports from a variety of sources warned that the 5th Viet Cong Division was planning a major ambush. When word came that the guerrillas of the division's 274th Regiment were on the move, the Blackhorse Regiment's commander, Col. William Cobb, began to pull in his detached squadrons. It was this move that triggered the chain of events that was to cost the 274th dearly.

The first squadron, equal in size to an armored battalion, began to go through Long Binh on the way to Xaun Loc, early on November 20. The 105mm self-propelled howitzer battery went on to Xaun Loc, but the rest of the squadron, delayed by foul weather, was trapped in Long Binh overnight, and they used the time to top off fuel tanks and pull maintenance. Their plan, initially, was to move out at 0700 the next day, but things were already beginning to come unglued . . . and the 274th VC main force regiment was moving into place.

Midway between the provincial capitals of Bien Hoa and Xaun Loc, Highway 1 drops into a streambed and then rises out into open rolling ground, with tall grass and some few paddies. On the north side of the highway, there was tall grass that could hide a standing man. Rising out of that sea of grass like a green island in a shallow sea, was a square kilometer of jungle. On the southern side of the road, the trees of an old rubber plantation had been almost smothered by new jungle growth. Past this, a cultivated banana field continued for about 300 meters, almost to the edge of the hamlet of Ap Hung Nghia.

The VC commander, a canny old warrior, placed his ambush in classic style, with an impressive amount of heavy weapons. Ranging along the south side of the road, from the jungled plantation through the banana grove and actually into the hamlet, he placed small groups of riflemen, B-40 rocket gunners, and machine-gun nests. In the classic VC pattern, he placed 75mm recoilless rifles at the ends of the kill zone to destroy the lead and trail vehicles, and trap the bulk of the convoy in his concentrations of weapons; 300 meters back in the jungle were his 82mm mortars, ready to fire on call. Scattered in huts along the road were heavy antiaircraft machine guns that could take American aircraft under fire.

Seemingly, he'd thought of everything. He'd placed groups of riflemen on the north side of the road to take out the inevitable American truck drivers who would try to take cover, and he'd even set up a protected escape route with bunkers that would delay the inevitable pursuit. The position of his command HQ was on the crest of a hill 500 meters south of the actual kill zone, and from here the VC commander could see the whole site. It was a good professional plan, but one of Murphy's rules of war is that "war is full of unpredictable amateurs."

Another thing was that the 274th Regiment had never seen an ACAV. The concept had been proven south, in the Mekong River Delta, but VC formations were sedentary military units, each with responsibility for a given area, and apparently there wasn't as much communication between them as there should have been. The designers at FMC (Food Machinery Corporation) had taken one look at an ARVN-modified M-113 and gotten busy. Now the TC station was fully armored, both wing guns had armored shields, and there was a 40mm grenade launcher included in the armament of the five-man crew. The stage was set, and the players were moving into the wings.

By 0600 at Long Binh, the convoy was formed and ready to move out, but there was no commander. At roll-out time, 0700, there was still no commander and no armored escort. By 0800 even more straggling trucks and some staff and clerical types joined the convoy, which was now oversized and unprotected. At 0840, First Lt. Neil Keltner, commander of 1st Platoon, Troop "C," 1st Squadron, was tagged for the job.

Moving quickly, he got his four tracks and four from the troop's 2nd Platoon under way. Somewhat to his surprise, he found, sandwiched in among the trucks, a stray ACAV from "A" Troop and quickly adopted it. He now had nine ACAVs to defend a convoy that had swollen from 50 to over 80 vehicles, all wanting protection to Xaun Loc. There seemed to be at least one of everything in the U.S. vehicle inventory.

At 0920, standing in his hatch, Keltner gave the signal to move out, and the huge convoy lurched into motion like an arthritic, spastic snake. Almost immediately, there were problems. For the march, Keltner had placed his ACAVs in pairs. A pair each at the head and tail of the convoy and two pairs equidistant down the length of the line of trucks. He'd put his own vehicle with the second pair, about 20 trucks back from the head of the convoy, where he could, hopefully, see the whole string at one time.

The problem was that the drivers were inexperienced and that some of the heavily laden trucks were slower than others. These two factors caused an immediate accordion effect to ripple through the clusters of trucks as they alternately speeded up, stretched their intervals out, and then slowed down and bunched up. As they passed through the hamlet of Ho Nai, right outside the gate of Long Binh camp, a VC lookout flashed word to the 274th Regiment that the convoy was at last under way. Runners trotted down jungle trails to tell the gunners to get ready.

The great convoy hadn't been on the road for a whole hour when a message flashed into Blackhorse HQ—a roving LRRP (long-range recon patrol) had spotted the 274th's combat command post and radioed its location in. The regimental S-2, Major Brookshire, immediately pinned the coordinates on the map, drawing the obvious conclusion: AMBUSH. In one minute he had radioed a message out to the squadron's TOC (tactical operations center) at Long Binh. Orders began to fly over airwaves and along wires, and in short order, the squadron's light aerial fire team was in the air and on the way. Already an L-19 aircraft with a FAC, or forward air controller, was overhead. Everybody had been warned, except Lt. Keltner, who was just then working his lead trucks through a Vietnamese National Police checkpoint.

Then his radio crackled with urgency. "Suspected enemy activity at coordinates 289098." Not really worried yet, Keltner nonetheless radioed the FAC to verify the convoy's head in relation to the new coordinates. Looking up, he could now see two FAC planes, as one was low on fuel and a new one had come to relieve him. Just as the FAC Major Stefanelli radioed that the head of the convoy had passed the suspect area, ACAV C22 came on the net reporting contact and incoming fire. Reacting to his earlier training,

Keltner decided to run the convoy through the small-arms fire and get as much of it out of the still-unknown kill zone as possible.

Still on the move, Keltner ordered his own gunners to spray into the banana grove, and then a mortar round fell on the road between his track and the one following. That was the stray track, A34, and the round did no damage. Now the oversized convoy and the amateurish drivers were working to Keltner's advantage. The line of 80 ill-matched trucks was too big for the size of the ambuscade, and already half of them were clear and out. The main fire was supposed to have been triggered by one of the 75mm rifles taking out the last vehicle, which wasn't even in sight yet. The 274th Regiment had just unwittingly bitten off more than it could chew. One of the regimental traits of the Blackhorse is an almost inhumanly fast reaction time, and at Long Binh, the rest of "C" Troop was roaring out the gates at full throttle, even as the gunships were lifting off the pad.

In the kill zone, eight trucks were trapped because the first one of them was carrying a heavy load and couldn't get out of the way. ACAVs C18 and C13 were in the kill zone with them and were firing into the banana grove with everything they had, including the 40mm grenade launcher. The VC, all surprise lost, were firing everything they had at the hapless trucks, but the drivers kept moving and the "shotgun" riders were firing into the right side of the road. The din was now overwhelming as hand grenades were thrown at the trucks and the truckers threw their own grenades. Drivers, steering with one hand, fired pistols with the other and lobbed grenades of their own.

ACAV C18 took a round from a recoilless on the side of its loading ramp but kept going. The trucks immediately behind C18 and C13 stopped, and the drivers dove for cover, weapons and helmets in hand. Ahead of the two ACAVs the eight trucks were still desperately trying to get clear of the kill zone. C18 then took another recoilless hit in the side. This hit started a fire and wounded the ACAV commander. His crew pulled him down into the track and another man took over the .50. Now another 75mm round hit the heavily laden lead truck in the fuel tank. The vehicle exploded violently, killing both the driver and his gunner. The burning remains of the truck lurched to the side of the road, but its trailer remained on the road partially blocking it. While the crew of C18 kept up the fire, the wounded commander radioed the situation to Keltner.

Keltner, now clear of the kill zone, sent off a quick report and then turned to reenter the firefight, just as C18, smoldering all this time, burst into flame, and on order of the critically wounded sergeant, the crew bailed out, except for the driver, who continued to drive the burning track down the road until killed. Even as C18 fought to its death, C13 moved off to protect one of the trucks, which was under a hail of grenades and small-arms fire. The ACAV raced to put its armored bulk between the truck and the enemy fire issuing from the banana grove.

Another recoilless rifle fired and sent a fuel truck up in flames. As C13 passed the truck another round exploded against its right-hand shield, destroyed the machine gun, and killed the gunner, wounding everybody but the driver. Another shell hit the engine compartment, and C13 began to burn also. At this time in the war, the tracks were still powered by gasoline engines and terribly vulnerable to fire. Burning but still fighting, C13 made another 1500 meters, clear out of the kill zone, and then the crew abandoned their vehicle, moments before it exploded.

With the passing of the second ACAV, there was a sudden silence, for a few moments, and then the hidden VC gunners began methodically blowing up the stalled trucks with their recoilless rifles. Now the few truck drivers and their shotgun riders were alone in the ditches alongside the road, alone and unprotected. They were fighting as best they could, but expected to be overrun and killed. Only minutes had passed, though, and the FAC pilots had been busy. There were still two of them, and they'd put white phosphorus marking rockets where they'd seen movement in the VC positions. When the little Bird Dogs pulled up out of their marking runs, a gunship, the only one fully operational that day, made its first pass, right over the top of the embattled truckers. The VC antiaircraft gunners now opened up on everything that flew, damaging one of the FAC ships but not, somehow, managing to hit the gunship.

Then the regimental light fire team homed in on the column of smoke from the burning trucks and began their runs. While the helicopter firing runs were in progress, the FAC people had managed to divert a preplanned air strike for the South Vietnamese Army. Now three F-100s with bombs and napalm came streaking down out of the sky onto the VC positions. The ambush was beginning to break up, as 500-pound bombs and napalm came down into their carefully prepared positions.

Lt. Keltner, meanwhile, had ordered his lead ACAVs to take the unhit part of the convoy on to Xaun Loc. Then taking C10 along with him, he turned back to the fray. Coming upon the burning C13, he dropped C10 off to protect the wounded crew and went on in . . . alone. Although his high speed—about 35 mph—protected him, a 57mm gunner managed to get a hit, after five tries, wounding both Keltner and one of his wing gunners. Then he found out that the hit had also knocked out his intercom and radios. Now the only way he could communicate was by using a PRC-10 portable radio that had been strapped to the inside of his cupola. The only individual on the particular frequency was the FAC, and this provided, for a while, a last fragile link from Keltner to the rest of his command.

When he reached the still-smoldering C18, Keltner stopped only long enough to remove the weapons and check for the crew. Finding no one, he continued on to where the truckers were holed up in a ditch. Calling for another medevac, he went on down the line, to where he could take over track C23, which had an operable radio. His wounded gunner had since died of loss of blood and was left with the truckers. Now, commanding from C23 and accompanied by his original command track, C16, Keltner returned to the first group of drivers, who told him that most of the fire was now coming from the north side of the road. By now a pair of F-5s were orbiting the site, and Keltner quickly vectored them in on the new target area. Suddenly, it was over and the relief column of ACAVs was rushing into the kill zone as other Cav units spread out over the fields, hunting for the fleeing survivors of what had once been a proud regiment of the VC main force. The VC commander's plans had been thorough, though, and the Cav never did quite catch up with his now thoroughly mauled regiment.

The full squadron was now out on sweep with all three Cav troops and the tank company beating up the bushes, picking up the occasional survivor of regiment 274. All the captives evinced sheer terror at the amount of firepower that the ACAVS, new to them, had put out. Late that afternoon, November 24, the squadron returned to Blackhorse Base for a slightly delayed Thanksgiving dinner.

Adapted from a U.S. Army Center of Military History book titled Seven Firefights in Vietnam.

SFC CHARLES HAZELIP
BONG SON, RVH, 1967

In the spring of 1967, "A" Company, 1-69 Armor, was part of the 3rd Brigade of the 25th Infantry Division. The battalion, however, had been cross-attached to the 4th Infantry Division, which was headquartered at Camp Enari, near the provincial capital of Pleiku, in the central highlands of Vietnam. While both of these divisions were conventional in makeup, the 1st Cavalry Division on the coastal plain was decidedly not. It had been reconfigured as helicopter-borne light infantry.

The 1st Cav could lift all of its infantrymen by helicopter at one time, but had no heavy armor, or even APCs, with which to fight hardened sites. The Cav relied heavily on helicopters for mobility and firepower, backing these up with TACair and its own artillery. They had, however, been taking an inordinate amount of casualties working against bunkers and trench networks in the Bong Son area. They needed tanks and "A" 1-69 was picked as their armor support.

We road-marched from the central highlands through the

infamous Mang Yang Pass, where a French armored column had been ambushed and decimated by the Viet Minh. The company continued through An Khe where the AirCav was headquartered, down to the coastal city of Qui Nhon. Here we were loaded onto LCMs that were just large enough to carry one tank and its crew. We then sailed up the coast to the Bong Son River, where we were unloaded and came under operational control of the 1st Brigade of the 1st Cav.

The Bong Son Plain stretches roughly 30 kilometers along the coastline of Vietnam and is roughly triangular in shape, about 15 km wide at the base, tapering off to a narrow valley at the northern end. On the west, it is bordered by the An Lao Mountains, and on the east by National Highway QL-1. About 10 km farther east is the coast of the South China Sea. The area once supported about 80,000 people, but most of these had been resettled out of what had become a war zone, and at the time we arrived, there were only about 12,000 farmers remaining. Mostly, they were old men, women, and children—there being a noticeable absence of military-age males.

The problem was that most of the villages had "bombproof" bunkers that the natives said were only for their protection from artillery and bombs. Strangely, those bunkers had firing slits, baffled entrances, and interlocking fields of fire. Many of them were connected by WWI-style trench networks, and we found tunnels that went from one hamlet to another. The entire area was crisscrossed with streams, rice paddy canals, and dikes, but during most of the year the land would support tanks. The main obstacle to trafficability was the network of streams, but we solved this by having the 8th engineers use their bulldozers to cut many tank ramps into the streams.

They also helped us with the bane of a tanker's existence, mines and booby traps. We normally had an engineer team of four to seven men with us and they swept for mines at the crossings and blew many in place with their demolition equipment. Every tank in the company had hit several track-breaking mines, some as many as seven or nine times. Getting blown up periodically was simply an occupational hazard.

"A" Company operated out of a major LZ named English, near the town of Bong Son at the southern end of the plain, and we built a company base at the bottom of the large airstrip. Usually there was one platoon in there at all times, undergoing tankers RR&R—rest, repair, and refit. The other two platoons would be either at LZ Geronimo at the northern end of the plain or at LZ Uplift, some kilometers south in another valley. My platoon's normal base was Geronimo, a high, windswept, dusty hill with usually one company of infantry, one battery of 105mm artillery, one or two 40mm tracked antiaircraft guns, and a platoon of tanks in residence.

About 2230, one hot muggy night in early May, I was sitting on my tank turret atop Geronimo, comparing the moonlit valley laid out before me with my map, identifying prominent terrain features, and comparing them with the map. This is a habit that I have always had as I believe that you can't lead if you don't know where you are. Wherever I went, on or off the tank, my map case went with me.

As I was studying the terrain, I began to notice that south and a bit east of our LZ, flares were going off. Somebody had contact. Then I began to see tracers, both red (ours) and green (theirs) crisscrossing the rice paddies. Then there were intermittent explosions, grenades, and claymore mines. Then the valley began to be lit up with bigger flares than the little hand-launched infantry flares. Mortar and artillery flares began to glow into existence, and the Bong Son plain was now an eerie sight. Now I could see the lights of helicopters circling around the periphery of the area. Something was definitely up, and I knew that somebody would be calling for tanks soon. I notified my platoon leader, a fine lieutenant, that it looked like 1/12 Cav, who had that area, was in contact.

He agreed and told me to monitor the infantry command net on my auxiliary receiver, which I was already doing, and went up to the battalion TOC. While the platoon leader was gone, I heard that several units were in contact over a fairly wide area, and there were desperate calls for armor support. As usual, that was us, because there simply weren't any more tanks in the area. I immediately passed the word to mount up, and the tankers were already getting ready, disconnecting their sleeping tarps from the fenders, cranking engines, and checking ammo supplies. By the time the lieutenant came back with a march order, we were, so to speak, leaning forward in the saddle. I had already started our engineer minesweeping team down the long twisting trail to the valley floor.

He told us that the unit in contact was "C" Company, 1/12 Cav, and that we were to move out immediately. The enemy unit had definitely been identified as NVA, not Viet Cong. We were up against a fully competent military force, not local guerrillas. We had good visibility with a three-quarter moon and flares all across the contact area. We got down the trail and out onto the valley floor in good order, but the next task was to get across a stream, and we were stopped by a steep bank on the other side. The stream crossing, which we had been using, was about 20 feet wide and about three deep, but there had been some recent rains and the water had washed out the far bank.

As platoon sergeant, I was lead tank and promptly got stuck in the mud on the far side. Since we habitually ran with tow cables hooked up, the tank behind me easily pulled us out. Then, standing hip deep in muddy paddy water, we dug into the far bank and began to place explosives, of which we always carried plenty. We used a cratering charge to blow a hole in the far bank, but the ground was simply too soft and muddy to hold a 52-ton tank. We must have waded across four of five times to set explosives, but I always got stuck. We couldn't get across the stream at that point. This was counterproductive.

At this time we had no infantry to secure us and were terribly vulnerable to fanatics with satchel charges or RPGs. Things were starting to get a bit hairy, and I told the platoon leader that there was another, better crossing nine or ten km south of here. He agreed and said to lead out, which I did. We, at this time, had only four tanks as one was down for repairs, up on Geronimo. Eventually, operating by terrain inspection off the map, I found that crossing in the night, a feat of which I was quite proud at the time. Once across, we then had to cut back as we'd come a bit south of the battle raging behind us.

At that time, my platoon and I were feeling more than a little bit nervous as we'd been in situations just like this before—off into the dark with no infantry into a night infested with VC or worse, the North Vietnamese Army. That, however, was the way we had to fight most of the time, and we simply did it, no questions asked. The last time was up in the highlands when the Special Forces camp up at Duc Co had been attacked by a full regiment of NVA. It had gotten so bad that with three out of four tanks immobilized by mines, we had to button up, call TACair in on top of us, and then shoot the survivors off each other. This was starting to feel the same way.

These thoughts went fleeting through my mind, and I was determined not to get caught the same way again. We'd been on the move, though, and after finding the crossing and having the engineers sweep it, we were on the other side. We were almost home free, which was the time you had to be really alert. We came up on Charlie Company's push (radio frequency) and were vectored in to their position, which was a semicircle facing a village. No sooner had we gotten into position than we got orders to link up with an infantry platoon and move west and south to the other side of the village where there was an abandoned airstrip, and set up a blocking position.

This was accomplished, and we spent the rest of the night adjusting artillery illumination and dealing with the intermittent sniper activity. Usually, this is what the VC or NVA did while they were withdrawing or repositioning their forces. They'd set up a screen of snipers to discourage patroling or scouting, and harass the attacking force while they moved their platoons around. These were extremely competent people.

About an hour before dawn, all contact ceased. An armored-and-infantry-combined sweep was organized and conducted through the village we had cordoned off. We found the usual bloodstains, abandoned gear, and what not, but no bodies. At this point, almost as an afterthought, a decision was made to sweep through the other section of the village, on the east side of the airstrip. I say as an afterthought because we were told to sweep through with one platoon on the way to selecting a PZ, or pickup zone, to extract the infantry to LZ English. Supposedly, this operation was over.

A brief conference was held between our lieutenant and the

infantry platoon leader, and the decision was made to mount the infantry on the tanks to speed things up. When we reached the hamlet named An qui (1) they would dismount and begin the search. A word is necessary here, about those little hamlets. They were family compounds, which made up the villages, and if the name of the main village where the headman lived was An qui, then the rest of them were simply numbered. The previous night, we had been facing An qui (3).

We moved out in platoon box, two tanks abreast, with two following, infantry on board. With this formation, no matter what happened, we could get at least three 90mm guns to bear instantly. As we approached the hamlet, we came upon an irrigation ditch about eight feet wide and four deep, which was spanned by a coconut-log bridge that could take one tank, just barely. We had to use it but the problem was that, for a few minutes, we were channelized into one point. We had to cross one tank at a time. This we did, carefully, each tank crossing and then fanning out to one side to secure the next one over. I crossed first, cut left, and took up a firing position, just in case. Two more tanks crossed with one to go when it happened.

There was a long, sustained burst of MG fire to my left. I turned and saw our infantry jumping or falling off that tank as sustained AK-47 fire began to eat into us. The fire was so heavy you would not believe it. It sounded like a giant kettle drum was being beaten, and we were inside of it. A nervous NVA machine-gunner had triggered off a battalion-sized ambush, and we were in the kill zone. My fourth tank cut to the right, hit a mine, took an RPG round, and was immobilized, although it could still fight.

We were in a cross fire, taking casualties right and left, at close range, about 15–20 meters. *The SHIT is ON,* I remember thinking to myself. I immediately ordered a full assault, right into the village, and we moved slowly forward, cannons thumping out 90mm HE canister and HEP, while every machine gun we had yammered between cannon shots. We were firing as fast as the guns could be loaded, and a good loader can feed the breech as fast as the gun comes out of recoil.

The first few minutes of a well-designed ambush are characterized by chaos, panic, and a total loss of coordination and communication, and at that time the tanks were the only elements working. The infantry that had not become casualties were all down prone, looking for concealment and getting organized. The first thing you have to do is get control of your people and move them out of the kill zone. This can be done by fire and movement, which the tanks were providing. Soldiers will usually respond to anyone who sounds like he knows what he is doing, and they could see that it was safer behind the tanks than anywhere else.

The initial shock hadn't worn off yet, though, and I couldn't get enough infantrymen on the move. Now we were firing directly into ground-level bunkers and spider holes, and were beginning to get the upper hand by sheer firepower. The only people to follow me into that hellhole were my engineers—all six of 'em. Four were already casualties and being carried out, to be medevacked later. While all this was going on, the two platoon leaders, mine and the infantry's, were reporting what was happening to the infantry CO and requesting help in the form of fire support (ANY kind), medevac, and ammo resupply.

Communication was a problem as usual. Since everyone was on the same push and everyone was trying to talk at the same time, nothing could get through. In a situation like this, every message is urgent, to whomever is sending it. Radio procedure gets disregarded as the RTOs (radio telephone operators) report that so-and-so is hit and needs medevac, they are taking sniper fire, etc. Sometimes the only way to get through is to stick your head out of the tank and yell at the infantry squad leader on the ground to get his people in gear.

The infantry platoon leader had reported to his boss, and the rest of the company was double-timing it to us, but they were a thousand meters away. When they finally got there, they were exhausted and needed a short breather, especially in that wet tropical heat. They were full of fight and took their breather as they maneuvered into position by squads and fire teams. Fire had broken out everywhere in the hamlet, and there were hundreds of broken-off coconut stumps that acted just like WWII-style dragon's teeth and would peel a track off or belly-up a tank. The drivers lived in a lonely world of their own while the turret crews fought.

Only men who have been close-in ground fighting at hand-grenade range can understand what it is like to be in a life-or-death struggle for not just surviving but winning. The action was so close that I got blisters on two fingers of my left hand . . . from pulling hand grenade rings and dropping the grenades around the tank.

The heat was another problem. Figuring a starting temperature of about 100 degrees inside the tank *before* the action starts, you can see that we were working at the limits of human tolerance. The heat of the cannon and two machine guns raised the temperature inside that tank to unbelievable heights, even with the turret blower full-on and the engine drawing its combustion air from inside the hull. The stench of burning powder and cordite was awful, and the smoke and dust from the guns coated all of us with grime. We couldn't wear shirts, and everybody was working stripped to the waist. Our eyes were constantly burning and sweat ran in muddy rivers off our bodies. The smoke can get so thick that you can't see across the turret.

Every 10 or 12 rounds the tank would clutter up with 90mm casings, and we had to break off firing to dump these out so they wouldn't jam the turret. Then the loader had to reload the ready rack from the hull storage while the driver and TC kept a nervous watch outside. A good loader is worth his weight in gold, especially one as good as mine was. I didn't have a gunner then, and operating a turret with just the TC and loader requires a high order of teamwork, with the loader doing 90 percent of it.

All I had to do was pick targets, traverse the main gun and yell out for whatever type of shell was needed, lay the gun and fire it. It was the loader, sweating and stumbling around the turret, grabbing the shell and feeding the cannon, while he serviced the temperamental coaxial machine gun, changed barrels, and made it work.

While fighting my own tank, I also had to control the movement of my other two mobile vehicles and work along with the infantry. It was the tanks that determined the course of battle. We had the firepower and the advantage of a higher viewpoint and telescopic sights. We picked the course of battle, and the infantry went along with us, covering our vulnerable flanks so we wouldn't be knocked out by some suicidal attacker with 50 pounds of explosive strapped to his chest.

It seemed like it was us against the world, but help was on the way. Medevac choppers had been landing behind us in a small one-ship LZ, getting out most of our wounded. The dead would go last. Several batteries of artillery at LZ English and other places were standing by, and ARA (aerial rocket artillery) ships were on the way. Back at English, resupply slicks were hooking up to preloaded cargo nets of ammo, medical supplies, and water. The Green Machine was in motion.

As soon as one of Charlie Company's sister units could be loaded, it would be air assaulted into blocking positions around the hamlet. This having been accomplished, we were ordered out to resupply and began loading up the dead and wounded onto our hulls as we backed out of there. We were now down to a few white phosphorus shells for the 90s and we fired them into the ground to create a smoke screen to hide our withdrawal.

As we backed out of the village, ARA ships and gunships arrived and began to make rocket and MG runs. We backed out slowly, covering the infantry, who'd gotten the word first. The barrels of our coaxial guns were glowing almost a cherry red, and rounds were going tumbling out as we'd shot the rifling out of the barrels long ago. In the first five hours of that contact, I burned out three MG barrels. As we eased on out of there, the gunships had to go back to refuel as a UH-series helicopter, the famed Huey, can only fly for 155 minutes—it burns one gallon per minute.

Now, though, the artillery had gotten registered and was beginning to turn that hamlet into a moonscape. Meanwhile, I had a chance to fill in my own company commander, who back at English was getting a bit frustrated at not being able to lead his own tanks. That was the nature of that war though; it was essentially a series of small unit actions. Our CO had already done what he could, getting ammo, water, and supplies out to us, and now he informed us that armored reinforcements were on the way. He'd gotten our "reserve" on the road.

As may be seen, "A" 1-69 was spread pretty thin. Our reserve was the platoon of broken-down tanks that had been in English pulling repairs, followed by the tank retriever that was necessary to keep some of the cripples running. In addition, our own medics were on the way, in an armored ambulance, and our senior medic was rated for light surgery.

The infantry company commander informed us that he'd be ready to reassault about an hour after the artillery fire had been lifted. He also added that as a final gesture, a concentration of tear gas would be fired to draw the NVA out into the open while we went in. *Fat chance.* About this time a flight of F-4 Phantoms rolled in, hot to get their licks in. They used their normal cloverleaf pattern, and on each pass dropped 250- and 500-pound bombs and napalm, finishing up with 20mm gun runs.

After they had finished, the artillery dropped the promised final concentration and the tear gas, and we went back in. Our other platoon of tanks had arrived and been briefed by our platoon leader. We shifted to the right, and they went in to our left. We were on line, in good order, with two infantry platoons, but there was a full battalion of main force NVA in there and they were full of fight. The enemy commander had reorganized, through his tunnel and trench network, and was determined to contest every foot of ground.

No one who has ever fought the NVA will ever question their courage or tenacity. This was a veteran, hard-core NVA battalion that was well trained, superbly led, and well equipped. They were some of the finest light infantry in the world, and the fighting was close in, brutal, and murderous. This was not the kind of combat that the Patton-series tank was designed for. They were designed to kill other tanks at a range of several miles. This, however, was the kind of brutal fighting that the U.S. Marines had had to do in the Pacific several wars ago. The tanks were always in the forefront, with the infantry right alongside, but do not think that it was a well-planned coordinated assault.

The only way to describe this kind of fighting is as a semi-organized brawl. There was no finesse, no grand strategy or tactics involved. I am sure we committed every tactical error in the book, and maybe invented some special for the occasion. But we were, by God, getting the job done.

No one had time for the niceties of fire control when shooting point-blank into a bunker right alongside a machine gun that was trying to kill you, or shooting right into a spider hole with the 90mm at maximum depression. We'd see a sapper coming at us with a satchel charge and shoot him with a grease gun (M-3 submachine gun), and see the dust jump from some NVA that boarded over the side when you shot him with a .45 that you pulled from a shoulder holster.

Every time there was even the slightest break in our lines, the NVA would come swarming in to counterattack, either individually or by squads, and our infantry would shoot them off our backs while we smashed the enemy's bunkers. The grunts couldn't have lived in front of our guns, but by now they'd follow the tanks anywhere. They kept us alive, we kept them alive, and together, we broke that NVA battalion.

It takes a lot of guts to do what those kids did. I have heard a lot of postwar critics whine about the caliber of our men, but they just don't know what they are talking about. They weren't there. They weren't involved in the knock-down, drag-out type of combat that we lived through and won. In 1967, we still had the best professional army that the nation had ever fielded, before the rot set in. Those young men were tough as whit leather and there was no give in them. They were the pride of our nation and, man for man, the best fighting men on this planet, and even today I will fight the SOB who tries to say otherwise.

One other little point while I am on this. Someone once said that there are no atheists in foxholes . . . and no bigots either. I have seen young Southern white boys fighting and dying right alongside hip Northern blacks, saving each other's lives, day after day. Race isn't the problem; the problem is individual behavior, and the battlefield is the leveler. Adversity is a great builder of cohesion.

That fight continued through the afternoon until we again

ran low on ammo and had to withdraw. We backed out in good order, bringing our wounded and dead with us. The U.S. Air Force returned and made pass after pass with 250-pound bombs until the place looked like a lunar landscape with gray dust and bomb craters everywhere, and still the NVA fought on. While the air strike was still on, we started to set up a night cordon of the village. The 1/12th's "A," "B," and "D" Companies had been air-assaulted in to blocking positions to prevent any escape from that village. In other wars, units were defeated; in this one, many were simply exterminated.

We'd had two tank commanders killed and four crewmen wounded, and we'd gotten replacements from our headquarters section. Our maintenance people, as usual, did a superb job of repairing combat damage to our tanks. They worked all through the night under intermittent sniper fire. Resupply choppers came in with more ammo, and the artillery pounded the hell out of that village, but in the small hours of the night a short round killed two of our own riflemen.

Just before dawn, the infantry started to gear up, and they were loaded for bear. Each rifleman carried about 400 rounds for his M-16, and four to six fragmentation grenades. The grenadiers carried their M-79s and up to 70 rounds each in bandoliers. The machine gunners had 1,200 rounds each distributed about their squads. Their canteens were full, and all nonessential gear was discarded and stacked. There was a sense of quiet determination, and the riflemen and tankers exchanged a silent thumbs-up. This time we were going in to finish it. The artillery let up, and we moved in. Slowly, carefully, eyes scanning for hostiles, we slid forward.

The village was a smoking ruin. Practically every tree had been blown down, fires were everywhere, and patches of fog mixed with the battle smoke, before the sun began to burn it off. This time we were more settled down, more methodical. The enemy fire built up, and we started taking casualties. Bunker after bunker was depopulated and then destroyed with satchel charges. Trench line after line was run over and consolidated; the fighting was just as fierce as yesterday, but there were no locally concerted attacks. The enemy was running out of manpower. This time, positions taken were not lost. Around noon, the firing had tapered off until only single shots were heard, and the last pockets of resistance were mopped up.

Now came the grisly task of finding and recovering our dead. Some had lain in the trenches for as long as 36 hours, and we had to find them and identify them and get them onto ponchos or into body bags. My platoon of tanks and "A" Company, 1/12 Cav, searched the whole area, right out to the base of the An Lao Mountains, finding only discarded equipment. Most of the infantry was air-evacced out, but you can't do that with a 52-ton tank, so we stayed out on the plain for a while . . . as usual.

A few days later, my platoon was brought back to LZ English for a much-needed maintenance break, and a couple of us had to attend an awards ceremony held by 1/12 Cav. There wasn't much left of Charlie Company. Out of a whole company of infantry—that's four platoons of about 38 men each—I counted only 37 men left standing. A lot of good men fought and died out there. Seldom talked about but never forgotten, this was their war, and they deserve better from the "official" histories.

Adapted by the author for this book from original material submitted by Charles Hazelip.

22

THE SIXTY-NINTH ARMOR

FIRST LT. JOHN MOUNTCASTLE

One of a tank's lesser-known capabilities is its ability to act as an instant artillery piece. Up until the advent of the Abrams tank, every American main battle tank carried an elevation quadrant and an azimuth indicator that allowed it to drop shells with great accuracy anyplace within the range of its gun. One of the last units to use this capability was the 3rd Platoon, Bravo Company, 1-69th Armor, under command of First Lt. John Mountcastle. Here is his story of what might have been the last "Redleg Platoon" of the armored force.

Darkness came swiftly to the central highlands of Vietnam. With sunset two hours past, the heat of the day began to fade. A slight welcome breeze dried the sweat-soaked fatigues of the infantrymen manning the perimeter of the firebase. The night sounds of the dense forest surrounding the position were only faintly audible over the hum of the generators supplying electricity to the HQ bunkers. It was April 1967, and

American soldiers of the 4th Infantry Division were settling down for another night along the Cambodian border.

Occasionally the querulous voice of a soldier or the clink of metal striking metal came from the dark forms in the center of the base, or the flicker of a filtered flashlight revealed outlines of sweating soldiers carrying long shells over their shoulders to the five tanks. The laboring ammunition bearers made little noise, speaking in subdued voices as they carried their loads to the tracked machines. Then, once the turrets were full, the soldiers sank wearily down on the sand-bagged revetments, smoking carefully cupped cigarettes, awaiting their next orders in silence. It would not be long in coming.

As they rested, their lieutenant made his way to the thin sliver of light that marked the FDC, or fire direction center. His return signaled an end to the break, and the troops soon mounted their vehicles. Under the red glow of the dome lights in the turrets, they checked the fuses on their shells, and waited for firing orders. Within minutes of the lieutenant's return, they came.

"FIRE MISSION! 15 ROUNDS, HE, DEFLECTION, 84 LEFT; QUADRANT, PLUS 150, AT MY COMMAND FIRE!"

For five minutes, the elevated gun tubes of the tanks blasted shells westward into the night sky. While crew commanders relayed orders from the lieutenant, gunners checked elevation quadrants, pressed the firing triggers, and sang out, "On the way." Loaders stripped to the waist and streaming sweat bent low and fed rounds into the breeches of the elevated guns. Finally, after the mission was fired, the crew commanders announced, "Rounds complete!" The sudden quiet, coming so soon after the noise of firing, seemed to echo its own presence in the night air.

After a moment, the cry of "Brass" went up from each hull and empty shell casings were handed out to be stacked behind the tanks. A few minutes for rest, then another fire mission, loading, firing, and unloading the brass, until 200 rounds had sped into the night. Only then did the exhausted crews have time to think of sleep or of the guard duty they would all pull in the five hours of darkness left till dawn. These "artillerymen" were actually the tankers of the 3rd Platoon of Company "B," 1-69th Armor, and as their former platoon leader, I well remember our efforts to "put steel on target."

During much of 1967, the 4th Infantry Division Artillery was hard-pressed to provide the level of support demanded of it. By augmenting the firepower of DivArty, we tankers had demonstrated the flexibility that characterizes armor operations. The missions were nearly always performed at night and was in addition to a primary responsibility of supporting the infantry battalions in daylight Central Highlands search operations and escorting truck convoys through ambush zones.

The use of tanks in an indirect fire role was certainly not a new idea in 1967. Tank guns had augmented artillery fires in WWII and Korea. I was aware of this, but was still surprised when told that my platoon would be the test unit for a new and challenging mission. The battalion commander of the 1-69th Armor, then LTC Paul S. Williams, explained that we must exploit our capability to support not only infantry but artillery units. We were still a new concept, and all of our "Black Panther" troops were solidly behind Col. Williams in his campaign to convince other commanders that we could do something other than escort convoys.

Training began immediately. Using our gunnery manuals and assisted by an artillery officer on loan, the 3rd Platoon delved into the mysteries of indirect fire. We learned how to position our tanks, investigated the M2 aiming circle, which is a glorified surveyor's transit, and rapidly grew proficient in laying our gun tubes exactly parallel. NCOs who had given themselves over to the "co-ax and canister school of gunnery" took great pleasure in demonstrating their knowledge of fire control instruments gained years before on the tank ranges in Germany and at Ft. Knox, Kentucky.

The firing tables for our 90mm high-velocity guns proved to be no problem for the artillery advisors, and after some practice in setting time fuses on our HE rounds, the 3rd

TANK ACES

(Redleg) Platoon was ready for its first live-fire mission as an artillery battery. Within a few days we road-marched to the Special Forces base at Plei Me. There, under the watchful eyes of our artillery mentors and the local 105mm battery, we took up firing positions. By running the tanks up on to a dirt berm, we increased the elevation available over that of the gun mounts.

We fired 100 rounds on the first mission. Our target was an enemy base area in the dense jungle of the La Drang Valley, 12 kilometers to our southwest. Using our firing tables, which were somewhat different from those of the 105 howitzer, the FDC computed our elevation and deflection settings and then assured area coverage by giving us a different set of figures for the last 50 rounds. The entire mission went off without a hitch, and we were gratified to hear that an aerial observer had reported good target coverage. In addition, the compliments from the kibitzing artillerymen of the 105 Battery, who had been our teachers, boosted the platoon's collective ego. It seemed that there wasn't anything that a tanker couldn't do.

The business of serving two masters, working both day and night, demanded a great deal of both men and machines. In the course of a night's firing, an entire platoon rotated through the loader, gunner, and tank-commander positions as the fire missions came in, in order to spread the load equitably. In spite of the obvious strain, my tankers took obvious pride in being among the hardest working troops on the firebase. As a platoon leader, I gained priceless experience in operating independently, many miles from our parent unit.

When the 4th Division received additional artillery support, we were relieved of indirect fire mission. As we departed Plei Me, the "Redleg Tankers" could take credit for performing a challenging mission in a most professional manner. It was with a sense of honest pride that we announced to one and all: "Rounds complete!"

Adapted from an article in the Artillery Journal, *by Maj. John Mountcastle.*

ACTION AT BEN HET
March 3, 1969

The Ben Het Special Forces camp, west of the city of Dak To in the northern highlands of the Republic of South Vietnam, stood on a barren, dozer-scraped hill overlooking the juncture of the borders of Vietnam, Cambodia, and Laos. In addition, the camp had the task of securing military road 512, which was its only land route to the allied main base at Dak To. Also, not coincidentally, the camp was within patrol and artillery range of the Ho Chi Minh Trail.

At this point in history, about a year after the infamous Tet offensive of 1968, the communist supply line into the Southern Republic was being systematically choked off, and they were in danger of losing their grip on the prized rice fields of the south. The decision of the local NVA commander had been to eliminate the reinforced Green Beret camp by invading it with tanks, which had proved fairly successful before, at the Plei Me Special Forces camp, some years earlier. His nemesis here would be also, as before, the battered M-48s of the 69th Heavy Tank Battalion.

In early February, the NVA had started battering the vulnerable camp with long-barreled Russian 130mm guns, which many experts consider to be one of the best artillery pieces on the planet. For weeks, the big 70-pound shells had been leaving their privileged sanctuaries in Cambodia to come howling down on the bunkered base at Dak To, sometimes as rapidly as one every 45 seconds. No one dared get more than a few steps from a bunker, and there were many casualties, some fatal. Fortunately, the communist guns were sited where their muzzle glow could be seen against the heavy jungle and the cloud cover of the gloomy weather. The men all knew the flight time from "flash to bang" and would simply count rapidly while running for a bunker. At the end of 18 beats there were two choices, be in a bunker or hit the deck and pray as the ground jumped under you.

At this point in time, Green Beret patrols out in the jungle reported seeing Russian-made PT-76 scout tanks moving south through Laos, and the American commander put in a call for the best antitank medicine he could find. The prescription was Company "B," 1-69 Armor under Capt. John Stovall, which was already at Dak To.

February 25, 1969: When Captain Stovall rode his jungle-battered, rocket-gouged 50-ton steed up the access trail into Ben Het, he led a platoon of hardened tankers second to none in the world. As was usual for the 69th, when they were shifted from one AO (area of operations) to another, the company base had been placed next to the airstrip and helipad at Dak To. Tanks burn a lot of combustibles, and the resupply usually has to come in by cargo plane and go out to far-flung platoons and even lone tanks by helicopter. When the call from Ben Het came, Capt. Stovall simply mounted his lead tank and took a platoon out personally.

What he saw at Ben Het wasn't overly heartening. In addition to the beleaguered 12-man Special Forces "A" team, there were three 175mm guns, a pair of 40mm "duster" tracked antiaircraft guns left over from the Korean War, and assorted indigenous infantry. These troops were three companies of Civilian Irregular Defense Group (CIDG) native troops, who'd been trained and equipped with assorted weaponry by the Special Forces team. The camp had been under almost constant attack for about a week—the situation wasn't at all promising.

Bravo Company, 1-69, was, as usual, strung out over quite a bit of distance, as one of their missions was to secure the road links around Dak To. That meant a mix of convoy escort and strong point duty (sit by a bridge and look dangerous). Stovall had a reserve platoon back at Dak To, but it was understrength and its tanks were in various states of repair. The captain and his 1st Platoon leader immediately placed their tanks on the camp's perimeter and had the crews begin digging and sandbagging their positions. Almost immediately, they too came under long-range artillery fire and had to work their guns in counterbattery fire, shooting back at the hidden communist weaponry with their long 90s. Between the platoon's guns and the three 175mm cannons, some reduction in the communist fire was effected, but those 130s were never silenced.

For a long week, the situation remained unchanged. The tanks and their enemies exchanged long-range gunfire, and the NVA probed the defenses with night attacks. These would consist of companies of light NVA infantry trying to sap their way through the base's concertina wire and minefield defenses while the defenders shot at them and the guns from Cambodia tried to keep the CIDG soldiers in their holes. After the tankers arrived and began ripping the attackers with canister shells, this practice died off, as did much of the shelling. During this period, casualties in the emplaced tank platoon were "slight," amounting to nine scratches, which didn't remove anyone from duty, and one medevac—the platoon leader.

At this point, short on officers and getting suspicious about the lessening of enemy activity, Captain Stovall, who'd returned to Dak To to take care of Bravo Company's business, got worried about the slackening of attacks and came back to Ben Het, setting up a command post in an abandoned bunker. The first and second of March proved to be disconcertingly quiet. The abnormal silence was broken by mortar fire and recoilless rifle fire when the supply convoy arrived on the first of March. That night the Special Forces team sent out patrols of CIDGs led by American noncoms. They found nothing. Throughout the next day, they waited and waited.

At 2200 hours on the night of the second, platoon sergeant Hugh Havermale, of Berkeley Springs, West Virginia, slid out of the night and into the bunkered CP and reported to Captain Stovall that his men could hear engines and tracks to the west of the camp. Somewhat alarmed, Stovall accompanied his platoon sergeant to the wire and scanned the area west of the camp with a starlight scope, which amplified local light about 80,000 times. They could see nothing, and due to the sound-deadening effect of the jungle, they couldn't exactly pinpoint a location. All they could hear was the sound of unidentified vehicles running their engines for a few minutes, then shutting down. They could tell, however, that the engines were considerably larger than truck engines.

On March 3, enemy activity remained low, and three CIDG patrols were sent out, this time to operate as outposts. At the daily intelligence briefing, Stovall was informed by the camp commander that an attack was imminent and that the enemy was known to have armor capability. The last time Americans had crossed guns with communist tanks was in Korea, 16 years before. In the meantime, the communists had developed several more generations of tanks while the 69th was still using the M-48, a development of the M-46, which had fought in Korea. Since then, Russia had developed the T-54 and its derivatives, the new and deadly T-62 family and the PT-76 patrol tank. Which enemy tank, Stovall had to have wondered, would it be? He was just about to find out.

At 2100 hours that night, the camp's central hill began receiving heavy and accurate recoilless fire from at least two locations out in the distant rain forest. By 2130, heavy mortar bombardment, probably from man-packed 82mm models of either Russian or Chinese manufacture. Suddenly, in between the shell bursts, the tanker's sensitized ears picked up the engine sounds again. This time much closer and roaring with assault power. Then they picked up the distinctive clatter of tracks. Now there was no doubt at all; they were going to receive an armored assault!

Again they scanned desperately with their single starlight scope, to no avail. One tank switched on its 75-million-power searchlight on infrared light while the gunner almost poured his eyes into the magnifying sight. Again, there wasn't a trace of enemy armor although small groups of sappers could be seen, working on the wire. Suddenly there was a flash about 800 meters out, where a cluster of antipersonnel mines had been laid in a defile. The gunner switched his sights to the fireball. TARGET! A tank was outlined in the flames. Rapidly he counted. Three tanks and some kind of open tracked vehicle were illuminated by the fire. Like hunting cobras drawn to the heat, the three 90mm tubes swung to the hostiles and began lashing out with HEAT rounds. *Jackpot.* Those tanks were right in front of the target, rock which the American tankers had been using to zero and range their guns. This was a known range to target and the long 90s struck with deadly accuracy.

Other tankers, whom Stovall had brought to set up his HQ, instantly went into action, firing auxiliary weapons to help the CIDGs, who were now under attack and firing their preplanned final protective fires. The armor battalion medics had set up shop and were treating Americans and Vietnamese alike when Stovall, nervously standing beside his HQ, monitoring the radios and scanning the hell storm, got more good news. A fourth tank had been sighted, approaching the thinly defended airstrip side of the camp. Then a radio report from an outlying CIDG post came in describing an eight-to-fifteen-vehicle column approaching from the Cambodian borderline to the west of them.

Stepping into the CP, Stovall picked up a field phone, spun the crank and ordered the camp's small mortar squad to fire illumination rounds. Almost instantly he heard the hollow bonking sound of an 81mm behind him, and in a few seconds, the night was eerily illuminated by half a dozen magnesium flares, each descending on its own little four-foot parachute. Now one of the tanks had taken up searchlight duty, lighting targets for its mates. The necessary protection of night was rapidly being stripped from the attackers.

The mind-numbing thunder of a working tank platoon became even louder, if possible, and it was death to even walk to the side of the steel chariots as enemy fire was ricocheting from their flanks, and even the muzzle blast of a tank cannon is lethal. Eyes staring into the wicked tracery of battle, Stovall could see at least two enemy tanks take direct main gun hits and begin to burn fiercely as their ammo and fuel cooked off. Somebody'd already gotten the tracked carrier and it too was on fire.

To get a better view, Stovall, a tall gaunt Kentuckian, leaped to the back deck of one of the tanks. As he stepped behind the turret into relative safety, a large fireball, followed by a body-shaking concussion, erupted from the front slope of the hull. They'd just taken a cannon hit from a tank's main armament. The blast flung Stovall from the deck and landed him in a tangled heap. The tank commander, Sgt. Mike Stewart, was blown clean out of his turret and dropped helpless and bleeding 10 feet to the rear of the tank. . . . That's also a 12-foot drop.

The loader and driver who'd been on top of the turret, manning its top .50-cal machine gun were killed instantly, blown down and to the side of the rocking, smoking hull. Although the tank had been put temporarily out of action, crews from other tanks and Bravo-Company-HQ types rushed to fill its fighting positions, and in a few minutes, its weapons were again doing business with the NVA.

Suddenly, the night was again filled with the clattering roar of tank engines and tracks. Could this get worse?

The perimeter's wire gate was rudely jerked open by a tanker from the 69th. Bravo's reaction platoon, under Lieutenant Ed Nichols, rushed through the gap and into firing positions alongside the now almost exhausted 1st Platoon. Enemy fire was now down to almost nothing, and an AC-47 "Spooky" gunship was on station, harassing the enemy retreat with its Gatling guns, shattering them wherever they formed into an inviting target. For the remainder of the night, the perimeter was quiet, save when some nervous rifleman saw a bush walk and took a shot at it.

Next morning, Sgt. Havermale took a patrol out to investigate their opponents. They found two badly shot-up PT-76 hulls and a completely smashed tracked carrier. Further patrolling turned up several damaged and abandoned vehicles. No one ever identified the enemy unit, nor has anyone ever figured out, thus far, just why the NVA tried an attack on this particular camp. The attack was spurious, lacked assault infantry, and the usually wily and competent NVA hadn't even laid an ambush for the relief platoon. Given the reputation and known effectiveness of American armor, it seems doubtful if the enemy had known of the existence of a platoon of the big M-48s at Ben Het. Possibly they came in straight off the trail and went in unbriefed.

Capt. Stovall was medevacked and survived, as did the tank commander, Mike Stewart. Bravo Company sustained two killed and two wounded in that battle. The M-48 that took the 76mm main cannon hit was not seriously damaged and continued to patrol the highlands. Once again it was proved that the best defense against a tank is another tank.

THE LAST BATTLE
Sgt. James Russell
"C" Company, 1-69

January 8, 1970: For nearly a year, Charlie Company had been my home in the central highlands of Vietnam, but that period of my life was almost over. Within the next month, my tour would be over and I would be leaving the 1st Platoon forever, taking with me only my memories. I had already made plans for a five-day leave in Australia, coupled with my last three-day in-country R&R. I had chosen to use both of them together so that when I left the field for the last time, it would be permanent. Little did I realize that morning that I would get neither leave nor R&R.

A little before 0900 hours, my M-48A3 tank had completed its routine morning rumble down Highway 19 and crawled up onto the embankment, barely off the pavement, for another boring day of strong point duty, guarding a stretch of road with our guns. From my TC cupola, I monitored the radio net as my crew prepared themselves for the long hours ahead of us. As I listened to the activity on the net, though, I became more apprehensive. An infantry unit was in contact in an area that was just down the road from us. Usually, unless contact was broken, it would result in a call for us and our firepower. The contact wasn't broken, and we were called out.

These were not Viet Cong; these were the same professional North Vietnamese regulars that we'd been fighting for a year or more, and they were dug in and entrenched in a hardened position. When we got to the contact area, we were formed into a platoon wedge, facing north into the tree line. Dismounted infantrymen took up station between our Patton tanks, and we began to move forward at a walking pace. Suddenly one of the infantry sergeants yelled, "Watch it when you go in. The bastards are in the trees, too."

If he had seen NVA in trees, it was probably so that they could shoot American tank crewmen. However, due to the density of the cover, we couldn't secure hatches, nor could we even use our sights. Tank commanders, including myself, had to expose ourselves from the waist up, reaching back down into the turret to control the guns with the TC's override control. There was no need for a gunner in these kinds of operations. My loader would feed the gun, and I would fire it. The driver would just drive.

Continuing our slow movement northward, I placed my hatch in the upright position to cover my back. As soon as we entered the forest, we began drawing automatic weapons fire. Now the radio headset in my helmet is full of constant yelling. As the radios are keyed, I can hear cannon and machine-gun fire, adding to the confusion. Flipping my headset back to intercom only, I order the crew, "Freeman, turn right 30 degrees," and the hull moves forward and to the right. "Chapman, release the safety, prepare to fire." I sense motion in the turret beneath me and hear the single word "UP." The cannon is now ready to fire. I pick a target on the hillside, a place where somebody could be hidden.

I yell the warning, "On the way," and the tank bucks in recoil as the 90mm fires. Noise and smoke from the explosion fill the air as she settles back on her suspension. We fire again and continue. A quick look back assures us that the infantry are still with us. Each time we fire, the smoke makes it harder to see. When the smoke clears, I pick another target, such as a clump of trees or bushes where somebody might be hiding, and fire again. The other tanks do the same.

Each tank carries 63 rounds of 90mm ammunition. Three are HEAT rounds in case we run into more enemy tanks, like we did in March up at Ben Het. The rest of the shells consisted of canister, beehive, HE, and WP. We had two types of canister, the older kind that was in a black can and contained about

1,800 little steel cylinders and a newer green can type that was full of fléchettes. Firing our 90mm "shotgun" with both types of canister shells would open paths in the brush that you could drive a tank through. As tree tops and other debris fall, I see two enemy soldiers crumple to the ground . . . and two more still up and running. They were in the path of our shells and shouldn't be alive. Both are dressed in faded green fatigues, wearing pith helmets and carrying AK-47s. With ammo belts crisscrossed over their shoulders, they run for cover. I was caught so off guard that I failed to shoot right at them and could only send a shell into the brush after them.

We continued moving slowly through the cannon smoke, and all of a sudden, there it was, the enemy's fortress . . . and it was tank proof. The NVA had chosen an excellent position— a steep hill covered with scattered trees and large boulders spaced too closely for tanks to pass through. My driver moved us up the hill as far as possible, but the large boulders prevented us from going any farther, so we continued to fire from our enforced stationary position.

Without warning, our tank began to roll backward! Instinctively, I ducked down inside the turret as the tank gathered speed. Flying backward down the steep hillside, 52 tons of steel had so much momentum that even after reaching level ground we continued to roll through the brush and trees, flattening everything in our path. I could only grit my teeth and hold on. Finally, after what seemed forever, the tank came to rest. I had assumed that my driver had been hit and lost control. "Freeman, Freeman," I yelled, "can you hear me? Are you all right?" He responded with a simple "yes," and I asked, "What the fuck happened?" Freeman answered in a shaky voice, "The transmission went out, and I couldn't hold it with the brakes."

My heart was still pounding when I raised back up to see where we were. An infantryman ran up shouting, "Move up, move up, you ran over some guys!" I suddenly felt sick. After all that's happened in the last year, now this. Jesus Christ . . . God . . . no.

I watched the grunt check under my tank; in a moment, he reappeared and shook his head. I couldn't hear what he said, but he waved his arms and ran off, and I knew that no one had been underneath our tank. I keyed the radio, calling the platoon leader. "Charlie one-one, this is Charlie one-two. My transmission went out, I can't move." A disembodied voice came back. "Charlie one-two, this is one-one, we'll get one to tow you in a little while."

We couldn't move, but we could still fire while we waited for help. I had Chapman change to high-explosive shells since we would be firing from a distance. I tried using the gun sights, but the smoke in the air prevented me from seeing anything. I had to climb halfway out of the commander's hatch in order to see anything. The whole top of the hill was almost engulfed in a blue-gray smoke, and behind the hill was the black smoke of the napalm runs from the air strikes. In the midst of all this chaos, helicopters were hovering at treetop levels and attacking in front of us. One of the choppers took a hit and went spinning down into the smoke. Later on, I heard that most of the crew survived.

We finally expended all of our main gun ammo and were now down to the co-ax and the .50, and we were running out of internal ammunition. Chapman had more ammo stored on various points outside the turret and he climbed out to resupply as I worked the guns. As he was climbing back in, an RPG hit on the right front of the turret, and suddenly I felt my face go numb. The rocket hadn't penetrated, but shrapnel had splattered in all directions. I immediately dropped down inside the turret for protection. I couldn't see out of my left eye. It was like looking at a TV screen after the station has gone off the air—just a white fuzzy nothingness. I sat on my TC seat and saw that my pants and the front of my shirt were splattered with blood. I worked up the nerve to raise my hand to feel the side of my head to see if it was still there. It was, although my hand came back covered with blood.

I suppose it was my way of looking for courage, but I recalled a story my father had told me about one of his experiences in WWII. He had been an artilleryman and had sustained a head injury during a fire mission. I remembered him saying how the blood from his forehead had run into his eyes, making him think that he was wounded in the eyes. I managed to convince myself that what happened to my father had happened to me. I had no way of knowing that my wounds were far more severe, at the time.

Looking up at Chapman, I could see his face twisted with pain. He had been hit in the arm. "Get the first-aid kit and wrap it up!" I yelled without using the intercom. Then, via the intercom, I checked on Freeman, who had not been hit. I hit the radio transmitter. "Charlie one-one, this is one-two. We've been hit." The lieutenant's voice came back. "This is one-one. How bad?" I replied, "Not bad, but we need a medic." A third voice came on the net, a medical unit. "Where are you, one-two?"

"I'm the tank at the bottom of the hill," I answered. "Help's on the way," came a reassuring voice. Meanwhile I helped Chapman wrap his arm, and he bandaged my eye. Not wanting to sit and think about my injuries and in an attempt to psych ourselves up, I said "Hey, fuck these motherfuckers, let's fire." We reloaded the .50 and resumed shooting. As we fired, two medics came aboard, over the back deck.

Once on board, they ushered Chapman and me down inside the turret, where they quickly examined and rewrapped our wounds. With the battle still raging and our radio still cluttered with yelling and screaming for more tanks, more men, and more ammo, they told us to leave the tank and head for an evacuation point behind the line of vehicles. While we were being escorted by the medic to the ground, another tank from our platoon pulled up to our disabled machine to hook it up and tow it off. I waved as we scrambled by.

Upon reaching the pickup location, Chapman and I had to crouch down to avoid small-arms fire. We noticed several other men—along with some medics—already standing by at the site. The first chopper came in, and the stretcher cases were loaded without problems. As we stood up to board, a burst of bullets flew overhead, and we dropped to the ground as the bird sped off. Within seconds another came in but was driven off by gunfire. The pilot circled around and came in once more. This time, Chapman and I ran for the bird before it even touched down. My head was throbbing and my eye was burning as I ran for the aircraft. The bandage slipped over my good eye, blinding me, but I pushed it back up and saw a figure standing in the door of the chopper, beckoning me to hurry.

When I reached the chopper, that beckoning hand reached down and pulled me into the ship, which lifted off as I stumbled head over heels into the aircraft, finally slamming into the opposite side. Still drawing fire, I could see the tanks and the battlefield getting smaller and smaller as the medic apologized for manhandling me into the bird. When we reached the main base camp, they put me on a stretcher and—for what seemed like a lifetime—I was able to completely relax. Nobody was trying to kill me. Much later, when I was in a hospital in Japan, I learned that good ol' Charlie 1-2 had died the same day that Chapman and I were evacuated, towed off to company base to be cannibalized for spare parts.

Less than three months after this battle took place, I was on my way to being medically discharged from the army, the 1/69th Armor was redeployed from Vietnam, and its colors retired. The 69th was the first heavy tank unit sent to Vietnam, and it was the only one ever to have engaged enemy armor during the whole period of the war.

RETURN TO VIETNAM
MIKE STEWART, AUGUST 10, 1994

Twenty-five years after Captain Stovall and I were medevacked out of Ben Het, I arrive over Ho Chi Minh City, formerly Saigon. This time, though, I am not flying in a chartered American airliner. I am riding Air Vietnam. The plane is a bit timeworn, a mysterious fog issues from the A/C vents, and the navigator has hair down to his waist and wears an earring about the size of a quarter. Times do change.

Coming in over the tip of the peninsula, I can see three rivers that appear to have shrunk somewhat since I was last here. The banks seem to be silting in and the channels are narrowing. As we come in low over the city, I can see that almost every piece of sheet metal left over from the war seems to have been salvaged and put to use as roofing material. The city is huge and still growing, and the need for materials outstrips the supply.

Although new tourist hotels are springing up all around the city, I am booked at the old Saigon Hotel. It's affordable, clean, and has good room service. Your laundry even gets returned. The in-country rep books me in, and then I am on my own for the rest of the night. After a shower and a shave, it is time to explore Ho Chi Minh City. I will be leaving for Nha Trang in the morning, with car, driver, and interpreter. That will be my first stop on the way to the old battlefield at Ben Het.

First I went to the ninth-floor bar of the hotel to get my bearings, since it has a good view of the city, which I remembered from the old days. Then down nine flights of stairs (the elevator died some years ago, like much of the city's machinery) and out the door. Suddenly I'm in another world. The streets are alive with the countless sights, sounds, and even smells of the Orient. Street vendors are selling everything that one could imagine . . . and most are trying to avoid the tax collectors. Much of the goods for sale has come into the country via the back door. The old Ho Chi Minh Trail was once a smugglers' path, and it is back in business. The black market is overwhelming; I'd need my own small plane to haul back all the stuff that I want to purchase out of those stalls.

After some hours of wandering and remembering, I find myself at the wharf by the floating gardens. Tour boats and sampans, some engine-driven, some sculled by old mama-sans, seem to be most of the night traffic. Pretty, all the moving varicolored lights, but they hide a crying need. The "People's Republic of Vietnam" may have a yearly master plan for the country, but the harbors and their equipment are going to need a lot of attention before they can meet the expanding expectations of the nation. The infrastructure of this whole country is in a shambles. Somehow, though, the beauty of the city that was once known as the Paris of the Orient shows through.

The car, driver, and interpreter arrive, and we head out of Saigon, driving north over incredibly beat-up roads. Turning onto National Highway 1, we are soon passing through rubber tree plantations and past the beautiful countryside of Vietnam. Lushly green rice paddies are dotted with thatch-roofed houses, small clusters of cattle, and the ever-present water buffalo. The shoulders of the road are used to dry food, so the driver must be careful not to run over someone's next year's supplies. Driving is an obstacle course to which one must pay close attention. The larger the vehicle, the more right of way it has. Working horns are a must, and one should be a competent mechanic before heading out on these roads. Reliable help and spare parts are few and far between.

At the end of the first day's run, at the city of Nha Trang, Mr. Hein, my interpreter, takes me to a favorite restaurant for dinner, and we are seated near the street by an old wooden fence. The place is already full of diners and, it being a hot evening, sweat is already pouring off me. Then the waiter brings a hibachi full of hot coals so that we can cook our own meal to personal taste. While more of a sauna than a dinner, the food was excellent.

After a morning swim at the hotel's private beach, I showered with fresh water, had an excellent breakfast, and was on the road again. The familiar names clicked off in my memory. Tuy Hoa, Vinh Hoa, Qui Nhon, and Bong Son, where the 69th had fought so many battles, and then back to Qui Nhon for another night, and then the trip up to the highlands. We'll be running up QL19, the French-built road that, in a series of switchbacks, climbs the Annam Cordillera to the city of Pleiku. As we take the grade—ducking countless ditty wagons, log trucks, and overloaded buses (they still tie pigs, chickens, and children on top)—I think back to running this gauntlet in an M-48 tank . . . about three times, I think.

Now we've passed An Khe city and are approaching Mang Yang Pass and, although I see the incredible beauty of these cloud-filled green mountains, my internal RAM is replaying bridge security memories and mortar-filled nights followed by sniper-filled days and armored jungle patrol. Then the roadsides suddenly swarm with my old enemies, the NVA, who are only on peacetime maneuvers. As shivers run down my back, I roll the window up, finding the scenery on the other side of the road to be of much more interest.

Another night in Vietnam, this time in the highland city of Pleiku, where the old 4th Division base of Camp Enari was located. I can see Dragon Mountain, and this gives me my bearings. From here I could find anyplace in our old area of operations. Accommodations here are distinctly inferior to those down on the coast. The "hotel" is lacking in all areas of service, but we make do, although the car has to be garaged in a locked stall. Next morning, after some complications with the local government, we take off toward Dak To. Now there is a policeman in the car with us, and we have had to get permission from the district montagnard chief.

This land is burned into my memory. We pass the place where Archie lost his leg, where Bowers and Doc Eller hit those mines. My senses are now on full combat alert. The last time I was here, I'd been ambushed, and there was a raging battle going on. Capt. Stovall and I had been blown from the back of my tank by an NVA tank cannon and almost killed.

The land has all changed, yet not really; there are just different structures on it. It took two hours and 25 years to go the 16 klicks from Dak To to Ben Het.

I take off walking up the hill. Then the cop informs me that the area is still mined and dangerous. Oops, stop and walk backward, very carefully, breathe deep sighs of bad days long ago, and let the new peace of this place envelop me. I've taken a few pictures of the valley from Cambodia that those tanks used to get to us. I request and get permission to take a couple of handfuls of earth with me. With Anderson, Goss, and McGee on my mind, could I do less? I wanted to bury a 69th memento up there, but couldn't pull it off. I had thought to wear my 69th cap for some photos, but was informed that although it would make a lot of people very happy, it might make some awfully mad. When in Rome, is the ticket, I think.

Evening is soon to come, and I must return these extra people to Dak To. We must get back to Pleiku by dark. I never did ask why, but no one travels by night. I'm quiet as we arrive in Dak To, still shrugging off parts of that old movie in my mind. Ten thousand miles and a quarter of a century. I'm back. I did it.

* * *

TANK ACES

From 1975 to 1991, the U.S. Army lived under an undeserved cloud, slowly healing its wounds in an era of budgetary constraints and low prestige. With the draft gone, the military had to fight for recruits with better living conditions and higher salaries. Slowly, oh-so slowly, they came back. With the goad of the old Soviet Union's militant adventurism, Congress grudgingly funded new armored vehicles. And pundits in the media immediately attacked both the Bradley and the Abrams as overpriced and too technical for the soldiers.

Nothing is more expensive than a tank that loses wars, and no machine is too technical for a generation that grew up with *Star Wars* and video games and computers. With engines that drive them at highway speeds, laser sights, satellite navigation, and guns that fire depleted uranium slugs, the new mounts of our armored cavalry came howling out of Saudi Arabia against the best tanks Russia had ever built and shot them to scrap metal. That operation was truly a Desert Storm.

23

THE DESERT STORM

The land that is now called Iraq has hosted the wars of the peoples of antiquity since record-keeping began. Herodotus, whose *The History* has come down to us intact, begins his record with the story of two petty city-states that were fighting a war that neither understood. They had inherited it from their fathers because that was how life was lived in those times. All the way down the long biblical centuries, the Sumerians, Hittites, Babylonians, Medes, Persians, Chaldeans, and Parthians all left blood and chariot tracks on the desert that was once fertile land. The land now seems made for war, and in this century, the place of the chariot is filled by the main battle tank. Where chariot horses once grazed, oil wells and refineries now produce, among other things, tank fuel.

After WWI, Great Britain partitioned the possessions of the decadent Ottoman Turks, who were the pitiful remnant of the great Islamic conquerers, into wholly new nations. Unwashed barbarian camel herders who lived in the ruins of Babylon and Nineveh were suddenly declared to be sovereign nations. Then the oil that was under that land became necessary to our increasingly mechanized culture, and Western wealth poured in by the barrel. One would have thought that, under enlightened, Western-educated rulers, those undreamed of riches would have gone for schools, universities, industries, and irrigation projects to enrich the peoples of those lands. Wrong, they bought new weapons, revived ancient feuds, and went joyfully to war. George Santayana once said, "Those who cannot remember the past are condemned to repeat it."

Since America, after pumping our own internal oil resources out of Texas and Oklahoma to fuel much of the Allied effort in WWII, was now dependent on Middle Eastern oil, we had to have a policeman in the area to stabilize the situation. After much deliberation, we backed the Shah of Iran and made a modern power out of ancient Persia. For a time, there was a sputtering peace in the area, but under pressure from self-castigating liberal think tanks, President James Earl Carter dropped the ball and allowed the Shah to become unseated, and the rest is history.

Megalomania runs deep in Middle Eastern blood, and without warning, Iraq turned from a seven-year war with Iran and threw its mechanized barbarians against tiny Kuwait. We had showed weakness and indecision in the form of a waffling ambassador named April Glaspie, and one more Mesopotamian maniac smelled a cheap victory. With little or no warning, he rolled a thousand tanks into Kuwait, announced that its history was annulled and that it was now merely a department of Iraq. Then the looting started. An entire small nation was subjected, before the world's eyes, to an ancient Middle Eastern tradition: rape, pillage, and plunder. Then someone finally noticed that, if he weren't stopped, Saddam Hussein would be the sole owner of over half the world's proven oil reserves. . . . And America burns one tanker load of oil every three hours. Japan manages to squeak by on one supertanker per day.

Stung into action at last, America did the only thing possible. Due to budget constraints, the only force that we could move instantly was the 82nd Airborne at Ft. Bragg, North Carolina. Paratroop infantry without their tanks against heavy armor. How did they hold? They should have been only a speed bump in the desert against a dozen divisions of tanks. Nuclear blackmail was the only answer.

Saddam Hussein was allowed to know that if he hit that division, which was only a thin red line in the sands of Saudi Arabia, he could expect nuclear retaliation. Whether or not President George Bush was bluffing, no one will ever know, but by the time Saddam Hussein began to rattle his tanks again, he had a sky full of hi-tech aircraft that worked over his defenses for six months. True, airpower could stop his advance, but it could not make him retreat, nor could it make him surrender. The only thing a man like that understands is a tank in his courtyard and a man with a rifle in his office. That was about to happen. Almost.

While the paratroopers held the line and the U.S. Air Force and Navy pounded southern Iraq, while Saddam postured and the Alliance dithered, the tankers played hurry up and wait. The 1st Armored Division (1st AD) in Germany first shipped out its tanks and then, on January 6, 1991, shipped the tankers from Hamburg, West Germany. Kenneth Patch, a tank commander in 1st AD Forward, would be one of the first to go in on the formal invasion. For over a week in Saudi, Patch and his men waited, pulled detail, and sweated the SCUDs at a camp called the "Dew Drop Inn." Finally, their tanks arrived.

EXCERPTS FROM THE DIARY OF KENNETH PATCH, 1st AD

JAN. 17, 1991, PATCH DIARY

Our tanks are here. All right, no more grunt stuff. They told us that a detail from another outfit is unloading the boat and that when our tanks were off, they would call us. It sounded like they had their shit together but they didn't (nothing new). We got the call around 1530 and got on the buses and left around

1600. We were all still thinking that the tanks are unloaded, and we could just pick them up. We got to the port, and found our boat, U.S.S. *American Falcon,* from San Francisco, California. There was an E-7 in charge, and he said that he was very short on people and needed help to unload the ship. We all walked on the boat, and there was junk everywhere; this was obviously going to be an all-night job.

We started to unload trucks, PCs, Bradleys, M88s, helicopters. Then we got to the tanks. They were at the bottom of the boat, and they had to haul them up one at a time on a lift. It reminded me of the movie *Top Gun,* where they brought the F-14 up on a lift. Anyway, the guy said that he can raise four to five tanks in an hour. All right, we only had 58 tanks to raise, so that should have only taken 10 to 15 hours. It got very hot and smoky down there because we had to drive the tanks to the lift, and the ventilation sucks. I had to leave there three or four times to go and get some fresh air. We were done about 0600 the next morning, and the carbon monoxide headaches were killing me.

We quickly inventoried the tanks to see that everything was still there, and then lined up and drove them back to the Dew Drop Inn. When we got there, we put more fuel in them and then pulled some maintenance. That night my crew went to bed around 1700 and slept till the next dawn. Then we were up for two days working very hard getting the tanks ready. Then we waited for a few days to get the tanks painted from European colors to desert colors. Then we waited for tank transporters (that's a truck that's *bigger* than a tank to carry it), to take us about 500 klicks to the tactical assembly area (TAA).

While Kenneth Patch and his crew were getting their tanks ready for war, one small unit was already across the infamous Iraqi desert barrier and in combat with the enemy. "I" Troop, 3rd Squadron, 3rd Armored Cavalry Regiment, had been on a routine patrol when they got a call from a group of Saudi border guards who had a small problem.

THE FIRST FIREFIGHT
"I" Troop, 3/3 ACR
Captain Johnathan J. Negin

Third platoon, "I" Troop, 3rd Squadron, 3rd Armored Cavalry Regiment made the first ground contact, small as it was, on January 22, 1991. Our mission was to conduct a screening operation on the right flank of the 24th Infantry Division. Since our final destination was over 100 kilometers from our assembly area, we'd brought along our long-range antennas and laid on additional supplies. Unfortunately, also because of the distance, we'd decided to leave our 4.2-inch mortar track behind, and later on we had cause to regret this decision. There were times when we wished that "Blue Seven" and Sgt. James Kennedy's indirect firepower were available.

We did have one unexpected "attachment," when our regimental commander, Colonel James Starr and his Bradley crew took this opportunity to conduct the traditional leader's reconnaissance with our platoon. We also had a ground surveillance radar track from the 66th Military Intelligence Company, commanded by Sergeant Todd Morgan, along with us.

We moved out on a clear cool morning, heading northwest over rocky, sandy, sloping terrain. Observation was outstanding as we paralleled the berm between Saudi Arabia and Iraq. Along the way we encountered an MP squad securing a main road northward to a small town that had been under Iraqi mortar attack. We were in unsecured territory, although Col. Starr informed me that allied aircraft were scheduled to take out those mortars that evening.

As we neared our objective, Corporal Alvin Gage, the gunner for track I-32 (#2 Bradley, 3rd platoon, "I" Troop) spotted something on the horizon about five kilometers to our west. I maneuvered the platoon from a staggered column to a wedge, and notified Col. Starr that I was sending a section forward to investigate. The colonel also went forward. As

Bravo section got closer to the object, they identified it as an abandoned "lo boy" trailer. Also, near here, they identified some Saudi border guards near the first vegetation that we'd seen all day.

The platoon was now moving in a wedge formation, which, from the air, looks rather like a squashed "M" shape. By now Col. Starr was dismounted and talking with the Saudi captain. In the dusky distance of the next ridgeline, we could see unidentifiable equipment on the enemy side of the berm, which was now clearly visible down the slope to our front. Remarkably, there was also a large two-story building in the valley below; it was the first structure that we'd seen in days.

Col. Starr quickly briefed us that there was a Saudi border patrol engaged in a firefight in and around the building to our front, and requested our assistance. How could we refuse? As we headed down the gradual slope, we could see that the shallow valley was densely covered by scrub and scattered bushes, affording decent concealment and some cover. The far side of the wide valley was at the limit of our vision, some 10 kilometers distant.

The day had become overcast and dim as Col. Starr prepared us for what was about to unfold. He ordered me to have the platoon close all vehicle hatches, move out on line, and prepare for contact as we slid down to the berm. We readied our weapons and our minds as we intently scanned the valley below. We pulled into hull-down positions along the berm, and I looked into Iraq for the first time. The berm was five to six feet tall, consisting of bulldozed rocks and dirt at a formidably steep angle. I sent my observers (dismounted crewmen) forward for local security.

Across the barrier, scattered Saudi soldiers moved in and around the lone structure. Border-guard trucks pulled out to the west as we arrived. We caught glimpses of the enemy as they ducked in and out of the dry leathery vegetation. Due to the relative quiet of modern American machinery and the lively exchange of fire between Saudis and Iraqis, we had achieved surprise on the battlefield. The enemy could not have been ready for what was about to happen.

Col. Starr calmly directed us to scan for targets, but he

ordered me to let him know before we engaged. After a few moments of scanning, though, I heard the report of a 25mm chain gun to my right. Col. Starr had spotted something and was reconning by fire. I took this as a sign and commanded my troops to engage any targets that presented themselves. Col. Starr continued to engage at intervals, and my Alpha section told me that they were engaging a bunker and troops in the open at about 1800–3000 meters with HE rounds. Col. Starr radioed me to control my fires as he'd observed tracers flying high into the air. I had to tactfully remind him that this was normal for HE at extended ranges. We'd never practiced at these ranges in training. Sgt. Terry Miller, commander of I-32, said that he actually saw enemy soldiers trying to dodge the slow, arcing shells that they could see coming in at them.

Alpha section thoroughly covered the bunker with suppressive fire. "It just lit up," Sgt. Mason later told me. Now the only enemy that we saw were fleeing into other bunkers, which would easily have been in range of the 4.2 mortar that we'd left behind.

After he'd saturated an area to his front, which had been the source of some fire, Col. Starr moved out with his Bradley. He was trying to flush out enemy soldiers that were trying to hide in the dense vegetation. Tracers began hitting all around him, and he requested that I send a section to assist him. He was shooting across the berm into Iraq, and we'd already identified a low spot in the earthen rampart that we would be able to cross. The situation developed suddenly into a hasty attack.

Sgt. Steve Ruch, in I-35, initiated the assault by quickly crossing the berm and dashing to the enemy's flank, coming down on them from their west, or left, side. Sgt. Peter Baez, in I-36, had trouble negotiating the berm and was 500 meters behind I-35. It was not a flawlessly initiated attack, but it was taking shape. With both Bradleys gone from my left flank, I instructed my dismounted scouts to concentrate on that area. If we could get across, so could the enemy. I cautioned them to get a positive ID on any suspected hostiles before they engaged.

Col. Starr later said that we were under small-caliber mortar fire at the time, but I hardly noticed, being busy trying to find a place to cross the berm. Alpha began to cross just as I-35 reached the temporary objective, and I ordered them to hold in place and scan alertly and report. Suddenly I-35 came under fire as it moved through those clumps of scrub, and Sgt. Ruch's excited voice came over the radio. "I've got casualties in the back! My track's full of holes!" *Welcome to the war, Lieutenant,* I thought. The word *casualties* hits hard. *God, let them live.*

I told Sgt. Ruch to return to the berm area and treat his casualties; I directed I-36 to continue the assault and informed the colonel of my decisions. He agreed with me, and we anxiously watched as I-35, driven by Pfc. Kelly Ocon, headed for relative safety. Sgt. Ruch then reported that his track was full of smoke and that both his scout observers had received leg wounds, one serious, one minor. Pfc. Ocon skillfully, if not too gracefully, got I-35 across the berm through a hail of fire. It was a determined effort and a tribute to the teamwork and training of the crew.

Back on our side of the berm, the slightly wounded soldier, Corporal Mark Valentine, a combat lifesaver, both stabilized the wound of Specialist Trey Garrison and treated his own. Amazed, we counted 15 holes of differing sizes in I-35, mostly medium to large machine-gun holes with one small-caliber AT weapon of some older type. Luckily most of these rounds either didn't fully penetrate or just didn't hit anything sensitive on the way through.

Meanwhile I-36 closed in on the objective. The enemy, disheartened after subjecting a Bradley to such heavy fire and then seeing it just drive off seemingly undamaged, began to raise their arms in surrender. I-36 stopped on the near side of the position and dismounted three scouts to collect the prisoners. Dismounts from Col. Starr's track went forward to assist. Suddenly I-36 opened up again, swiftly and savagely. Its gunner, Sgt. Bryan Hunt, had spotted a heavy machine-gun crew in the brush, getting ready to open up on the EPW (enemy prisoners of war) collection. He destroyed them with 25mm fire and that was enough; the enemy didn't care to provoke any further attacks. It was time to withdraw and reconsolidate.

We brought the prisoners back across the berm, mounted on the bow of I-36, and Col. Starr contacted our regimental aviation troop for a flight of Blackhawk helicopters to evacuate the prisoners. While waiting for the birds, we systematically disarmed and searched the prisoners. They were between the ages of 18 to 45, well armed but poorly equipped. Some were frightened, but others resigned to their fate.

Once the Blackhawks departed with the EPWs, we returned to the vegetated area on top of the ridge where we'd first encountered the Saudis and settled in for the night. Col. Starr arranged for an aerial resupply. This had been a long day, and night was falling as I assembled my commanders for a short after-action review and got ready for the night laager. After night settled in, the ground radar track, an M-113, reported ground activity in the valley across the berm, and we remained on alert against any possible counterattack. Col. Starr called for two of our OH-58D scout helicopters and an A-10 attack aircraft, and they drew some fire as they worked over the area. We girded for a tense, yet uneventful, night. The Army had trained us well.

Reprinted and adapted with permission, from Armor Magazine.

JAN. 24, 1991, PATCH DIARY

We left the Dew Drop Inn at 0600 in the morning, with the tanks on the transporters and us in buses, headed for the TAA. We drove all night at about 20 mph, and then took our tanks off the truck and left for the TAA, which was still about 35 kilometers away. This is the first time that I have seen the desert here because every time we move it is at night. There is nothing here to look at, and I mean *nothing* to look at. It is very flat, and they tell us we can see for 30 miles.

We'd sent off an advance party to set up a company area and pick places for the tanks, but not much had been done when we got there. So we spent the rest of the day setting up tents and commo nets and so forth. The next few days we worked on company maneuvers and battalion maneuvers. The battalion CO wants to know what will happen when we go to war, so we have to practice.

TANK ACES

The tanks are holding up good out here, not many problems. The other day, we went to the range and shot-in our guns. One service SABOT main gun round and 50 rounds of 7.62 ammo for the machine gun to zero them. We are fully uploaded with ammo: 40 rounds of main gun ammo, 10,000 rounds of MG ammo, and 1000 for the .50. I have never seen so much ammo in my life.

We have an operations order. It just doesn't have a time or date. Other units are to breach the obstacle, then we are to roll through it and do a movement to contact. That means that we find them and kill them. It sounds dangerous, but it is really safer. It is hard to hit us when we are coming at 35-plus miles per hour. We are going right through the neutral zone west of Kuwait and into Iraq.

They have about 75 phones here, about 30 minutes from our tent area. The other night I went to call P. J. and the boys. I would have called home, but it was about 1400 in the afternoon there, and I don't think Sneaks would have answered it. I will try to call when the folks are home.

I found out where we will be at; it is supposed to be a secret, oh well. We won't be at the Kuwait border. We will be west of Kuwait about 75 miles. We are on the Iraqi border, and we are going to be the "point" for the task force. The 1st Armored "D" Division will be to our left and back, 3rd AD and 2nd ACR is to the right and back. They said that out of everyone, 2nd AD Forward (that's us) will be the closest to the border. I think the reason why is that we have the M1A1 heavy tank; that's the newest version of the Abrams tank. We are the only ones that have it. Don't I feel special? The other thing they told us is about the helicopters that defected over here. The news has been reporting that it didn't happen. Well, it did. They said that there was an Iraqi general involved, and we have been downplaying the situation.

FEB. 9, 1991, PATCH DIARY
They gave me another mission briefing. We are moving away from here and going to our forward assembly area, or FAA. Rumor has it that we will stay there about eight days and that on 21 Feb. we will go in. During those eight days, they will hit

the area that we are going through with air and arty. There is a four-foot wall of sand that is the boundary between Saudi and Iraq, and from that wall to the Iraqi defenses is about a half mile. 1/41 Infantry is going to clear that area, and then part of the 1st Infantry is going to breach the military obstacles. Once that is done, we will form a task force with part of 1st ID and go on through to the other side and set up a blocking position just in case of a counterattack. We will have two tank companies and two infantry companies from 1/41 Infantry.

The Iraqi force close by the area is small; it has a company of T-55 tanks and some infantry and artillery, so we should be able to handle it with few casualties. Once we start through and set up, 1st ID, 2nd Cav, and 3rd ID will go through and head north—don't know how far. Then the British will come through and head east. Then we wait until someone runs into problems, and we will go and help the one with the most problems. This is called a "flexible mission." Sounds like a plan. It will be a cluster fuck.

LETTER HOME
Ken Patch

13 Feb. 1991

Dear Mom and Dad:

Hi. Sorry I haven't written, but I have gotten so many letters from other people that it is hard to keep up. I was going to call today, but last night they told us that the phones are off limits to us. In two days we are going to our attack positions. By the time you get this letter, I will be in Iraq. I am on radio watch. It is 0300 in the morning. I don't know why I am watching from radio, it can't walk away. But anyway, I can see flashes from bombs going off. I can't hear them but I can see them. I have counted about 25 planes so far. To get to our attack position is about 90 miles away. The artillery and 1/41 units are going up there today, and they will start bombing and clearing the zone tonight. They have over 42,000 rounds to drop on them. It is starting to get busy around here. We are getting ready to go. There should be a really good artillery show.

I have gotten a few letters from you. No boxes yet. They said the reason why we don't get much mail is because they are using most of the trucks to haul ammo and food. They are starting to give us what is called M.O.R.T.E., or meal open, ready to eat. They are a Hormel meal in a cup and okay when warm. When they are cold they are really BAD. Well, I have to go, I have to get ready for a PCI (precombat inspection). I will write you when I get to the forward assembly area. This should be different.

Love ya lots and miss you,
Ken

P.S. HAPPY BIRTHDAY TO BOTH OF YOU.

FEB. 24, 1991, PATCH DIARY

Well, we are off to war. We are in the process of moving up to the breach site. We won't attack until tomorrow. We are moving everything up and setting up for the night. The marines took a prisoner, and he was wired with explosives and blew himself up. I just got another update. The people in front of us captured a tank company, and one of their people was wired with explosives and he blew himself up . . . I will shoot them all. I will not send my people out there to search them. Behind us is a battery of Patriot missiles, and there are seven of them with 20 missiles each. Don't have to worry about SCUD attack.

1400 Hrs—We just went through the berm. I am sitting in Iraq. The forward units have about 700 POWs already. There has been no movement of the other Iraqi units to come over and help. It's been a walk in the park, so far.

While Patch's unit, 2AD Forward, was working its steady way into Iraq, another outfit had walked right into a hairy situation. Ghost Troop, 2nd Squadron, 2nd Armored Cav was right in the path of a steamroller.

24

GHOST TROOP

2ND SQUADRON
2ND ARMORED CAVALRY

One of Murphy's laws of war is "No battle plan survives contact with the enemy." The 2nd Armored Cavalry's campaign in Desert Storm was to be no exception. A perfectly planned operation would begin to come unstuck because of the success of two Marine divisions and one battleship. As originally planned, the plan of campaign was a deliberate movement to contact from an assembly area west of Kuwait, in the so-called neutral zone. At that time, the 2nd Squadron (equivalent to a battalion) was commanded by LTC Mike Kobbe.

FEB. 23, 1991
The squadron was organized for battle with a few attachments and detachments. A combat earthmover from Company "A," 82nd Engineers, was attached to each of the platoons of the three cavalry troops of the squadron. The troops are named, Eagle, Fox, and Ghost and are composed of a mix of Abrams tanks and Bradley scout vehicles. Hawk

Company is a tank-only unit. The squadron's integral artillery battery was under operational control (OPCON) to 6/41 Field Artillery, in direct support. Ghost and Fox Troops each had an EPW team with Kuwaiti nationals to broadcast surrender appeals and interrogate prisoners. By 1500 hours, the berm had been breached in dozens of places, and the squadron's way was open; instead, they received orders to hold in place.

FEB. 24, 1991

At 0700 hrs, the squadron moved out in a deliberate zone reconnaissance toward Phase Line (PL) BUSCH. There was no contact, and they established defensive positions. At 1000 hours, regiment informed 2nd Squadron that there would be no further movement until the next day. *Where, they must have wondered, is our war?* On the way, as it turned out. The lead armored elements of two Marine divisions had run head on into the Tawakalna Division of the Republican Guard, shooting it up with old M-60 tanks. Worse, the battleship *Wisconsin* had been offshore beating up Baghdad with cruise missiles and dropping 2000-pound thumpers into the Guard. They wanted out of Kuwait SCHNELL. And they were headed right at where Ghost Troop would be.

At noon, the squadron was given orders to move out northwest, toward objective MERRELL. At 1430, they moved out in diamond formation across PL BUSCH toward PL DIXIE and OBJ MERRELL. Fox was leading, Ghost on the right, Eagle on the left with Hawk Company in reserve. Right alongside Hawk were the three firing batteries of 6/41 Artillery. So far, no serious problems. Soon they were inside OBJ MERRELL, and Ghost and Fox were accepting mass surrenders of Iraqi troops who'd already been tenderized by ground attack A-10 "Warthog" fighters.

FEB. 25, 1991

At 0630, regiment initiated a 10-minute artillery prep on MERRELL, and the squadron resumed its attack. By 1230 hours, the squadron was at PL LITE, having come a further

24 kilometers against light resistance. At 1400 hours, Ghost Troop engaged and essentially destroyed a Guard's recon company that had gotten too close to it. That company was equipped with Russian MT-LBs, a lightly armored tracked vehicle with no resistance to chain-gun fire, let alone a 120mm HEAT round. First Lt. Mecca, Ghost Troop's exec, brought six of them in as trophies. At 1500 hours, regiment ordered the squadron to halt along PL BLACKTOP just a few kilometers short of a longitudinal line on the map called 73 easting. At 2100, regiment ordered the 2nd Squadron to set up a three-sided defensive position along PL BLACKTOP.

FEB. 26, 1991

At 0620 hours, the squadron moved east to its newly assigned blocking position, with Eagle in the north, Ghost in the south, Hawk in reserve, and Fox guarding the squadron rear. At 0800, Ghost engaged the rest of the MT-LB–equipped recon company. The Iraqi commander of this force had trained at Fort Benning and should have known better. Regiment halted the squadron and began to rearrange things. Ghost Troop was now tied in with Iron Troop, 3rd Squadron of the 2nd ACR, and the regiment was moving across the easting lines. Then VII Corps gave orders to shift the whole regiment south to make room for the 3rd Armored Division to pass through. Eagle and Hawk were then shifted farther south, leaving Ghost Troop leading Fox Troop in the north with a large corridor in between.

At 1500, the squadron received an abrupt change of plan. They were to continue the attack east. They moved out at 1525, and after having no contact at the 60 and 65 eastings, asked for permission to continue on, which was granted. At approximately 68 easting, Eagle ran into prepared defenses with infantry in bunkers and dug-in tanks in revetted positions, the famous "Pita" emplacements. Both Eagle and Ghost ran into and bypassed minefields. Then a sandstorm hit, followed by the lead elements of the Tawakalna Republican Guards Division. The Battle of 73 Easting was on.

"A certain part of you just dies," First Lt. Keith Garwick

said. "Somebody trying to kill you so desperately for so many hours and coming so close. We just couldn't understand it, we still don't understand it; those guys were insane, they wouldn't stop," Garwick said of the Iraqi Republican Guard. "They kept dying and dying. They never quit . . . they never quit. If the rest of their army had fought as hard as the Tawakalna Division fought, we would have been in trouble." Garwick is a West Point graduate and a native of Fresno, California.

Pfc. Jason E. Kick from Pembroke, Georgia, was driving a Bradley that morning, and he remembers that the day was still wet from an overnight rainstorm. He'd dropped out of high school and joined the army at 17. He'd gotten his GED in Basic Training and was talking of going to college. At age 18, he was the "young buck" of the platoon. He carried a small tape recorder and was talking into it. He wanted to send the tape home to his mother.

"We expect contact at any time," he told his mother in a slow drawl, speaking into the recorder. It was a little after 0800. "The units that were in Kuwait, the ones that the Marines have driven out, are headed directly our way. And reinforcements, instead of going back into Kuwait are also headed our way. So, unh, we're gonna hit a lot of shooting." At 0830, Ghost Troop spotted an enemy vehicle and blew it apart, admitting later on to "a little overkill." They just didn't want any of that recon company to get any messages off. "All I can say," Kick told his recorder, "is better them than me. It sounds cruel, but it's true."

By 1530, they'd killed several more personnel carriers and at least three tanks. A sandstorm was raging, driven by a hot dry wind out of the south. Off on their right, Eagle, Iron, and Killer Troops were already fighting dug-in Iraqis. Ghost Troop's commander, Capt. Joseph Sartiano, from San Francisco, had a bad feeling about all this, and pulled his light Bradleys back and put his tanks farther up front than normal. Garwick, the Bradley platoon leader, was in position behind a small hill by 1645, overlooking a wide shallow valley that the Arabs call a wadi. The more they looked, the more enemy troops they saw.

"We've pulled up on line now," Kick told his tape recorder. "We're engaged in a pretty decent firefight right now . . . we're shooting again. I can see what we're shooting at, but I can't see a vehicle. This is chaos here, total chaos." Battle commands flooded the radios, then Pfc. Kick again. "I can see smoke on the horizon, that means we killed something. What it is I don't know. White One, that's the platoon leader, you can hear it in his voice, he's all shook up. Time 1654, that sound is the co-ax firing. . . . Time is 1710, we're still in contact. . . . There's a few PCs here and there, mostly infantry. I just spotted the biggest damn explosion at about 12 o'clock from us. I don't know what the hell it was."

Garwick's platoon had killed nine personnel carriers and the enemy had now started shooting back. Now artillery was falling around the Bradleys. "A tremendous volume of small-arms fire hit the berm to my front," Garwick said. Iraqi infantrymen ran forward and were mowed down. The enemy gunfire increased, but some of it was on their own men. Kick's track was on the left of the platoon, then Garwick, then two more, with Captain Sartiano's tank section right behind them. At 1740, Garwick saw three tank rounds hit the ridge in front of him, each shot closer to the Bradleys on his right. The last one hit. "One just got one of our guys!" Kick shouted into his recorder.

Spc. Patrick Bledsoe, 20, from Oxnard, California, was driving the right-hand Bradley, number G-16. All he saw was shooting. "We were in a little wadi," he said, "but the top of the vehicle looked out over the top of the valley. We were kind of skylined. . . ." The Bradley's gunner was 23-year-old Sergeant Nels A. Moller. His coaxial machine gun was jammed, and the track commander was working on it when he looked up and saw troops coming at them, real close. "You got troops to the front?" he asked Moller.

Suddenly there was an explosion. From his seat down in the turret, Moller couldn't see right outside. "What was that?" he asked. According to Bledsoe, that was the last thing Moller said. There was another explosion, showering sparks across the front of the Bradley, and Moller was dead.

"It was just like somebody hit us with a sledgehammer," Bledsoe said. He jumped out and ran behind the Bradley. The other sergeant was slightly wounded. Friendly tanks, Sartiano's, were now firing directly over them at the oncoming enemy, and the concussions of their guns were terrific. Bledsoe jumped down, as there was yet another explosion. Pfc. Jeff Pike, 21, of Binghamton, New York, was driving Sartiano's tank, and he believes that explosion was Sartiano's gunner shooting the T-55 that killed Moller.

Bledsoe tried to get away. "I low-crawled up to the other track and knocked on the back door, but they didn't hear me. I went up to the driver's hatch, the driver opened it, and I said, 'We got hit, I think Moller's dead.'" G-16 had taken two tank hits from a 100mm gun and hadn't blown; it was just sitting there, smoking. At 1750, Kick spoke into his recorder. "It was one-six that got hit. The gunner of one-six, Sergeant Moller, is dead. The TC and observer are on one-five right now. Sergeant Moller was killed at, time about 1740." He paused a moment and added, "Can't let this . . . can't let this get us down at all, or we're gonna die. And he wouldn't want that, he don't want that. . . . But I'm scared."

Garwick told his men to keep firing. All around them on the hill, artillery, tanks, and machine guns were firing. More were destroyed, more fired, more came. "This is chaos," Kick reported at 1804. "Total chaos . . . got nine dead vehicles out front, enemy vehicles. And got more coming."

The sandstorm had worsened, Garwick could see only 50 or so yards with normal vision, but the thermal sights cut through some of the murk. With those, he could see about a half mile. He could see them before they saw him. Two more enemy tanks were coming. Kick watched them get hit three times, just minutes later. "Boom, hit. Hit and kill. He hit it. That's revenge for Moller, you son-of-a-bitching Iraqis. God I hate them. Sergeant Moller was a good guy. That's four Iraqi PCs killed for this track alone."

Garwick's scouts told him that 12 more, possibly as many as 25 more, tanks were coming. Iraqis down in the valley would leap out of their disabled PCs and run at Garwick's platoon, firing their rifles . . . getting killed. All Kick could see was rounds going downrange. Spc. Chris Harvey from Virginia Beach, Virginia, looked out of his track. "All I saw were things burning for 360 degrees, nothing but action."

Garwick called for the Air Force, but the planes were diverted to another mission before they got to Ghost Troop. Instead, Garwick held off the tanks by calling in the artillery and rockets, pounding each wave as it appeared on the far ridge. "It looked," said the squadron's executive officer, "like Armageddon."

One of Garwick's main problems was that the radios were so busy that he couldn't call through. Several times he had to jump out of his Bradley and crawl over to the artillery observers to tell them in person what he wanted. On one of these occasions he had crawled halfway to the arty observer's vehicle when a round of airburst went off just on the other side of it. He and the artilleryman, a Sgt. Fultz, ducked under Garwick's Bradley. . . . Another wave of tanks was coming in. For a few minutes, Garwick said, "we just sat there crying, just shaken, until we could get back out from underneath the Bradley. The airbursts were coming right on top, ricocheting around us. We were in a corner of hell. I don't know how we got out of there. I don't."

More than once, artillery saved Ghost Troop. Helicopters helped kill tanks, and near the end, when the troop was desperately short on ammunition, Hawk Company came in to relieve them. In its 100 hours of combat, the regiment destroyed (conservatively) 100 tanks, about 50 personnel carriers, and more than 30 wheeled vehicles—and that's before counting the damage done in Ghost Troop's sector. The equivalent of an Iraqi brigade was destroyed that night, and it was the first defeat of the Republican Guard.

FEB. 25, 1991, 0600, PATCH DIARY

I am on my way in, today we should see the enemy. I am not too worried, mostly troops; they have the RPG 7 (rocket-propelled grenade, model 7), which can stop the tank maybe, but can't kill us.

0748: We are attacking at 0800. We are on PL COLORADO.

We did a relief in place with the people from Ft. Riley. We are going to Phase Line NEW JERSEY. Once we get there, 2ACR will replace us, this is WILD.

1344 hrs: We are at PL NEW JERSEY. On the way up here, we captured 10 Iraqi; they were dug in and we took a tank-powered mine plow and just dug them up. They didn't give us much of a problem. 3rd AD, 2ACR and 1st ID are all heading north and we are waiting for the British to come through. . . . They just told us that a brigade of Iraqi tanks and BMPs are coming toward us and we must get ready.

FEB. 26, 1991, 0900, PATCH DIARY

The Iraqi never came yesterday. They stopped and set up a blocking force. Last night we opened up our lines and passed the UK Royal Tank Regiment through us. They are going after them. 1st Armored Division, 2nd Armored Cav, and 3rd AD are going after the Guard, we will fall in behind them and be the reaction force. We probably won't see anything today. Yesterday we took 28 EPWs, nine of them were officers. . . . We moved all day, most of the night and hit a defensive belt about 2300 hours. They told us that we could attack at midnight. "Oh great," I said to myself, "I might get shot by my own people, this should be fun." We hit them and they were where the briefing said they would be.

There was heavy fighting all night and I killed a T-55, it was totally destroyed when I hit it. It went up in flames. We got seven altogether. It was pretty intense out there, with big bullets flying everywhere. We took over 150 POWs. Our task force lost two Bradleys, ATGMs got them. I don't know if anyone got hurt. When we went into battle, I was more worried about friendly fire than enemy fire. I have been in this tank for 24 hours. We stopped for three hours to eat and refuel. Right now we are heading back south to Kuwait. Maybe we can get some beer. Let's see what happens.

What was happening was that the whole Iraqi army had been cut off and was being destroyed piecemeal. The following three vignettes have been extracted from *Armor*

Magazine, the house publication of the Armor School at Fort Knox, and were compiled by the public affairs officers of the units concerned with the action. . . . Especially interesting is the fact that an antitank missile can be shot out of the sky by the tank at which it is aimed.

SCOUT PLATOON, 4/34 ARMOR

Two Bradleys, HQ 21 and HQ 26, commanded by Lt. James Barker and Sgt. Chris Stephens, rolled forward through a pitch-black overcast night. The date was February 26, 1991, and the war was only hours old. Ahead of them, they could hear the sound of heavy engines and the distinctive rattle-squeak-clank of Soviet-built armor. At least one tank was coming. Using his night-vision goggles, which amplified what little light was available 80,000 times, Lt. Barker suddenly spotted a T-72 coming over a low rise to their front. That item of hardware has a 125mm cannon, and the little Bradleys were no match for it. Alongside the tank, Barker could see several dismounted infantrymen trotting along.

Stephens also spotted the vehicle, reported it, then let go with both his TOW missiles. The first missile, which has to be steered by the gunner, missed. The second one was low, only knocking off a roadwheel, but not killing the tank. Then Stephens opened up with his 25mm chain gun while Barker launched another TOW. The third missile was the executioner. It slammed into the front slope of the T-72, set off a massive internal explosion, and blew the turret clean off the hull. The sky began to light up as secondary explosions reflected off the low overcast.

Suddenly the platoon sergeant, Dennis McMasters in HQ 21, another Bradley, reported that Stephens was taking incoming fire from an undisclosed location. All he could see were the ricochets bouncing off the hull. Then something got through the armor and Stephens's ammo began to cook off and explode, with the crew still in the vehicle.

Pfc. Frank "Ranger Bob" Bradish was in the crew hatch of 2-6, reloading the TOW launcher when the incoming rounds struck. He lost part of his right hand and took several other wounds. Stephens was wounded in the head and legs. Pfc. Adrian Stokes took several life-threatening wounds in the abdomen and groin. Sgt. Goodwin was hit in the chest. Suddenly, Pfc. John McClure was the only unwounded crewman. McClure and Bradish were now the only functional crewmen, and they got straight to work, dragging their fellows out of the crippled Bradley.

Bradish reported to Lt. Barker while Goodwin climbed out of the after-hatch and McClure pulled weapons and flares out of the ammo racks. Bradish needed to set off flares to mark their position for rescue, but he couldn't open them with one hand. Finally he ripped them open with his teeth, stuck them in the sand, and stroked the igniters. Bradish, now worried about his own hand wound, nonetheless told McClure to keep working on Stokes and Goodwin. Then they heard the rumble of more enemy tanks coming.

Meanwhile, Lt. Barker had radioed the battalion HQ for tanks and an ambulance track, which weren't far off. An Abrams with the governor off and the hammer down can do about 70 mph, and it wasn't overlong before Sfc. Craig Kendall brought his platoon into the fray. A medic track pulled up alongside 2-6 and Sgt. Sergio Nino, a medic, immediately took over from McClure. He went first to Stephens, who was ominously still. "Is he gone?" asked the recon platoon sergeant McMasters. "I'm afraid so," Nino answered, and then turned to finish treating Goodwin and Stokes. Nino and his partner, Michael Gindra, tried to give a plasma infusion to Stokes, but he had lost too much blood and died on the sand beside the Bradley.

Then Bradish, who had waited until his friends were treated, told the medics that he needed help, too. He'd lost part of his right hand, taken shrapnel in the groin and a bullet through both thighs. How he had been able to run around popping flares, radioing for help, and tending his wounded comrades, no one could figure out, until Bradish explained: "I shoot left-handed."

3rd PLATOON, 4th SQUADRON, 7th CAVALRY

Just to Barker's north, a cavalry platoon, again mounted in Bradleys, had to go head-to-head with T-72s and took some serious damage. Commanded by Sgt. Roland Jones, 3-6 took a hit and was disabled, prompting the platoon leader to pull up alongside the crippled track and rescue the crew. Lt. Michael Vassalotti tells the story:

"Sergeant Jones called in contact with enemy infantry on the ground and then with a BMP armored personnel carrier. Sergeant First Class Ivery Baker, my platoon sergeant, also called in a BMP and dismounts, then the Bravo section leader called in another, and I immediately reported to my company commander. By the time I called in, though, the first BMP was in flames because Baker had fired on it. By the time I finished calling in all three sightings, all three enemy vehicles were destroyed.

"Jones, in 3-6, had by this time gone forward and taken up a firing position. We moved up with him and then made way for our second platoon to move through us. In the process, we went blank on ammunition and had to reload the ready racks from hull storage. Second Platoon took the heat off us while we pulled back and around them to the right and began reloading."

Sgt. Jones now picks up the narrative: "Lieutenant 'V' came over the net, saying that we had to move south about 800 meters. As we were shifting, my loader was reloading the TOW launcher. When we took up position we engaged another BMP with the chain gun and then another tank with the TOW. We were getting low on ammo, so I told my driver to pivot under the turret so that my loader could get at hull storage. Then I realized that we were still up front, so I changed that to an order to back up.

"There was a noise that sounded like we lost a track, so I told him to stop. As soon as we stopped, we took a 12.7mm round in the transmission and lost all power, and I called for evacuation. When 3-1 arrived, my track took another round, either an RPG or a SAGGER, and my driver took some shrapnel from that. We got evacuated into 3-1, but on the way back to the supply-and-resource area, we were engaged by a T-72 and took two main gun SABOT rounds right through the hull. When the first round hit, I was only scared. When the second one hit, that terrified me. After the second round, I knew they had a bead on us, and I waited for the third."

Miraculously, neither of the two pig-iron SABOT projectiles hit anything sensitive, including human flesh. They just went in one side and out the other, causing only minor flash burns to the crew and their passengers. Then another Bradley crew took out that T-72 with a TOW missile, and Vassalotti and Jones got the hell out of there.

COMPANY "A," 4th BATTALION, 18th INFANTRY

By the morning of the 27th, the American forces were curving back south toward Kuwait, but the war wasn't over yet. Sgt. Marvin Rutherford, a platoon sergeant in Alpha Company tells this story: "In the early morning hours of February 27, we saw what we took to be a flare coming down, but it kept getting closer and closer. It was an antitank missile coming directly at us."

Fortunately, Rutherford's gunner, Spc. Donald Barker, had his turret pointed in roughly the right direction, and when Rutherford ID'd the missile, he put his crosshairs on the flaming speck and shot it out of the sky only 200 meters from impact with their hull.

For Rutherford and his men, the fight was just beginning. "We didn't know what we had gotten into," he said. "They had tanks in the trench lines, and they were dug in and hard to see. Again, my gunner got on them, and we started whipping HE, TOWs, and AP on them."

Rutherford's commander, Capt. Charles Forshee, shot at one Iraqi tank with inconclusive results, then killed a T-62 with their TOW launcher, and then two armored personnel carriers with the 25mm chain gun. Forshee looks back on the battle as one of no contest. "We killed stuff that was blind to us," he said later. "Shooting blind men in the dark."

And with first light came mass surrender. The Iraqi troops wanted no misconception of their intent. "They carried large white sheets or sleeping mats or anything that was white, and just walked in en masse," said Sfc. Michael Jones, another Alpha Company platoon sergeant. As the EPWs came closer to the victors, the U.S. troops began to question some of the things they had heard about their "elite" opponents. "They were scared, really scared," said Spc. James Singleton, an infantry soldier. "One group looked like they had been digging through garbage cans, because they had pieces of our food here and there. The guys that we took looked like they had been planning their escape for quite a while."

FEB. 27, 1991, 1545, PATCH DIARY
We are on the last leg to Kuwait. We are attacking a military complex that Iraq built. It is going to be city fighting. . . . Never trained for this. I have been up for two and a half days, going on three, I am very tired and dirty. Today we captured another 150 POWs. They just give up, don't really blame them. One POW asked, "What took you so long?" He lives in the States and had gone back to visit his mother, and the Iraqi army took him and sent him to fight in Kuwait. So far we have killed about 70 tanks and taken about 1000 POWs. . . . This task force is very low on fuel.

FEB. 29, 1991, 0930, PATCH DIARY
Never made it to the military complex, don't know why, everyone got about six hours of sleep last night. This morning they told us that, at 0800 hours, a cease-fire was in effect. Our mission was to go about 30 kilometers to a road and set up a blocking position. We were to destroy everything in our way, but shoot it before 0800. We killed about five more tanks and

took more POWs. I guess it is over and I made it. I didn't know what was going to happen. I have only one tank kill to my name. We went 319 kilometers from the berm, and I have been in three countries in about 56 hours.

MAR. 1, 1991, 1930, PATCH DIARY
We are set up in Kuwait. Our mission now is to sweep a certain area and blow up any ammo left behind. We did that all day. We went down this highway, there are a lot of cars and Iraqi military vehicles destroyed. They found a truck full of dead Iraqi soldiers that were pretty torn up, heads missing and stuff like that. We blew up some more tanks and BMPs today. I went into a lot of bunkers to look for ammo and weapons. Some of the bunkers are pretty nice in there—furniture and carpets, even. Those must have been where the high-ranking officers stayed. We are clearing all the way to the coast and then back up; this will take about a week; there is a lot of stuff out there.

I found out yesterday that one of my friends, Ssg. Applegate was killed by friendly fire. Three 120mm main gun rounds from "A" Co., 2/66 Armor, hit his tank. He was married with two kids. I knew his family real well. I think there were four people from 2AD Forward killed, all by friendly fire, none by enemy fire. Iraqis can't shoot at night.

MAR. 15, 1991, PATCH DIARY
Everything they told us is on hold because a few days ago we moved back into Iraq. We are just inside the border. We are doing a show of force, so that they will sign the peace treaty sooner. We have a screen line set up and a roadblock up. No military is allowed to pass through. Two one-star generals tried, and they weren't too happy when we wouldn't let them. Today a bus came to the checkpoint and a little girl had a hurt arm, and I fixed her up and gave her some candy. I felt good about helping her. We have been blowing up all their stuff left in our sector. My tank crew burned up about ten trucks, blew up four water tanks, and ran over one truck and water tank with the tracks. We are making it so that they can't use it again, and it is fun just running around messing everything up.

I wish we could get to a phone. I would really like to talk to my family. I haven't talked to them since the war started. I know they know that I'm all right, but I would like to tell them myself.

LETTER HOME
Ken Patch

Mar. 15, 1991

Hi Mom and Dad:

I am back in Iraq. We went across the border yesterday. Why we are here, I don't know yet. It is midnight and I am on radio watch again. We have set up a screen and a roadblock. No military goes through. We see a lot of them. We search them and their cars, and send them back the other way. One car came up and it had a pair of one-star generals in it. They were trying to get to the military base close by and we didn't let them. We treated them with respect and told them "You can't go through." What could they do with three tanks looking at them? They left smartly.

We are sitting about 5 kilometers west of a ship channel that leads to the ocean, it's called Khawr az Zubayr, and if you look on a map you might find it. It is for ships to come in and unload. I don't know how long we will be here. I haven't heard the news for weeks, and I have no idea what is going on. We have been told that about the end of the month they'll sign the treaty, so we just run around and blow stuff until they sign it, and then we'll just take our turn to leave.

I am doing fine, I got lots of boxes from you, but please tell Dad to write the right APO number on the right box. I got a box that was going to Pam, but it had my APO on it. So I ate the cookies and read the soap opera books, and cut out all the coupons so I can go to Kuwait City to shop, HA. Thanks for the stuff in the boxes. Everything you sent travels well. I smiled when I saw the root beer candy, I haven't had that in a very long time. I have to go now, thanks for the boxes

Love,
Ken

P.S. Please send some more of the packet coffee, that works great.

MAR. 20, 1991, PATCH DIARY

We did a relief in place this morning, by a unit from the 3AD. We moved back into Kuwait. Tomorrow we have a 78-mile road march north back into Iraq. We will sit in between here and KKMC (King Khalid Military Complex). The reason is that we might replace the 82nd Airborne up there, or we will sit there until the peace treaty is signed. Yesterday was an interesting day. We had one platoon watching this missile site that we had found. The site was for antiship missiles that the Iraqis had stored. There is a town about 1000 meters away and there were a lot of people around.

Well, late in the afternoon some Iraqi soldiers came out and started shooting at the people. I know they shot one old man that I could see. We could not shoot back because they were not shooting at us. So we sat there watching and begging higher up to let us engage them. We never could. It was hard not to shoot back. There were a lot of Iraqi soldiers moving around in the town. Later on, one Iraqi soldier came out and wanted to defect. He said that they were shooting innocent civilians and he wasn't going back. It was depressing just watching them shoot people, and you can't do anything about it.

APRIL 25, 1991, PATCH DIARY

It is over with, I should be out of here by the 6th of May. They did send us back into Iraq one last time, we were up by Highway 8, the road that goes to Baghdad. We didn't do too much up there, sat around and took some more EPW. We were up there for a few weeks, and helped out some families that needed help. We didn't get any mail up there, I guess because we were too far north. Everyone else was on the way out of here. It is very depressing when you don't get any mail. A person can do without a lot of things, but needs mail. When you go through something like this, you need to know that they haven't forgotten about you.

The move back here was a three-day trip, with a stop-off to unload ammo and make the tanks safe for shipping. We are outside of KKMC, and it is very dusty here because of all the tank movements. The dust is now a fine powder, so when the wind blows, we have a dust storm. Last night, we had a bad one and I couldn't even see the person sleeping next to me. I could hardly breathe, the dust was so thick. I am so used to being dirty that it doesn't even bother me.

We have been here for a week. They have tents for us to sleep in. They have a rec center, PX, phones, Wolfburger stand, and a mess hall where you can sit down at a table and eat. I haven't been able to do that since the war started. We have been getting the tanks ready to ship back. We only work until noon because it gets too hot. It gets up to 110 or 115 degrees every day, and in the afternoons, we go sit in the tents and sweat. But the war is over!

A NEW TYPE OF WAR

When Ken Patch and the rest of the Desert Storm troopers came home from Saudi, history began to creep up on the American military. It now seems as if we are going to have two distinct armored forces. The big divisions can handle the Saddams of the world, but, unfortunately, the resources that civilization depends on can be throttled by petty warlords as well as desert potentates. Not only that, but the military is now being tasked with what is euphemistically called OOTW, or "operations other than war." Under this acronym come peacekeeping, international varmicide, famine alleviation, and noncombatant rescue.

While Russia, traumatized by the failure of their weapons and doctrines in Iraq, hides behind the Ural Mountains and rebuilds, other hot spots around the world continue to simmer toward the boiling point. And we are not ready. No nation, not even the so-called UN peacekeeping force, has a small, tight, hot unit that is designed to go into a bad situation and put it to rights.

Lebanon, Panama, Grenada, Libya, Angola—the list of potential trouble spots goes on and on, and every time piecemeal solutions are tried, Americans wind up carrying the ball. The Middle East, Africa, and parts of South America and Asia are seething cauldrons, and sooner or later, the UN command will dial USA-911-TANK and the tankers will be sent out one more time. That is precisely what happened to Captain Michael Campbell and the USMC provisional tank platoon when Operation Restore Hope tried to salvage famine in Somalia. The Marines were once again put on history's front burner, and they were magnificent.

25

MOGADISHU, SOMALIA

January 3, 1993
USMC Provisional Tank Unit

Somalia, as a nation, was and is an accident waiting to happen. The people make up an intensely proud warrior society with absolutely no tradition of Western-style democracy. They are tribally minded and clannish. Their loyalty is to the local warlord, not some vague Western idea of "government." Blood feuds, clan wars, fights over water and grazing rights, or wars just for the hell of it are embedded in the culture. The neighboring Ethiopians, who know them best, have a saying: "Where there are two Somalis, there is a fistfight, three are a riot, and four will start a war." Into this volatile environment, America and Russia had been pouring modern weaponry for about a quarter of a century. This was a recipe for disaster, and in 1992, the inevitable happened.

Leonid Brezhnev once told the corrupt and venal dictator of Somolia, Siad Barre, "We are after the oil storehouse of the Middle East and the mineral treasure house of Africa and we shall have them." When Russia's grandiose dreams of empire went down the tubes, so did most of its puppets, including Siad Barre. The next thing that happened was that his Russian-trained army came apart and took their weapons out into the hills and set up as warlords. And in the resultant turf fights, all the land that had been farmed was stripped of crops by the warring factions.

Almost automatically, starvation set in, as one of the worst droughts in history further compounded the situation. Then the media and the relief workers raised the world's attention threshold, and the decision was made to go in and straighten the mess out. . . . That had been tried before.

Three nations—Britain, France, and Italy—had tried and given up in disgust, decades ago, but America and the UN had to give it one more shot; the results were predictable. The U.S. ambassador to Kenya, Smith Hempstone, described the problem very precisely in December of 1992, when the project was first launched. "The Somali is as tough as his country," he said, "and just as unforgiving. Somalis are natural-born guerrillas. They will mine the roads. They will lay ambushes. They will launch hit-and-run attacks. . . . They will inflict and take casualties." We had been warned, but few listened.

Into this situation, the USMC provisional tank platoon was dropped. Two Marine tank crews from 29 Palms Base in California were all there were, for a while. Captain Michael Campbell and SSgt. Daniels were in charge of six other assorted crewmembers and 30 tanks without crews . . . to support the 40,000 UN combined joint task force, Somalia. Captain Campbell describes the first day of operations.

It was 1500 when LTC Biszak and Col. Klimp came to see me at the port and told me that we were now designated the "Provisional Tank Command of Task Force Mogadishu," Capt. Campbell remembers, and they asked me how many of the 30 tanks that I possessed could be manned. I know that I will never forget the look of shock on their faces when I told them that, with the eight tankers we had in Somalia, I could make two crews of four. The question then became how many tanks would we need and how could we possibly man them with partially qualified tankers? SSgt. Daniels and myself were the only qualified tank commanders in the group, and the two next most senior tankers were both brand-new corporals. The rest of the Marines were drivers. They were however, the cream of the crop of our 1st Tank Battalion regimental combat team at 29 Palms. I had worked with every one of them as their company commander, and that experience would pay off in unrealized proportions.

I directed SSgt. Daniels to set up a pair of two-tank sections and a crew of four for the M88A-1 tank retriever. Next he was to find out, of the Marines available, the best qualified to fill the 12 vacant positions. Then he was to formulate a plan to teach them the basics of tanking, including battle drills, gunnery, and loading. As I departed with Col. Klimp for MARFOR headquarters, I had to tell him that he had just six hours to accomplish the foregoing because I had just been informed that we were going to occupy an attack position at 0200 the next morning!

What made all this possible, and necessary, was the depth of despair and degradation into which the country had sunk. The Somalis had so destroyed their country that they saw the Americans as the avenging saviors in clean white hats. Now the rule of the "Technicals" would be broken.

That term needs some explaining. When the UN workers and the news media hacks first began going to Somalia, they quickly found out that they could go no place without an armed vehicle and a guard unit, which were for hire. Somehow they could not bring themselves to designate the hiring of armed guards and bully boys on their expense accounts, so they just listed them as "Technical Assistants," and the term stuck. Within days the USMC tankers found themselves being referred to as the "American Technicals." Captain Campbell now continues.

We did not trust the Somalis, and they were understandably leery about us, intimidated by our aggressive posture. We took no quarter and gave no quarter. If the tanks or anyone else was threatened by a hostile Somali, the rules of engagement (ROE) allowed us to take any necessary actions to protect our lives and those of the people in our charge. We fired nearly 6,000 rounds of small-caliber ammo during this phase, either to kill a Somali attacker or to use our exceptional accuracy to give a clear-cut warning: "I could have killed you but I did not: Either stop what you are doing and leave the area . . . or die."

The Somalis invariably chose life, and we were able to defuse many tense situations. With only four M1A1s and our tank retriever, we could not only continuously protect the unarmored and relatively unprotected forces working with us, but also we could bolster perimeter security at the soccer stadium and act as "backbone" for a robust reaction force. We did, however, become bullet magnets. From the time the tanks came off the ship and were parked on the dock until we were reembarked, three and a half months and 2,000 miles per tank later, they were constant targets of harassment and sniper fire. (Sometimes I really thought that they shot at us out of boredom—thinking that they could not hurt us—like a kid throwing snowballs at a car.)

Knowing this, anytime any part of the task force was engaged, a tank would move to a position to draw fire away from the less-protected unit. We were so successful at drawing fire that every water can, every oil can, all of the fenders, most of the headlights, and many of the vision blocks were destroyed by shrapnel or small-arms fire. The Marine infantry began to affectionately call us "bullet magnets" or "animals" because we could shrug off most fire like some great prehistoric beast. Not for anything would they have traded a supporting section of tanks, but they didn't dare get too close to us out in the field.

At our base in the Mogadishu soccer stadium, however, they would come around to socialize and view the battle scars on our hulls and turrets. Even there though, they had to be careful. We took sniper fire when we were parked outside the stadium, which we called "Fort Apache." One incident from this period stands out in my mind. I had just been *officially informed* that Operation Restore Hope was a humanitarian mission and *not combat,* when several rounds of rifle fire ricocheted off a nearby tank.

I quickly mounted up on my own tank and got into radio contact with our own sniper team up on the third deck of the stadium. They had spotted the snipers, and with SSgt. Daniels as wingman and our ever-present AH-1W Cobra and UH-1N gunships flying close air support, I left the stadium in hot pursuit. We acquired a group of Somali men running at high speed and chased them back to their village on top of Hill 104, a long-suspected base of operations of marauding criminal thugs and their families. Upon reaching the hill, I dismounted and, covered by my wingman, stalked over to a group of 12 to 15 sweating, winded, but now unarmed Somali men who were clustered around their elder. He graciously asked me what he could do for the U.S. Marine Corps. Still angry from having been shot at while being informed that we were not in combat, I told him that he could stop shooting at us.

Of course he denied any involvement, saying he had no quarrel with the USMC and denied that his men had been the shooters. This was a patent lie. I then assured him that for his safety as well as that of all other Somalis, we could not allow attacks to go unpunished. . . . If we were shot at again, I would surely come directly to Hill 104, crush his homes with my tanks, and kill his entire group. If he wanted to fight, then we would fight. Of course, this was pure bluff, but the next morning the huts were gone, as were the people, and a large number of weapons and ammunition had been left behind to show good faith. The sniping stopped, but I often wonder what I would have done if it had not.

In addition, the tanks acted as the bulwark of the quick reaction force. During patrols and on offensive operations, the tanks always led. We went through so many walls that we had to chain railroad ties across the bows of the tanks or lose our fenders like the tanks did in Vietnam. The trick worked great. Another contribution to the task force was our true night-fighting capability. There is little doubt that there would have been much more fratricide if the tanks had not been players.

For instance, as Col. Klimp returned from his nightly embassy meeting with MARFOR, he was fired upon and possibly ambushed near a 90-degree turn that we called Checkpoint 7, in spite of the two accompanying armed Hummers. While withdrawing back to the embassy, he called us for assistance. Simultaneously, there were also reports of armor, infantry, and "technical" activity in a large open area bordering this same road, known as the 21 October Road. At this time the heavy reaction force of two platoons of Marines in Amtracs, and our tank platoon was activated.

The plan was that, as usual, I would lead the tank platoon, and Capt. Bob Bruggeman, CO of "C" Co., 1/7 Marines, would ride with his platoons. We were told that there were no friendly forces anywhere near Checkpoint 7 or in that field. The order was given, "Move to an assault position and attack through the long axis of the field." We left Fort Apache within five minutes, but were both wondering what the ambush had to do with a supposed build-up nearly a mile away. This was in almost total darkness; the only people who could see anything were in the four tanks with thermal sights. Everybody else was effectively blind.

At this point in time, with the UN operation just beginning, it seemed that everyone wanted to get into the act, and there were a lot of little lost battalions running around loose. International forces from many nations were coming in at all hours, and there was not then, nor has there ever been, a UN command structure in *any* host country, unless that force was American-commanded *in its entirety,* from the very beginning. As it was, nobody knew with any degree of certainty where any of the other units were, and this led to many very scary incidents . . . like the following one.

As we closed on the field, my gunner called out. "PC left flank, range 580 meters. . . . Sir, this field is swarming with Zekes (probable hostiles), digging in every 10 meters. I estimate at least 50 and at least 3 more technicals closer to the buildings on the far side of the field."

I reported this information to the TF operations center and was told to engage, but something didn't feel right. Somalis don't normally dig in. Captain Bruggeman had monitored this transmission and informed me that his lead vehicle was closing on my trail vehicle. We crept slowly forward about 200 meters, and immediately the Zekes realized that something was wrong on the road to their front. Some sort of general alert was raised because *all* their weapons systems suddenly oriented on us and we began receiving small-arms fire. We were just about to "develop" the situation when the bravest man I have ever seen stood up out of his hole, slung his rifle, and stood rigidly at attention, staring down my tank. This was no Somali irregular!

There was some intense discussion between SSgt. Daniels and me over just what the proper procedure should be. I wanted to wait while my higher HQ urged attack over the radio. Just then I heard the most memorable sentence in my life. "Animal, this is Endstate, what is happening?" Colonel Klimp had called me to clarify the situation. I gave him a sitrep and the geometry of the situation, and to a Marine he knew nothing about, he asked, "What do you think?" Shocked, I told him that Captain Bruggeman and I had misgivings about this maneuver. With the aid of my thermal sights, I wasn't convinced these were the bad guys, despite the bullets dinging on our hulls.

Twenty seconds from our projected assault time, he asked, "Animal, do you know where the Moroccans are?" I replied that, as far as I knew, they were at the airport where we had left them. There was a sudden flurry of communications, and then I was informed that the Moroccan coalition force had left the airport at night and occupied their new compound without informing TF Mogadishu of the move. . . . The man in front of me was a Moroccan infantry sergeant!!!

What could have been a bloody-awful international incident was averted by the existence of a tank unit. Those four Abrams tanks were the only items of hardware in Somalia with full all-weather and night-fighting capability. Just as in Vietnam, though, they had been told that they weren't initially necessary. While we in Vietnam were told that "it ain't tank country," Capt. Campbell and his men had been told that this is a "humanitarian mission." Tanks, however, have the ability to just sit and analyze a situation, while any other force would have had to return fire, causing intense fratricide. You can be a lot more humanitarian when you are bullet- and RPG-proof.

The "American Technicals" were defusing a nasty situation, but taking horrendous personal risks in the process. They had to allow themselves to be shot at without shooting back—most of the time. The Somalis had effectively wrecked their nation but were too proud to like being rescued, and the tanks were convenient targets of their rage. . . . There's got to be a better way. Captain Campbell now continues.

What we were doing was not war, and it was not combat. While we never stopped reporting both enemy contact and engagements, being engaged in the first 45 days was so routine that it was hardly discussed after the initial report. In spite of all the rounds expended, I would suspect that we inflicted no more than 12 casualties, while running off many hostiles, protecting coalition forces and defenseless members of the population. With a clear conscience, I can state that anyone who was hit by tank fire in Somalia was armed, fired first, and then was given the opportunity to stop. If he made the wrong choice, he deserved what he got.

As the days progressed, word quickly spread that the tanks were not meant to be toyed with and, perhaps more importantly, that we could not be drawn into firing indiscriminately into an area. A favorite Somali tactic was to infiltrate into a neighborhood friendly to U.S. or UN forces and fire at a foot mobile or motorized patrol from within an otherwise supportive crowd, hoping to draw indiscriminate fire and get civilians killed while they slipped away. Initially, after being fired upon, we would very carefully kill the attacker. We promptly found out, however, that intentionally missing would quickly defuse the situation. If the tanks could receive fire and shrug it off, then the force as a whole gained validity and legitimacy for trying to keep the peace. . . . Many times, the sniper would actually wave at us, smile, and walk away.

The tanks up to this point certainly owned the night, and we began to make the actions of the invasive bandits very difficult. Somalis rewarded our efforts with children cheering and adults expressing their gratitude as they moved freely in their own city again. This positive attitude would at times be challenged by a lone troublemaker, caught in the act by the "Silent Giants." Faced with the choice, he could run and lose his treasured pride or opt to stand and face Goliath. Facing down an M1A1 tank at 50 paces wasn't crazy to the Somalis. These people deeply respect acts of individual bravery. Luckily, the score remained grossly one-sided in these little unrecorded title bouts."

Gradually though, the attitude began to change. For days, we had not received a shot, and with their stomachs full and commerce returning to their city, the Somalis began to resent us more and more, wondering just what we were still doing in their country now that the danger was over. The Somalis have absolutely no concept of neutrality, and they assumed that if we were not aiding one neighborhood against another in their ongoing feuds, then we must be helping their enemies, even to the point of planning to bring back their hated despot: Siad Barre.

To confuse us further, we began to get mixed signals from home. We had stopped the banditry, alleviated the suffering and starvation, and gotten food to the people. Now we were told that before we could leave, *all* the weapons had to be seized and more local infrastructure had to be in place before we could transfer authority to the UN and the newly forming Somali police. To put this into perspective, try to imagine disarming San Diego, California, which at 1.5 million inhabitants, is about the same size as Mogadishu.

In February of 1993, we were ordered to go house to house, block by block, and confiscate all weapons. We quickly found out that when a Somali is disarmed, his neighbors will kill him and his family. I was told that entire families were killed, once we took their weapons of self-protection away from them. We saw entire neighborhoods simply disappear. As we patrolled, the smell of decaying human flesh was ever present, and I saw numerous cases of scavenging after the owners had abandoned everything they had owned . . . or been killed for it. The Somalis who had their weapons seized were *much* worse off, after our arrival to help them, than before we had taken their only means of defense from them. The only forces which did not receive these orders were the Australians and the Italian contingent.

A strong case could be made that this point in time is when the infamous "mission creep" set in, and the task of the Americans changed from feeding to fighting. Possibly the change of administrations in the U.S. had something to do with that decision. Just as in Vietnam, there was another batch of bright-eyed, bushy-tailed, save-the-world whiz kids in the White House, and their good intentions, as usual, paved the road to hell. Captain Campbell and his tankers drove that road, right into the flames. Listen to the man.

It all came to a head on February 22, the most dangerous and scary night of my life. The day had started with peaceful demonstrations, but by evening, the Somalis had erected neighborhood barricades and were burning tires and trash. The revelry was getting out of hand. The army had a HMMWV "hummer-jacked," and had lost two five-ton trucks to marauding bands. A company of infantry manning a vehicle checkpoint was receiving pressure from about 1500 angry Somalis and could not make it back to the stadium without assistance.

SSgt. Daniels was already out on his first scheduled route-clearance patrol and somewhat dryly advised me that "the natives were restless." As I left the stadium, the route was so lined with women and children that it was impossible to button up without greasing the tracks with Somalis. My instructions were to move along the Via de Italia to link up with LTC Getz, the CO of the 1/7th Marines, and his "B" Company and bring them back to the stadium. As we approached the first intersection, the light from bonfires forced my driver's night scope into the self-protect mode, turning it off and effectively blinding him, and the heat and fumes from burning rubber and trash forced my loader and me into the turret.

Then snipers began shooting at us from the roofs, and

women and old men began pelting us with rocks. The median that divided the two sides of the avenue had been filled with Somali shops so that we had about a foot of clearance on both sides of the tank for the next 2,500 meters, which forced us to weather this withering assault.

When we got to the trapped Marines, there were no Somalis around them. Major Fleck, 1/7 S-3, or operations officer, informed me that within the last 15 minutes the crowd had moved back from them, back toward the direction from which we had just come. *"No kidding?"* I asked him.

Then the decision was made that I would take my section around the loop of major roads that connected the port, the airport, the embassy, the university, and the Joint Support Compound. When we moved out, everything that could burn was on fire. As we smashed through barricades, Somalis would shoot at us or throw grenades, firebombs, or rocks. It seemed as if every neighborhood had a communal bonfire and that they were trying to outdo each other. It was up to our two tank sections and our phenomenally brave, but unarmed, young tank mechanics in the M-88 to keep on knocking them down to let them know that we weren't intimidated. We made the loop, receiving fire from the same buildings near the same checkpoints as before, while we plowed through rebuilt barricades.

I did get concerned when my wingman threw a track by turning too sharply in the soft sand, but his driver was able to drive it back on again. I also worried when I got a car stuck under my tank and dragged it along for nearly a kilometer before we could shake it loose. When we completed the loop and once again reached 1/7 Marines near their old position, we were told to "DO IT AGAIN." Reduce obstacles and show the Somalis who was in charge.

That was a scene from the very pits of the inferno. Four tanks and a tank retriever, in groups of two or three, driving through burning obstacles, debris in the tracks threatening to pull them off, gas turbine engines shooting eight feet of flame out of the exhaust plenums. RPGs, Molotov cocktails, bullets, and rocks bouncing off of the tanks, TCs and loaders standing up to take the abuse in the thin but unconditional hopes that we wouldn't run over a nonbelligerent.

We finally escorted 1/7 Marines back to the stadium over a different route, and then continued to "show them who was boss" until about 0300, when the Somalis simply got tired and went to bed, unimpressed. We went back to Fort Apache, pulled what maintenance we could, and slept until 0730, when we received another call. About 2,500 Somalis were rioting at a Pakistani-controlled food site, and I was told to take two tanks and go aid them. I told the regimental S-3, or operations officer, that the only people I would be helping would be the rioters since the tanks now very clearly only inflamed their anger. He replied, "I know, but no one else can get to them; they are cut off, and the Somalis want their weapons and vehicles in exchange for their freedom."

When we got about halfway there, a crowd of demonstrators made children lie down in the street to block us. We called for a translator to be brought forward in an LAV (light armored vehicle—a wheeled armored car).

Through the interpreter, I tried to talk to the elder of the group, and he informed me that [he believed] that the U.S. was colonizing Somalia, stealing their personal property and their natural resources, and was emasculating them by taking their personal weapons away. What the U.S. and the puppet UN were doing was making slaves of the Somali people. We were bringing back Siad Barre. The ships were not bringing in grain, food, and medicine, but were leaving with able-bodied Somalis as slaves. We were seen to be on the side of one warlord, while the Italians were on the side of another, and for those reasons, I would have to drive over the women and children if I were to continue. Eventually, though, the interpreter managed to convince the elders of our honest intent, and we were allowed through . . . by that group at that time.

Captain Campbell reported this conversation to his HQ and was told to take another route to the besieged Pakistanis, which he did. En route, they were told that the

RALPH ZUMBRO

Pakistanis were now safe but that they should now proceed to the embassy, where a large group of Somalis were demonstrating against the seizure of their arms. On the arrival of the tanks, the Somalis went completely wild, throwing everything not attached to the ground at the tanks and again prostrating themselves in the path of the tanks.

Faced with a populace gone mad, Captain Campbell had no choice but to leave, and took his small tank unit back to the stadium to shut down for the night—or until something serious occured. En route, he picked up six more stray vehicles that had been looking for help. As he approached the entrance to the stadium, he found his way blocked by a crowd of approximately 100 old men and women. When Captain Campbell stood up in his turret to try and explain his passive intent, the whole crowd, on signal, launched a barrage of rocks that drove him down to the floor of his turret with a broken helmet and a broken jaw. . . . These were the same people that had been seen starving in refugee camps only months before, showing true Somali gratitude.

In April 1993, the Somali three-and-a-half-month tour of the provisional Marine tank unit was over, and they were shipped back to the States. What happened to Captain Campbell and his tankers should not happen again. There are many places in the world that are not worth the life of one American soldier, and Somalia has certainly proved to be one of them.

If the Powers That Be see fit to send Americans, they should be afforded the protection of American tankers. The tragedy of the Bakhara market, six months later, could have been lessened or possibly avoided, if we had had just *one* platoon of American tankers in the area. Nobody else, including the Russians, the British, or even the Germans, react as fast as Americans, especially tankers. Time after time, history has proven that the fastest way to terminate a battlefield catastrophe is to simply radio the nearest Yankee armored unit. Usually, within less than a minute, the great rumbling beasts are heading out of the firebase gate, crews still half awake as their officers get their orders over the radio. The Battle of Bakhara Market cost us 18 rangers and pilots killed, 78 wounded, and several very expensive helicopters shot down. The solution should have been very simple, as it was in all the other wars: Call for the tanks!

THE END . . . FOR A LITTLE WHILE

EPILOGUE

History can be viewed as one long succession of dishonest politicians getting honest soldiers in trouble. Nicollò Machiavelli once wrote, "Gold will not always get you good soldiers, but good soldiers can always get you gold." As long as that attitude guides many of the world's rulers, our shining cities are hostage to would-be conquerors. Europe still looks nervously eastward. The petroleum of Kuwait is only one tank drive away from the acquisitiveness of a better-armed neighbor. And our wealth and freedom are coveted by half the world's population. Thus history has always been and thus it will always be, unless we evolve into a tamer species. For the foreseeable future, though, the only prescription for armed greed is extremely competent professional soldiers.

Soldiering may not be the world's oldest profession, but it can lay claim to being the second oldest. The most ancient civilizations of which we have record, Sumer and Akkad, were taken down, not by mounted horsemen, but by chariot-driving Scythians, who had invented the crewed fighting vehicle back in the Bronze Age. No one has quite pinned down the catastrophe that ended civilization that time, but the arrival of the armed chariot and the oared fighting ship certainly helped matters along. Infantry may be called the "Queen of Battle," but the fighting vehicle, whether chariot or tank, is the "King of the Killing Zone."

There are cycles in history, from which no nation is immune. Just as Alexander's phalanxes were disrupted by India's elephants and the armored knight was taken down by the long bow and the rediscovered phalanx of the Swiss cantons, the massed infantry of WWI was stopped and murdered by the machine gun, barbed wire, and controlled artillery. Then came the invention of "His Majesty's land ships," and once again, the armored crewed vehicle was King of the Killing Zone.

When Captain McGuire took his tank "Ju-Ju" off into the blue, he was beginning a tradition of independent action that American tankers carry on to this day. He was also following in the chariot tracks of Celts and Romans who'd fought over the riches of Europe thousands of years earlier. The little Renault two-man tanks and the giant land ships restored the mobility of battle and again made winning a war possible. Before their advent, the so-called Great War was merely a giant bloodbath that was well on the way to consuming that whole generation of European youths.

Who can possibly know how many Einsteins and Carusos were shredded to red mist and doll rags in those trenches. There may have been minds in those armies that could have built starships for us. From that viewpoint, the tank is a machine of mercy. It allows commanders to make decisions that end wars instead of merely shoveling men into a grinder.

When the political discussion of the fate of civilization was taken up again in the late 1930s, technology, driven by war and knowledge, had almost perfected the new chariots, and the lessons learned in WWI were put to violent use by the Germans. Germany, it should be remembered, was the only nation on earth that had been subjected to "Tank Terror," and they'd taken the lesson to heart. Throughout the experimental decades, they'd studied the lessons of the Great War and the writings of western writers such as J. F. C. Fuller and Charles de Gaulle. The result was *blitz-*

krieg, or lightning war, and in 1939, the world was set on fire, only months after Neville Chamberlain proclaimed, "Peace in our time."

George Santayana's comment "Those who cannot remember the past are condemned to repeat it" seems more and more valid today. In 1939, the smallest armies in the industrial world were those of Portugal, Poland, and the USA, a point that we are rapidly approaching today, due to the need to fund "social programs."

What saved us then was our superb manufacturing capacity, already being geared up for war, and the gallant delaying action of Great Britain. The Battle of Britain bought us time to get our tank and aircraft production lines running, and the long travail of the tankers of Bataan threw the Japanese timetable completely off. They never completed that island shield and never linked up with Rommel, as the Axis had originally planned. Once our locomotive factories began churning out Sherman tanks, that war was as good as over. It was won, in large part, not by generals, but by manufacturing capacity. "Rosie the Riveter" deserves a larger place in history than she's been given to date.

In the space of only four years, this nation cranked out 100,000 assorted armored vehicles, and almost half of them were Shermans. We shipped 7,000 tanks to Russia, some in the Murmansk convoys and some overland by way of Iraq from the Persian Gulf. Granted, the Sherman was not the best design of the war, that honor being fought out between the Panther and the T-34, but it was designed for assembly-line production. We buried the enemy with 54,000 30-ton monsters with a reliability factor like none other in the world.

Stories are told of tankers who fought across North Africa, made the Normandy landings, and rolled into Germany in triumph—in the same tank. Russian crews tell of rolling their red-starred Shermans from Moscow to Berlin, and then being put on the trans-Siberian railway and moved across 11 time zones to chase the Japanese out of Korea. This is not a bad record for one machine, and the durable beasts are still fighting in the world's backwaters today, partly because they are almost unstoppable.

The Sherman would climb until it fell over backward, and it needed that trait in places such as Italy and the mountainous backbone of rocky Korea. Sometimes it acted as a battle taxi or ambulance, carrying its attendant infantry into battle and tenderly shielding their wounded inside the armored hulls. More than one tank has come home with blood running out of its belly hatch! Col. "Jeb" Stuart, who commanded the Marine tankers on Okinawa, tells it best:

"They went in together, they fought together, and they stuck with each other . . . alive, wounded, dead, maimed, crying in anguish or triumph, limping, bleeding . . . no matter how, they came out together."

On Okinawa, as in no other battle, the tank-infantry team had been so efficient, so tight, and so unbeatable. They'd learned their lessons well. As the Shermans rolled forward, smashing bunkers and mowing down fanatic charges of Japanese infantry, the Marines and soldiers stalked warily beside them. When a suicide warrior came rushing out of cover with a satchel charge, Molotov bomb, or magnetic mine, riflemen cut him down. When a tank got boarded by hostiles, the riflemen picked them off.

When the riflemen ran low on bullets, a single yell of "AMMO" was sufficient to cause a bandolier of cartridges to come sailing out of the turret or be dropped from the belly hatch. When the tanks shut down for the night, the grateful riflemen tucked in with them, helping with the unending maintenance. The tankers and riflemen, who were now about half tankers themselves, took equal turns at night watch and used the tank's carrying ability to haul rations, stoves, medical supplies, and whatever. They lived in each other's pockets and together were unbeatable.

It took a whole war to learn that simple lesson, and after every war, it gets lost in the planning for the next "big one," and the tankers and the grunts have to bleed for the knowledge all over again. Korea, Vietnam, Desert Storm, and now even in Somalia, the lessons have to be learned again, because they are not taught.

What saved us in Vietnam was that, after Korea, we'd finally learned that the only way to stop communism is with armed might, and that meant, for the first time in our history, a relatively large standing army, with professional soldiers who could carry the traditions from one war to the next. Those old troopers carried in their memories, lessons that had never been captured in the training manuals.

This writer went into the army in 1957, and I was trained by men who'd fought in "The Big One," men who'd rolled tanks across Europe or parachuted into St. Mere Eglise. Men who'd driven Shermans up Korean mountains, and in one case, spent a year in a North Korean prison camp. When my turn came in Vietnam, I proudly passed the old hard-learned lessons on, even as I learned new ones. Vietnam, however, was a very different kind of war from any that we'd fought before, as much a paper-and-propaganda war as a fighting-and-dying kind of war . . . and we got snookered.

What has to be understood is that *WE DID NOT LOSE THAT WAR*. The Viet Cong admit it, the North Vietnamese Army admits it, and every veteran that came home from there knows it. Only our liberal academicians and media won't admit it. That war was given away by inept politicians who literally snatched defeat from the jaws of victory. Or was it stolen?

In 1962, Vietnamese President Ngo Dinh Diem, resentful of the "white glove" attitude of his media critics, told his advisor, Sir Robert Thompson, "Only the American press can lose this war." Sir Robert was the British counter-guerrilla expert who had been instrumental in de-communizing Malaysia some years before and knew how to deal with communist revolutionaries. With his advice and American aid and might, we beat them into the paddies.

Leonid Brezhnev, Ho Chi Minh, and even Vo Nguyen Giap all stated that they could not win against the Americans on the field of battle and that the war would have to be won on the streets of American cities. And it was. In the late 1960s and early 1970s, the street mobs in our country were doing what no communist force had ever been able to do in the field: defeat the American army. And we read about that in Vietnam. Always remember this: We *knew* what was going on back in the States.

From June of 1967 to June of 1968, I served in what became the most decorated company in the U.S. Army at the time. Company "A," 1-69th Armor won the Valorous Unit Award, the Vietnamese Distinguished Unit Citation, the Vietnamese Cross of Gallantry with palm, and the U.S. Meritorious Unit Citation. Regardless of what came over the TV screen on any given evening, the communists lost. I was there, and I saw the Viet Cong die. I was one of the ones who buried their bodies with my own dozer tank.

On Tet, January 1968, the communists launched a massive offensive aimed at taking all the district capitals and discrediting the American efforts. It failed miserably. That misguided endeavor cost the VC 100,000 men. They were utterly broken as a military force and never again took the field for offensive operations. Instead, they were used as guides and auxiliaries for the North Vietnamese Army, which was then coming south in record numbers.

It is not a well-known fact, but there are two Vietnamese races in that country. The Annamese, or South Vietnamese, and the Tonkins, or North Vietnamese. Simply put, the Northerners, under Ho Chi Minh, invaded the South, with Chinese and Russian backing. When the Americans were in charge of the war, we stomped them into the ground and then gradually "Vietnamized" the war, turning all our hardware over to the Viets.

In 1972, after we'd left and against all treaties and agreements, the Tonkins sent an army of 150,000 men and 600 tanks out of that sacrosanct DMZ and invaded the South. It was reported by our press as a "resurgence of the guerrilla war." The South Vietnamese, with a little help from our helicopters, which, with some CIA people, were about all we had in country at the time, fought the Tonkins to a standstill. Their own figures admit to *another 100,000 dead soldiers.*

Yet again, that war was won, this time under the direction of President Nixon, who still had the power to bomb the aggressive Northerners into signing nonaggression pacts . . . *which they did,* in Paris, January 23, 1973. For the first time in history, a communist nation had been forced, with a gun to its head, to stop enslaving men and killing women and children. At that time, Vietnam was a free nation. But, at that point in history, our internal politics *again* cost us an already won war, just as they had 20 years before in Korea.

With the North Vietnamese communists on the run, the Watergate scandal, oh-so-conveniently, pulled the rug out from under Richard Nixon. The timing of that scandal was a little suspect, though. It was just too perfect for some of the parties concerned. In order to find the perpetrator of any given act, all you have to do is ask, *Who benefits?* Whose ships now anchor in Cam Ranh Bay? Who gained from the senseless demonstrations of historically and politically ignorant students? The Russians, whose socialist dogma is still prated upon in our universities.

In his book, *The Real War,* Richard Nixon made the following statement: "In April, May, and June of 1973, with my authority weakened by the Watergate crisis, retaliatory action was threatened but not taken. Then Congress passed a bill setting August 15 as the date for termination of U.S. bombing in Cambodia, and requiring Congressional approval for the funding of U.S. military action in any part of Indochina. . . . The effect of this bill was to deny the President the means to enforce the Vietnam peace agreement by retaliating against Hanoi for violations."

As a result, the funds that had been destined for the South Vietnamese became diverted into the "Great Society," the biggest pork barrel in history. At a time when the Tonkins were rearming at a rapid rate, the South couldn't even move all of its tanks at the same time and medical orderlies were washing and reusing bandages. In 1975, when the Tonkins tried again, ARVN infantrymen were limited to about 20 bullets per man and their tanks were out of fuel. World oil prices had quadrupled due to the Arab oil embargo.

On March 4, 1975, while we were still embroiled in the Watergate hearings, the North Viets launched four complete army corps, with brand-new Russian equipment, south out of the DMZ. For the record, that is more men and equipment than we put ashore on D-Day in 1944. We could not even protest the invasion because we'd been kept in the dark by a media that saw 700 Russian tanks as a "resurgence of the guerrilla war."

That war was not lost, it was trashed by ignorance and a lack of national will. Fortunately, the next war was more clear cut, and wonder of wonders, all the experts agreed that this, at last, was real *TANK COUNTRY*.

Desert Storm proved several things very conclusively to the world. Remember the critical furor over the alleged flaws of the Abrams tank and the Bradley fighting vehicle? Those critics are strangely silent now, as silent as the Iraqi tank commanders who had their turrets blown off from distances as great as six kilometers. That kind of war—clean, distinct, and open—we can always win. It is the dirty little wars around the periphery of civilization that get us in trouble. General Schwarzkopf's "Hail Mary" is a military maneuver as old as time, and the valor of our soldiers is a civic virtue as old as civilization. It is unfortunate that our soldiers got stopped in their tracks at a time when, as we now know, Saddam Hussein was just about to flee for asylum. As has been mentioned before, the UN has never won a war. Possibly they are afraid of the responsibilities of victory.

Now, as in Somalia, the U.S. finds itself tasked as global 911 and the question is often asked, why us? Why should the rest of the world think that they can simply pick up a phone and dial, USA-911-TANK? The answer is, who else? What other nations have the power to step into chaos and resolve a situation? *Can we even do business in the world that would evolve without a policeman?*

We are the last superpower and have inherited the responsibility for some level of global stability. That mantle was once worn by the great powers of Europe, but they shed it in their own eternal struggles for dominance. The great nations of history spent the greater part of this century eating their substance over politics, and have proven their unfitness to rule. Twice we had to bail them out and give of our lifeblood to put them back on their feet. They cannot handle global responsibility.

If we don't pick up that responsibility, who will, and will their interests coincide with ours? Do we really want the small nations that are decivilizing themselves dominated by a resurgent Soviet Union or imperial Russia? Or militant Islam? The old Roman sage Vegetius said it best: "Who desires peace, should prepare for war." And in this day and age, that means Tankers.

NO

PLACE

TO

HIDE

A Novel of the Vietnam War
by
GERRY
CARROLL

Available from Pocket Books

POCKET
BOOKS

1063-02